Dedicated to
the children of
the world who
read these stories
with resolve that
it will never
happen again.

The publication of this book was made possible through the contributions of the following people and foundations:

Mr. & Mrs. Jerry Miller

Mr. & Mrs. Marvin Friedberg

Mr. & Mrs. Paul Hirschbiel

Mr. & Mrs. David Kaufman

Mr. Mark Dreyfus

Mr. & Mrs. Tavia Gordon

Mr. & Mrs. Alvin Wall

Mr. & Mrs. Arnold Leon

Mr. & Mrs. Kenneth Brethauer

The Tidewater Jewish Foundation

In Loving Memory of Pincus Paul

In Loving Memory of Reba & Sam Sandler

A special acknowledgement must be extended to the thousands of contributors to the **United Jewish Federation of Tidewater Annual Campaign**. Each year they extend their generosity to the community supporting programs that have an immeasurable impact on improving our society as a whole, and the Jewish community in particular. The publication of this book is a natural outgrowth of the important programs sponsored by the Federation's Community Relations Council in its effort to promote the Holocaust as a vehicle for tolerance education. The funds received from the Federation's annual campaign – as well as other grants and contributions to specific Holocaust Commission programs – enable these important activities to continue into the future.

To LIFE:

STORIES OF COURAGE AND SURVIVAL

TOLD BY HAMPTON ROADS HOLOCAUST SURVIVORS, LIBERATORS & RESCUERS

Published by the

UNITED JEWISH FEDERATION OF TIDEWATER

To Life: Stories of Courage and Survival

Copyright© 2002
Holocaust Commission,
United Jewish Federation of Tidewater
Virginia Beach, Virginia

ISBN 0-9714787-9-1

Printed in the United States of America
First Edition

Cover design and illustrations
by MaryAnne Katz

"L'Chayim" by MaryAnne Katz

TABLE OF CONTENTS

חי

*Chai, the symbol of life, will be used
in this book to designate survivors.*

The Holocaust Commission of Tidewater is a committee of the Community Relations Council within the United Jewish Federation of Tidewater. the goals of the Commission are:

To promote an understanding of the uniqueness and magnitude of the Holocaust, its unfolding stages and critical lessons.

To encourage tolerance of people of different religious, racial and ethnic backgrounds.

To serve as an Educational Resource Center for students and teachers to learn about the Holocaust, racism, and the dangers of prejudice.

To help students apply the lessons of the Holocaust and other historical events – discrimination, peer pressure, unthinking obedience to authority, indifference – to the moral decisions they make in their own lives today.

To promote understanding of the importance of participating in and preserving the democratic process.

To plan and sponsor the annual Yom Hashoah Commemoration for the entire community.

To organize and sponsor educational conferences that use the Holocaust and other experiences to help students become critical thinkers.

The Holocaust Commission serves as a resource for identifying books, audio-visual materials, curricula, and other tools for teaching the lessons of the Holocaust.

Members of the Holocaust Commission accompany local Holocaust survivors to schools, churches, and synagogues where they share their experiences with students.

How a community remembers its past is the single most important element in determining its future.

James Carroll

**Holocaust Commission of the
United Jewish Federation of Tidewater**
5029 Corporate Woods Drive, Suite 225
Virginia Beach, Virginia 23462-4376
www.holocaustcommission.org

FORWARD

by Yaffa Eliach

Dr. Yaffa Eliach, Professor of Literature, History and Judaic Studies at Brooklyn College, is the founder of the first Center of Holocaust Studies in the U.S. She is the creator of the most widely acclaimed exhibit at the U.S. Holocaust Memorial Museum, "The Tower of Life," a collection of 1500 photographs of the families of Eishyshok, the shtetl in Poland where she was born. Eliach is one of 29 survivors among the 3500 Jews of Eishyshok who were murdered by the Nazis.

At this moment in history, to publish a book about survival during the Holocaust is particularly meaningful and relevant. September 11, 2001, brought back very painful memories to survivors of the Holocaust, crushing their hopes that attacks on innocent people would never happen in the United States. For many Holocaust survivors, America became the beloved homeland, offering the promise of a safe and bright future. New York City, in particular, with its magnificent cultural life, its ethnic and religious diversity, became a symbol of the freedom and vitality of our nation.

After this American tragedy, the stories of Holocaust survivors, rescuers, and liberators will provide new insight into how survivors manage to rebuild their lives and to once again find hope.

The Holocaust was a watershed in Western civilization. For the first time in history, the Jews had no options for survival. Previously, Jews had the opportunity to survive by converting to other religions or immigrating to more tolerant countries. In many countries – Spain, Portugal, France, e.g. – Jews were expelled.

During the Holocaust, however, the definition of a Jew was based on whether one had "Jewish blood." Regardless of what faith one practiced, having one Jewish grandparent was enough to be considered Jewish. Nor were there countries where the Jewish people could find safe haven. Even the U.S. government turned away the ill-fated ship, the St. Louis, which had departed from Germany on May 13, 1939, searching for a safe port for its Jewish passengers fleeing the Nazis. Eventually, the St. Louis was forced to return to Europe. Even after the Liberation, England did not permit Holocaust survivors to enter Palestine ("Eretz" Israel) since it was under the British Mandate. The "illegal" immigrants were sent to camps on the island of Cyprus.

The establishment of the State of Israel in 1948 opened the floodgates to Holocaust survivors. Despite Israel's War of Independence, the wars of 1956, 1967, and 1973, and terrorist attacks through the present, during which some survivors and their descendents were killed, incredibly the survivors have built new lives.

The second largest group of Holocaust survivors was welcomed by the United States. As one of those survivors who found a new home in America, I established the first Center for Holocaust Studies in the USA, introduced Holocaust Studies on the American campus, and created the "Tower of Life" at the United States Holocaust Memorial Museum in Washington, D.C.

To Life: Stories of Courage and Survival is a collection of Holocaust stories by survivors, rescuers, and liberators who also have an American story to tell. All of those interviewed live in the Hampton Roads area of Virginia. Each personal account contains important

Moshe Sonenson holding his daughter, Yaffa, minutes before the Germans invaded Eishyshok.

and unique information, as well as particular elements about the destruction in various countries under Nazi occupation as experienced by people of different ages, situations, and backgrounds.

Esther Goldman, for example, is a woman of great inner strength, faith, and courage. Her story documents life in the forest, ghetto, death camp, and on the death march. It records her face-to-face encounter with Mengele, the "Angel of Death" in Auschwitz, as well as the indescribable pain when the Poles killed her younger brothers. Esther is also a model of survivors who rebuilt excellent lives in America.

Abraham Baum's testimony is extremely honest in depicting the negative attitude of many Poles towards Jews. A Polish policeman told him when he was fifteen years old, "It's time for you to pay the price." Unfortunately, this prejudice continued after the Liberation. About 2500 Jews were murdered by their Polish neighbors when the camps were opened and they were allowed to return to their hometowns. In no other country did such a tragedy occur.

Many Americans do not realize that 17 percent of immigrants to the United States actually returned to their countries of origin. Unwittingly, they left a place of life and security for a place of death and destruction. The stories of Hanna Schrob and Mary Sigillo Barraco represent such situations. At the age of three, Hanna's mother moved with her parents from New York back to Germany. Likewise, Mary Barraco, a devoted Catholic, returned to Belgium with her mother. Mary is among the Righteous of the Nations, assisting and saving many Jews. While many people lost their faith in God during the Holocaust, Mary understands it differently. "God did not allow the Holocaust to happen," she said. "It was man who had no fear of God."

The liberators, people like Rocco Russo — their stories are monuments to the men and women of the American armed services, their courage, their compassion, and their determination to serve as witnesses.

In these difficult days following September 11, 2001, perhaps Hanna Schrob has summed up best how our American survivors feel when she noted, "In spite of all of its troubles, America is the best country in the world … I feel so intensely proud to be an American."

God bless America.

Yaffa Eliach
New York City, January 9, 2002

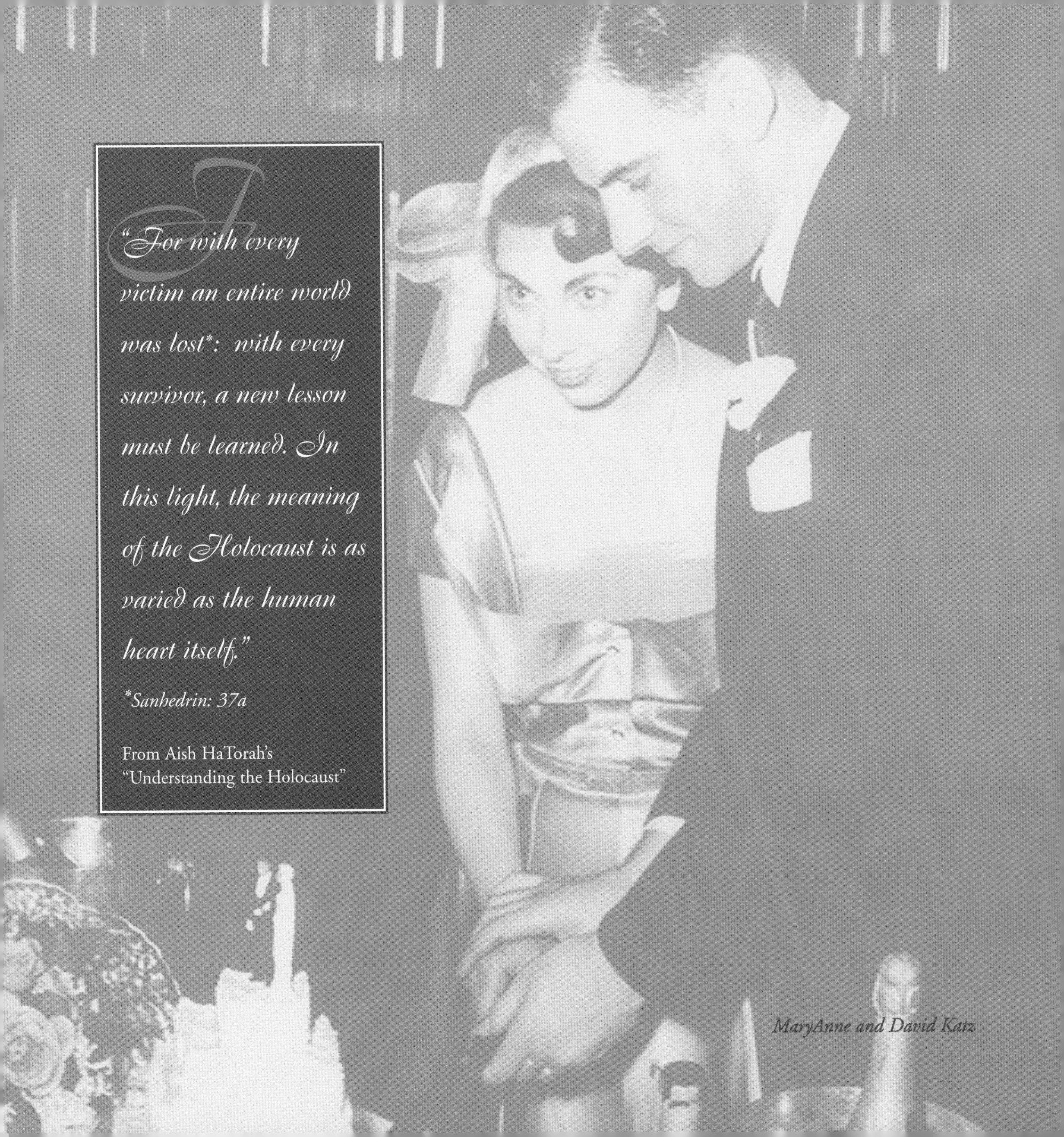

"For with every victim an entire world was lost*: with every survivor, a new lesson must be learned. In this light, the meaning of the Holocaust is as varied as the human heart itself."

*Sanhedrin: 37a

From Aish HaTorah's "Understanding the Holocaust"

MaryAnne and David Katz

TO LIFE IS A CELEBRATION!

It is a celebration which honors the memory of all those who perished in the Holocaust – faces and names which pass us by in a blur of pain; and a celebration for those who survived and returned to tell their stories as a testimony to life. They got married. They had children and some had grandchildren.

TO LIFE is a project which began in the Tidewater community in the late '70s, and culminated in three annual booklets which featured the stories of various Holocaust survivors in the early '80s. Other survivor stories were published in the *Southeastern Virginia Jewish News* and *Renewal Magazine* throughout the next 10 to 20 years.

TO LIFE is a compilation of all of these stories as well as many others which were not part of the three publications – all area survivors we could identify and who wished to be part of the book.

Photo by Stephen Jay Photography from the 1982 Supplement published by the United Jewish Federation of Tidewater.

TO LIFE also includes stories of area liberators, members of the military who were on the scene shortly after liberation; and rescuers, those who live among us in our community and risked their own lives to save the lives of Jewish people during World War II.

TO LIFE is more than a history of survivors who have lived in our community. It is a document that records a time when hate knew no boundaries. The Holocaust Commission is placing this book in all schools and public libraries in the Hampton Roads area in the hope that future generations learn to avoid the tragic consequences of hate and indifference.

TO LIFE contains stories that may not be easy to read, for some acts of cruelty are beyond comprehension. But the fact that there are those who survived, who were willing and able to share their stories, and who made new lives is a testament to the resilience and faith of man.

TO LIFE! MAY WE ALL COUNT OUR BLESSINGS!

Reba Karp
Editor

The Torah is a Tree of Life to those who grasp her,
Whoever keeps her is content.

Proverbs 3:18

Torah Scrolls

By Reba Karp

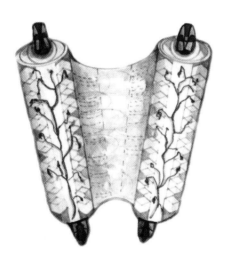

If only one had survived, it would have been enough. It takes only one Torah Scroll to tell the story and document the defeat of the Nazis' effort to destroy world Jewry.

One Torah scroll would have carried the message that the Jewish people live, and as Rabbi Israel Zoberman noted: "You cannot have people without the Torah. They are connected." Nathan of Nemirov was even more deliberate when he wrote: "Every living soul is a letter of the Torah, wherefore all souls taken together make up the Torah."

Just as Torah marks the beginning of life for the Jewish people, so it shall mark the beginning of our effort to honor our Holocaust survivors and celebrate their lives. *To Life* would not be complete without acknowledging the survival of the holy words contained in the Torah.

For many years the surviving Torahs plundered from Jewish synagogues by the Nazis lay uncared for in a Prague repository – 1,564 Torah scrolls piled next to one another, silent witnesses to hatred, sentinels of faith, waiting to once more spread the word of God.

An article in *Reform Judaism* described the scene, "rack upon rack; an ingathering – Torah Scrolls – in the hundreds," until a British businessman, Ralph Yablon, acquired them and arranged for their delivery to Westminster Synagogue in England on February 7, 1964.

Since then, many of them have been redeemed by congregations around the world, with more than 900 finding homes in the United States. Six of these redeemed scrolls are in Tidewater synagogues – Kehillat Beth Hamidrash and Beth Chaverim in Virginia Beach, Gomley Chesed in Portsmouth, and in Norfolk, Congregation Beth El and Ohef Sholom Temple, which has two. The seventh is housed in the Ark of Beth Sholom Home of Eastern Virginia.

For the members of KBH, their procurement of a Holocaust Torah began with an article noting that the Westminster Synagogue in London was looking for a home for Sifrei Torah rescued from the Holocaust. KBH's Holocaust Memorial Commission had been working on plans for a memorial wall in the synagogue's lobby and their vision included a Holocaust scroll, encased in Plexiglas, as a reminder of the survival of the Jewish sacred heritage.

The synagogue's board contacted Westminster and on October, 1980, KBH's secretary Judy Saperstein, the current vice-president, received a letter from the secretary of the Memorial Scrolls Commission in London. It stated that Torah No. 1113 had been saved and had been assigned to KBH on permanent loan. The shipping documents noted that the Torah would arrive in Tidewater on January 26, 1981 between 7:30 a.m. and 11:30 p.m. that day. However, the scroll did not arrived as scheduled for it had been temporarily "misplaced" and later discovered on a dock in New York. Eventually, the Torah did arrive in Norfolk and Leo Saperstein, Judy's father, went to the old Norfolk airline terminal to pick it up and bring it to its new home in the synagogue's ark.

However, KBH's Torah never came to rest in a Plexiglas case; instead, it was given a place of honor in the *Aron Kodesh* of the sanctuary. Although not for *halachic* use, its presence in the sanctuary reminds the members of their history and heritage. By a remarkable coincidence, the Torah scroll, which is about 150 years old, was rescued from a town in Czechoslovakia, just outside of Prague, the home of KBH's Past President Stephen Schechner's maternal grandfather, Julius Hauer. Schechner feels it is probable that his grandfather might have read from KBH's Torah during his Bar Mitzvah in December of 1938.

Beth Chaverim's Holocaust Torah, No. 526, is about 150 years old, coming from Brno, the capital of Moravia. It is written in the "German" style, 26 inches in height with 59 lines per column. This style was discontinued in the 19th century.

The present standard of 42 lines is the "Polish" style.

Czech Memorial Torah Scroll No. 62 is at Gomley Chesed in Portsmouth. This Torah was written in 1744 and confiscated by the Nazis from a synagogue in Trebic, Czechoslovakia. Trebic had been a Jewish community dating back to the year 938.

During the Holocaust, 1,370 Jews were assembled in Trebic and deported to Theresienstadt concentration camp; only 35 survived.

The family of Ella Caplan Brewer, in her memory, presented the Torah, a precious legacy, to Gomley Chesed in 1989. The Torah was presented by her husband, children and grandchildren and rededicated in the memory of Sol Brewer in 1993.

Two Torah Scrolls found their way into Tidewater by way of the family of Rabbi Benjamin Martin and Helen Martin and their children, Rabbi Bernard Martin, Cantor Stanley Martin and Elsie Martin. The first found a place at Beth Sholom Home on December 15,

The Twarda Synagogue is the only remaining synagogue in Warsaw. Prior to World War II there were over 300 synagogues in daily use in that city.
(United Jewish Appeal Photo Service)

1980. The scroll, No. 1343, came from the town of Divisov in Czechoslovakia and was written in the beginning of the 19th century. The mantle for the Torah was dedicated by Rabbi Benjamin and Helen Martin in memory of their beloved parents.

According to a letter to Beth Sholom Home from the Honorary Secretary of the Memorial Scrolls Committee of the Westminster Synagogue in England, the Committee's policy was to send Torahs in good condition only to new congregations in need of a scroll of their own. Although Beth Sholom's "prized and precious" Holocaust Torah was damaged and unable to be repaired, it was placed in the ark of Beth Sholom's sanctuary. It is used on specific commemorative occasions, giving the Holocaust Torah life and purpose.

The inscription on Congregation Beth El's Holocaust Torah Scroll, also a gift from the Martin family, reads: "Let it be enshrined in this synagogue and let those who see it remember that it was saved from the Holocaust, and that even though some of its letters have fallen away, it is aflame with life. Let them remember that this Torah is a symbol of the triumph of God and the Jewish spirit over those who wished to remove God from the world and wipe Judaism and the Jewish people off the face of the earth."

The above was taken from the remarks of Dr. Bernard Martin on the occasion of the presentation of this sacred Torah

אודה בה אפא פרד שערי לי פתחו

EMPTY ARK

A Holy Ark

without its

Torah occupants

is a synagogue

without its

soul.

(United Jewish Appeal Photo Service)

to Congregation Beth El by the Martin family in honor of the 60th wedding anniversary of his parents, Rabbi and Mrs. Benjamin Martin on January 2, 1982. Benjamin Martin was a Torah reader at Beth El and an active *mohel* in Tidewater for 35 years. Martin's son, Dr. Bernard Martin, was a reform rabbi and scholar who held the Abba Hillel Silver Chair at Case Western Reserve University and was chosen to chair the Department of Religion there. He died prematurely and unexpectedly 12 days after making the presentation on behalf of his father at Beth El.

The Beth El Torah, Hungarian in origin, came from a part of Czechoslovakia that was eventually incorporated within Hungarian borders. This was especially meaningful to the Martin family as their ancestry is Czechoslovakian.

According to records, the Beth El Torah was written by a scribe in the Hungarian town of Divisov about 200 years ago and read week after week by the pious residents of that community until they were transported to Auschwitz.

Ohef Sholom Temple is in possession of two Torahs from the Holocaust. Rabbi Malcolm Stern (of blessed memory) obtained the first Torah in the summer of 1957 while on a ten week tour of Europe. The Sterns were able to find a Torah at the Jewish Museum in London which had been left by a man from Czechoslovakia during the late 1930s.

Since he did not return to claim the Torah, the museum sold it to Malcolm Stern. After being restored in New York, it was presented to the temple. Rabbi Stern's wife, Louise, chose a blue mantle to cover it. It is currently the smallest of four temple Torahs.

The presentation and rededication of Ohef Sholom's second Holocaust Torah scroll was held October 10, 1969. It was a gift to the temple from Mrs. Julius B. Levinson in memory of her husband and parents, Mr. and Mrs. S. Kirsner. The Torah, written in 1890, was used by members of a synagogue in Breznice, Czechoslovakia. According to information provided by Ohef Sholom Temple Archives, it was confiscated and desecrated by the Nazis who intended to place it in their museum of "exterminated ethnographical groups." The Torah eventually found its way to the Westminster Synagogue in London. Rabbi Harold Hahn (of blessed memory), who was then spiritual leader of Ohef Sholom, contacted Rabbi Harold Reinhart of Westminster who assisted in the procurement.

To quote Rabbi Reinhart: "Our task, in addition to housing, studying, classifying, and where possible, restoring these Torahs, is to distribute them to synagogues throughout the world that they should find permanent homes in sacred Arks, to honor the divine Name, to memorialize the martyrs from whose synagogues they came and to bring light to future generations. Each scroll that we assign goes with a three-fold prayer: for the souls of the martyred millions, for the safety and honour of the sacred memorial itself, and for the blessing of the congregation."

Why has Torah survived when so many have sought to destroy its wisdom? Perhaps one of the answers can be found in Nahmanides' Commentary on Pentateuch when he wrote: "Every glory and wonder, every deep mystery and all beautiful wisdom are hidden in the Torah, sealed up in her treasures." ❖

"Every glory and wonder, every deep mystery and all beautiful wisdom are hidden in the Torah, sealed up in her treasures."

NAHMANIDES
(Commentary on Pentateuch)

Irving Althaus

73551

"Life goes on ..."

By Eric Futterman

The measure of a man's stature is ofentimes a matter of perspective.

Take IRVING ALTHAUS. Almost every single day since 1956, a customer could walk into the Newport News delicatessen owned by his cousin Sam and find this five foot four inch man dutifully creating Corn Beef on Rye sandwiches for lunch customers. Watching Irving dish out a steaming bowl of matzo ball soup or scooping out potato salad and artfully squeezing it onto a sandwich plate, probably would not make an onlooker feel intimidated or even impressed.

Yet piece by piece, over a period of a few hours, the people who take the time to get to know Irving Althaus realize this is a man who has indeed stood tall in the face and memory of horror.

The first clue to the stature Irving Althaus possesses is one that jolts many who understand its significance. The tattoo. Irving is number 73551. "That used to be my name. It's what they always called me," he half chuckles in his thick and lively native Polish accent.

The tattoo always strikes us, doesn't it? I remember once growing a bit impatient with an elderly man in a grocery store who absentmindedly knocked into my cart. In an instant I glanced at the number on his arm and was awash with grief and compassion.

For those of us who only know the Nazi Holocaust of the Jews by film or textbook, to encounter a survivor can be as striking as discovering a living piece of history.

Irving Althaus wants little compassion for what he went through and what he saw. He says he doesn't need it and I believe him. The conviction with which he says so adds yet another level of strength to Irving's stature. Especially when he reveals what he witnessed more than a half century earlier in Poland. The dark days of the Holocaust, Auschwitz, Birkenau.

Unlike many survivors who have been forcing themselves to shed the masks of fear and psychological trauma to tell their stories for the sake of history and humanity, Irving rarely exhibits the stuttering, tear-filled agony that normally pours out of these victims. He reports what he saw: the crematoriums, the hangings, the shootings, the starvation, the humiliation, with the detachment of a journalist. It can throw a listener off balance. It is as if this survivor believes the Holocaust was no big deal. But to believe that notion is to miss the point of Irving Althaus' apparent stoicism.

Irving Althaus

I first met Irving in 1995 when I interviewed him for a documentary on Virginia Peninsula area residents who were Holocaust survivors, witnesses and American soldiers who helped to liberate the concentration camps.

Irving and his cousin Sam spent three years in Auschwitz and Berkenau respectively. His great fortune at being a skilled electrician made him useful and therefore spared him from certain execution on dozens of occasions, including several times when the infamous doctor, Josef Mengele, stared down at Irving and ordered him out of the death line and back to work.

We spoke with the camera running for more than thirty minutes. In tersely told stories, Irving Althaus painted the all too familiar picture of Nazi terror. He did so without embellishment because he knew none was necessary. His words overwhelmed the listener with the emotion one would expect to find in the storyteller.

"They could gas 2000 people at one time, " he says. "Big crematorium. Pushed them in, undressed, pushed them in. Put in the Zyklon B gas, close the door and they were gassed. When they opened the gate the bodies … blood came out from the nose, ears and everything. It was awful, awful.

"But one time when the Hungarian transport came in, they couldn't burn 2000 at one time. They used to burn them outside. It was awful, the smell. I had to fix a fence behind the crematorium. (They were) burning bodies right in a big pit … smell and the smoke. … I couldn't finish the job. I was coughing. I can't see nothing … the smoke choking me."

One of the most frequently asked questions about the Jewish people and their reaction to Adolph Hitler's legalized hatred and murder in the camps, concerns the perceived lack of forced resistance and escape attempts. Irving's explanation was as quick and profound as the response of his captors.

"You couldn't resist. It was pointless. For example, take our group. If I went out working with people and somebody escaped … not only will they hang me too, they bring his family from the outside, lay him out so everybody can see. Grandmother, grandfather, uncles, everything. So resistance was very, very out of the question."

Irving's insight in the documentary has made him a celebrity of sorts on the Virginia Peninsula, a mixed community with a strong economic base in shipbuilding, and an assortment of families from all walks of life. The Jewish Community of the Virginia Peninsula, which stretches from Williamsburg to Newport News to Yorktown and Hampton, is small but intensely active and tightly knit.

Since 1996 more than 40 Peninsula-area public schools have used *To Bear Witness/A Living Testimonial of the Holocaust* to teach students about prejudice, survival, hatred and the dignity that must accommodate civilized life. Irving's account of his experience in Poland's worst camps is riveting, not for any overt emotional response, but for the startling clarity with which he presents his memories.

Sitting inside a synagogue, his small compact body still revealing the physical strength that was packed inside a younger man decades earlier, he deliberately told his story: "I was working back near the crematorium. 1944. (They were) bringing Hungarian Jews there. Transporting day and night. And a truck with children and women pass by in the back gate. A few children fell out. The truck stopped. The officer asked me to give him a hand, to put them back on the truck. They asked me … the women know … they asked me if they are going to death. And I didn't say nothing. I just couldn't say nothing. I couldn't answer at all."

"They had a feeling. They asked me in Jewish, are they going to death? I just couldn't say nothing. And they went. You could see it right there. Few hundred feet. Always stick in my mind. I couldn't say nothing."

It is a story that moves viewers to subtly shake their heads at the impossible position in which Irving Althaus found himself on that day in 1944.

Still, the recollection represents only a small obstacle to the fulfilling life Irving Althaus has lived since the end of the war. He refuses to allow the Holocaust to dominate or even drive his days. In fact he is steadfast that his real local celebrity status comes from the

Winter of 1944.

Photo by Hugo Horvath

thousands upon thousands of lunches, breakfasts and dinners he has served to this shipbuilding community. "When they had parties at the place, they invite me. They say come in for a drink. Very nice people. Treat me very nice," he says fondly.

In retirement, Irving has breakfast three days a week with former customers, who he considers friends. And he speaks glowingly of the way this blue collar community welcomed a small, hard working Polish speaking Jew who was new to the American shores. "At that time my English was very bad. People were nice to me, very nice. Met a lot of people. Everybody from the Mayor to the police department … very nice."

Very nice. It's almost Irving's mantra. Certainly not the kind of phrase one would expect from someone who faced down history's cruelest individuals.

Irving arrived in America in 1949 and moved to Newport News to work as a non-union contract electrician. When the contract ended he got his first taste of the new Jewish Homeland, Israel, while delivering cattle by ship from Newport News to Haifa. "That was a bad time," he says. "January, 1950. People still living in tents. All the people started coming from Europe. It was very bad then, very bad."

Newport News was not so. When Sam started the Althaus Delicatessen, which operated successfully for more than 40 years, he and Irving began a relationship with a community Irving holds in very high regard. It is not uncommon to hear, in both the Jewish and non-Jewish community, "We're lucky to have him."

That's what drives Irving Althaus. His friendships, which are considerable, his happy retirement, his passion about the former Althaus Delicatessen and his disdain over the fact that a good corn beef sandwich can no longer be found on the Peninsula since Sam sold the restaurant.

"Life goes on," he says, stating it at once as a living philosophy and a lesson to anyone who is willing to listen. While he has seen the worst humanity has to offer, he has also seen the best in America, which he calls, "… the greatest country. Freedom, everything. I enjoy it. No problems. I get along with everybody, Jews, non-Jews everybody. Never had a problem."

Says the man who lived three years in the most notorious concentration camp created by Hitler and his Nazi subordinates, "I am not bitter."

Fifty-five years after tasting freedom upon his liberation from Auschwitz, Irving returned. He eagerly shows off a videotape taken by his cousin's son, New York actor, Harry Althaus, of his trip during the Spring of 2000. Much of the tape shows Irving, Harry and a guide traveling through Krakow and Ciechanow, Irving's hometown.

They are seen touring Auschwitz. Again Irving surprises a listener. Instead of allowing the scene to dominate his psyche, he laments on what he believes is the inadequate care that has been taken of this museum. "It's not kept up. All deteriorated over there. Weeds are growing. Not kept like a museum should be."

Visiting a place of one's youth and at the same time being forced to recollect unspeakable horrors, one would expect

A Plea to Survivors

Tell me all you know, parents,

don't hold back,

I'm getting old myself.

Every piece you share is precious,

though painful it remains.

A people's puzzle,

reflection of your own,

can be perceived in full

only if you reveal what begs

to be hidden, forever veiled.

Rabbi Israel Zoberman

a flood of emotion. Not from Irving. "No, I've seen it before. Didn't need to see it again." Even when pressed, he cannot say that the experience of coming back moved him.

Irving says the only reason he went back was because Harry asked him to return. Harry and his father had tried to get to Birkenau several years earlier but the travel plans didn't work out. It was important to Harry, as it is with so many children of Holocaust survivors, to make that connection to his father's past.

"Without question it was the most extraordinary gift I've ever received," says Harry. "Here is this man, he (recently) had had eye surgery, he is 75, we were going to three different cities in ten days, packing and unpacking, *schlepping* to these places. We were getting up really early in the morning, trucking out to theses places and walking around. He got a pretty bad cold between Warsaw and Krakow. At Auschwitz he really wasn't feeling well. But you never would have known that.

"And he was doing that for me because he wanted me to see it. Here's this guy doing all this and you're an adult and he's treating you like you're his kid and he'll do this for you no matter what."

The trip afforded Harry the opportunity to visit the barracks where he believes his father Sam was interned during his time at Berkenau. In the video Harry made, he takes viewers down a long road to the barracks, scoops up a small pile of dirt into a plastic bag and brings home a sample for his father.

Unlike Harry, who was taken aback by the experience, Irving appeared unfazed by it all. "I didn't know how he was going to react," says Harry. "When we were getting close to this charged situation I was a little nervous. (I asked myself) what have I gotten this guy into? He's going along with this but what if it's too much for him? Do I know him well enough to know what to do about that?"

Yet Irving never showed any emotion besides his disappointment that a shed where he did a lot of work during his time at Auschwitz had been removed.

Again, it's easy to perceive Irving's stoic nature as that of a man who has blocked it all from his psyche. But Irving Althaus is fully aware of the significance of it all.

The vast majority of survivors I have personally known say they can't watch films like "Schindler's List" or read books about the Holocaust. It is far too disturbing and takes them back to the darkest moments in their lives. Not Irving.

"He's read just about anything everybody wrote about the Holocaust," says Harry. "He always had a voracious appetite for information without emotional attachment to it." Irving even said that about himself at one point. "I don't get emotional about this."

"Death March" by MaryAnne Katz

With that knowledge comes an ability to make a quick analysis. When asked what he thinks of the fact that a synagogue located a short distance from Auschwitz had been recently renovated and was now operating, Irving's response is painfully matter of fact. "For who? I mean maybe the tourists stop by, that's all." Irving Althaus is all too aware that the Nazis did their job well. Many towns in Poland never recovered the Jewish populations that were so efficiently devastated.

While Irving proudly proclaims that Poland is "making a comeback," he has little desire to be in attendance when that comeback is complete. "Why should I? I don't have anything there."

Irving also knows that anti-Semitism still exists in Poland, despite the monuments and the museums. He believes it exists in the United States as well, but not as much on the surface and not as dangerously. When asked about the possibility of a Jewish Vice President (Joe Lieberman) becoming a reality, the shrewd, practical nature of a

survivor emerges. "I don't know. If he's doing a good job he's not going to get no credit. If he messes up, they could say 'the Jews did it.' That worries me."

In the video of his trip to Poland, it becomes quickly apparent that Irving ultimately took over the duties as a tour guide to his hometown because, even after a half century, he knew every street and every ancient building. Once again, he shuns any attempt to get him to reveal emotion. He's more excited about the highway conditions of a place that was in shambles when he last laid eyes on it. "Yeah all the signs (are) beautiful. (And the) service stations. They got nicer service stations than here."

Indeed. Irving Althaus appears to tell his story of the Holocaust impassively. Yet, the reaction from listeners is quite the opposite and not just from his young cousin Harry.

When we completed the interview for the documentary back in 1995, I thanked Irving and huddled with Ettalea Kantor who was President of the United Jewish Federation of the Virginia Peninsula and who coordinated the project, along with our video production crew to set up the next interview. A few minutes later, as we were engaged in conversation, I could see out of the corner of my eye Irving putting on his modest trench coat and heading out into the early winter evening. I excused myself and trotted out after him.

I knew that dredging up the memories of mass murder, of seeing childhood friends tortured and gassed, of humiliation and starvation took a kind of bravery few of us could understand. I wanted to express to Irving my gratitude for helping to write the true story of the Holocaust.

"Oh, it's nothing, no big deal," he said with a wave of his hand. "Anytime. Just call me if you need me." Once again Irving Althaus spoke without the flood of emotion one would expect from a survivor who has shared his story. I watched him step up into his bland, utilitarian van and drive away. At that moment I realized that my eyes were flooded with tears and my heart engulfed in the sentiments Irving never appeared to express himself. Instead he evoked them in me, as he has in hundreds of others, giving us all a lesson of immense value while elevating his already impressive stature. ❖

'Courage, ma fille!'
MARY SIGILLO BARRACO

By Richard Marten

"In Gand Prison I was beaten on a Wednesday and my whole world was taken from me. As I was dragged through the corridor, a priest, his face beaten to a bloody pulp, managed to say 'Courage, ma fille!' I was thrown back into my cell. After a little while I heard tapping on the pipe. It was the bloodied priest in the cell next to mine. 'I will pray for you,' he whispered through the pipe.

"Exhausted, and in more pain than I had ever experienced in my life, I fell into a deep sleep. I dreamt I was with Arthur Libre, my fiancé. In my dream he was going ahead of me into a dark tunnel, into which I could not see. Suddenly, Arthur looked at me, then proceeded again. He turned around several times more. On the fourth turn, Arthur stared at me intently. 'Attendez pour moi. Voici. C'est la derniere.' (Listen to me. Here. This is the last one.) Then he kissed me and I saw the light and a star and woke up praying in a corner of my cell. Arthur was executed by firing squad at 7 o'clock in the morning." The date was October 21, 1943.

In the Spring of 1940, having subjugated Poland, Adolf Hitler turned his attention west, launching his fierce war machine against France and the neutral countries of Holland and Belgium. These nations were no match for the Nazi blitzkrieg, which shrieked through them with minimal opposition.

MARY SIGILLO BARRACO was 16 years old when the Wehrmacht marched into the Belgian city of Renaix. Their tanks, mortar and jackbooted soldiers broadcast a sinister rhythm as they marched down the cobblestoned central street of the Flemish city. As the Nazis gripped the country in an iron fist of oppression and terror, Mary joined the underground resistance. Their mission was hiding fugitives and Jewish families, and rescuing British, American and Canadian airmen who had been shot down. She also smuggled passports, identification cards, ammunition and weapons until her ultimate capture and arrest.

She had been born in Lawrence, Massachusetts in 1923. Her father was an American and her mother, Belgian. Raised as a devout Catholic, she attended church regularly in Lawrence. Mary was an American who loved hot dogs and listening to classical music. As the Great Depression deepened, her father left for Canada to work, and her mother, with seven-year-old Mary, moved to Belgium, where they lived in Renaix (Ronse). Mrs. Sigillo went into business, operating a grocery store and a

Mary Sigillo Barraco

"*During the most*

trying times, I felt

God was always

with me.

He gave me

strength."

barbershop/hairdressing establishment. Mary studied classical music and opera at the National Conservatory of Music and Drama. In addition to French and English, she also became fluent in Flemish, Italian and German. In the years to come, the latter would serve her in good stead. In fact, it would prove invaluable.

In 1937, when she was 14, Mary's grandfather called her to his bedside. "I know that we will have a war," he prophesied. "I feel that the Germans are rising again. I am not going to be here and I count on you to protect your mother and grandmother." A philosopher, he talked to her about history and about his experiences as a prisoner in the First World War, and extracted Mary's promise to remember everything that he taught her.

Shortly after the Nazi invasion, traveling to the city to collect wages due her from the textile company where she worked, Mary encountered three German soldiers on a motor scooter, who stopped to ask directions. Without thinking, Mary instinctively guided them in the wrong direction. This was her first act of resistance to the foreign invader. Her next was even bolder: Mary saw that prisoners being marched through the street often had no shoes or were ill-clothed. She began sneaking into a building that had been converted into a prison camp. There, she helped prisoners escape and stole identification cards and other vital documentation.

Eventually, Mary and her mother began hiding escaped prisoners and Jews in their attic. "If you ask how many Jewish families we helped, I could not tell you because we were there to help everybody that we possibly could." Daringly, Mary took young Jews on the train, diverting attention from her charges by vamping with the Gestapo inspectors in the aisles. She brought escapees to the house of her two widowed aunts in Brussels. She located safe farmhouses where people fleeing the Nazis could hide.

At first Mary acted independently, smuggling civilian clothes and stolen potatoes to military prisoners by posing as a German sympathizer. "To get into the prison camp, I would make some coy remarks to the German guards who loved to be flirted with. I would always be able to go in." However, she soon affiliated with the Belgian resistance, writing an underground newspaper and helping to sabotage railway transports. While trying to blow up a train, a group of saboteurs – Mary among them – was discovered by a sentry. In the ensuing exchange of gunfire, one of their group was killed.

Mary and her fiance, Arthur, fled to France where they were betrayed by a fellow member of the underground. A Belgian partisan sold them for the equivalent of $12. She and Arthur were captured at 4 o'clock in the morning.

Mary was subjected to atrocious and savage torture that permanently damaged her, mentally and physically. Her jaw was cracked, her nose broken, her teeth knocked out. She was the victim of gruesome and bizarre medical experiments that left her sterilized. Her pelvic bones and vertebrae were damaged. She was placed in a steam chamber that burned her and later she was placed in a locker in a semi-crouched position for an interminable length of time.

In Brussels, at 347 Avenue Louise, known as the "Gestapo Torture Building," she was thrown in a bloody, damp cellar where she could hear the cries and screams of other prisoners being tortured. Mary managed to scratch two words on the walls of the cellar, *"adieu maman"* (Goodbye Mother).

"During the horrible interrogations, I never deviated from my cover story which was that I was a party girl who had left home for money and food and a good time with German soldiers," she said, explaining that as an American she had no access to rationing coupons which would provide her with food and clothing. Consequently, her cover story gave her an alibi for having food and clothing which she got from the resistance.

Against all odds, Mary was released on Christmas Day 1943. Immediately, she reconnected with the resistance, helping to rescue downed Allied pilots by providing them with forged identity papers.

"During the most trying times, I felt God was always with me. He gave me strength. In prison, the Germans would torture the prisoners by making us stand against a wall with our hands outstretched over our heads for hours. Schmidt, the commandant, would walk up and down the yard, rattling his keys. But with prayer, I was able to escape from Schmidt. Despite the fact that since childhood I had had a tendency to faint if I stood too long, I never fell down – I was even oblivious to the sound of the jangling keys."

After the war, Mary and her mother returned to Lawrence, where she met her future husband, Joseph Barraco in 1947. Two months before their wedding in 1949, at an informal dinner at her home, Mary had an opportunity to dine with two Belgian priests. During dinner, with her fiance sitting at her side, one of the priests, Father Deberghe, looked across the table and said, *"Est-ce que c'est toi, chou fleur?"* (Is that you, cauliflower?) Astoundingly, this was the very priest who was being dragged from the interrogation room at Mons Prison as she was being forced into it. At the time his face was bloodied, "almost unrecognizable and when he passed by he said, 'courage, ma fille,'" Mary remembers. Later, this same priest gave her comfort as she lay on the floor of her cell by whispering and tapping through the pipes -- their only communication line, "I will pray for you. I will always pray for you, *chou fleur.*"

Joseph and Mary Barraco were married April 24, 1949, with Father Joseph Deberghe officiating.

When asked how God could permit such a thing as the Holocaust, Mary adamantly replies, "God did not allow the Holocaust to happen. It was man that had no fear of God. I had faith in God, even with a broken heart, giving me the strength to stand all adversity. I cannot live without God."

Mary and Joe Barraco moved to Virginia Beach in 1950. They adopted a daughter in 1959. "The greatest joy in my life is my beautiful grandson, Lee Smith. He is 15 years old and it is for him and all the children that I am continually doing what I am doing today – fighting for freedom and spending a great deal of my time talking about tolerance and responsibility. That is what I am dedicating my life to. I never want another Hitler on this earth." ❖

Abraham Baum   *Photo by Echard Wheeler*

He Survived Six Concentration Camps
Abraham Baum
SURVIVOR

By Margie Marcus

As ABRAHAM BAUM'S story spills out in fragments, traces of his native Polish emerge through his dry, raspy voice. It is a story of aborted youth, of formative years stolen forever as a result of chance and circumstance: he happened to be born into prewar Poland, 15 years before Nazi insanity was to erupt into his corner of the world. Again, as a result of this same fortuity and circumstance, it is a story of his surviving the horrors in six concentration camps, equaling those described by Dante in his description of the Inferno.

Born in 1924 on a family-owned farm near Krakow, Poland, Abraham Baum's study at *Cheder* school was abruptly cut short by a war that was to disrupt the course of his whole life. As the oldest of seven children, the first part of his youth had been spent helping his parents scrape out a living to support their family. His father opened a grocery store to supplement their income from the farm. But being a Jewish merchant among Polish peasants with no sympathy for Jews was not easy. His mother kept a kosher home, tended the animals, and helped her husband in the store.

Nine-year-old Abraham was sent by his father to study in a *Cheder* in a nearby city. He would have preferred playing outdoors with his brothers and sisters;

he missed his family and hated the long hours of study away from them.

Life on the farm was brought to an abrupt halt when the family was forced by the Germans in 1940 to leave their farm and was assigned to a small apartment in the nearby city of Wielopo. This move was a shock that disrupted the pattern of their whole life, Abraham said. On top of that, for Abraham, at a time when most boys are flexing their muscles and exploring their strengths, it disrupted his passage from a child into a young adult.

The Germans had invaded Poland the year before, in 1939, during the High Holidays. As they conquered city by city, they stopped to burn whole synagogues full of worshippers. Abraham's father had volunteered to join the Polish army in 1939 to fight against the Germans and Russians. After being taken prisoner by the Russians, he was released within two weeks. On his way home he witnessed the remains of the burnt synagogues, which he described to Abraham. At this point his father shaved his beard and *payos* in order to look less Jewish.

Abraham got separated from his family after he escaped out the back door during a middle-of-the night raid on the apartment where they were staying. "The Germans pounded on the back door, and before my mother was able to open it (it) was already open." When the younger children started crying he woke up and looked down from his

HOPE
by Abbott Saks

"It can't be true what they have said"
(That they who enter they are dead)
On deaf ears mostly rumors fell
That here on earth were flames of hell
And as they trudged toward that gate
They pondered their uncertain fate
And searched about for ray of hope
In fear and anguish souls did grope
Until above barbed wire high
They saw the sign they might not die
In iron letters: ARBEIT MACHT FREI!

attic room. When discovered by the soldiers and questioned, he told them he was only 12 although he was actually 15, hoping that this would save him from the German labor force. The soldiers ordered him out the front door to join the men, but he disobeyed and ran out the back door. He managed to stay hidden until daybreak, when a Polish policeman finally caught up with him and told him, "It's time for you to pay the price." The year was 1940. He was 15, and for the next five years he was transferred from camp to camp, where "pay the price" he did.

In the policeman's custody he was escorted to the marketplace and deposited with the rest of the Jewish labor force being collected and guarded. His sister, not a candidate for labor, was able to bring him some shoes without fear of conscription. This was the last time he saw any of his family and he does not know what became of them.

The group assembled in the marketplace was taken to Mielec, "a freshly built concentration camp" situated behind a factory where planes were built. The sign above the gate read *Arbeit Macht Frei,* which translated as

"Work Makes You Free." Their clothes were taken away and replaced with striped prison garb. They were told that if they behaved, their families would be spared. "Masters of deception," Abraham called them. The fact that this was his first camp, combined with his youth, hit Abraham hard emotionally. He said that he felt torn up at this point and could see no justice. Two older cousins gave him comfort and at the same time tried to toughen him up. He said he soon became cynical.

Meals at this camp consisted of cabbage soup, with caterpillars from the cabbage floating on top. An epidemic of stomach typhus broke out in the camp; those too sick to work were shot if they were found in the barracks during working hours. Abraham was assigned to work on new German fighter planes in the factory. The Poles in the camp told him, "Your days of eating white bread and chicken every Friday and of cheating us are over." He learned by working side by side with the Polish people how much hate they had stored up toward the Jews.

Abraham was at this camp for "what seemed like a lifetime," but it was actually just shy of four years. Keeping up with events outside the narrow world of the camp took a back seat to the priority of daily survival. While there Abraham did receive a letter from his father saying that he wished the two could trade places, but he does not know how the letter reached him or where his father was.

During the summer he was 18, Mielec was liquidated and the prisoners were transported in freight cars, with only slits for windows, to other camps. The train stopped at a camp near Krakow where they stayed for two weeks; then, they piled back into the cars and headed toward Auschwitz. While the train stopped at a station, Polish passers-by promised water to the thirsty passengers through the slits in exchange for any jewelry they may have kept hidden. They took the jewelry but never brought back water. The packed train finally started moving. Meanwhile, the passengers were collapsing from the heat.

They wound up at Flossenburg, a transit camp in Germany. Faced with machine guns when the doors opened, half of the prisoners made no attempt to move out of the way. They had apparently died from the heat.

Much of the time Abraham followed orders blindly: "Half the time I didn't know where I was or what I was doing. I was just like an animal being pushed," he said.

Upon arrival at Flossenburg they were ordered to surrender all valuables. But this was one time Abraham did not obey orders. He did not give up his most valuable possession – a photograph of his mother. They were taken to a large shower room where ice cold water was turned on. Weak from the heat of the jimmy, everyone ran out from under the direct stream of the shock of the cold water. At this point, the Germans in charge jumped in with whips.

At Flossenburg for the first time, Abraham was exposed to prisoners guilty of crimes other than being Jewish. These other "crimes" ranged from homosexuality to murder. Each criminal wore a color on his lapel symbolizing his crime. The Jewish prisoners wore a number on their collars. "That number was what they called you. You actually forgot your name," he mused.

Abraham was among a group transferred to Auxburg, Germany, where work consisted of chopping down trees to clear the land. In order to get to the woods every day, a ten mile hike and travel by train was necessary. Eighteen-year-old Abraham grew weaker and weaker from the rigors of the routine.

"That number was what they called you. You actually forgot your name."

He was sent to a camp in Litmeritz, Czechoslovakia. When his group arrived, the Poles in charge told them that they had been waiting for the Jews and they were going to repay them for what they had done to the Poles in Poland. They were forced to watch the hanging of three escapees unfortunate enough to have been caught.

Litmeritz was situated next to a salt mine. The mine was cool in summer and warm in winter. But unfortunately, "in the winter I'd be on the outside and in the summer when it was nicer outside I was always inside the mines. As you lined up (for work) the stronger workers would always push you to the side," he said.

From Litmeritz he went to Leonburg, where "it was even worse. (The camp)

had no facilities of any kind," he said, "and plumbing consisted of water dripping from a pipe." This camp was located next to a factory where planes were manufactured in an underground tunnel which protected the planes from bombs dropped by the British and Americans.

"Every time a plane would come by they would drag us all out in the middle of the night," he said. He guesses that the Germans were trying to protect the factory by exposing the inmates.

The war began winding down. From this point on, the Germans were being pressed from all directions – "the Americans on one side and the Russians on the other," he said. "They continuously told us that there would be no witnesses. Most of us had reached the stage where we were too weak to work." In this camp the work consisted of carrying the dead.

He remembered developing holes in his hips as a result of lying on hard boards which formed his makeshift bed. "I guess I must have been too weak to walk around because I just continued to lie there," he said.

The last camp he was taken to was Dachau, where he was liberated by the Americans. When liberation arrived in April, 1945, Abraham had to be carried out. He heard other people yelling to catch the Germans who were in the process of escaping. "But all I could do was listen. I was just too weak. In

another eight or 24 hours I would have been dead, had I not received help," he said.

"I spent about six months in a field hospital being nursed back to health." Abraham said that at this point he could not even remember his own name, but somehow he was identified. Gradually, as his memory returned, the set of facts he recalled matched up with the identification that had been assigned to him

He remained for a few more months acting as an interpreter for the field hospital; then he secured a room in a private German home. After this he found himself alone in the world, feeling guilty for surviving. He never found out what happened to his family.

With no living relatives and no place to go, his thoughts turned to America. He had been exposed to the American soldiers' talk of home while he was recuperating. After five years of wading through red tape to get to America, he settled in Norfolk and has been living here ever since. He lives in the Ghent section of Norfolk. ❖

The Power of Labels
Reinhold Beuer-Tajovsky

By Lois Winter

> *"Around existence twine*
> *(Oh, bridge that hangs across the gorge!)*
> *ropes of twisted vine."*
>
> *BASHO*

REINHOLD BEUER-TAJOVSKY, a Gentile survivor of the Holocaust saved by Jews, has a special story to share. The story is one of the power of labels. The path of his entire life has been controlled by other peoples' perceptions as he was continually branded with a series of stereotypical names. For instance, in the Vienna, Austria of 1928, a child born out of wedlock was considered a bastard. His single, unwed mother, shunned by her family and relatives, had no means to support her baby. Reinhold, as an unwanted child, had to spend his childhood living as an orphan with foster parents and in institutions.

When the Nazis annexed Austria on March 12, 1938, Reinhold remembers that confusion reigned supreme.

Thousands of Jewish families were soon to loose their homes and possessions. While their children were instantly robbed of their past loving home lives, Reinhold was never to attain his wish for such an idyllic life. "Overnight everything changed as by the touch of a magic, albeit evil wand," Reinhold recounts. "At school we had to learn a new way of handwriting; German history and mythology replaced Austrian history, the Austrian anthem was replaced by the German anthem, even the name Austria was changed to 'Ostmark.' The times were very frightening to us children who did not really understand what was happening. Nazis in their army uniforms were everywhere with their menacing looks, their shiny black boots and their arrogant airs."

While his Jewish friends lost their pasts, Reinhold lost his longed-for home because of the immediate implementation of the Nazi Blood Purity laws. Promulgated in 1935, Jews were declared unfit to exist, 'Life unworthy of life,' as one top Nazi theoretician put it. "These worthless creatures," the Nazis wrote, "have to be put to death if they even 'kiss' a non-Jewish woman's hand. As for non-Jewish women who associate with Jewish men, they are to be considered infected, as with a deadly germ, and as such are to be punished with either imprisonment or with penal servitude." Like lepers, the Nazis branded these gentiles contagious with a deadly disease they called "Jewishness." Reinhold says, "Our Gentile status was changed to that of 'Jew-by-Association' and to save our lives, we too, had to emigrate."

Reinhold as a young boy in France.

"Overnight everything changed as by the touch of a magic, albeit evil wand."

Reinhold's mother and her Jewish fiancé left for Paris by train on the very night when the Nazis invaded Austria. Soon thereafter, the orphanage in which he was staying, reported Reinhold abandoned, and he was turned over to the new Nazi regime, which placed him in a home for incorrigible children. There he was beaten by the older boys who were training to become "Hitler Youths." On the infamous *Kristallnacht*, (November 1938) he remembers being forced to go with them to watch what happened to the Jews as the boys looted, burned and beat anyone they considered Jewish sympathizers.

In 1939, on his 11th birthday and speaking no French, Reinhold was sent to join his mother in Paris. Because they had a daily hand-to-mouth struggle for survival, his mother shipped him off to a foster family in Switzerland for safe keeping. "Unfortunately, the Swiss forced me to return to France after they mobilized at the outbreak of WWII in September of 1939," he says. "By 1940, during the fall of France, and the evacuation of Paris, my mother ended up in a camp in southern France, while I was swept up by a rescue organization called *Oeuvre de Secours aux Enfants* (OSE)."

As author Serge Klarsfeld, himself a hidden child survivor, put it "the OSE story is a model of the way Jews and courageous non-Jews fought the Nazis and the Vichy regime to save lives in occupied and unoccupied France." All together, France shipped over 70,000 men, women and children to death camps in Germany during the perilous 1942-1945 years. Over 10,000 of these victims were children. Reinhold was one of the few children survivors thanks to the OSE.

According to Reinhold, "Many of us hidden children owe our lives to one great lady, the Baroness Pierre de Gunzbourg. She provided OSE with millions of French francs in late 1939 to purchase villas and old, run-down, empty chateaux, like Chabannes, to house the thousands of displaced and homeless children streaming into France for safety from Nazi regimes in Germany, Austria, and Eastern Europe. For all her efforts and generosity, Mme de Gunzbourg's name has been lost to Holocaust history," he says. To perpetuate her memory, Reinhold, who is an artist, has memorialized her in a surrealistic abstract painting based on

Chateau de Chabannes in France.

Reinhold Beuer-Tajovsky
Photo by Susan Hirschbiel

the use of each of the letters contained in the words: *In Memory of the Baroness de Gunzbourg.* Describing his painting, Reinhold says, "As is the case with many of my surrealistic-symbolic paintings, the 'unmanifest manifested,' not only in the unique design of the memorial painting itself, but it even contains the letters O-S-E, showing how deeply entwined the two subjects are, from a soul's perspective."

While he was hidden in the Chateau de Chabannes, Reinhold developed a close relationship with Jewish Holocaust survivor, Charles Martin Roman. They met as children in a Paris train station, two of many being rushed out of the city ahead of the invading Germans by OSE. They became instant friends and were separated in August 1941 when Reinhold was among the 253 children

chosen to be sent to the United States, while Charles was left behind. Miraculously, the two old friends were reunited in 1997 after being separated for 56 years.

Reinhold's search for his own identity and a loving family did not end with his arrival in America. When it was discovered that he was a non-Jewish refugee, the Jewish placement organizations did not know what to do with him. During his first two years, he was placed in six different foster homes, attended four different schools in three different towns and two different states. That marked the beginning of Reinhold's homeless, rootless, transient life in America. At age 16, he had to go to work only to discover that he could not be employed in defense factories because he was branded an enemy alien, since his legal papers designated him to

be a native of Vienna, Germany – the enemy! He eventually joined the army and after military service, attended Columbia University in New York City. Reinhold is a WWII and Korean War veteran. He became a U.S. citizen in 1953. He is now retired from the U.S. Civil Service, the father of two, and makes his home in Newport News, Virginia.

His deeply repressed Holocaust memories returned to him several years ago when he came across a book containing the photo of a little girl whom he recognized from his days at Chabannes, but who had not survived. "When she arrived at the Chateau, she looked so forlorn, I remembered feeling extreme compassion for her. Seeing her photo again overwhelmed me with severe survivor guilt," he says.

Charles Martin Roman and Reinhold, friends from OSE days, discuss Reinhold's painting titled "Memorial to OSE and the Baroness Pierre de Gunzbourg."

"If mankind, the animals, the plants and our earth are to survive, the Reverend Martin Luther King's dream of freedom, peace and justice needs to become everyone's dream."

Since this incident occurred during the celebration of Passover, it triggered the question for Reinhold, "Why me? Why was I saved? For what was I saved?"

The answer to that question is revealed in his most recent painting entitled, "Lives Unworthy of Life" in which he epitomizes man's eternal struggle with the cosmic forces of light and dark. Extraordinary intellectual and technological advances were applied in the service of the most sadistic, brutal and inhuman behavior imaginable. For millions, enslavement, genocide and the Holocaust became a literal "Hell on Earth."

Reinhold's most enduring label is survivor. As one survivor of man's greatest inhumanity to man, he concludes, "If mankind, the animals, the plants and our earth are to survive, the Reverend Martin Luther King's dream of freedom, peace and justice needs to become everyone's dream. Only then will we usher in the prophetic words of Isaiah, the age when "… the wolf will dwell with the lamb, and the leopard will lie with the kid" and when "… they shall do no evil, nor will they destroy." ❖

"Memorial to the Ten Thousand Hidden French Children" based on an actual photograph of a mountain made of clothes outside a crematorium in Europe.

Rabbi Israel Bornstein
To Life!
By Lynda Gonsenhauser

Rabbi Israel Bornstein
Photo by Stephen Jay Photography

RABBI ISRAEL BORNSTEIN (of blessed memory) served B'nai Israel Congregation in Norfolk for 47 years before moving to Manchester, England in 1999 to live with his sister and niece. His love of Judaism, Israel and the Jewish people was not only expressed in words, but in deeds.

He was born in Copenhagen, Denmark and later studied as a youth in the renowned Rabbinical School of Kamenieze, Poland. His father was a cantor, *shochet* and a Talmudic scholar. So esteemed was his reputation that he was elected *shochet* of the Frankfurt, Germany community. Despite the honor, his father declined due to the rapid rise of Nazism.

"This one decision probably saved our lives," Rabbi Bornstein said in an interview which appeared in the 50th anniversary *Tribute Journal* of B'nai Israel.

Rabbi Bornstein's mother, the daughter of a cantor and *shochet*, could recite and sing the entire High Holiday services by heart. His sister, Mina, was blessed with an operatic voice and was even accepted into the Royal Conservatory of Opera in Copenhagen, but as Rabbi Bornstein noted, "our father blocked it."

Recalling life for Jews in Copenhagen before World War II, Rabbi Bornstein noted, "Although I came from an Orthodox home, Orthodox life in Copenhagen was not booming. Jews enjoyed complete freedom and acceptance in Denmark." However, as elsewhere in Europe, things began to change once Germany invaded. "Since the Danish government surrendered under honorable conditions, the king promised that the Jews would be left alone. Still we felt insecure. It was like living under a cloud. More and more,

we began to hear what was happening in middle Europe. It soon became apparent it would overtake us all."

Finally, on Rosh Hashanah 1943, Hitler issued direct orders to round up all the Jews in Denmark. Thanks to a tip-off from a German diplomat, George Ferdinand Duckwitz, the Jews escaped with the help of the Danish people. Rabbi Bornstein's family fled to Sweden where they remained until the end of the war. During this time, he supported himself as part-time cantor, having been trained by his father. He also worked for an import/export firm as a Nordic language expert.

In 1946, after the war ended, Rabbi Bornstein came to America, where he taught and studied at the Ner Israel Rabbinical College of Baltimore under Rabbi Jacob Ruderman (of blessed memory), by whom he was ordained. Later he earned a Master of Philosophy

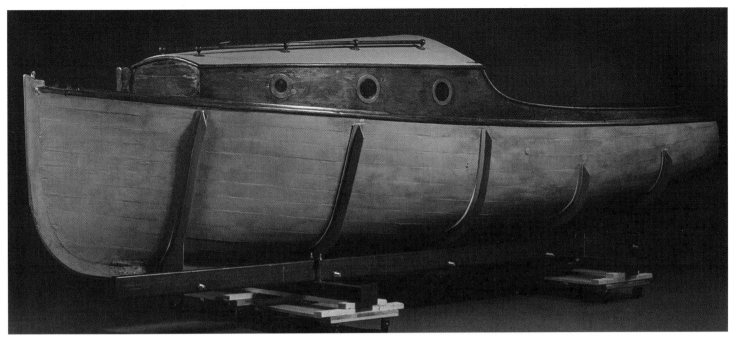

Among the German-occupied countries, only Denmark rescued its Jews. Jews were hidden in homes, hospitals, and churches of coastal towns. Danish police refused to cooperate in arrests. In October of 1943, 7,220 Danish Jews were brought to safety. The Danes thus proved that widespread support for Jews and resistance to Nazi policies could prevent deportation. The clandestine rescue of Danish Jews was undertaken at great personal risk. This boat and several others like it were used by one of the earliest rescue operations code-named the "Helsingor Sewing Club." Photo by permission of U.S. Holocaust Museum.

degree from Georgetown University. More than 125 of his sermons have been published by the Rabbinical Council of America.

In 1949 he came to Norfolk to serve as a cantor and associate rabbi at B'nai Israel Congregation under Rabbi Joseph Schecter. In 1961 he became a full rabbi and served until his retirement in 1989, when he became Rabbi Emeritus.

In the *Tribute Journal*, he noted: "We have to accept on faith that we have been elected as a people to be a religious and spiritual catalyst for the entire world. To the question how do we promote the spiritual, we must go back to Jewish law. We live today in an age where despite technological advances and modern comforts, we feel a lack of intimate contact with God and the Divine which we want to bring back into our lives.... "

Regarding the need to reconnect more Jews to their heritage, he said, "For us to be successful, we must extend our love and understanding unconditionally. Every Jewish soul is an off-shoot of the divine and must be recovered." ❖

Rabbi Israel Bornstein
died February 27, 2001
in Manchester, England.

"We have to accept on faith that we have been elected as a people to be a religious and spiritual catalyst for the entire world."

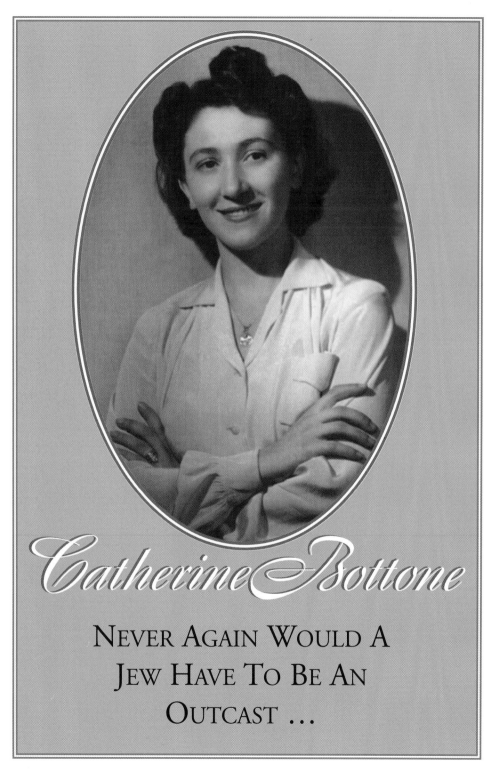

Catherine Bottone

Never Again Would A Jew Have To Be An Outcast ...

Editor's Note: The following is a copy of a talk given by Catherine Bottone at the Ohef Sholom Men's Club Archives Brunch on January 17, 1999.

"The impact on me of the 1948 Recognition of the State of Israel"

For Millennia, Jerusalem was in the dreams of the Israelites. It is repeated in all our daily prayers. Israel has therefore existed in our hearts and wishes from time immemorial.

So that finally in 1948, when after a long fight against all odds, the Zionist dream obtained legal status, this was a world-shaking event for every living Jew.

What can I say, how can I say what it meant for me? Coming from Europe and being a few decades older than the group of American "Baby Boomers" I am talking to, I will try to point out the event from a different angle.

Let us compare the difference in our background. You are Americans. America is a federation of 50 States, but it is *ONE COUNTRY* – guided by one Constitution, speaking *ONE LANGUAGE*, and having a basic legislation valid in the *ENTIRE COUNTRY.*

The Jewish presence in America dates back to almost the beginning of U.S. history – and though it has certainly suffered some anti-Semitic trends, there is no legislation limiting the right of a Jew to be a Jew at the level he chooses to be. He is a U.S. Citizen with all the rights of a citizen.

The scenario in Europe at that time, and still presently, is totally different. There are many nations– independent of each other, each speaking a *DIFFERENT LANGUAGE,* being governed by a *DIFFERENT SET OF LAWS,* Monarchies, Republics, with each country bestowing their citizenship rights on the inhabitants.

Wars and political upheavals, revolutions, dictatorships have shifted and changed borderlines in an always different jig-saw puzzle. My own biography can be an appropriate example. It may seem to you that I am talking completely out of context, but I assure you that all this background will

Catherine and her brother.

be perfectly connected to my reaction at the recognition and the birth of Israel as a State.

I was born in 1920 in a city called Fiume, in the northeastern tip of the Adriatic Sea. The city, with a population of about 50,000 people, had been an important southern port of the Austro-Hungarian Empire up to 1918, when the Versailles Treaty cut the city from its previous links. Between 1918 and 1920 a furious civil war among the mixed ethnic groups living in Fiume (Austrians, Hungarians, Croatians, Italians) brought about the 1920 "Bloody Christmas." The Italian, Gabriele d'Annunzio, a soldier-poet-adventurer at the head of his legion, won out against the various ethnic groups and Fiume was declared a *FREE CITY.*

I was six weeks old during the Bloody Christmas and my parents went into hiding taking refuge in the basement of a big coffeehouse. After six years of being a free city, in 1926, Fiume was annexed to Italy. At the same time, the city was divided in two. The borderline was a river separating the western side of the city from the eastern half, which was named Sussak and became part of the Yugoslav Monarchy. So I became an Italian citizen at age six (of course, through my parents). This was already my second citizenship. I grew up in Italian Fiume, was raised in fascist schools, proudly wore my fascist uniform, and was integrated in the surrounding society. Fiume had a high percentage of almost 1,800 Jews (about

Catherine's mother with a Jewish GI who helped her family during the War.

3%), mostly Ashkenazi, as a result of the Italian-Austro-Hungarian previous position. In all of Italy there were then less than 40,000 Jews, mostly Sephardim. They settled and grew in Rome before the Christian era, brought as slaves by the Roman conquerors of Palestine. If there was any anti-Semitism it was essentially due to the existing presence of the Vatican in Italy. During the domain of the church, Jews had the role of doing jobs or work that the Church believed to be below its dignity, like collecting taxes. Yet, collecting taxes was important to the church. But this position singled them out at the same time as objects of contempt and often ridicule. They were restricted to living in the Ghetto, where they had to re-enter by sundown before it was closed for the night. The Ghetto was finally abolished and opened only in 1870, when the Italian Monarchy restricted the Church to the Vatican City, and chose Rome as the Capital of Italy. The social and intellectual progress of the Jews, the free access to education, the professions and the military developed only after 1870.

The Ghetto population evolved quickly, thus filling the gaps the previous restrictions and segregation had created. The feeling of "different" diminished, though the Jews remained still a tight religious group, and mixed marriages were not usual.

I did not hear about Zionism until my puberty years. I came into contact with Zionist youth movements only during a trip to Romania in 1935, to visit my mother's family. In Romania there was a large Jewish presence and therefore also strong anti-Semitism, well orchestrated by the fascist Iron Guard. I had the occasion to see my Romanian cousins having Zionist gatherings with a lot of hora dancing and talk of Palestine. In Italy we were too few and widely scattered, nor was there any discrimination to motivate rebellion or change. Hitler was already in power and after he annexed Austria, Fiume became a point of passage to the first refugees from Austria's Dachau Concentration Camp, who fled to my city, from where there was clandestine

sea transportation arranged illegally. Although I saw this happening in front of my eyes, I could not identify with it personally, but my emotions and sympathy were deeply involved.

In the fall of 1937, my brother, then barely 15, was admitted to the Fascist Navy Cadet school just opened in Venice, where he attended this elite school in his third year of high school, 1937/38. By September 1938, he was ready to start his second year at the Cadet School. On September 1, Mussolini promulgated the infamous "Racial Laws" by which, from one day to the other, the Jews of Italy lost all their civil rights, and were gradually divested and deprived of all means of livelihood. For people deeply set in the fabric of Italian life in its quiet world,

Catherine's parents and brother in Italy, 1945.

and totally unaware and unprepared for the danger looming over them, everything was even more difficult.

I go back to 1938. The Jews of Fiume became a target of the racial laws. The gravity of the consequences was that all Italian Jews lost their civil rights. Jews of Fiume were also *DEPRIVED OF ITALIAN CITIZENSHIP*: the law, in fact, decreed that Jews naturalized after 1919 were automatically to lose their Italian Citizen status. Fiume became Italian only in 1926, seven years after that cut-off date. My entire family, as well as all Jews, lost their *CITIZENSHIP*. I was still under 18, a minor with no individual rights, a dependent of my father. Kicked out of school, out of jobs, with no present or future, we all turned to alternative emergency planning.

Relatives in the USA supported our plan to join them in New York. This possibility existed only for the young ones, since our generation had been born in Italy, while our parents were born in Hungary, Poland, Transylvania, all with closed immigration quotas according to laws set by the USA in 1924. So, we had to separate from our parents.

The thought of going to Israel was an ideal desire, but there was no Israel, only illegal and dangerous entry. So we chose America. But again, one needed a valid passport in order to stamp a visa on it. As a minor I could not even apply for a stateless passport. The tears of my mother moved to pity a person from Fiume who was a VIP in one of the State Departments in Rome, and he produced two temporary Italian passports, one for me and one for my brother. Four of my cousins also immigrated; two with a Hungarian passport issued by the Hungarian Honorary Consul in Fiume, and two with Nansen stateless passports obtained by probable bribe or rare human solidarity.

Jews had no land of their own, no nation to turn to. They were subject to the whims of the powers ruling over them. They had no court to turn to for justice. We were boats lost in a sea of trouble and danger. The temporary Italian passport with no return, permitted us to obtain our immigration visa and come to the USA in October of 1939. In June 1940, Italy declared war on the Allies and we were promptly issued "Enemy Alien Certificates" by the U.S. authorities. My brother was not admitted to evening courses at City College of New York because of his enemy alien status. At the same time, our father, in Fiume, was imprisoned as an enemy, and later sent to forced residences in small towns on the Adriatic coast, where they had to be monitored daily by the local political authorities.

Luckily, they survived without falling victim to the Nazis. In 1944, I became a naturalized U.S. Citizen. The Second World War ended and the new Italian government abolished the racial laws and re-instated Italian citizenship for the Jews who had lost it. In the years between 1939 and 1942, many refugees who had succeeded in getting out of German-occupied nations tried to find a haven and afterwards became victims of the then prevailing limitations in immigration. Some people speculated on the despair of these persecuted persons and took advantage of their needs to get them false entry visas that turned out to be invalid. A huge number of them, after begging for consideration, were turned down. Entire ships full of refugees, after unsuccessful attempts to obtain landing permits, had to travel back to Europe.

After Pearl Harbor, my brother and my cousin volunteered to join the 10th Mountain Division of the U.S. Army. On December 1944, they were sent to Italy to fight. My cousin, who was not yet 21, died during the American offensive on the Gothic Line in the Appennines. My brother survived the horrors of war.

I had married in 1942, had a daughter, and in 1948 I divorced and went back to Italy to my parents who could help me raise my child. I knew that as a single mother I would not be able to care for my child, so it was certain that I had to stay in Italy for several years. Again, destiny had made a decision for me that had heavy consequences.

Here I can add another facet to what I came to call "the ballet of my citizenship." And I think you will be shocked and surprised at what I will

Photos of family and friends from Catherine's personal collection.

"For Millennia, Jerusalem was in the dreams of the Israelites. It is repeated in all our daily prayers. Israel has therefore existed in our hearts and wishes from time immemorial."

read to you from the last page of my American Passport. "If you are a naturalized citizen of the United States you may *LOSE* your citizenship by residing for three years in the country of your birth or former nationality, or by residing for five years in any other foreign state." Can you believe this? In 1948 I was back in my country of birth, so I lost my U.S. Citizenship.

In 1964, a tough and courageous Jewish Refugee from Austria, Angelica Schneider, sued the USA because it had two types of citizenship. A *NATIVE* American could spend his entire life out of the USA without limitations while a *NATURALIZED* one would lose it after an absence of three or five years. The U.S. Supreme Court declared that it was unconstitutional to have two types of citizens, and the last page of U.S. passports no longer carried the sentence I have previously read to you. Of course, I wanted my U.S. Citizenship back; I had not given it up. It had been taken from me against my wishes. Yet the re-instatement was not automatic: you had to apply for it and justify yourself. But this is already another story.

It is under these circumstances and after all these vicissitudes, when in May of 1948 I rejoiced at the recognition of Israel! Never again would a Jew have to be an outcast, be denied civil rights by a political decision of the country of residence. Jews, finally, had a *LAND*; all they had to do is go to *THEIR NATION* and they were automatically citizens of Israel. No one could deny

them this right. Now we were not only a *PEOPLE*. Now we had *OUR NATION*.

Fifty years have gone by since that momentous 1948. Israel is there still fighting for its right to the Land of its Fathers. It is a thin strip of land surrounded by enemies; it has created a nation starting from scratch; it has revived the national language; it has a heroic population that with dedication, persistence, ambition, genius, and initiative has earned the admiration, and often the envy of the modern nations.

We are accused of having double allegiance, and it may be true, but the truth is that our roots, the deepest ones, the ones that remain the same even if transplanted, are in our attachment to our inalienable Jewish faith and tradition. To this deeply felt Jewishness we are tied, regardless of whether we are Orthodox, Conservative, Reform or secular Jews. ❖

EACH DAY A DAWN OF NEW HORRORS
Bluma Kushner Bromberg

By Reba Karp

BLUMA KUSHNER BROMBERG is an attractive impeccably dressed woman. Her entire appearance bespeaks a quiet and dignified lifestyle.

But it is a facade, for while many of her contemporaries in America and other western countries were in college or getting married and setting up homes, she was confined in ghettos and labor and concentration camps.

She speaks softly, covering up insecurities which she admits are hard to keep in check when the memories of those years take over.

"I am nervous," she said softly before letting herself go back to times she would rather forget. But she feels she has a responsibility to future generations and to the world at large to record her story, for she doesn't believe the truth of what happened is totally believed by all; for indeed, weren't the crimes in themselves totally incomprehensible to the civilized world, she questions?

"I wanted to escape, but where could I go? I never believed people could do so much to other people and not feel something … although I wished many

Bluma Kushner Bromberg
Photo by Stephen Jay Photography

times not to get up in the morning, I wanted to survive to tell others what it feels like to be a Jew," she said.

Consequently, no matter how tortuous her life became, she never entertained the notion of taking her own life. What truly kept her going was the hope that she would survive to belie the German's oft-spoken threat that "no Jews will be alive in the future."

Although she wanted to live, she did not fear death, for it was commonplace.

As penned on November 20, 1942 in a diary of "E.K." found in liberated Dachau, "these pages that I now begin to write would lead to certain death if they were found. But what is death? How few of those I knew here are still alive today, how close to death we all stand. I can die here any moment even if I take the greatest care … why should I not endeavor, even in the midst of these conditions of this cruelty, to tell this gruesome story that no longer gives us goose flesh."

And so Bluma Kushner Bromberg tells her story of an odyssey in hell.

Before the war she lived near Vilna, Poland with her brothers and sisters. In all there were seven including her parents – a happy middle-class Jewish family. Her father, who was a merchant, owned farmland which he rented to Polish farmers. She was about 16 or 17 years old when she got her introduction to German cruelty – the systematic search and seizure of property from the Jewish population.

What could they do as they stood and watched as their possessions became the

Bluma and friends in Austria before the War.

property of the Third Reich? To speak up, to protest would earn the butt of a rifle blow on the face, in the stomach. So they watched in quiet, sober fear. At first, the Germans settled for Jewish plunder and when there was nothing else left to take, they went for Jewish blood.

"They took property first and later took people … not all at once, but in small groups." Those who did protest or those they did not want to take "they killed, just threw them on the streets and shot them."

Her painful journey through horror began when she and members of her family were brutally tossed on trucks and transported to the ghetto. She remembers: "Five families in one room … maybe 18 people, no sanitary conditions … children crying, squeezed in, sleeping on the floor. … "

THE RAVINE

Hear the words of Yevtushenko
Who through deep silence heard the martyrs' cry
Whose pen would chisel in the mind
A monument that they not die
Though snows may blanket Babiyar
Hear the words of Yevtushenko
Who said what history was to say:
No fury, flood, no force on earth
Will still that cry or wash that blood away.

Abbott Saks

Some tried to escape, to get across the border to Russia. Those caught were beaten to death.

Punishment for those living in the ghettos was special "just because we were Jews," she said, recalling the hours they were forced to stand barefoot in winter in swamp water while they bore the brunt of brute cruelty. "To save bullets they would throw small children (those a year and younger) against tree trunks," she said, "where they were left, dead and dying." The children's mothers were forced to watch as they stood helplessly in line.

Those taken outside the ghetto for work details never knew if they would return. "We thought, if we could die a normal death, it would be a blessing." The first in her family to succumb was her father, who died of a heart attack while living in the ghetto. Later her brother would be killed while trying to escape.

And as their emotions became numb, they tried to gather strength from within. "We could not believe it, we waited day by day; maybe it would disappear."

Ghetto life for her and her family ended as abruptly as it began. Two groups were selected. Her group went to a labor camp. The other was stuffed into box cars and buried alive, she later learned.

What remained of her family, two sisters, a younger brother and her mother began a new countdown of days

Welcoming the Red Army.   *Photo by Hugo Horvath*

Bluma and her first husband, Saul Kushner.

One day in particular stands out in Bluma's mind – the day she last saw her mother and younger brother. The call was out for mothers with small children to assemble for transport to Auschwitz. They clung together, but only for a moment before her mother pushed Bluma and her sisters away. She would not hear of their going with her, for she believed that by parting it would increase their chances of survival. Later Bluma would be separated from her sisters at Stutthof.

But, before they parted, Stutthof would dawn with new horrors. Before being introduced into the camp's already existing population, the new inmates were deloused and deprived of their clothing and personal items. Then they were issued new clothing, which in many instances was to further humiliate them rather than cover their bodies.

"So many had been killed in Stutthof," Bluma said, that a casual shifting of the foot in the ground would unearth a tooth, a bone or a shoe from someone burned and buried. She was in Stutthof from February of 1944 to June of 1944.

Before Bluma reached Stutthof however, she was literally dragged on foot, from one place to another, as the Germans sought to escape the advancing Russians. It was during this interval that she slept out in the open wherever she fell, unless they found a barn, or were in temporary camps and behind barbed wire.

in hard labor. "We had to lay stones for roads, using mallets and picks." The fate of those unable to work is well-known – beaten with the butt of rifles or shot in the head.

No one had enough food, even the SS men in charge of the laborers. So she survived by begging food from neighboring farms for herself and her German captors. "We couldn't run away, for where would we go?" she questions as she explains her reason for returning to the camp.

Although they reasoned it wasn't much, it was an existence. Surely the war would end and sanity would reign once again.

In June of 1944 she was transferred to another labor camp from Stutthof and forced to work on roads once more until she was liberated in May 1945.

When liberated by the Russians she was living in barracks in a forest. "More than half were already dead, lying next to the living. This I will never forget as long as I live."

Many lived to be liberated, only to die shortly afterward of dysentery caused by trying to eat food their systems were not ready to digest. Although liberation had been a much-dreamed of moment, for Bluma, as well as for many others, it proved to be disappointing. "I questioned if it were true, if it was really over. I didn't want to be alive. I didn't have anyone."

And she had nowhere to go. When she regained some of her strength, a Jewish man in the Russian army helped her and a few other women to return to Poland where she encountered more brutality in the form of a band of murderous Poles and Germans who were still determined to kill Jewish people even though the war was over. So she fled once more. "I didn't know where I was going. I was just moving, looking for a safe haven until I could get to Israel."

In Lodz she met her first husband Saul Kushner, also a survivor, and they were married. Later they decided to move to Norfolk because Kushner had family living there. "My first husband escaped a premature ghetto grave by digging his way through dirt and dead bodies and then joining the partisans. He took part in raids against the Germans and Poles," she said.

Until they moved to Norfolk, the Kushners lived in Belgium where her daughter Irene was born. Irene and her husband, Joseph Weintraub, have one child, Emily. After Saul Kushner died, Bluma married Alexander Bromberg.

Both of Bluma's sisters survived and are now living in Israel. One, she said, returned after the war to Poland for a brief stay, living with her uncle who was later killed by a Pole.

"I will never return to Poland even if they gave me a free ticket … not even for a million dollars will I ever return," she concluded. ❖

Irene and Joseph Weintraub

Emily Weintraub

Photo above, Bluma lighting a candle at Yom Hashoah.

Photo right, Alexander and Bluma Bromberg.

A Yahrzeit in Words
Harry Bromberg

By Reba Karp

Harry Bromberg   *Photo by Stephen Jay Photography*

Yehiel De Nur, a survivor of Auschwitz, who has written five books on the subject, among them *House of Dolls*, chooses to write under his concentration camp number Ka-Tzetnik 135633. The reason is simplistic and is based on a special need for identification, for he notes: "My name, Ka-Tzetnik 135633 is not just a pen name – I see myself as a chronicler from the planet of Auschwitz. … "

Another survivor, HARRY BROMBERG of Tidewater, expresses his "pain at being liberated" in similar terms. With liberation and relief came fragile joy – and how could it be expressed otherwise than fragile in a person weighing only 75 pounds and suffering from malnutrition, mental exhaustion and lack of identity? When the joy of liberation subsided, he looked around for a familiar face or landmark and found none. He had survived six years in hell while his family had been murdered.

He had become an alien on his own planet. "The question was, 'Where will I go?' I had no one else in the world."

The liberation became a bittersweet victory. "My family perished in Treblinka." A few almost made it to the finish line. "My brother and his son hid in a hole in a village during the war. They were killed three days before liberation. My youngest brother, he was only 13 years old, was killed in a similar manner, while hiding, sold out by the Poles."

He wants to tell his story, a *yahrzeit* in words. Before the war he worked in Warsaw in a small shoe factory where tips for shoes were made and where leather was processed for sale to shoemakers. His family lived in Stanislaw, 40 kilometers away. The year was 1939.

"When the Germans marched in, they took all the young Jewish people and locked them in a church for three days. We had no food, no water, no facilities."

His words are Spartan and he rushes through events as if speed can diminish the pain of remembering. When the Germans finally opened the door to the church, they began the systematic mental and physical abuse of the young Jewish people which was to characterize the Third Reich and stigmatize an entire generation. "They tried to cut off the beards of the religious with their bayonets," he said, adding that they also struck the now weakened and unprotected bodies with their rifles and inflicted whatever torture was at their disposal.

He fared better than most. "They put me to work pushing trucks. The roads were impossible for trucks to get by." But he realized he could not long endure, for his captors viewed him merely as a Jewish body without a man

When the joy of liberation subsided, he looked around for a familiar face or landmark and found none.

inside. and as such was only to be used until he could not be used any longer.

He tried to escape several times, finally getting across the river to Byelorussia, Russian-occupied Poland. He and a friend made it to Stolpcy where they worked in a factory until 1941, living in the fields, men without an address. "We were caught in the middle. We were refugees, people without a home."

But his restricted freedom was short, for when the Germans arrived, they sought out the Jewish people and put them in ghettos, a panorama of horror, punctuated by the knowledge there was nowhere to run.

He recalls the time when the Germans put a call out for all the ghetto Jewish children. "The mothers who didn't want to give up their children were bayoneted, other children were thrown

from five to six stories up onto the trucks below."

Conditions were crowded, food was scarce, if at all, and death was commonplace. Although it was routine to evacuate Jews from the ghettos for mass executions and massacres, no one became apathetic. The will to survive kept many alive. He was later transferred to a smaller ghetto in Dworez, where his profession as a shoemaker spared him. "After we were led out, those left behind – the women and children – were killed," he said.

"We were taken away in box cars to a work camp in Krasny Bor" (Red Forest). There his job was to mend the shoes taken off dead and wounded German soldiers. "Some still contained part of the foot or toes of the last to wear the shoes," he remembered.

His grizzly task was made all the more difficult by the imposition of a quota, which if he fell behind, earned him 100 lashes, administered with an instrument of torture similar to three water hoses tied together with wire. "I still have some of the scars," he said quietly.

"Rations were a small loaf of bread for ten people and soup made with water and sawdust. Many became ill with dysentery and died."

Other memories of Krasny Bor are living nightmares which return at unsuspecting moments. "During count each morning as we stood in the snow, we were hosed down with water.

"I saw potato peelings in the latrine. I was so hungry, I dug them out."

When the Russians broke through the German lines, he was once more placed in a railroad box car with 120 other humans, without food, water and sanitary conditions for 14 days and 14 nights. The cars only moved by night; during the day they were at a stand still by the side of the road or at a railroad station. It was summer. "At the stations, we would beg the Poles for a little water. The reply was always the same. 'You damn Jews, you're soon going to fry in a crematorium.' We were not far from Auschwitz," he said.

"I feel the Germans put their most infamous camps in Poland because of the Polish people. They had organized groups called *Endeks* who grabbed Jewish people off the street and beat upon them."

By the time the boxcar reached its destination about 70 percent had perished. Due to lack of space some of the dead were still in an upright position when the doors were opened. There was no room for them to slide down, for they had been shoved up against one another for Germanic Teutonic expediency, as if inanimate objects rather than human beings.

In 1942 Bromberg found himself at Majdanek where once more his profession as a shoe maker spared his life. The scene was a familiar one when he arrived – the shoemakers, laborers

"Faith Bridges the Pit," by MaryAnne Katz

and carpenters were herded into one group – all the others went to the crematorium.

"Thoughts centered on getting enough to eat and drink. We didn't have the strength to commit suicide. No one thought they would ultimately survive. The goal was to live one more day. Those who lacked the desire for that one more day, threw themselves on the electric barbed wire which circled the camp."

Even in the midst of their struggle to survive, the Jewish people tried to establish a system among themselves in which rules prevailed. Bromberg remembers incidents in Blyzn to support this inner striving for order. "We worked repairing and making shoes … quotas had to be met, food was scarce." But what they had was evenly distributed. Portions were weighed, and in order to avoid arguments, all portions were cut and distributed as each turned his or her back. "This way no one could say another had gotten a bigger share."

An epidemic of typhus broke out while he was in Blyzn. "Hundreds died. Our barrack, number 9 was on a hill. I had to crawl on my belly to reach it. I didn't have the strength to walk." When the strength to crawl on his belly finally failed him, he was tossed into the "hospital barrack," an enclosure where the dead and dying lay indiscriminately one upon another. "I was on the floor, covered with dead bodies … I tried to

crawl over them." What was left of his strength grew less with each futile movement. He was trapped in a web of arms, hands, legs and hair of the dead and dying.

A hand reached out. Someone pulled him from the pile and placed him upon a platform. "Somehow I survived." The same man, one he refers to as a "doctor"

After the war, Bromberg tried to find the man who had miraculously saved his life. He had disappeared as strangely as he had appeared.

brought him a little food, a little soup. "I don't know why or how. He appeared so tall. Even after I was released from the hospital, he told me to come back and see him, that he would give me part of his food."

"It was like God saying I had to live."

After the war, Bromberg tried to find the man who had miraculously saved his life. He had disappeared as strangely as he had appeared.

From Blyzn he was transferred to Krakow and from Krakow to Mauthausen where he was subjected to two weeks in quarantine, a systematic attempt to further humiliate them. The men were kept completely naked … forced to sit between each other's legs. It was back-to-back torture. Bromberg recalls that in an inhuman effort to get the Jewish men closer together during the initial line-up, German soldiers would hit each man in the stomach in an effort to get him to pull in tighter.

And so they sat through the night, not only unable to find a restful position in which to sleep, but unable to move any limb beyond a limited area. To some, sleep came in the nightshades of death.

As the Russians approached in 1944, the inmates were marched to Ebaenze, Austria. Those who couldn't walk, were shot. Bromberg learned later that the people in a previous transport had been put on a boat which was deliberately gutted so the Jews on board would drown.

Ebaenze, which was surrounded by mountains, "was like being in a hole. We felt, as we looked around, God cannot find us here."

The Jewish people died by the thousands at Ebaenze, Bromberg said. "The crematoriums couldn't burn them fast enough. Many were buried outside the fence."

But the dwindling number of survivors held on. Liberation was not far away.

"We were warned not to go if the Germans wanted to put us in an underground shelter where ammunition was made," he said, explaining that the very next day the German soldiers tried to coax them into the shelter, telling them it was for their own safety.

"We refused to go, we knew we were going to be blown up." Consequently, the Germans were ready to machine gun the inmates when the American tanks broke through. The Germans on the guard tower were killed, others surrendered.

"We ran out, even kissed the tanks," he said, remembering that after the initial jubilation, reality took over. "We had lost everything. We were left with the feeling that life was not worth living … I didn't have anyone. I didn't have anywhere to go."

The Americans gave him food, which he tried to eat, although his system wasn't ready for food. "I felt like I was dying. They took me to the hospital.

I remember, even now, they gave me medicine which smelled like turpentine."

Later, he married his wife, Paula, who was liberated 30 miles from him, in a displaced persons camp. When his wife got pregnant, he realized it would be difficult for them to get to Israel and he turned to an uncle in America for assistance. He wrote letters to every Jewish newspaper as well as other American newspapers looking for his uncle, asking his help. By chance his uncle read of his plight and helped him get to America.

The Brombergs, who now live in St. Louis, Missouri, have two children, a daughter, Dr. Susan Bromberg Schneider who lives with her husband, Dr. Robert Schneider, and a son Al Bromberg. The Brombergs also have three grandchildren.

Even now, many years after liberation, Bromberg finds it difficult to sleep through the night without painful dreams.

But despite the horror which returns in his dreams, "I still believe in God," he said. He is a Survivor. ❖

"I still believe in God," he said.

ANNA BURK
Chana Shapiro Berkowicz

Edited by Elena Barr Baum

Anna and Charles Burk of Norfolk, were once known as Chana Shapiro Berkowicz and Chil Berkowicz. This is Anna's story, part of her testimony to a reparations committee for Holocaust survivors. Her husband's story is also in this book.

Before ANNA BURK and Charles were married on June 7, 1946, Anna resided with her widowed mother and her two sisters in Pokroujus, Lithuania. They lived in a building that her mother owned, in which she operated a small hotel and a grocery store. After graduating from high school, Anna was helping her mother with the businesses, and as a family, they were quite comfortable financially.

Due to the Communist occupation of the Baltic States, Anna and her friend, Rita Sands, left home in January of 1941 to seek employment in the city of Kovno. They were joined by Anna's sister, Ruth, on June 21, 1941. Upon Ruth's arrival they saw that the Nazis had invaded the city and were also bombing it by air. As flames engulfed the city, the women rushed into a house near the station, where they waited in hiding with other Jews for two days.

Realizing then that there was no way for them to return home to Pokroujus, they headed for Vilna, Poland by foot. When they reached Vilkomir, Lithuania, the Nazis, parachuting into the town, made them return to Kovno. There they were ordered into a large building full of other Jews, and commanded not to leave except to pick up their rations from a local store. Getting to the store was its own humiliation, as they were forced to walk in the gutter in single file. For this treatment, they were rationed a piece of bread, some grits, and salt.

On July 15, 1941, Anna and her sister, Ruth, entered the Kovno ghetto, and were forced to wear the black and yellow cloth bearing the Star of David on their chests. The ghetto was enclosed a month later with barbed wire; reflectors were strategically placed, and it was heavily guarded by Nazi, Lithuanian, and Ukrainian police. Anna and Ruth, at that time, "lived" with eight other people in two small rooms, sleeping on the floor. Twice a week they would get rations from the Nazis, as the ghetto had no shops. They got the same bread, grits, and salt, and once a week they received some horse meat, some rotten herrings, and rotten potatoes, which gave the ghetto a particular stench.

The ghetto's commandant, a man named Jordan, was known for his

Ruth, Anna and Charles after the war in Vienna.

"*All of the Jews were 'roused' at 5 each morning and lined up by the gate that served as both the ghetto's entrance and exit.*"

Needless to say, none of the workers was compensated financially for the forced labor.

After about two or three weeks in the ghetto, Anna and the others were ordered by Commandant Jordan into the courtyard. There were two rows of Gestapo men facing each other, and the ghetto residents had to walk between them, and were further ordered to the left or the right. The procession began at 6 a.m. and lasted for about 12 hours. When the line ended, those on the right, like Anna, Ruth, and the others, were ordered back to their quarters in the ghetto. If separated family members tried to reach each other on the other side, they were beaten unmercifully. Those unfortunate souls ordered to the left were subsequently taken under guard out of the ghetto, shot, and thrown into graves which the Jews had been compelled to dig as part of their "work."

In 1943 Anna, still in the Kovno ghetto, contracted typhus from the unsanitary conditions and her weakened condition after two years of forced labor. At age 24 she dropped to 65 pounds. She was confined to her room for three months, where she was treated by a kind doctor who came to see her, unbeknownst to authorities. The Jewish police, or *Judenrat*, also covered for her, so the Nazis would not know she was absent from her work shifts. After three months, Anna returned to work at the airfield. She soon learned that the Nazis had killed her mother and her other sister.

cruelties. All of the Jews were "roused" at 5 each morning and lined up by the gate that served as both the ghetto's entrance and exit. From there, they were divided into groups of several hundred, and walked to designated working areas by Nazi police carrying guns, whips, and clubs. Anna was assigned to work building the Kovna airfield, where she dug ditches, mixed cement, carried steel beams, and pushed wheelbarrows filled with dirt, stones, or cement. As she performed these and other chores, their Nazi overseers beat her and the other Jews at will.

Another cruel "job" she held involved unloading trains of food for the military, for which she left the ghetto at 6 a.m. and did not return until 10 p.m. or midnight. The only additional food she and her compatriots were given during the workday was some watery soup made from potato peelings.

Local survivors celebrating a holiday together after the war - from left, Mr. and Mrs. Drucker, David Sendowski (at table), Clara Sendowski, Sabina Okun, Bobby Burk, Anna Burk, Jack Drucker (at table), Abe Okun, Reila Sendowski, and Chaim Sendowski.

On November 30, 1943, Anna was ordered from the ghetto to Gifangen Lager, previously a Lithuanian military installation in a Kovno suburb. There, about 1,500 men, women, and children were housed in a large, brick building, with the women and children on the first floor, and the men on the second. The camp itself was surrounded by barbed wire and each corner had reflectors. The daily routine there was equivalent to that at the Kovna ghetto, with the Nazi police always on guard.

In July of 1944, Anna and Ruth were two of about 50 women loaded onto a boxcar. Men were loaded into other cars, and the train set off for several days with hardly any food and no ventilation, and eventually arrived at the concentration camp at Stutthof, Germany. Walking into the camp, Anna saw the crematorium, and something behind it that looked to her

like a mountain. But as she looked closer, she realized that it was a huge pile of shoes and clothing left behind by the people who had lost their lives in the ovens.

Camp Stutthof was surrounded by electrified barbed wiring, and had hundreds of police with clubs, pistols, and machine guns. The new prisoners were taken into a large white building, where they slept on the floor. The next morning the Nazis marched the men away, and an hour later ordered the women into the yard. They were taken into a building and ordered to strip naked. The guards ordered them into another room, and they had to walk naked. The officers then ordered the soldiers to go through Anna's and the other prisoners' hair and mouths and other parts of their bodies, to find out whether they had hidden any money or jewelry.

In a third room, each woman had a pelvic examination by a doctor to determine whether they had hidden any valuables internally. After this horror, they were herded into yet another room and promised a shower, but only a few drops of water came to them. Then they went to another room where mounds of clothing were on the floor, and were told to take one garment, whether it fit or not, and then pick a pair of shoes. From the time they entered the building to be searched until they picked up their "new" shoes, 24 hours had passed, during which they had no food or drink. There was just one huge line of people walking from room to room.

After this process, Anna was taken into a wooden barrack housing hundreds. Each barrack had only one small door, so only one person could enter or exit at a time. Like other camps, there was electrified barbed wire encompassing the prisoners' world. But Anna was kept on the move. After three weeks at Stutthof, she was taken on a small ship with 500 women to Dorf Stainort, where they were housed in shelters made of what looked to her like heavy cardboard. Each was round and housed about 50 women, who slept on the straw-covered ground. There were no sanitary facilities. Here Anna was again forced to dig trenches and bunkers for the Nazi military.

On January 21, 1945, Anna got up to report to work as usual, and was told that they were to be taken to a new place to work; but as the Nazis were talking, the bombs kept falling, and she thought that the Nazis were bombing the prisoners. She and the other women who survived the bombing were forced to walk, presumably toward their new work area, which they did without food or rest, and those who fell by the wayside were simply shot by the Nazis.

Those who survived were forced by Nazis into various buildings. Anna and her sister found shelter in a haystack in the loft of a barn. Before leaving, the Nazis bayonetted the haystacks, seeking stragglers. Luckily, the two were not found. They hid in the haystacks for seven days, surviving on icicles. Slowly the prisoners began to recognize the singing of Russian songs. Soon Russian soldiers arrived and asked the women who they were. When they told the Russians they were Jews in Nazi servitude, the Russians told the Jews that they were free, and that they need have no further fears. This day, which Anna would always remember, was January 24, 1945. The place was Rewodzik, Poland.

The Russians took them in trucks to a deserted village in Poland where the Jews, most of whom had barely any clothes on their backs, were told they could enter any home and make themselves comfortable. Anna and Ruth stayed there for one week. Then the sisters and four other women decided to return to their hometown of Pokroujus. They only got as far as Bialystok, Poland, in an open-topped railroad car. There the train stopped, and they were told they could disembark for a while, as there would be a considerable delay.

They walked into the town, and noticed some other Jewish people. Those Jews advised them to remain there, since Bialystok had a Jewish Committee that would advise them where it would be best for them to go. Anna and her comrades took the advice and remained there until after the Passover holidays. Then the Jewish Committee sent them to Budapest, Hungary, where they stayed for two weeks. It was the first time in almost four years that Anna was treated well and lived like a civilized human being. The refugees were given food and clothing, and examined by real doctors.

They then traveled to Ludus Kibbutz, from which they were planning to emigrate to Israel. Instead, because of Ruth's illness, they headed for Vienna and resided in the building which was formerly the Rothschild Hospital. They remained there until June 5, 1946. While in Vienna she met Chil Berkowicz, who would become her husband. Shortly thereafter, the newlyweds immigrated to the United States of America. ❖

Anna's sister, Ruth Igdal, has a story in this book. Anna died in February, 1998.

The Burk's son, Franklin Robert, at his Bar Mitzvah at Temple Israel. At left is Rabbi Joseph Goldman.

CHARLES BURK
Chil Berkowicz

Edited by Elena Barr Baum

CHARLES BURK, *formerly Chil Berkowicz, spent the entire time between September 1939 and January 1945 either in hiding from German occupation in Poland, in labor camps, in Jewish ghettos, or in concentration camps. The following is his story of his life from September 1942 through the liberation, in his own words, slightly edited. His wife, Anna, has a story in this book.*

I was born in Dzialoszyn, Poland on December 3, 1918. My mother Rosa died when I was seven years old, and my father, Mordka, later remarried. A few years after graduating from public high school, I think it was about 1934, I decided to go to Czestochowa, Poland, where I became a tailoring apprentice. I worked with my teacher, Mr. Novak, until the Nazis invaded Czestochowa on September 2, 1939. At that time, my father and his wife were still living in Dzialoszyn, while I had my two single sisters living with me. I had worked my way up to earning the equivalent of $50 per week.

On September 4, two days after the Nazis came into our town, they burned down all of the houses on our street, and we all ran in panic. Later that day, the Nazis took all of the Jewish men and herded them into churches (since they had burned the synagogues), and we sat there for the whole night. The next day they marched us to a military camp, where I was registered and examined, and after three days I was released. I had no home to go to, so I went searching for my sisters, whom I found at the home of a relative, Baruch

Sterling. I stayed there, too, for a short time, until we were told that anyone whose house had been burned should register for housing. By the time we were given a room, our father had joined us, as Dzialoszyn had been badly bombed and was in shambles, and my stepmother had died in the attack.

A *Judenrat* or Jewish police "force" had been formed, which reported the Jews to the Nazi in charge of the city and we were issued ration cards. I was now unable to find regular employment, so each morning, like the other men, I reported to the *Judenrat* office at 7 to be assigned to work. Some of my assignments were in military installations, where I had to uproot barbed wire (placed there by the Poles, in their now dashed hopes of keeping the Germans at bay). I also had to load and unload carloads of food products, carry bricks, and do clean-up jobs for the Nazis. All the time we worked, the Wehrmacht, the SS Storm Troopers and the Junda Maria surrounded us.

The Nazis soon gave orders that all Jews were to be moved into the Czestochowa ghetto by March of 1940, so my father

Photo above: Charles Burk in Rome, 1946.

Top right: Berkowicz family in Poland before the war – Charles is the young boy in the front row.

and sisters and I entered the ghetto, which was open but heavily policed. No one was permitted to leave, except under guard. Upon arrival, we were all ordered to wear a white band with the Star of David on our left arms. Every morning I continued to report to the *Judenrat* for assignments, and I

continued to do the same laborious work I had done while living outside the ghetto. The rations were very small, and the ghetto was overcrowded with about 40,000 Jewish people, many of whom had been brought in from other parts of Poland.

I lived there with my family until June of 1940, when I was taken in a cattle car with several hundred young men to Lublin. From there we were ordered by the SS Storm Troopers to run seven kilometers to Midanek, while they rode bicycles, motorcycles, or horses. As I ran, I saw several people fall to the ground, as the Nazis had shot them. Lublin was a pit stop, from which I was assigned to the labor camp at Chrubieshof, Poland. I was taken there by truck, and I remained there from June to September 1940.

At Chrubieshof we lived in barns formerly housing horses and cows, and were watched over by Ukrainian and Nazi police. We were roused each morning at 4 and were ordered to do gymnastics, after which we were given a black substance they called coffee and a small piece of bread. We were then organized into work battalions, carrying shovels, scythes, and other heavy equipment to build a road. We began the work of leveling the hills for the roads to be built at 7. We walked the few kilometers to the work site under Gestapo and Ukrainian guard, while they toted guns, whips, and clubs.

While at this labor camp, I was beaten so severely over the head that I suddenly felt everything in front of my left eye turn black. I never reported my injury, however, for fear of being shot. I never regained vision in this eye.

— 43 —

In September of 1940, while I was working and the overseers were talking to one another, I ran to a house near the road where I worked, and I hid until dark. That night I began walking, and continued to walk each night for two weeks, while hiding out during the days. At the end of two weeks, I was back in Lublin, where I reported to the *Judenrat*, who ordered me to go to the Czestochowa ghetto. When I reported there, using a different name so I wouldn't be found out, I learned that my father and sisters were still there. We stayed there together until September 1942. During this period, I was assigned to work in a fur shop, making heavy garments for the German army, which was attempting to move into Russia.

The day after Yom Kippur in September of 1942, we got up and reported to work as usual. The ghetto, which was usually surrounded by Jewish police, was this day filled with hundreds of Ukrainian and Nazi police, and storm troopers. They had come to liquidate the ghetto, a process that took two weeks. I was called with the third liquidating group and was loaded like cattle into a boxcar with 110 other people. By month's end, we reached Austrotung Camp, Treblinka, Poland.

After I had left the Czestochowa ghetto, I heard that the Nazis had shot my father in his room, because he was too sick to walk. My younger sister remained in a new camp in

"That night I began walking, and continued to walk each night for two weeks, while hiding out during the days."

Czestochowa, after the liquidation of the large ghetto. My other sister was sent, like I was, to Treblinka, but was exterminated.

When we reached Treblinka, we were ordered into an open area, and commanded to take off our clothes. I was given number 831, and wore it (in

cloth, but not tattooed) on the left side of my chest. I was chosen for work, and not immediate extermination, so I was sent to a wooden barrack, where I was crowded into a room with about 200 other men. That night I slept on the bare ground.

My work at Treblinka was to search clothing for valuables. I stayed only until mid-October of 1942. I felt that death was no worse than my life there, so although the camp was surrounded with barbed wire, I took the chance to run away. I hid with two other men in a mound of clothes. When the guards policing the area were far from us, we ran and jumped over the barbed wiring, and just kept going. For a month during the days we hid and we walked at night, until we reached the new camp at Czestochowa. This time I registered under my own name, Chil Berkowicz,

Charles and Anna Burk's first day in Virginia. Charles' sister, Stefa Korn, is second from left.

A gathering of the Burk and Igdal families in Norfolk, Virginia, 1955.

as I knew they had no records of me from the liquidated ghetto where I had previously served.

I went to the office where the Czestochowa prisoners reported for work, and was ordered to work in a labor camp Rakow in November 1942. I continued to live in the small ghetto until the Nazis dynamited it in 1943. Afterwards, the Nazis set up a barbed wire-enclosed camp in Rakow, which was heavily guarded by the factory's police. I now lived at Camp Rakow, which was actually a steel mill. At first I worked in the mill making wires and railroad tracks for German industrialists and the army. Later on, a tailor shop was set up to make army uniforms and I was given an assignment as a tailor. I put in 11 hours of work per day, and received no pay, only very small rations.

One day in the middle of January in 1945 we were not taken to work, but were ordered to walk under very heavy guard. The guards carried handguns, machine guns and other weapons. When we reached the railroad station, they pushed us into the cattle cars and one of the Nazis told us that we were on our way to Buchenwald. When the train was twelve miles out of Czestochowa, I again took a chance on escaping by breaking little bars in the window of the boxcar, and I jumped from the moving train. I found myself in the small village of Ostrow, where I hid out for a few days. I could hear bombing all around me. After two days, I could not endure the hunger any longer, so I emerged from my hideout, and learned that the Russians had taken over the area.

I returned to Czestochowa, Poland and remained there from January 16, 1945 to May 4, 1945, under Russian domination. I then decided to run away from the Russians, and I finally reached Vienna in September of 1945. There I entered the Rothschild Hospital, which had come under the charge of the American Joint Distribution Committee. I was given food, clothing, and other necessities. I remained there until November of 1945, and then went by train to Linz, where I entered the UNRRA (United Nations Relief and Rehabilitation Administration) Camp Bindermichl.

While in Vienna, I met Chana Shapiro, whom I married in Linz on June 7, 1946. We immigrated together from Bremerhaven, Germany on the ship, Ernie Pyle, January 3, 1947, and reached New York on January 16. We came soon to Norfolk, Virginia because I had relatives who lived there. ❖

The Burk's had one son, Franklin Robert, who died in 1997. Charles Burk was founder of Anjay Fashions. He died December, 1969.

PHIL CAMINER
Excerpts From My Story

By Phil Caminer

Phil Caminer *Photo by Susan Hirschbiel*

… It was not until I was eight years old in 1933 when Hitler won his first election to Reich-chancellor that I became aware of being different from my playmates and yesterday's comrades.

You see, everyone would fly his party's flag at election time, and we, as most of the people in my neighborhood, would display the black, red, and gold of the democratic Weimar Republic. Upon the declaration of the election results, a mob of youths in our area banged on our door, screaming, "You damned Jews better take your flag down or else …" This was my introduction to an awareness of religion. Being Jewish did not have any particular meaning or significance for my life until then.

(Not that I didn't sense unhappiness because of being Jewish but I was not aware that my being Jewish caused the unhappiness.) … There was no safe

place in my childhood. I had a grandfather, a kinder man never lived, and surely with him I would have felt safe but he was picked up off the street, deported to Poland, not to be heard from again.

I had a grandmother on my father's side, also kind and gentle, and generous. She would give us cough drops, the closest thing to candy she could afford, but her husband would get angry at her for using her allowance on us in this manner.

… a train is leaving Berlin in late July 1939, less than 45 days before the war breaks out. I am on it, leaving Germany for England (where my mother was waiting for us) as part of one of the last "Kindertransports." It is *verboten* for parents to come to the station to say their "good-byes." The Nazis would not want to have people

witness the sight of families being torn apart. However, the train stops at every local station along the route and, at the next stop is my father. I do not know how he got off from work. No longer part owner of the family business, but now he is a conscript laborer. How did he manage to get there? What is that package in his hand that he is obviously trying to give me? He calls through the closed window that I should open it and stands helplessly by while I am restrained from making that last contact with him. We are under orders not to open any windows or look at or talk to anyone under threat of being removed from the train. I cannot heed his pleading nor am I sure that he understands that I appreciate his final "I love you" to me. The train pulls out. Two or three years later, he is dead in Auschwitz. This scene stays with me and comes, again and again, every time I think of my father. ❖

Dana Cohen
"... one long chain of miracles"

By Lisa Bertini and Reba Karp

Dana Cohen   *Photo by Susan Hirschbiel*

Holocaust survivor DANA COHEN'S childhood in Lwow, Poland began on a pleasant note. Her father owned a saw mill and the family was able to enjoy the comforts of their society. Those early years were filled with wonderful memories of playing with her cousin Mira and being soothed to sleep by lullabies from her nanny, Magda.

Dana's mother, Freda Sygal (of blessed memory) also enjoyed the comforts of city life. Evenings were spent attending the theater or discussing the "fine arts" over a glass of wine with friends in their beautiful home.

Hitler's rise to power caused all that to change. Before her death in 1994 at the age of 90, Dana's mother attempted to write her story and leave it as a legacy for future generations.

One paragraph stands out: "After a month's journey in cattle cars and in the most unhygienic conditions one can imagine, the disheveled humanity consisting mostly of women and children, more than 40 in number per car, landed in Kazakhstan, the famous hunger steppes. Our struggle for survival for nearly two years in detention could be described only in terms of one long chain of miracles." When she later related her experiences to the English authorities, she was received with a large dose of skepticism and disbelief followed by the comment, "If all this you say you went through is correct, you could not possibly survive."

As an adult, Dana visits the Katyn Forest Memorial where her father was murdered.

Despite her early life of comfort, Dana said her mother was a strong woman. She was determined to survive.

Their odyssey began early in the morning of April 13, 1940. A group of Russian soldiers stormed into their home, confiscated their apartment and personal belongings, and carted Dana and her mother onto a lorry for a trip to a train station. Their destination was Siberia and, subsequently, forced labor.

Still clad in their night clothes and coats, they quickly collected whatever jewelry and small possessions they could carry before being packed into a cattle wagon for their nightmarish journey through Russia, Siberia and Kazakhstan. They only had each other. Eight-year-old Dana did not have the chance to say goodbye to her grandparents or favorite cousin and playmate, Mira. She would never see her home again.

Dana remembers crying, but her mother did not. Freda, who had been so vivacious and outspoken, said very little during those weeks of transport.

They spent their first year of exile in a village among natives of Mongolian descent. The Kazakhs (not to be confused with Cossacks) built their huts half buried in the ground to prevent them from toppling over during snow storms.

The Russians formed labor gangs consisting of women and children to build stables, dig foundations, and to perform other field work – all without payment and little food.

"The only reward we ever received for the hard labor we were compelled to perform was a meager ration of an unedible lump of black rubber which they called bread," Freda Sygal wrote, explaining that if the job did not live up to expectations, "the bread was forfeited and one retired for the night exhausted and starved."

To supplement their meager rations, Dana learned to steal potatoes from fields belonging to the native villagers. She remembers the hunger – a terribly dry emptiness and inability to feel her insides. She remembers it being constant. It just became a part of life, she said, explaining that it was not anything you got used to, just something you had to face each day. Because of the pain from hunger, she would look forward to those potatoes and that simple ration of black bread.

The summer passed with hard work, starvation and hopelessness. Before Dana and her mother were taken from their home in Poland, her father had been mobilized into the Polish Army. He eventually ended up in the infamous Katyn Forest where he was murdered. Their lifeline to the civilized world, however, continued with "care" packages from family members. These became part of their key to "survival."

"With winter approaching, many of us decided to cross the river to Petropavlovsk and seek shelter with the Kulaks, so called 'wealthy Russians.' Like ourselves, they had been deported from the Volga Region during the revolution," Dana's mother recorded.

She remembers the hunger – a terribly dry emptiness and inability to feel her insides.

Using her wit and ingenuity heightened by the desire to survive, Freda obtained a small corner in a kitchen of a Russian peasant for herself and her daughter to spend the cold nights. This she purchased with the exchange of clothing, tea and money received from her family. Ironic as it may seem today, the mail did arrive at their isolated outpost.

The peasant family consisted of four adults who stayed with them in the same kitchen by day and retired for the night in an adjoining room. "There was no privacy at all.... " In addition to the freezing, starving humans, the kitchen was refuge for a newly born calf. It ate one of their woolen scarves and caused Freda many moments of worry. She wrote, "I was not concerned with

Dana's parents.

the loss of the scarf. I was frightened that the calf may get ill and I would be blamed. Luckily there were no consequences and the calf was in sound health."

Her world within the kitchen became a hard bunk consisting of a few planks of wood joined together. This served as a chair, table and bed. Bartering was the known currency. There were no shops with goods where one could make necessary purchases, even if one had money.

"One had to be resourceful in order to survive.... Many died that winter from hunger and cold, the two biggest enemies of mankind," Freda Sygal's journal notes.

During that first winter Dana and her mother met a young Pole about 19 years old who was dying inch by inch from cold and hunger. "He lived a day-to-day existence until the final defeat mercifully arrived, bringing his sufferings to an end. Life was cheap." With the ground frozen, his remains were buried in the snow, only to be dug up in springtime by hungry dogs. His body was subsequently buried beneath the ground, minus his limbs.

Summer brought good news. The Russians had broken their alliance with the Germans. With the Germans advancing into Russian territory, the local authorities suddenly released them. "We simply ceased to exist as far as they were concerned. We could come and

go wherever we pleased," Freda Sygal wrote. However, "they did not bother to provide us with transportation to take us to the railway station across the steppes." They were all but forgotten.

Those in the position to rationalize the situation knew that they had to make the crossing before winter. Since nothing could be accomplished individually, the surviving families agreed to travel together and share expenses. The plan was to reach Samarkand, in Uzbekistan.

Dana's mother was forced to sell her "steadily dwindling meager possessions" to pay for her share of the travel expenses. Sadly, she parted with her wedding ring, the last link to her past. She rationalized, "any price for freedom, not yet achieved, was worth the sacrifice." Jointly they hired a lorry which took them across the monotonous steppes to the railway station.

The group reached the Dzangistobe Railway Station late at night. It was told that the next train was not due for a couple days and would be surely overcrowded with Russian refugees fleeing the advancing Germans. "With sagging spirits we settled for a three-day vigil at the station … on the fourth day the train puffed into the station … crowded with people on the steps clinging to the cars for dear life."

The scene that followed, described in detail by Freda in her records was "beyond description." With her child and a few bundles in her arm, she made her rush to the train. "I was suddenly lifted into the air, practically suspended between two pushing masses, struggling to reach the coach. By sheer force of the impact, I was carried to the door and pushed inside. I reached the goal and this was all I really asked for."

However, she was forced to leave her trunk with all her food, clothing and important identification papers on the platform with a young Kazach. For a few rubles, he had promised to hand the trunk over to her. Instead, he vanished with "my precious valise containing all my belongings."

Dana and her mother learned to be survivors and since there was no other option, they continued on their course. When she reported the theft to the train personnel and a Red Army soldier, neither seemed concerned.

At Tashkent they were told to disembark and wait for another train heading for Samarkand. "The wait extended into three full days spent literally on the streets. There was no shelter or food provided for us. We huddled together outside a recreation center for the Red Army soldiers. A search for food and water began…. We soon realized that there was no authority, country or human organization interested in our lot. The Russians responsible for our reluctant presence in their country, turned their backs on us." The only "organized"

thing they had done for the refugees, Dana's mother wrote, was to deport them to Siberia.

"We lay on the streets stretched out on our bundles, practically chained to them, to protect them from thieves circling around us like vultures."

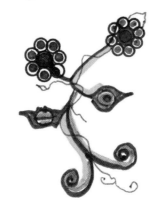

When they finally arrived in Samarkand, it was with great fear and trepidation. Dana and her mother had lost their identity papers. "I felt a kind of constriction welling in my throat from exasperation as to what would happen to me and my child," she wrote, if the guard checking papers did not believe her story about the stolen valise.

Still living by her wits, in desperation Freda pulled out an old train ticket and handed it to him. Luck was with her, the guard, overworked and exhausted from the heat and pushing crowds, with merely a glance allowed her to pass and join a family who had traveled the distance with her. They were offered temporary shelter in a room where 14 people, all ex-deportees, were stretched out on the floor asleep.

Since she had no papers, the landlord asked her to leave the next day. "I was on the street again, with my sick child and without documents, food, shelter or friends, nowhere to go and nobody to turn to for help in a hostile world," Freda wrote. "Up until that time we were a kind of community closely knit together by sharing the same fate … I just found myself abandoned by God and man alike."

In desperation she entered a tea shop and sat down at a table next to a Polish prostitute. Upon hearing Freda's story, the young girl extended human kindness by offering shelter for the night and the promise of bread, raisins and blankets.

Freda Sygal feels this act of kindness became a turning point. "Thanks to her I am here to tell this story. She was a guardian angel. I did not even know her name. It should be 'Mercy.' With her deed, she convinced me that a warm heart is to be found where it is least expected and where one would never dream to look."

More help, albeit somewhat limited, came from a Russian family of six adults. In order to save Dana's life, the refugee family from Bessarabia agreed to provide shelter even though they barely had room for themselves.

"It was the zero hour. The agreement called for sharing all of the expenses equally, not in the usual sense, but as two families. That meant that I had to

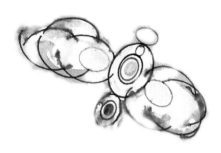

"With her deed,

she convinced me

that a warm heart

is to be found

where it is least

expected and where

one would never

dream to look."

pay the same for the two of us as they did for six." All food was obtained on black market. This additional burden forced Freda to barter her last few possessions.

Then one day she gathered enough courage to go to the town hall and explore new possibilities. Since the town was teeming with refugees, she took her place in line and braved herself for a long wait in the chilly air.

Finally, she reached the office and related her story using the "worst Russian language ever told." The weary clerk, mistaking her for a Red Army soldier's wife, issued her new documents. He also provided her with food ration cards only available for Russian Army families.

"I would never have dreamed … of such an outcome to my escapade, as the ration cards meant bread and bread meant life. Giddy with the unexpected success, I ran out of the office and flew home on wings of sheer ecstasy, all the time blessing the Kazach at the Dzangistobe station for stealing my trunk with the original Polish papers…. Despair had turned into joy…. "

Dana said she and her mother shared many experiences connected with their survival. One incident was connected with typhoid caused by lice and unsanitary conditions. She vividly remembers the time she contacted a kidney infection and her mother could not get a doctor to treat a young Jewish

girl. In desperation, her mother convinced a woman doctor to leave the hospital to look at her daughter, huddling on a street corner. After lightly examining Dana, the doctor stated that Dana would not survive.

Here again, as in many other instances, they beat the odds.

Freda was not to be discouraged by limitations. She placed Dana in an orphanage so she would receive more care than Freda could provide. Dana received regular meals each day and wasn't subjected to hard work.

Eventually, Freda learned that there was amnesty for all Polish refugees in the Soviet Union. The Polish officials would not accept Jews for transport out of Russia. In the interest of survival, Freda changed her last name and assumed the facade of being Catholic. She taught Dana to cross herself and adopt new mannerisms that would permit them to leave. Dana even received the sacrament of communion.

Dana was assigned to leave on a transport scheduled to depart two weeks before her mother's train. Although Freda had prepared her daughter for the separation, she had not prepared herself. It was too terrifying for the mother to let go of her daughter's hand. Two soldiers had to pull them apart.

The train moved down the track with Freda screaming, "Danusia!" and Dana crying, "mother, mother!"

After many harrowing experiences and painful separations, Dana and her mother ended up in Koja, Uganda. They lived together in a hut on Lake Victoria, where it was safe to assume their Jewish identity again. Freda helped form a hospital and later became one of the administrators.

Dana attended a Polish school formed in the camp and had many pets including a monkey and a crocodile.

When she was sixteen, Dana left for Nairobi where she attended Remington College, an English secretarial school.

In 1958, Dana moved from Nairobi to Washington, D.C. Shortly thereafter she met her future husband, William. The two were married in 1963. They are currently living in Norfolk and have one son, Michael. Freda moved to Norfolk in 1965 and lived here until her death in 1994.

In Russia, Freda and Dana learned how the moral code could be stretched and interpreted to meet one's particular needs. The Russians did not hesitate to deprive them of everything that was dear to them and to ultimately leave them to suffer on the streets.

Dana's mother held onto the hope that "eventually, maybe, mankind will solve its real or imaginary problems by means other than cruelty towards old people, women and children."

In the book that Freda started, she explained that she did not feel guilty for her actions brought on by desperate situations. "In a semi-starved condition, there is no place for morals. What remains is the drive for survival. A concealed potato in the hem of a skirt did not keep us awake at night repenting our sins. A sleepless night could be only attributed to pangs of hunger, which could not be appeased with a few meager potatoes.

Many times I have wondered if deportation to Siberia did not prevent my child and myself from perishing in the German gas chambers. From the two evils, mine was the lesser one." ❖

Dana's husband, Bill, a liberator, has a story in this book.

Dana's Nanny, Magda

Dana and her mother, Freda, in Africa, 1943.

BILL COHEN'S *unit was among those liberating Dachau Concentration Camp in Munich, Germany in April of 1945. As the army advanced, Cohen remembers that "we knew what we were going to see, but actually seeing and smelling death was a different thing," he says.*

"You could smell death two miles away. We were coming up over a hill and you could feel it. It was an urging. You couldn't get there too quickly," he says, adding, "as if an hour was going to save another life."

"U.S. Army intelligence had a good idea of what to expect because the Russians had liberated a few camps prior to that and General Eisenhower had issued an order to secure the camps and see what we could do." Cohen was part of the Third Army, an armored unit. Although he was only a sergeant he was allowed to ride with the colonel into the camp because he spoke French and "knew German," he adds.

"When we saw the immensity of the situation, we radioed back for more doctors. Being Jewish made it a personal war. There were my own people there. We got them out and into a hospital as soon as possible."

At that point, the German guards had two choices, he explains. Either become more human and try to help or kill as many as possible to get rid of the evidence. The guards at Dachau chose

William Cohen
"Being Jewish made it a personal war . . ."
By Reba Karp

William Cohen

"They looked at us, some too far gone to know they were being liberated."

Bill's wife, Dana Cohen, a Holocaust survivor, has a story in this book.

the former and helped to carry out some of the prisoners on stretchers.

Cohen recalls the stares from the victims as they drove through. "They looked at us, some too far gone to know they were being liberated. They just stared," he says. When some of the more alert saw the Magen David arm bands on the chaplains, they broke down, he adds.

He notes that before entering the camps, the non-Jewish soldiers were indifferent, but once they entered the camp and saw the condition of the prisoners, they took a willing and active part in helping. "You can't get over the fact that it's your people," he informs, adding that he remembers later meeting members of the Jewish Brigade in Paris on leave. "I hate to think what would have happened if the Jewish Brigade had

seen what we saw. They would have massacred the Germans."

Cohen was a freshman in college when he went into the army. He distinguished himself on November 4, 1944, by risking his life to save fellow soldiers wounded in a minefield. He was commended by his commanding officer Lt. Col. Willard N. Wallace who wrote, "… Disregarding personal safety and at considerable risk to yourself, you entered the minefield to render aid to the wounded men and to remove them from further danger.… After performing first aid for the surviving soldiers you carried both of them from the minefield in two trips through the danger zone.… I commend you for this meritorious service which reflects great credit upon yourself and upon the Armed Services of the United States." ❖

Advancing American troops.   *Photo by Hugo Horvath*

John Compton leads the 82nd Airborne Marching Band in England, 1944

LIBERATOR
JOHN COMPTON:

An "All-American Soldier"

by Eileen Frey

Just as one note builds upon another to create a symphony, each of a person's experiences builds upon those preceding to orchestrate whatever one needs to get through the moment at hand. So it was for a young man working in an Army gunpowder factory, Hercules Powder Company, in Radford, Virginia, when the Japanese bombed Pearl Harbor, an event that catapulted so many American young men into the armed services.

"I, like most Americans, was totally incensed about a most cowardly act," declared John C. Compton, Jr., born March 17, 1920, and hailing from West Virginia. Like so many young men ready to conquer the evil forces of the world, he wasn't going to wait to be drafted into action.

Wanting to train as a pilot, he excitedly volunteered for the Army Air Force. Unfortunately, a doctor examining him claimed he had an eye problem that would prevent him from realizing this dream. This former Boy Scout and musician, who to this day says there has been no corroboration of that doctor's diagnosis, instead let the Army know he was available for action, and two months later, on March 24, 1942, he was inducted. Fate led him to basic training at Camp Claiborne, Louisiana, where he became a member of the 82nd Infantry Division Artillery, nicknamed the All-American Division.

One day he and some other troops were asked to assemble. While waiting for someone in authority to appear, on a

— 55 —

hunch Compton uneasily asked one fellow, "Do you have any musical training?"

"Yes. I play in a band."

"Oh, no. How about you?" he asked another. "Were you ever in a band?"

Getting an affirmative answer, he continued around the room and received the same sorts of responses. Just as he suspected, he and the others, because of their musical backgrounds, were to form the 82nd Infantry Division Artillery Army Band.

Compton, of course, was no stranger to different types of bands. From ages ten to twelve, this self-taught musician played bugle in a drum and bugle corps. He played saxophone in junior high school during the Depression, played in his high school marching band on Friday nights, and by 11th grade taught himself to play clarinet and performed in a professional band on Saturday nights. Not surprisingly, he went to Bluefield College on a music scholarship. When, during his sophomore year, he became leader of the band and was able to book it for dances and other events outside of college, he was also receiving a second music scholarship. All this training made him a perfect fit for an army band.

Instead of regarding this as an honor, Compton voiced displeasure since he knew he wouldn't spend his days leisurely rehearsing and perhaps giving a

few performances here and there. No, he and the others would be sloshing through the swamps of Louisiana as part of basic training, and then, while the rest of the 82nd enjoyed "down time," he and his band would be practicing their marching band, regimental band, and swing band routines. There would be no rest for the weary.

Everyone knows the leader of a marching band is its drum major. Not a one of the forty or so band members had ever been one, so Compton stepped up for the job. Now what was he going to do? After all, there was a certain amount of skill attached to that position. Fortunately he encountered a tech-sergeant, from a cadre that helped form new organizations, who trained him in just two hours to be the drum major for

this new group that would march and play whenever called upon.

When Compton one day was ordered to lead the band and the rest of the 82nd Division Artillery in an unusual formation during which the band took center field while half of the soldiers lined up on either side, he was mystified. The purpose started to become clear, he remarked, as "General Omar N. Bradley pointed his finger at all the men to my right and stated, 'From this day forward, you people will be called the 82nd Airborne Division.' Then he turned to the men on my left and said, 'From this day forward you will be the 101st Airborne Division.' I turned to the man next to me, Abe Joseph on bass horn, and said, 'What the hell is an airborne division?' He

"Yes. I play in a band." says John Compton.   *Photo by Charlie Meads*

whispered back, 'Some guys who jump out of airplanes.' It was beyond my understanding."

Nonetheless, about half the band, Compton included, volunteered to become paratroopers because they considered themselves soldiers first and musicians second. They wanted to take care of army business in the most professional way possible. General Joseph Swing, however, refused them because he thought they were trying to get out of the band, and band members were difficult to find.

It was on to Fort Bragg where General Maxwell Taylor and General Matthew B. Ridgway actually encouraged the band members to volunteer for glider training. Compton and his men did. This training was invaluable, for, as Compton said, "Whether you volunteered (to learn how) or not, overseas everybody got in the gliders and flew. I chose my squad of guys, and since I was qualified, I felt much safer in the gliders than I did in the C-47s," which is where he packed all the band equipment and music before assigning men to ride atop the crates as well. "With the C-47s so heavily loaded, I felt we in the gliders (which were towed) stood a better chance of surviving a crash." He was right. Maybe it was good fortune that disallowed him to become a pilot in the first place.

In April, 1943, after the paratroopers and glidermen trained, the 82nd's first stop overseas was North Africa where

John Compton visits with his mother while on leave in Norfolk, Virginia.

most of the Germans had already been scattered. While waiting to head into Europe where the action was, Compton and his swing band were playing one night to the enjoyment of a famous performer in the audience. Bob Hope was so impressed with this group that he asked the band to leave their division and travel with him. Needless to say, permission … not granted. How different and perhaps more pleasurable their army enlistments would have been had Compton and his men not continued to Sicily and other parts of Europe where they would learn more about Germans and their atrocities than anyone would want to know.

"Before I joined the war, no, I didn't know what was happening to the Jews in Europe," Compton replied when asked. "Word was out, but I didn't think too highly of what I had heard. I thought that maybe this was a bit of propaganda. I knew of abuses but didn't know about deaths. How could anyone think these rumors could be true?"

As Compton moved through Sicily, Italy, the United Kingdom, Normandy, Belgium, Holland, and France, he became more of a believer, and he and the other soldiers learned to trust no German, living or dead. Fast forward to the winter of 1944-45 when General Dwight D. Eisenhower ordered the 82nd in for the Battle of the Bulge. Compton described what happened. "He sent the 82nd to the northern flank near Elsenborn, Belgium, but I ended up in Stavelot (a town in southeast Belgium near the German border) where there had been a fantastic battle. There were blown-up German tanks and the Germans' dead soldiers all over the streets. I understand an outfit of combat engineers created most of this damage." As Compton and his men passed through, they knew not to roll over the body of a German corpse because there was likely to be an explosive beneath. That wasn't the only place danger lurked.

One of Compton's assignments in Belgium was to take twelve men and search for German land mines hidden beneath deep snow. Compton's leadership abilities shone through when he was able to round up area citizens who had seen where the Germans had planted the mines. With their help, he and his men were successfully able to mark the sites with sticks and rags. This ability to employ the services of a citizenry would appear again, just at the war's end, but few, if any, of the citizens would eagerly embrace his requests.

In that same brutal winter, another assignment led Compton to his first one-on-one encounter with victims of German intolerance. With a few of his men, he set out in a jeep from Stavelot to search for shelter in an abandoned home in the countryside. Before too long, they came across a farmhouse that appeared vacant, but as Compton headed to the front door, he had an uneasy feeling that someone was inside. With his rifle poised ready to fire, he knocked twice and received no response. His intuition prevented him from opening the door because German soldiers could easily be on the other side ready to kill him and his men. He didn't abandon the house; instead he barked, "I am an American soldier. If you don't open this door *now*…"

Immediately the door flew open, and there stood a pregnant woman sheltering four children. "I thought you were German until I heard you speak," she cried, terror in her voice. Relieved that she had not fallen into German hands, she continued, explaining that she had been a school teacher in Holland until the situation had become

The Jewish children, bare-legged in the heavy snow, that Compton's troop helped during the winter of 1944-45.

too perilous for these four Jewish students. She had been hiding them in Holland until she decided to flee, trying to get the children as far away from the Germans as possible. The five of them had been following American troops and somehow had persuaded Army drivers to transport them to Belgium. Unfortunately, they ended up in the middle of the fighting there. "I thought we had finally been discovered." Since the Germans had just left the area, the woman and children could safely remain in the farmhouse. The Americans, though, would be staying there, too.

The only one warm room in that farmhouse was the kitchen, occupied by the woman and children. Compton, careful to avoid impropriety because he knew this woman was frightened to death, ordered his men to stay in the remainder of the house, completely avoiding the kitchen, which was off limits. Of course, the rest of the house was frigid. The floors on which

Compton and his men would sleep were layered with ice, so the men employed some basic survival skills Compton had learned in Boy Scouts, not the Army, which enabled them to keep their feet dry and to set up their bedding on ice and still sleep warmly.

Sleeping warmly was the biggest, but not the only, concern of the men. Using abandoned houses in the area as supply depots, they scavenged for their bedding supplies, food, and fuel. While they were at it, they collected supplies for the woman and children, too. Then they coexisted at the farmhouse until Compton and his men received orders to move on. Before moving on, Compton advised the woman to stay put. He and his men restocked her supplies and departed.

After soldiering through the winter, Compton and his men returned to Stavelot in the spring of 1945. "I don't know how she knew we were going to be in Stavelot, but there she and the children were, waiting for us so that she could thank me and the men for what we had done. It was delightful! At the end of their visit," he continued, "we rounded up chocolates and other treats for them and then arranged for the motor pool to get them back to the farmhouse." Thus closed a bearable chapter of the war.

Shortly, the 82nd was crossing the Elbe River and corralling the 162,000 German soldiers surrendering to their 6,000 men. The war in Europe was rapidly coming to an end, and the

Germans felt safer in American hands than they did in Russian hands. For a while, Compton and his fellow band members had to guard the Germans who were held in a field, secured only by machine guns set up in each corner, until the captives could be moved on to prisons elsewhere.

Compton's next duty involved traversing the Elbe River on a pontoon bridge to reach Ludwigslust, a town in southwest Germany. Thus opened perhaps the worst chapter of the war, a chapter that would haunt Compton and others for years to come.

The focal point of Ludwigslust was an enormous, grand palace, a testament to Germany's power and glory. Across from it lay a peaceful town park undisturbed by the ravages of war. The townspeople went about their daily routines as if nothing were out of the ordinary while a group of medics from the 82nd left town to liberate Wobelein, a prison camp nearby. What they would encounter was too awful for words.

Wobelein was not a labor camp where Germany's enemies worked like pack animals and died. Wobelein was not a camp where a daily selection determined who would dig his own grave before being shot or who would be gassed and then burned in the crematorium. Wobelein was simpler, very low maintenance. The Jews and others assigned there were simply locked up and left to starve to death.

The medics who arrived on the scene saw stacks of corpses with holes in the torsos created by the living who had the strength to rip the corpses open with their bare hands and scavenge the organs for food. There also happened to be some SS guards who had not fled before the Americans arrived. While descriptions of the atrocious scene filtered back to Compton and the others in town, some of the liberators allowed prisoners with any strength at all to attack the SS with clubs and kill them; however, even the taste of sweet justice could not remove the taste of bitter horror.

An interrogator, Sergeant Nick Nichols, disclosed to Compton all that the Americans had seen and heard at Wobelein and what they planned to do. Filled with anger, disgust, and indignation, Compton begged to be included. That is how he came to lead an Army round-up of the citizens of Ludwigslust and set them to the task of digging two hundred graves in the beautiful town park and making crosses, many with the Star of David in the center, to adorn them. How could these people have ignored what was

German civilians forced to dig the graves and to bury the victims of Wobelein on the palace grounds.

happening at Wobelein, and how could they have objected to this labor?

Object they did. While Compton was supervising this project, he noticed two of the diggers muttering in German and casting venomous looks his way. "Hey, Nick. What are those two talking about?" he asked.

"You. How cruel you are and the nerve you have demanding this."

"You tell that guy that if he looks at me again, I'll take away his shovel and gloves, and I'll see that he digs this grave with his bare hands."

After Nichols relayed Compton's menacing message to the Germans, no one else openly objected to the forced labor. Beneath the unblinking gaze of

the mighty palace, the Germans created the cemetery that housed two hundred corpses carried to town from Wobelein.

Next, just two days after V-E Day, under American orders, every German in town had to respectfully report to the park for a memorial service to honor the victims of Wobelein. Each had to face up to his tacit agreement to allow the abuse and murder of fellow human beings when he listened to a moving eulogy delivered by the chaplain, Major George B. Woods. Compton's job was to go with other soldiers from house to house in Ludwigslust to shoot on sight anyone who dared be absent.

Meanwhile, American soldiers were not feeling righteous and jubilant about their part in exposing the Germans. Many, like Compton, had difficult questions for the chaplain. "How could these people know what was happening and allow it? How can there be a God who would allow this? Where is God? Show Him to me!" they furiously demanded.

Reflecting recently, Compton said, "I couldn't believe there was a God in heaven who would let this happen to these people." There were rumors about the Jews and others that most people dismissed before Compton ever entered the war. "It's probably just as well we didn't know the truth. We might have been brutal to the women and children in Germany as well, so bitter were we towards the Germans. As it was, we just refused to fraternize."

THE CHAPLAIN'S BURIAL ADDRESS by Major George B. Woods

"We are assembled here today before God and in the sight of man to give a proper and reverent burial to the victims of atrocities committed by armed forces in the name and by the order of the German Government. These 200 bodies were found by the American army in a concentration camp four miles north of the city of Ludwigslust.

"The crimes here committed in the name of the German people and by their acquiescence were minor compared to those to be found elsewhere in Germany. Here there were no gas chambers, no crematoriums; these men of Holland, Russia, Poland, Czechoslovakia, and France were simply allowed to starve to death. Within four miles of your comfortable homes, 4,000 men were forced to live like animals, deprived even of the food you would give to your dogs. In three weeks 1,000 of these men were starved to death; 800 of them were buried in pits in the nearby woods. These 200 who lie before us in these graves were found piled four and four feet high in one building and lying with the sick and dying in other buildings.

"The world has long been horrified at the crimes of the German nation; these crimes were never clearly brought to light until the armies of the United Nations overran Germany. This is not a war as conducted by the rules of warfare. This is murder such as is not even known among savages.

"Though you claim no knowledge of these acts you are still individually and collectively responsible for these atrocities, for they were committed by a government elected to office by yourselves in 1933 and continued in office by indifference to organized brutality. It should be the firm resolve of the German people that never again should any leader or party bring them to such moral degradation as is exhibited here.

"It is the custom of the United States Army through its Chaplain's Corps to insure a proper and decent burial to any deceased person whether he be civilian, or soldier, friend, or foe, according to religious preference. The Supreme Commander of the Allied Forces has ordered that all atrocity victims be buried in a public place, and that the cemetery be given the same perpetual care that is given to all military cemeteries. Crosses will be placed at the heads of the graves; a stone monument will be set up in memory of those deceased. Protestant, Catholic, and Jewish prayers will be said by Chaplains Wood, Hannan, and Wall of the 82nd Airborne Division for these victims as we lay them to rest and commit them into the hands of our Heavenly Father in the hope that the world will not again be faced with such barbarity."

Chaplain Reid of the 82nd Airborne Division

After this incident, except for having to entertain the Russians, Compton and most of his band members had no further obligation in Europe. They had accumulated enough time in the service to find themselves headed home in the fall of '45. Home again did not mean business as usual because Compton had lost both music and faith.

Regarding his musical talent, Compton explained, "The Army played me to death. I was all over Europe doing Army stuff by day and then playing gigs until one or two in the morning. When I got home, I was totally burned out and quit playing music for forty-three years." Music is undeniably a part of his fabric, however, and he finally started playing again, ten or eleven years ago, with Don Case's Satin Sound Orchestra. He also plays with the Tidewater Concert Band.

Regarding his faith, Compton replied, "I had a rough time understanding how God allowed the brutality that occurred during World War II." In fact, when Compton first arrived home, he lacked motivation and wanted to do little else than go crabbing, drink beer, and read. "Then one day my aunt gave me *The Robe* by Lloyd C. Douglas. I started reading and didn't stop until I finished. Reading that book brought me back because I saw the parallels between what happened to the Jews and what had happened to Christ. The methods were different, but the experience was the same."

To see John Compton, both modest and effervescent today, no one would suspect that he had ever had to deal with war and its effects. Part Boy Scout, part musician, part munitions maker, part soldier, part gliderman, part

leader, he had the experience, and experiences, that brought him through World War II changed but not defeated. Although Compton considers himself no more accomplished or heroic than any of the fellows Carl Sigman wrote about in his song about the 82nd, "All-American Soldier," his symphony is truly moving. ❖

John and Georgenia's grandchildren: Michael Drye, Draper, Olivia Ann, and Quillen Bender, and Thomas and Ellen Weaver

Ann Weaver, Georgenia and Gina Bender

The Compton Family: Vince and Susan Pilato, John and Georgenia, Denis Drye, Betty Compton, Clay and Marsha Compton, John Eli and Chaya.

— 61 —

Wallace Dreyer

No amount of rumor, reportage, news reels or indoctrination prepared me for such a spectacle.

Wallace Dreyer
LIBERATOR

By Eric Berryman

Wars have always been fought by ordinary men of modest rank. While generals may strike heroic poses, gather medals and write their memoirs, triumph or failure on the battlefield is decided by the performance of common foot soldiers. It was so 25 centuries ago at Marathon and over 50 years ago when Americans fought their way across Europe into the heart of Hitler's Germany.

Wars have always been fought by ordinary men of modest rank. While generals may strike heroic poses, gather medals and write their memoirs, triumph or failure on the battlefield is decided by the performance of common foot soldiers. It was so 25 centuries ago at Marathon and over 50 years ago when Americans fought their way across Europe into the heart of Hitler's Germany. The general pronounces grand strategy and geopolitical complexities. The infantryman's world, on the other hand, is narrowly focused on a few familiar faces, his physical discomforts and personal fears. The last highlight might be no more recent than yesterday's mail call and the future goes only as far as the next objective. His existence takes on the qualities of numbered chips in a bingo caller's basket. But it is to men like these that the rest of us owe our freedoms.

Private First Class Wallace Dreyer, photographer and former undergraduate, enlisted in the army at the University of Texas in 1943. By August, 1944, in the role of a Forward Observer he embarked in New York City aboard the troopship ARGENTINA, along with the rest of the 26th Infantry Division, 104th Regiment, 1st Battalion, Massachusetts National Guard. A month later, somewhere near Nancy in eastern France, he met his first hostilities. The 1st Battalion's job was to move along the front (much of it included the old Maginot Line, in fact), clearing out the Wehrmacht's formidable array of steel and concrete pill-boxes and other pockets of resistance.

In October, Moncourt Woods had to be cleared of the enemy, and the strong points in the hills of Bezange La Petite. A contemporary Regimental account of that action is worth recording.

"The infantry was moving forward. They entered Moncourt Woods and moved against the crossing fire of well placed and protected machine guns, and the planned fire of mortars, as they sought the protection of the earth. They moved and fought in the best tradition of foot soldiers. But the machine guns were well placed and well concealed, and difficult to get at. And the tanks couldn't move because there were mines and booby traps in the woods and the roads leading to it. When night came, the infantrymen dug in to hold what they had taken, and they did. But they were only one third of their way....

"Fire and movement, independent, aggressive action against the machine gun positions. Just as the book tells it. And it worked out just as the book says it will. The German was killed in his foxhole and behind his guns.... By fire and movement and close personal combat, the foot soldier had taken ground from the enemy ... a fight had been won."

What a splendid thing to have participated in the liberation of France! If only symbolically, that act may be among the second World War's few instances of panache.

Now they had fought their way to the gates of the Reich. PFC Dreyer, long since awarded the distinctive Combat Infantryman's badge, and his battalion crossed into Germany at Merzig, on the Saar River. From there they battled on to Alezy and Oppenheim, then around Darmstadt and northeast to Fulda. From Fulda they began to work down to the south and east and by April,

1945, they had reached the Bohemian Forest, on the Czechoslovakian border.

On April 23, they liberated an Aussenlager (satellite camp) of the central concentration camp at Flossenburg. It was Lager 15, on the edge of the small village of Schwartzenfeld. There were hundreds of these satellites throughout Germany and German-occupied Europe. Their purpose was to serve local industry with skilled and unskilled slave labor; payment for the work performed went directly to the Party and the SS. The Jews among these slaves were deliberately worked to death. That was documented policy. At war's end, the SS commonly resorted to executing

those who had survived and so it had been at Schwartzenfeld.

Dreyer's regiment found the bodies of hundreds of Polish Jews who had been murdered in the last days of war, and were either left in heaps in and around the camp or covered over in collective burial mounds. Someone, perhaps the regimental commander, ordered the graves opened and the dead placed in individual coffins and decently buried.

Dreyer did not enter the camp, he simply remembers its wooden buildings and tin roofs and he remembers with undimmed clarity how it was to be in the middle of so much death. Great burial mounds and heaps of bodies

American troops in France.   *Photo by Hugo Horvath*

stacked limb upon limb and how impossible it was to count the numbers. Some 400 yards outside the camp was piled high with the dead. Not much to reckon with in the staggering statistics of that era's genocide, but more than enough to impress upon Dreyer what it was he had been fighting for and against.

"No amount of rumor," he said, "reportage, news reels or indoctrination prepared me for such a spectacle. With a kind of dawning awareness I understood the nature of the foe and the dimensions of his crime."

The villagers were bringing survivors out of the camp. If, indeed, "survivor" is a creditable term, for Dreyer remembers them as wretched souls and tiny, shrunken people. Most could not even stand and none could eat solid food. They were being fed one part milk to ten parts water; that is all their bodies could safely absorb. They were being treated "like new-born babies," Dreyer recalls, adding, "That night the Red Cross arrived, and the regiment went on."

Other elements of the 26th Infantry Division uncovered the site of an atrocity in nearby Wiesenfeld: the bodies of Russian and Polish slave laborers who were shot because they were too ill to move quickly enough when the SS attempted to evacuate some of the camps. Still other American soldiers found a treasure in art objects hidden deep inside a local

salt mine. In blood or greed, lust knew no bounds.

And so the war came to an end.

Wally Dreyer became known locally and nationally for his prints made from "found" objects, and for his photography. He taught at Old Dominion University and in the summer he could be found in his

Hermitage Museum studio, teaching art to junior and senior high school students as part of the Norfolk Public School's Summer Enrichment Program. His wife Gay was a sculptor, painter, printmaker, and poet. Her works have been exhibited in some of America's finest museums. ❖

Reprinted from *Renewal Magazine*, 1985. Wallace Dreyer died in 1993.

Wallace Dreyer

An Interrupted Childhood
The Story of Alfred Dreyfus

By Rebecca Tabakin

ALFRED DREYFUS admits that he and his family were "very lucky." Their story is like that of so many other Jewish families; but, they survived to tell the tale. Sometimes it was their quick decision making, determination and timing that saved them all from Hitler's Final Solution. Other times it was the kindness of strangers.

He grew up in Germany, the son of a well-to-do businessman who owned a second-generation boxboard container factory manufacturing cardboard boxes for consumer items such as fancy candy, cigarettes and shoes. His family lived in a villa across from a beautiful park. In 1933, his mother employed a cook, maid and cleaning lady as well as a nurse to help with her three children – Alfred age nine, Henry age seven and the youngest, two-year-old Roger. In March of that year Hitler came to power.

Dreyfus remembers a day in primary school from that year as if it were yesterday. There were only two Jewish children in his class, Dreyfus and

Alfred Dreyfus

Photo by Susan Hirschbiel

another boy. He recalls, "The teacher screamed at us, 'You dirty, stinking Jews. I want you out of here.' You can imagine what that was like for this other fellow and me as it was in front of the whole class. Then, at the class break some of the kids beat us up. I told my father what happened at school and he said, 'You are not going back to that school.' Of course, my parents complained but the school said nothing can be done about it. It was the last day of my formal schooling for awhile."

The school incident became the deciding factor that the family was going to have to move. "Roger and my parents left for Strasbourg, France while my brother Henry and I were sent to live with our grandfather who owned an upscale kosher hotel in Baden-Baden, Germany. When we were sent to Strasbourg, we resumed school again, but this time at a Jewish school, and we were taught how to speak French," remembers Dreyfus.

Strasbourg was an industrial center that had been a part of Germany at one time or another in its history and the Dreyfus family felt at home there. Dreyfus' father found a partner who was of German-Jewish descent who provided the capital, and his father provided the technical expertise. But, businesses were all feeling the effects of the imminent war. The German-speaking Dreyfus family were foreigners and as such were merely tolerated. When they arrived, they initially lived some miles from the Rhine River in an apartment on the border between Germany and France.

"We stayed there until 1938, until it became inevitable that there was going to be a war. Then we hid 20 miles from the Rhine River outside of Strasbourg for about two months in a hotel. In the next months, we were forced to move often. Cousins took us in some 60 miles away in the mountains in

Luneville. Meanwhile, my father tried to start a new factory in the outskirts of Paris, but without a partner and with little money, it was a struggle," Dreyfus remembers.

In March of 1939, the family moved again to a new home in Pontoise some 25 miles north of Paris. Shortly after the outbreak of World War II, the entire family was arrested, their crime, "enemy aliens." There were so many people arrested that day, they filled the soccer stadium. Although the mother and boys were sent home after one day's internment, Alfred's father was to remain in another camp for over a year.

Shortly thereafter, the French government recruited the young Dreyfus and a lot of other young men to attend a crash course in tool making. "They needed these people desperately to fabricate ammunition and guns. I

Photo above - Dreyfus and Roos box-making factory in Muggenstrum, Germany in the early 1900's.

Right - Alfred and Henry with his father, Manfred Dreyfus, in 1930 in Rastadt, Germany.

graduated and received my certificate, and made plans to pick up my new official tool kit. I never got to pick up my tool kit because four days later the German army came through Belgium on their way to Paris and beyond. That June of 1940 the town of Pontoise was bombarded by planes everyday. It wreaked havoc in that little town. But, yes, we were very lucky," says Dreyfus shaking his head. "There was a 150-foot-high rock behind our home with a cave in it. To us, it was our air raid shelter. We stayed there day and night because the bombardment came periodically.

"One day we sneaked back into our house to eat a real breakfast. Neighbors came to tell us that the Germans were less than a day away. There was pandemonium! The streets were filled with people – the French army and civilians – all fleeing, going south. My

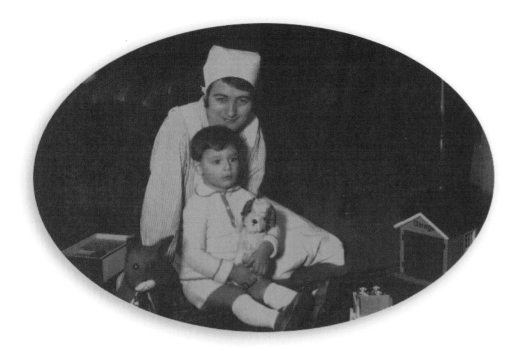

Top photo - Six-year-old Alfred with his nanny in 1930.

Photo above - Alfred's maternal grandparents in front of their kosher hotel in Baden-Baden.

everyone to get out. They said, 'No more trains were leaving from here. Get out of here. The station is a prime target for German bombs. There is no shelter here. For your safety don't stay here. You must leave!' We didn't know what to do, but my mother saw one train about five rows down the tracks. She made us walk there and get on the train, where we collapsed.

"There were other people on the train, including another Jewish family. At 5:30 in the morning the train started to move. We didn't know where we were going. Two days later we arrived in Toulouse in the south of France. The people in charge of the town's affairs fed us and let us sleep on the floor of the train station. The next day they took us and other people from the train by truck to a tiny village of 250 people, all farmers, in Lamothe Capdeville on the Aveyron River near Montauban. The people didn't know what a Jew was, and no one asked us. They just made extra room for fellow citizens. We were told the miller had given us a place to stay.

When we got there we soon found out that our new home was where he once kept his pigs! We stayed in that one room and slept on some hay over the concrete floor. I was able to work for rations at the mill or in the general store in the village center, and I went fishing every day so that we would have food. We didn't know what had happened to our home, or where our father was, but once again we had been lucky."

mother decided we would go to Paris to see what happens. On the way, Henry and I got temporarily separated from my mother and Roger." Before they were separated, the German planes consistently and relentlessly attacked the people fleeing south. "It was a carnage," Dreyfus remembers. "For some reason we all had the good idea to see a cousin of my dad's family in Paris. We were tired, hungry and very scared. There was no time to count ourselves lucky when everyone said that the Germans would be in Paris shortly.

"The only way to go south was to take the train. When we got to the railroad station it looked like there were millions of people there. It was incredible! *Everybody* wanted to get out. In the midst of all these frantic people, the people who worked there were telling

While the boys enjoyed the country, life was not easy for their mother. There was no running water or toilet facilities and their quarters were infested with mice and no way to control them. Alfred's mother was worried about their father, and added to her worries were her fears about the new occupants of their barn-home, Moroccan soldiers known as the Zouaves. But her fears were allayed when the Zouaves befriended the boys, and brought the family meat and sugar when they could find it. Alfred provided the family with protein by fishing daily. The boys were especially fascinated by the Zouaves' strange customs. "We were invited to the end of the Ramadan celebration. I cannot forget the sights and smells of the goat roasting on the spit and watching the soldiers as they danced themselves into a frenzy at the end of their 40-day fast. They were fierce anti-Nazis, and to us, those soldiers were special people."

Their father had been in internment for a year when the Germans took over the camp. First, they released the non-Jewish German prisoners. Dreyfus still feels that "somehow my dad, who spoke German, talked the camp commander into letting him go before the Gestapo was to interview him. He went back to our home in Pontoise only to find the breakfast table with food half-eaten."

He recognized that his decision to stay in the apartment while awaiting news of his family was dangerous. About 3:30

Alfred, at right, with his father Manfred, his brother Henry, mother Emma, and cousin Gerard Dreyfus, in "best" Internment Camp in 1943.

a.m., his father heard a loud banging on the door and shouting. "My father had the foresight to have purchased a rope ladder, which he used to climb down from the third floor bedroom window. Then he made his way to the cave his family had used as a bomb shelter. The police did not find him." Once again, a member of the Dreyfus family had escaped.

Many months later, while sitting at a café on the Champs-Elysees, someone walked by Dreyfus' father's table who recognized him. His father told the man that he was waiting in Paris in hopes of hearing the fate of his family. Much to his amazement, the man said, 'I know where they are.' The Dreyfus family was reunited again in late 1941 in Lamothe Capdeville. They moved to a small house and resumed a more normal life. They even had a Jewish neighbor several miles from their home. The adults were not allowed to work, but Alfred and Henry were given odd jobs to earn food rations.

Henry Dreyfus, a friend and Alfred Dreyfus in the last Internment Camp in Switzerland just before liberation in 1944.

Alfred in front of his home in Rastadt, Germany, which he revisited in 1993.

Several months later the family was saved again by the kindness of a stranger. Dreyfus will never forget "a man with an Austrian accent came up to me when I was working at the general store, and took me aside. 'If I were you, I would disappear tonight. They are going to arrest a lot of people.' That night at 3:30 a.m. the Vichy French Police with Gestapo supervision arrived by truck, knocked on the door of our home, then broke it down looking for us. My family had exchanged some of my mother's crystal and jewelry with a farmer and we hid in his hayloft. We were not detected."

Two months later they escaped by taxi to Toulouse where Alfred's father was able to procure some false identity papers with the help of his former secretary. Every car was stopped by *gendarmes* to check identity papers against a list of wanted persons. Dreyfus recalls, "When our taxi was stopped, we all sat there terrified. The taxi driver, who guessed our situation, said, 'They are right.' The *gendarme* waved us on without looking at our papers. If he had, he would have seen they were stamped in large letters, JUIF ETRANGER, Foreign Jew. We got past that close call, but there was more terror to come." Then they went by train to Lyon.

"Terror was with us every minute of that trip to Lyon. The French *gendarmes* and the Gestapo made arrests in every car in that train, at numerous train stops during a ten-hour train trip, including the one that we were in.

When we arrived in Lyon, Henry and I went to stay at the local Jewish center gymnasium while our parents and youngest brother stayed with some friends. Conditions at the gym were terrible. I couldn't sleep, and at 4:30 a.m. in the morning I told Henry, 'we have got to get out of here.' Later that day we heard that the Gestapo had come shortly after 5 a.m. and arrested everyone in the gym," finishes Dreyfus.

The Jewish community let it be known that there was an underground working to smuggle families into Switzerland. The Dreyfus family made the necessary contacts, and worked their way to the border. The night before they were to be ferried by boat across Lake Geneva, the smuggler and his passengers were arrested and several people were killed. So, the family paid a smuggler to taxi them by way of the mountains. To the family's horror, the driver drove off the road, deep into the woods, and stopped near the bottom of the mountain. Inside were a band of smugglers who demanded that the family go up in their hayloft and await their decision as to their fate.

Dreyfus' father managed to pay off the smugglers with the last of their valuables and they were taken through the snow and the mud up the mountains on foot. Dreyfus shakes his head when he recalls, "We were at the border above the tree line about 6-7,000 feet up and it was snowing. My poor mother had street shoes on.…"

No sooner had the family stepped on the footpath on Swiss soil, than a Swiss soldier appeared from hiding behind a boulder, and arrested them. They were interrogated at the police compound with hundreds of other refugees.

"It was another miracle that we were allowed to stay. 95% of the people were sent back! Only if families had a child under 12, then the whole family was allowed to stay. Everyone had false papers so it was very difficult to prove that the child accompanying a family was theirs. But for our family, we were lucky because my father's aunt and her daughter, who were Swiss nationals, lived in Zurich. They confirmed Roger was only 11 years old and we were all five of us one family." After the war, Dreyfus says he learned that the policy which allowed the family to stay was in effect for only five weeks – the same five weeks that his family used to make their escape from France.

"But we were not free." says Dreyfus. "We were separated once again and sent to labor in camps. The only time we had it good was when my brothers, father, mother and I were all reunited into one camp for two months. The camp commander was a Swiss Army officer and he couldn't have treated us better.

"At the next camp where Henry and I were sent, the commander must have been a Nazi sympathizer because the food was insufficient and we were always hungry. We were forced to work hard in snow, ice and later in ankle deep mud. It was bitter cold, with icy winds. They got us up in the middle of the night and worked us hard. Luckily we were there for only eight months. The next camp was better. We were building a road and the food was adequate. We boys fared better than my father whose health was broken by all the years of worry and incarceration for his age. My mother and Roger were released first from the camps. Roger lived with a very nice Swiss Jewish family and my mother was a maid for another Jewish family. Again, we were very lucky."

When the war ended, Dreyfus boarded a Liberty ship and left his parents and brothers behind to make a new life in the United States. ❖

Alfred lights a memorial candle at a Yom Hashoah commemoration.
Photo by Betsy Karotkin

Dreyfus family in the Atlanta home of Claudia Levi, Alfred's daughter. The photo was taken in 1997 after Alfred gave his personal history to the "Shoah Project."

FRIENDSHIP THAT EXTENDED BEYOND HISTORY'S CRUELEST HOURS

Charles Elder

By Lisa Richmon

Moving beyond survival through history's cruelest hours, Harry Grundmann may look back but he won't talk about it. What this retired Australian businessman will talk about is the man who helped him and his wife Anna recover from Nazi persecution 56 years ago.

That person is Charles Elder, a Tidewater resident and a member of the Board of Directors of the United Jewish Federation of Tidewater. During World War II, Elder served in the 71st Infantry Division of Patton's Third Army. He remembers those times well, which prompts him to say, "It is not easy to forgive the Germans." In 1945 Elder's unit was at Dachau, two to three days after its liberation. He also remembers "blowing the locks off the gates" of a satellite camp of Mauthausen, where the prisoners were worked and slowly starved to death. Later in August, 1945, he was transferred to the Office of Military Government for Bavaria in Munich.

In September of 1946, Elder heard from a distant relative who told him that his niece Anna had survived Auschwitz. After liberation Anna had met and married another survivor, Harry Grundmann, and they had made their way to Munich, where they were living. Using his military government influence, Elder was able to locate the Grundmanns just ten days after Anna had given birth to twin boys, Max and David.

Charles Elder

Elder, displaying a gentle yet passionate manner today, describes that first encounter as if it were yesterday. "I found them living in squalid conditions in a bombed out section of town which was off limits to American military after dark. As a military government officer, I was able to intervene to get them on their feet, focusing first on decent housing."

He explained that the Bavarian government provided housing for victims of Nazi persecution by requisitioning apartments or houses occupied by individuals who were identified as Nazis. These Nazis would have to "double up" with other Nazis. Since Elder was a military government officer, he was able to expedite this process in three days.

The Nazi, whose apartment the Grundmanns were to occupy at first refused to leave, but after a personal visit from Elder, moved out the next day. Once the couple was settled in their apartment, Elder then helped them establish a normal life and served as a link between the Grundmanns and their family in America.

In 1947, Grundmann started a small business, buying and selling used Rosenthal china. In 1952, the family emigrated to Australia. Grundmann worked in a textile factory for three years and then went to work for a company selling chinaware to specialty stores. Four years later, he started his own chinaware business. Never looking

German village   *Photo by Hugo Horvath*

back, Grundmann became the largest importer of upscale imported chinaware and glassware in Australia and New Zealand.

Many years went by and the Grundmanns lost contact with Elder. As fate would have it, 15 years ago Elder, through a distant relative, met an Australian woman who knew Anna and Harry, triggering their first contact since 1946. Shortly afterwards, Grundmann called Elder, promising to meet him when he, Anna and his grandson, Adam, came to the United States on an around the world trip in honor of Adam's Bar Mitzvah.

"This was my clue to how successful he had become," Elder said.

In 1993, Elder and his wife, Shirley, made a trip to Australia. Anna had, subsequently, passed away. The twins – Max, who took over the business in Melbourne, and David, a physician in Brisbane, were eager to become acquainted with the Elders. Harry, who was fully retired, was living in Australia's Gold Coast. The reunion was unforgettable. But, because the Elders were on a tour, they were only able to be with the family one full day and one evening. The Grundmann family, however, was insistent that Charles and Shirley return to Australia for a "proper visit."

In 1994, the Elders returned to Australia for a seven-week stay, dividing their time between Harry and David on the Gold Coast and Brisbane and Max and his family in Melbourne (with time out for excursions to the Blue Mountains, the in-land Myall Lakes and Singapore.)

One highlight of the Elders' visit to Australia was attending the Australian Championship basketball game, when the North Melbourne Giants, owned by Max, won the title.

Harry, though, appeared "solitary and subdued," without Anna by his side, Elder remembers, explaining that she had worked with him in their business from the start. Years after her death, he still mourns the loss of her vivacious presence, he added. Walking privately on the beach with Grundmann, who was 83 at the time, Elder found he was still reluctant to discuss the war years, the Lodz Ghetto or the concentration camp. "He simply chose to show how deeply grateful he remains for my help to him and his beloved Anna in 1946," Elder added.

An extended family connection had been established. In the past years, David Grundmann and his wife, Melissa, were in California for a medical convention and spent three days in Norfolk, visiting with the Elders.

Sadly, Harry passed away in 1999. But the deep bond between Harry and Charles Elder has continued with Max and David, Harry's sons. ❖

Charles Elder as a young soldier during World War II.

Marie Knowles Ellifritz
A Nurse's Story

By Reba Karp

Marie Knowles Ellifritz

"*O*ur evacuation hospital … was a place where a handful of doctors, nurses and GIs tried to hold back the escaping book of life."

Marie Knowles Ellifritz may be one of the few people who was obligated to visit the perimeters of hell, and yet, chose 32 years later to return and allow the ghosts of man's inhumanity to man to reenter her consciousness.

That is not to say that they ever truly leave, but as a registered nurse, she has had to learn control – to separate – that which can be avoided from that which must be faced.

She acknowledges that death is a natural order of life, when it is in its natural order – age or disease. But when inhumanely caused by external agents, it ceases to be understandable or acceptable.

Her story began in May 1945 when she was a member of the 130th Evacuation Hospital assigned to care for the victims of Mauthausen Concentration Camp in Austria. Theoretically it ended – or more exactly reemerged, in December of 1977 when she returned to Mauthausen.

She described the almost indescribable beginnings in an article which appeared in the Newport News and Tidewater Federation newspapers in 1976: "Our evacuation hospital was a series of cots and air mattresses under tents and sky where God gave superhuman endurance to his helpers and the victims of the devil; it was the place where swollen-bellied children ate a piece of bread and vomited; it was a place where women and men forever closed their eyes in escape."

And it was a place "where a handful of doctors, nurses and GIs tried to hold back the escaping book of life." Ellifritz was part of that scene in a hospital which had to be "elasticized to accommodate the 1500 half-starved Jewish men, women and children that became our patients."

She recalls that the first couple of days in the camp were spent preparing for the survivors. "And then they came – stinking, bewildered, staggering, naked human beings. They were almost like animals, without fur.

"I had to tell myself over and over again that these were human beings encased in what was left of a human body, bringing with them only their faith in God and the storehouse of their brains."

And then in December 1977 upon her return, she once again tried to describe the incomprehensible which must lie just beyond the limits of the human vocabulary.

"As the train lumbered along from Vienna towards Linz, Austria, I wondered if I had made the right decision. Several people told me … that perhaps the emotional trauma I would subject myself to would not be worth it. But then, those people had not been there 32 years ago. There was no way of telling them that it had been hell then and now perhaps I would find solace for my troubled conscience, troubled for I never understood how my world had let it happen.

"Even for the patients who knew they would be dead in a few short hours or days, liberation in May of 1945 was a joyous time – a time they were free of Nazism … a time of breathing fresh air outside the confining walls of the camp, a time of sharing with the American liberators the joy of sudden freedom.

"Those who died there would not see the end of their 'wandering in the wilderness' with the formation of the State of Israel in 1948 …. The dead would know from their vantage point, however, that because of their suffering and death, a State of Israel would be possible. It is always a greater sacrifice to lose your life, if by losing, something is made greater."

She remembers the site of the 130th Evacuation Hospital as "a large wheat field – somewhere in once beautiful Austria; it had no name. In sharp contrast to the gently waving wheat, my stringy hair poked out from beneath a combat helmet.…"

Today, looking back from the vantage point of a mother, she realized his "goodness, his kindness, his gentleness reflected, not the five years in a concentration camp, but rather in his mother's love and … teachings before she was put to death in a gas chamber."

In 1977 the walls of the camp were as she remembered them. The one difference then was the quiet. "No Russian prisoners burning their barracks, no celebrations of Polish weddings, no moaning that goes with suffering, no gaunt, haunting faces searching for compassion.…"

On October 27, 1981, Ellifritz, R.N., a member of a medical panel on the Holocaust for the U.S. State Department, had another time to try to express her feelings as an American woman and nurse who had to deal with the full gamut of emotions.

"The emotional trauma … was beyond belief – as Americans and as women we never before had been subjected to such inhumanity to man.… Clinically, it was a matter of sorting the dead from the living, deciding who would live for at least three days or more and to make all those we found comfortable and begin the process of treatment. A tent to keep the patient dry, an air mattress to give them a place to lie down, a blanket to help keep them warm, pajamas to give them a sense of dignity, a small amount of food to nourish them and plasma to preserve the remaining life and begin them on the road back to living.…"

Cast aside by all involved, she remembers, was concern for their own physical and emotional well-being. "Some of us did get sick from the dysentery that the patients had … from the TB exposure – from the emotional trauma – but most of all it was the sickness of the heart – of being a witness to the results of man's inhumanity to man.…"

Other memories surfaced during that presentation. Pride at being an American and part of the liberation, and as such winning the immediate trust of many of the survivors. For others, it took the rest of their lives for them to accept their freedom, for in reality many died within a few days of entering the camp. It seemed that when they realized "they were truly free at last … they simply closed their eyes and died in peace and freedom."

In 1985 at the time of this interview, it was 40 years since the 23-year-old Second Lieutenant in the U.S. Army Nurse Corps stepped onto the perimeter of hell and dared to look over the barrier through the eyes of her patients. But even as her memories are filled with the sharp blacks and greys of suffering, she sees the blue summer flowers gathered from the wheat fields which bordered the evacuation hospital. She terms it "love at first sight" as she reaches for words to convey the tenderness of her association with a 10 or 12 year-old Jewish boy who called her "Sistra."

"I called him 'Junior' … for the lack of something better."

He brought her flowers and helped her keep fragile sanity. They did not speak the same language, "but the looks and deeds of a child are universally understood. His gentle offerings were a response to casual American friendliness. He never knew the years of stifling memory those small deeds would cause…." Today, looking back from the vantage point of a mother, she realized his "goodness, his kindness, his gentleness reflected, not the five years in a concentration camp, but rather in his mother's love and … teachings before she was put to death in a gas chamber."

And so a friendship out of mutual need developed – his for the surrogate for a mother he had lost, and hers for a bit of gentleness in a world that reflected the brutal side of man's nature. "Even when

I was sent to work in the Lager hospital, it was his practice to see me off each morning and to wait for my return to our tent city each evening. I knew Junior waited, I did not know why. But I liked him to be there …."

One day she was to return and Junior was not waiting. "The hospital seemed empty," she said explaining that a number of the patients, including Junior had been transferred. Later that week she received word that Junior had asked that she come visit him in the new camp, a few miles away. "I promised myself I would visit Junior – tomorrow. My tomorrows somehow became the hurried yesterdays of life."

Today that promise is a whiplash which still stirs within her. "Was I too tired, too busy or too young and immature that I did not go?" she questions.

She still has a photograph over 40 years old and shows her as a young woman between two camp survivors. One of them is Junior.

"The photograph will brown with age, and the wonderful but sad memories … will fade, along with the horror of dying war victims. But my love for Junior lives on." ❖

Reprinted from *Renewal Magazine*, 1985.

Marie Knowles Ellifritz with Junior and one of his friends.

Simple Luck or Perhaps a Kind of Courage
BENNY FEFER

By Patty Slotnick

The question still haunts BENNY FEFER in moments of quiet reflection; why did he survive? Why was he the only survivor out of his entire family? Why were he and one other boy the sole survivors out of 800 Jews from Rembertow, Poland? Some might say it was simply luck that made the difference, but perhaps a kind of courage came to those who believed death was inevitable. It enabled them to take risks that ultimately made the difference between life and death.

Moishe Fefer

Dora Fefer

In the few faded photographs kept by a kind neighbor and returned to Benny after the war, one can glimpse the vitality and joy of the Fefer family. Benny's father, Moishe, was clearly a man of proud bearing. He was a pharmacist by education, and had served with distinction in the Polish military during World War I. He had been awarded a medal for heroism, unusual for anyone, let alone a Jew. His mother, Dora, was a beautiful woman, her gentle eyes shining with intelligence. Her family owned a wholesale grocery business that she took over and ran successfully when her parents retired. Benny, born Salek, and his twin brother, Josek were handsome boys on the cusp of young adulthood when they were swept up in the Holocaust. Their adored baby brother, Majorek, appears in the pictures as a carefree and playful four-year-old.

The Fefer family was comfortable and prosperous but they had always had to deal with anti-Semitism. It was a long standing and vicious part of Polish

Josek, Moishe and Benny Fefer

history. The Fefers were originally from Warsaw but moved to the suburb of Rembertow to try to escape the worst of it. Even there, they encountered persecution. Polish bullies beat up Benny at school so frequently that his father finally transferred him to a private Jewish school. However, the Jews of Rembertow managed to coexist with their Christian neighbors. When the Germans first invaded Poland, edicts were issued which discriminated against the Jews, but few anticipated the lethal intent of the Nazis. The worst many could imagine was being forced to work in labor camps.

In 1940, the Jews of Rembertow were relocated into a ghetto. Because of Moishe's prominence and military

experience, he was made a ghetto police officer. Initially, it gave the Fefers a slightly better standing, but in the end it made no difference. All of the young people, including Benny and his twin brother, were organized into work units digging ditches. Fencing enclosed the ghetto but it was fairly easily breeched, especially by a boy of small stature like Benny. He would often sneak into the Polish section of town to obtain food and other necessities.

One summer day, Benny was out in the streets of the ghetto when the Nazis began rounding up everyone in the marketplace. He sensed something terrible was happening. He escaped through the fence and made his way to a friendly Polish woman's house. She quickly hid him in an attic room from which he could see the Jews of Rembertow being loaded into railroad cattle cars. He never saw his parents or brothers again. Moishe, age 39, Dora, age 38, Josek, age 17, and Majorek, age 4 were murdered at Treblinka in August 1942.

Benny was in a desperate state. His friend could not risk keeping him hidden. She gave him a little money, a cap commonly worn by Polish boys to disguise himself and sent him on his way. He struggled to reach a village about 50 miles away where a cousin lived. As he approached the town, he witnessed Nazis arresting and deporting all of the Jews. Over the next week, as he tried to reach various relatives in outlying areas, the same terrible scene was repeated. Benny managed to elude the Germans, but he had nowhere to go. Eventually, he escaped into the forest where he met up with a group of partisans. He remained with them for three or four months. He avoided towns and villages as much as possible, but there were times when he had no choice but to enter a marketplace in search of food. It was during one such excursion that he was betrayed by a Pole who shouted, pointing at Benny, "That boy is a Jew!"

After his arrest, Benny was sent to the Lublin ghetto and slave labor camp, where there was a large German air

One summer day, Benny was out in the streets of the ghetto when the Nazis began rounding up everyone in the marketplace. He sensed something terrible was happening.

base. Conditions were much more brutal than in Rembertow. He was compelled to clean out the last remaining quantities of gasoline left in tanker cars after they had been pumped out. Fuel was scarce; the Germans didn't want to leave even the smallest quantities in the bottom. Benny had to climb down into the tanker with a bucket and scoop up the gasoline. The fumes were overwhelming but if he attempted to come out before he had finished, he was screamed at and beaten.

Moishe Fefer and his youngest son, Majorek.

He and his campmates also had to load coal onto railroad cars. They had to meet certain quotas every day. If someone was unable to meet his goal, he was beaten and oftentimes, shot. A man named Mr. Shapiro worked next to Benny and was housed in the same barracks. Mr. Shapiro was older, weaker and had a difficult time keeping up. When Benny finished loading his pile of coal, he would help Mr. Shapiro complete his work. This small act of kindness prevented Mr. Shapiro from falling behind and possibly saved his life. Benny labored in the Lublin ghetto for 18 months until the middle of 1943. As horrible as living conditions were in the ghetto, his nightmare was to become even worse. He was deported to the infamous concentration camp of Buchenwald.

Words fail to convey the desperation, the stench, and the hopelessness experienced by those imprisoned in the camps. Benny remembers the consuming, never-ending hunger that became the driving force of all thought and action. On entering Buchenwald, Benny was ordered to strip and enter a delousing shower. His clothes were tossed aside, and no attempt was made to reunite a prisoner with his original possessions. Instead, he was thrown a ragged set of clothes, obviously belonging to someone else. In Benny's case, they were so ill fitting that two more experienced prisoners warned him he would be shot on sight if he tripped over the baggy pants and fell, appearing sick or weak. He was told to do whatever he could to shorten the cuffs.

When Benny reached the barracks to which he was assigned, he tried to fix his pants. While he was working, he felt a hard lump embedded in one of the seams. Easing an object out of the fabric, he discovered it was a large diamond someone had secreted away. He had to find a hiding place for this treasure. Benny knew he had to conceal it in such a way as to make it appear worthless because the guards regularly searched the prisoners' meager possessions for any valuables or contraband. He took a chunk of green, moldy bread and stuck the diamond inside. Daily, the guards just tossed it aside, ignoring the disgusting looking bread. Benny kept the diamond safe until hunger forced him to make a deal with a camp guard.

Many of the guards were brutal, sadistic men who didn't hesitate to abuse and torment the prisoners. There was one older guard, however, who was kind to Benny, telling him he had a son Benny's age. When this man was going on leave for a week to see his family, Benny approached him with a desperate proposal. Benny was literally starving. He gave the guard his hidden diamond and told him to give it to his wife. In exchange, he begged for a simple loaf of bread. The man took the stone and left without saying a word. When he returned, he gave Benny a loaf of bread. Benny hid it in his clothes, eating a little piece each day, making that pound and a half of bread last two weeks. "What good was the diamond to me? The bread meant much more, to me it was life."

Unfortunately, Benny was reduced to starving again very quickly. It is estimated that prisoners subsisted on about 500 calories per day, an amount incompatible with life for more than a few short weeks. Thousands of prisoners also died of diseases in their weakened state. Death became commonplace to Benny, he had no expectation of survival and no longer feared death.

Within the barracks where prisoners were crammed three or more per wooden bunk, meager portions of bread were distributed according to how many pairs of legs were counted on each tier. During one night, two of Benny's bunkmates died. Rather than alert the guards to their deaths, Benny left the corpses there for two more days, thus receiving their rations for himself. When he could no longer endure the stench, he was forced to report them dead. The ability to survive even one more day was dependent on just such whims of fate and fortitude, however horrible they seemed.

Workers in Rembertow Ghetto near Warsaw.

Frequently prisoners were asked to "volunteer" for special duties. It became clear early on that volunteering was very risky. Often people who agreed to do so never returned, but once there was a call for volunteers that intrigued Benny. It was a bid for auto mechanics, which Benny was not. In fact, he had never even ridden in a private car in his life. He was, however, starving, and he reasoned that mechanics might be given better working conditions and more rations. He stepped forward and joined a group of about 50 men all claiming to be mechanics. They were a diverse

group of many different nationalities and Benny was clearly the youngest by far.

The men were lined up for interviews with two engineers. Benny got at the back of the line. As each man finished Benny inquired about what was asked and what they had answered. It became apparent that the same few questions were asked over and over. By the time it was his turn, he knew how to respond. He was afraid they would think he was too young to be a mechanic, so he said he was an assistant. "I didn't know what a carburetor was, but I could answer their questions!" Benny was chosen for the work detail.

The next day, the prisoner-mechanics were given uniforms, loaded onto a train and taken a short distance from the camp. When they reached the factory, they were directed to remove tires from vehicles in need of repair. At this point in the war, the allies were actively bombing German factories. The prisoners' work was frequently

"Lest We Forget: The Holocaust" by MaryAnne Katz

crawled back to the prisoners' enclosure. He took the two old buckets used to deliver the watery soup they were served each day, and went back and filled them with peelings. "I felt like a million dollars. I felt good; my stomach didn't hurt. I did this for three months. For 10 to 12 people in my section." Benny survived to see liberation day in 1945.

The tragedy of liberation for many was still death. After months and years of malnutrition, disease, and abuse, many former prisoners were too debilitated to recover. Countless people died when they began eating too much food too quickly. Since their bodies were unable to handle a normal caloric load, they developed fatal dysentery and died. Benny was lucky. In the group of American soldiers who entered Buchenwald were two Jewish men who made a special effort to locate Jewish prisoners. They took Benny under their care and kept him from harming himself by eating too quickly. They arranged for his transfer to a Swiss hospital where he recuperated over several months. Later, he learned that his family had been killed in Treblinka; he had no reason to remain in Europe.

Benny was able to immigrate to the United States because he had a cousin living here. He immediately found work, but was drafted into the U.S. Army during the time of the Korean conflict. He was injured in the service but once he recovered, he was assigned

disrupted by air raids, and they were able to accomplish very little. In addition, there was no increase in food as Benny hoped. The prisoners were still maintained on starvation rations.

Daily, the workers were herded into an enclosure when the guards took their meal break. While standing around, someone noticed a manhole cover. Because Benny was the smallest one, he was enlisted to go down into the sewer and see where it led. "It was dark and smelly, with muck all around, but what did I have to lose? I wasn't afraid." Benny crawled along until he spied light seeping around the edges of another manhole cover. He carefully lifted the cover up and peeked around. He found himself outside the kitchen for the German guards, where the garbage was thrown out. All around on the ground were potato and vegetable peelings. He couldn't believe his good fortune. He duty in post-war Germany. While stationed in Berlin, he located the two Jewish soldiers, Sol Kopel and Herbert Laaefeld, who had liberated him. It was a happy reunion; they were delighted to see Benny healthy and well fed. He spent seven years in Europe. After a variety of challenging assignments, Benny asked for a more stable position. His request was granted by his commanding officer and Benny was made manager of the Officers' Club in Stuttgart, Germany.

When Benny was discharged from the army, he and his new bride, Margot, moved to Norfolk where he went to work for Fancy Foods of Virginia. As he and Margot settled into their new lives raising their daughter, Debbie, his memories from the Holocaust receded, but never completely left him. One day, while driving down Granby Street in downtown Norfolk he passed by a bus stop. Glancing out the window, he spied a familiar figure. He quickly circled the block and came to a stop. Standing there was his old friend and fellow inmate from Lublin, Mr. Shapiro. The two had a warm and emotional reunion. It turned out Mr. Shapiro was living in the Ward's Corner section of town with his wife who had also managed to survive. He was a long-time member of Temple Israel and was tutoring children studying Hebrew.

Margot and Benny Fefer

There may never be a satisfactory answer as to why Benny survived and so many millions did not. He did not set out to live an extraordinary life, but by all measures, he has. He is in his quiet way a hero. He overcame incalculable odds, not once but many times to reach where he is today. His ability to love, to raise a family and once again fully participate in life is the strongest statement possible against the evils of Nazi Germany. Perhaps Benny survived so that we all have a reason for hope. ❖

My Grandfather
tittle

Picture→

Portrait by Ryan Finder, Ted's grandson.

TED FINDER

Soldier of Honor and Dignity

By Donna Kenworthy Levy

TED FINDER of Norfolk is someone whose life has been a story of spiritual victory over despair. Born into an orthodox Jewish family in Vienna, Austria, Ted and his family fell prey to the Nazis. In March of 1938, Ted was arrested by the SS and taken to their occupied villa in the outskirts of Vienna. There he was imprisoned, beaten and tortured. He felt certain that only death awaited him.

What happened next, however, was the first of many miracles that were to occur in Finder's life. He had been incarcerated in the villa about a week when he noticed a hole in the fence. It became his exit to freedom. Not only did he escape, but he was never recaptured. By not returning to his

Miracle after miracle has been played out in the circumstances of his life. With each successive tribulation and ensuing miracle, Finder's relationship to God grew ever stronger.

Ted Finder

own home and by constantly moving about, he was able to elude the SS until the next miracle provided both him and his sister with visas to the United States. They arrived in America on July 25, 1938. After two and a half years of living and working at odd jobs in the Bronx, Finder was drafted into the United States Army, where his knowledge of German was put to good use. Finder became an instructor and

taught American soldiers how to recognize different ranks of German soldiers by their uniforms. He did such an outstanding job that he was given the Superior Instructor Award. He was the first non-commissioned officer to receive this honor.

Unlike the millions of powerless European Jews who were trapped and doomed to total victimization, Finder

had the opportunity to actively fight against the Germans. As a member of the 29th Division, he landed on Omaha Beach on D-Day. In the weeks that followed, he was kept at the front of the line because of his fluency in German.

One day he went to investigate some movement and found himself in a dugout with 45 German soldiers. With his gun trained on his prisoners, he

Ted and Bess Finder's three children, Roberta, David and Andrea.

"We must be grateful to God. Jews must hold on to their faith in God and in their religion. We must stay true to all our traditions. And it is important to visit Israel often. Israel is the key to our survival. We must have our own place to go, in case something terrible like Nazism comes back into power again. However, we must never allow anti-Semitism to destroy our faith. Then we would lose everything."

single-handedly backed them out of the dugout. For this great act of courage and bravery in combat, he was honored with a bronze star.

On September 14, 1944, in Brest, Finder was wounded in the head and chest by mortar fire, causing one of his lungs to collapse. (Ironically, this was the very same day that his mother, who was living in Italy at the time, was captured and sent to a concentration camp where she later died.) While lying on the ground suffering from his wounds, another mortar shell came his way and shattered his right elbow. At the time of this interview, he still had over 50 pieces of shrapnel in his body. Fearing death, he promised God that if he would survive, he would go to temple every Sabbath for the rest of his life.

It was at this time that Finder experienced his third miracle. Knowing he would probably be captured by the Nazis, he threw away his Jewish prayer book, and his dog tags, which had an "H" inscribed on them for "Hebrew."

When the Germans actually did capture him, they took him to a German field hospital, where they decided to amputate his right arm. Protesting to them in German, the doctors naturally assumed that he was German or Austrian. They wanted to know why he was fighting on the wrong side. He answered that his parents had relocated to the United States when he was a young boy. Never did they suspect that

Finder was a Jew. As it turned out, the German doctors inadvertently actually saved this Jew's life. Finder then convinced the doctors to let him keep his arm.

For many years after the war, Finder was reluctant to tell his story. When asked about that time in his life, his response was "others suffered more." Perhaps this answer also bespeaks his own inner torment over his survival and the brutal deaths of the Six Million. He does not know why he was miraculously saved and others were not. Yet, for whatever reason, he feels that his own survival was indeed *b'shert.*

The end of the war did not, however, bring an end to Finder's personal dance with death. Four more "life-or-death" dramas were yet to come his way. The first of these in fact directly related to his injuries in the war.

In 1952, Finder developed a cranial abscess from the shrapnel that was still embedded in his head. The doctors recommended brain surgery, but did not truly know whether or not he would survive the surgery. They forewarned him that even if he did survive the operation, he could be left blind or partially paralyzed. However, another miracle occurred and Finder was brought back from the brink of death with his vision and ability to move totally intact.

Fifteen years later in 1967, Finder suffered a severe life-threatening heart attack. Thankfully, luck was with him and he survived. In 1974, he had to undergo triple by-pass surgery. Again good fortune was with him. Then in 1992, Finder became very ill and had to have another triple by-pass operation. And as before, destiny favored him.

Miracle after miracle has been played out in the circumstances of his life. With each successive tribulation and ensuing miracle, Finder's relationship to God grew ever stronger.

Despite his argument that "others suffered more," in all fairness, it must be said that Ted Finder is someone who also suffered. He experienced loss of family, brutality, disfigurement, years of nightmares about the past, and much physical pain, along with the emotional guilt of surviving when others did not.

As someone whose life and family were directly affected by the Holocaust, Finder has been interviewed by both the Holocaust Museum in Washington, D.C. and Steven Spielberg's organization.

No one could endure all the difficult experiences that Finder did without becoming a philosopher of life in his own right. As he notes: "We must be grateful to God. Jews must hold on to their faith in God and in their religion. We must stay true to all our traditions. And it is important to visit Israel often. Israel is the key to our survival. We must have our own place to go, in case something terrible like Nazism comes back into power again. However, we must never allow anti-Semitism to destroy our faith. Then we would lose everything." ❖

Ted passed away on January 15, 2000. Ted is survived by his wife, Beth, his three children and six grandchildren. (Beth notes that ten of Ted's first cousins, who survived the Holocaust, are still living.)

Ted Finder and one of his grandchildren, Ryan

Sonia Floch
Working Hard Her Key To Survival

By Ellie Porter

SONIA FLOCH looks younger than her years. Her lovely, unlined face belies the pain so indelibly etched in her heart. The pain now is in the form of old memories. Long ago, the pain was caused by hunger, cold, monumental loss and dehumanization, and yet she considers herself one of the lucky ones. She survived.

She credits her survival to the ability to work hard. All her young life she was accustomed to hard work. It went with being poor. "Some of the women who came from more affluent lifestyles found it harder, if not impossible, to cope."

Sonia was born in Russia in 1919, but her family moved to Shavl, (Siauliai) Lithuania when she was two years old. Not long after, her father died, leaving her mother a widow with five children. Sonia had three brothers and a sister. She was the fourth child. Her younger brother was born two months after her father died. She vividly remembers how poor they were, how difficult it was for her mother to feed the children. She never had an orange unless she was sick.

Sonia Floch

Photo by Echard Wheeler

"Healthy people didn't eat oranges, unless they were rich," she recalls. "Today there is welfare, but then in Lithuania, people were too proud, it was better to go hungry than to ask for help."

After finishing Talmud Torah school, she went to work as a sales lady. Later, while attending a friend's wedding, she met David, her future husband. Shavl was a large town, but their courtship consisted of taking walks through the narrow streets. It was 1941 and they knew times were not good for the Jewish people. Hundreds of refugees were swarming into Lithuania from Poland and being taken in by Jewish families in Shavl and all other surrounding towns and villages.

"You find it hard to believe that something like this would happen. You keep praying for a miracle to keep it from touching your family," Sonia said as she recalled the early days of the war. Still Sonia and David were young and they dreamed of a better life. They decided to get married and live with her mother. Although the war was moving closer, they never thought of running. It took money to go anywhere and they didn't have any.

Two months after their March 9, 1941 wedding, the Germans took over Shavl and all Jews were quickly rounded up and moved into a ghetto.

Sonia's family managed to stay together. Sonia, David, Sonia's mother, sister, her

At the Munich Zoo, David's cousin, David and Sonia.

There was a double edge to the razor of danger connected with leaving the ghetto to work; one was the threat to the workers' lives; the other was the agony of not knowing who would be gone by the time they returned.

sister's daughter, two of her brothers and three other townsmen made up the ten people who lived and slept in one small apartment.

Memories of those days are painful. "There was fear every day. The Germans and the Lithuanians came into the ghetto, looking for workers. Some never returned."

Despite this threat, all who could work would assemble at the gate in the morning, hoping to be picked for work detail. "Of course everyone wanted to get out, it was a chance to find some food or some thing to burn to keep warm."

Otherwise there was little food and long lines and waiting to get even a meager portion of what was allowed through the gates.

Because she was young, Sonia got selected to work in a warehouse which shipped food to the German war zones. "We would load trains with grain, flour and hay. The kitchen would provide the warehouse workers with a meal of flour and water," she added.

There was a double edge to the razor of danger connected with leaving the ghetto to work; one was the threat to the workers' lives; the other was the agony of not knowing who would be gone by the time they returned.

"Every day there was another decree. One day it was for the newborn babies; the next day, the old. The men were the first to be taken out," she said. But Sonia's brothers and husband were either overlooked or spared because their apartment was located in the back of the SS headquarters and it was her family's responsibility to keep the headquarters clean. During the day the women cleaned boots, washed and stitched uniforms and peeled potatoes. They learned to survive and cope.

Ghetto residents were constantly being searched. Sonia recalls finding a sliver of soap on the floor and keeping it clenched in her fist while being subjected to a search – arms outstretched. Her heart raced thinking of what could happen if she were found with the sliver of soap. The quantity of water they were allowed was meager and she wanted desperately to feel clean and indulge herself with the luxury of washing with soap. "The fear I had over that piece of soap; but I managed to get away with it. Today I throw away slivers of soap, but I never do it without thinking of that moment."

For three years Sonia and her family managed to survive, working for the Germans and Lithuanians and trying to be invisible when decrees were posted. She recalls one particular incident which is especially painful. She was washing windows in the SS headquarters building and saw the booty brought back after a weekend of Jewish massacres. These massacres, she explained, occurred every Shabbat, beginning on Friday night as the Germans and Lithuanians moved from city to city,

town to town harassing and murdering the Jewish people. "I saw what they were doing to the Jews. I saw the sacks filled with Jewish property and it filled me with great sadness. Words cannot express my feeling then and now."

What everyone feared befell the remaining Jews of Shavl on July 24, 1944. All were rounded up and transported by truck to the train station. Sonia and her family remained clustered together and were herded into a boxcar: destination Stutthof Concentration Camp.

"We couldn't move. In desperation we fought with one another. We were for days without water, food and sanitation." The darkness, the cries, the stench and the ever pervading sense of fear of what was waiting for them at the

Sonia's husband, David Floch

Sam Kessel, Sonia Floch and Benjamin Kessel in Paris, 1946.

The Flochs and friends on New Year's Eve after receiving papers to come to America

end of the line was more than some could endure.

Sonia recalls that in contrast to what was occurring in the cars, the train passed beautiful countryside. But, if the ride was one in fear, what was waiting for them at the end of the line surpassed anything they could have imagined. When the doors opened, the armed Germans with attack sticks and vicious barking dogs were waiting for them. In their haste to get off the train, Sonia's husband left his coat, one of the necessities they had thought to take with them. Shoes and coats would be needed in case they were allowed to work. Sonia recalls that once her husband saw the reception, he said: "I don't think we'll need the coats here."

The sticks and dogs soon brought them to the separation area where Sonia, her mother, sister and niece were separated from her husband and brothers.

The German guards took the women's clothing and jewelry and they were methodically examined to make sure they had no hidden valuables on their bodies. They were told to advance to the bath houses and Sonia feared the worst. She had heard of the bathhouses with no water. She felt only relief when she saw water dribbling out of the overhead faucet. They were given tent-like dresses and led before a large pile of used shoes, the legacy of those before them who had perished in the camp. They were told to find a pair of shoes and then directed to a crowded barracks. Each wooden bunk served as a bed for two women. Sonia and her mother were together and next to them were her sister and niece, who had been forced from their home in a small town near Shavl. "The Lithuanians had killed all the men in their town," she added.

Sonia had no underclothes, no blankets, no food, the sanitary conditions were

intolerable and a drop of water was a precious commodity. She and her mother shared their body heat huddled together in the bunk. All women were subjected to roll calls, day or night, sometimes for hours at a time. They were forced to stand in the summer sun and winter cold … "just to torture us," she said.

Each day, inmates were marched out on the field for crematory selection. The old and the sick were singled out. The young women were picked for work details. In order to remain with her mother, Sonia would hide in the barracks during these selections.

The last selection for work was held in November, 1944. "I had to come out of hiding to save myself." But it was with a heavy heart that she left her mother and sister behind. "I knew I would never see them again." She learned later from a survivor that her sister and niece died from typhoid fever and her mother died after being beaten.

The women were selected to work on a highway project. Each morning they would rise at 4 o'clock and would be hauling rocks by wheelbarrow to build up the roadbed by 5 a.m. There were men on the project who would break the larger rocks for the women to haul. Their one meal at the end of the day consisted of cabbage soup or greens and water, chicory water and at times "a little bread." Fifteen women were crammed into a hut for sleeping.

Each month 10% of the road workers were sent back to the camp for extermination. "If you could still work, you were not sent back." The name of the game was survival.

In a surprise move, one of the SS guards taught Sonia a lesson in survival. He advised her to take a cloth sack and tie it around her waist every time she went to the kitchen. In this manner, she would be able to bring back a few scraps of food. She subsequently devised a system with a young Polish girl who worked in the kitchen and who had to feed the pigs. Whenever possible, the girl would place a sack with scraps on the fence not far from the pigs. And when the Germans were not watching, Sonia would slip that sack around her waist in place of her own.

Whatever food she managed to get in this manner, she shared with others in the barracks at night. It wasn't much, but it made the cold nights a little more bearable. At times it was so cold, Sonia recalls that her hair would freeze to the straw on the floor that she used for a bed. Her closest friend at this time was Freda Green, whom she had known as a girl in Shavl. "I stayed with her until we were liberated."

Sonia thought about her husband often. She had not seen him since being separated the day they arrived at Stutthof in July, 1944. "I didn't feel married," Sonia remembers. "We lived more like brother and sister, first with my mother and then crowded in one room in the ghetto at Shavl." As rumors spread through the barracks that the Germans were being defeated and the war would soon end, she began to wonder if she would ever see her husband again.

With the approaching Russian army, the Germans organized marches that led the

At times it was so cold, Sonia recalls that her hair would freeze to the straw on the floor that she used for a bed.

inmates from the highway project to one village after another. There was no food. It was cold. Sonia recalls the wooden shoes she was wearing with paper wrapped around her feet. She had made pants and a top from an old blanket. She and the other women would utilize any scrap of fabric, convert it into something to wear; anything to keep warm.

After marching for one month, they found themselves within 50 miles of Gdansk, where they were crowded into a tremendous barn where masses of bodies lay. Some were living, some were dead. Sometimes it was hard to tell the difference.

But before entering the barn, Sonia's hunger enabled her to find a beet. It had a strong taste, but she ate it anyway. Perhaps it was because she had not had food in so long, but the beet began to burn her throat. There was no water available in the barn, and her pleas for water to a particular German guard went unheard. But it was just one more discomfort that she had to endure.

Not long afterwards, she heard the sound of gunshots, which heralded her first glimpse of freedom – Russian soldiers sitting atop tanks and holding guns. The few remaining German guards were killed, one of them was the guard who had denied her a drop of water just a short time before. The date was March 10, 1945.

With the liberators came food, the first they had seen in a long while. Sonia recalls that her friend Freda excitedly grabbed a live chicken and held it up.

"I asked her what she was going to do with that chicken. We had no place to cook it." Later, and a little calmer, they settled for canned food, but were faced with another dilemma. "We couldn't find a knife to open the cans."

However, another survivor had one and their "feast" began. Sonia remembers that meal as only an act against starvation – it was either canned beef stew or corned beef.

Their initial relief at freedom was short-lived, for they were warned by the Russian soldiers that the war was still on and they had better flee. "They told us to take hand and foot and go home. But we didn't have any home," she said.

"You can imagine the confusion, where to go, where to get help, where to find loved ones?" Sonia wanted to get to a large city for she felt there they would be organized and offer assistance. Later, Sonia, Freda and another young girl made their way to a farmhouse where they found a horse and wagon. Soon, they were joined by eight others, seven women and one man. They decided to travel to Lowenbourg. Russian soldiers stopped them and sent the ten pathetic passengers in another direction. Their fear now was that the Russians were sending them to German farms in order to send food and cattle back to Russia. "Russians always took what they found."

Eight days after her liberation, Sonia came down with typhoid fever, although she had tried to be careful what she ate, knowing many were dying from the disease.

She became very ill and credited Freda Green with nursing her back to health. Although they did end up on a German farm, working for the Russians, they were paid a small wage for doing a variety of chores. Here Sonia was allowed to regain her strength. The stronger women rounded up stray cattle and washed them.

Traveling to America on the U.S.S. Ernie Pyle, 1949.

Sonia was eventually transported to another farm in Stolp, a town near Berlin, where she worked in a warehouse and was responsible for giving out rations for day-to-day cooking. Occasionally Sonia took the cattle to the slaughterhouse in Stolp. On one of these excursions, she met a tailor who was acting as an unofficial clearinghouse for D.P.s looking for loved ones. However, she never dreamed that one day he would come looking for her.

His visit to her was triggered by a man who had formerly lived in Shavl, who was looking for the wife of a man living in Munich. As he explained his search to the tailor, someone who knew Sonia overheard the conversation. The connection was made. The man was

carrying notes to Sonia from her husband and brother, who were seeking her whereabouts.

Sonia's friend told the tailor that Sonia was working and living on a nearby farm, and later that day the tailor delivered the two letters. From the letters Sonia learned that her husband and two brothers were living in Munich.

The incident obviously had an element of *b'shert* however, for just prior to the meeting at the tailor's, Sonia had a dream about returning to Shavl and finding two one-hundred dollar bills. When she reached for the money she picked up two letters instead.

But how was she going to get to Munich?

Sonia had no papers, only a little money the Russians had paid her. But the little money, and a lot of *chutzpah* got her to Lodz where the Lithuanian D.P.s had organized. There she received forged papers to get her into Munich. It was then June, 1946, 15 months after being liberated by the Russians in Stutthof, and she was on a train to be reunited with David and her brothers. "I sent a letter ahead, telling them when I would arrive," she said. However, when Sonia reached Munich, there was no one at the station to meet her, for signals somehow got crossed and it was the following day before Sonia and David found each other at the Jewish Agency office.

Their reunion was a mixture of "strange feelings," Sonia said, explaining that they tried to set their lives in order by making plans for their future together. Although the war was over, they had to wait three years for permission to immigrate to the United States. Eventually, they found themselves in

Norfolk where David had family. "We worked hard and started a new life." David and Sonia had two daughters, both of whom are married now. David passed away in 1980. One of Sonia's four grandchildren is named for him.

But Sonia remembers her early years in this country with pride. "We went to night school, summer and winter, to learn English. We worked hard and established a business and reared two daughters.

"After he retired, my husband did volunteer work for the Jewish Community Center, helping with Meals on Wheels and anyway he could." ❖

Photo above - Sonia, David and Ethel

Sonia and her brother, Sam

Four generations of the Floch Family

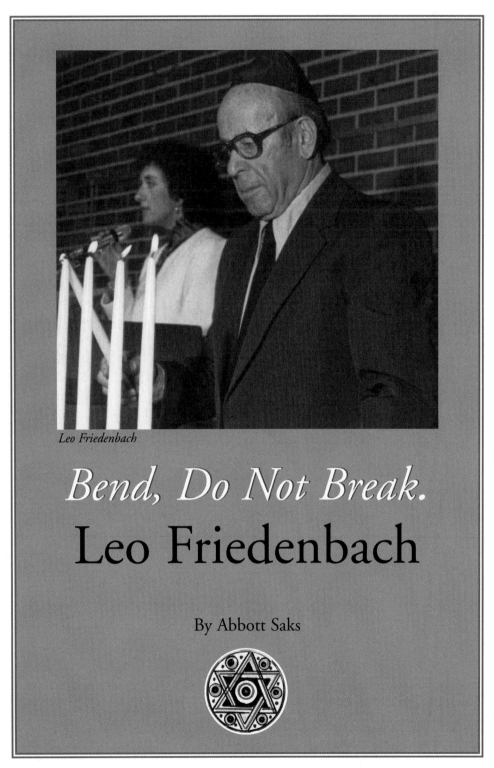

Leo Friedenbach

Bend, Do Not Break.
Leo Friedenbach

By Abbott Saks

LEO FRIEDENBACH was born in Galicia, Poland, May 29, 1903, when it was part of the Austro-Hungarian Empire. When he was two, his father died of pneumonia. His mother remarried, and an insensitive and uncaring stepfather all but ignored him, depriving him of the love and attention that should, in a better world, be every child's birthright.

He traveled back and forth from his small town to nearby Crakow where he received his schooling and *cheder* instruction. Prospects and economic conditions in 1921 were bleak and the young Leo made a wrenching decision: he would leave home and make his way to Vienna, the great economic and cultural heart of the empire. In addition to his mother and stepfather, he left behind five beloved siblings, four sisters and one brother whom he was never again to see. (Two of the sisters were from the second marriage.) The parents passed on of natural causes and all of the others and their children were swallowed up into the inferno of the Holocaust.

Jobless and without resources in Vienna, he had to spend time in a shelter for the homeless and penurious which, it is ironic to record, was home to Adolph Hitler in his own early days in the Austrian capital. Leo got a job as a worker in a fruit import company (Sudfruchte) owned by an understanding and helpful employer, Jakob Feuer, who befriended and encouraged his hard-working and eager-to-get-ahead young employee. Jakob's guidance was a key factor in Leo's building up his own imported fruit business. Feuer was to become one of the millions of the Nazis' victims.

Leo met his future wife, Edith Jonas, through a mutual friend on a blind date. She was a popular and musically talented young lady, an accomplished pianist who received her training at one of Vienna's conservatories. She earned a little money providing piano accompaniment during the silent films of the day. She also gave private piano lessons and played at nearby mountain vacation resorts with a young violinist who was courting her at the time that Leo met her. It was he, however, who played the more beautiful melody on her heartstrings and they were married in 1929. Kitty, their only child, was born in 1932. Leo's wholesale-retail fruit business prospered. He had many loyal customers, a much loved and dependable delivery horse and wagon, and a bright future that was not to be. When a newly hired delivery boy was worried about negotiating a many stop route, Leo reassured him: "Don't worry, Liezel, the horse knows the way by heart. She'll take you."

His enterprise continued to prosper even as Nazi persecution of the Jews was growing in intensity. More and more, Jews faced restrictions squeezing them out of and excluding them from business, educational and professional pursuits. He was forced to sell his horse but not before finding a buyer who assured him his faithful Liezel would be treated well. His business was

confiscated. His entire world was crumbling about him and the message was on the wall. For those unwilling to recognize it, the bloodletting and destruction of *Kristallnacht* made it painfully clear. Leo decided that he and his family had to flee the madness. The Friedenbachs twice came excruciatingly close to making it out of Europe. After much effort, paperwork and red tape, cousins in Norfolk had succeeded in sending to Vienna all the necessary documents for emigration. Leo stood in interminable lines, but never made it

inside the building to get the literal final stamp of exit and approval.

Their frustration was compounded later in Belgium when three other persons bribed the officials and took the Friedenbachs' place in line and left for the USA. They were left literally sitting on their suitcases. Just before they were deported to their deaths, Edith's parents wrote to Leo's cousins in Norfolk pleading for help to find safe haven in America. (The letter is preserved.) They asked nothing for themselves.

It Wasn't Just Strudel

By Stefan Grunwald

A small literary monument,
I'll set you here,
Mrs. Friedenbach,
I wished you were still around
to make that strudel for me.

Because into it you baked
the sweetness of our Europe,
 the tartness of who we are,
the spices of our language,
 the beauty of your soul,
the goodness of a mensch.

Oh beloved Mrs. Friedenbach,
this poem's only the topping
of my deep memories of you.

(Editor's Note: Mrs. Friedenbach, mentioned in the poem and in the photo above, was the wife of Leo and mother of Kitty Saks, a survivor featured in this book.)

Save the children was their only petition. Kitty's grandfather Adolph was a World War One veteran who had survived capture by the Russians and he reasoned that his service to his country would offer him and his wife some measure of protection. The two of them, he rationalized, would ride out the gathering storm. Hitler was just a latter day Haman. The Jews would outlast him as they did Torquemada and the inquisitors. The Nazi nightmare would pass, life would return to normal. With Hitler's demise, Nazism would just be one more painful memory on the road of the Diaspora and the woods and hills above Vienna would ring again with glorious strains of Strauss waltzes and not the sounds of goose stepping boots on the cobblestones of Vienna's streets. The grandparent's naïve myopia, tragically, was shared by too many.

Leo's plan was to get to Belgium and when possible to send for Edith and Kitty. He went by train to Aachen and with the help of guides made the precarious way across the border. As an unemployed refugee and without proper documentation, he was placed in an internment-work camp along with other refugees. Some of them had been with him braving the dangers of the illegal border crossing.

The work camp was at Merksplatz near the Dutch border. His early experience on the family farm in Poland and leadership qualities gained him the status of foreman of a work crew.

On the preceding page is a poem by Holocaust survivor, Stefan Grunwald, in which he lauds the strudel cake made by Mrs. Friedenbach. Below, is the recipe as remembered by her daughter, Kitty Saks, who notes that the apple strudel "was actually the original 'Jonas Apple Cake' which my mother made for him. It is the recipe of my late maternal grandmother, Antonie Jonas."
Since the measurements for the ingredients are not exact, Kitty lovingly recommends, "Make at your own risk!"

Jonas Apple Cake*
3 cups of regular flour
one stick sweet butter or one stick sweet margarine
one egg
one and half cup sugar and one package "Oetker Original" vanilla sugar
one and half teaspoon vanilla extract
one and half tablespoon baking powder
one lemon (juice only)
little water

Mix together and knead well. Roll out with a little flour. Put aside.
Filling: Peel (medium) five or six tart apples or Granny Smith - grate
No raisins
Mix with sugar, plenty of cinnamon to taste. Add a little vanilla sugar
Grease bottom of pan. Dust bottom with flour.
Spread the apple mixture on top, cover with another layer of dough.
Bake in 11x9x2 pan.
Bake until golden brown. Dust with sugar.
Voila - good luck!
*ingredients: approximate

Edith and Kitty also made the rail trip to Aachen. But their eventual border crossing was wrought with danger and difficulties. After several unsuccessful and frustrating attempts – they were more than once caught by border patrols and sent back to Aachen. They persevered and with the help of paid guides made it across.

"Home" for the Friedenbachs was a dingy one room apartment on Rue de L'Ascension. Leo worked at any odd job he could find. He, as many of the other refugees, dealt on the Black Market to put food on the table. Ironically, some of his customers were Wehrmacht soldiers with a few francs to spend on cigarettes, fabrics or any hard-to-get marketable items.

Letters from Vienna stopped coming in 1941. The last communication concerning the grandparents came from an aunt who informed them that they had been deported to Lodz. They suspected, but could not know for certain the awful truth. They learned after the war that the grandparents were gassed in Chelmno, the major annihilation center near Lodz. Leo's brother, sisters and their children were shot in the woods and dumped into mass graves. The *burgomeister* (mayor) of his hometown was the source of the horrific report.

On more than one occasion, quick thinking action saved Leo's life. Spotting a known informer being driven around the Jewish areas by the Germans to point out Jews, he ducked into a doorway and avoided certain detection. Once, he was caught in a roundup and IDs were demanded. Bearing a "yellow" card that identified him as a non-Belgian Jew, he was in mortal danger. Noticing that only the *apatride,* stateless, were being sent to and held in a corner of the crowded room, with *chutzpah* and bravado, he boldly and assertively showed his card at the desk placing his thumb on the spot that showed him to be *apatride,* and a Jew. Only "Poland" was visible and thus he must be "legitimate." In the noise and confusion the police official waved him on and he was breathing the air of the open street. He had moved quickly enough to dodge the bullet.

Miraculous would not be a hyperbolic adjective to describe the Friedenbachs' narrowest of escapes in August of 1943. The Gestapo, acting on a tip from a neighborhood informer, was literally at the door of their apartment. It was held closed by a latch that a kick would have broken loose. *"AUF!"* (Open!) they heard as the agent pounded on the fragile barrier that shielded them. The Gestapo, acting on an informer's tip, had raided the house. Several Jews were living in the building. They had been denounced for the going price of fifty francs. The providential remark of the landlady may have saved the day and their lives. Madam Luxen yelled up to him that the couple was out – "they are

working;" that could only mean they were not Jewish. The Nazis already had a carload and they believed their task was completed and they carried away their prey. None of those taken was ever heard from again. What occurred that afternoon was a most amazing twist of fate that proved to be a tragedy for one couple and salvation for the other, for included in those rounded up were two Jews who just happened to be visiting the downstairs neighbor. Subsequently, the Germans had the number they were after.

During the painful scenario, Kitty's father lay motionless on a squeaky bed. Her mother, in a pathetic move inspired by desperation, had put a bottle of aspirins on the table and was going to plead for Leo, who was "not feeling well." Giving up, she began to move toward the door to open it and face the inevitable. At this life-and-death moment Leo yelled to her with his eyes and a hand movement: "Don't do it" was the message – and she didn't, her fingers within inches of the latch. She froze in her steps. An interminable few seconds of silence followed and they heard the sound of footsteps going down the stairs.

However, the Nazis were back within an hour looking specifically for the "couple with the child." (Their daughter Kitty was already in a convent hiding.) By that time the Friedenbachs were in their new hiding place with others three blocks away, where Leo was to fashion a cleverly made false wall which could be an emergency hiding place should the

house ever be raided. Later, when one of those hiding with the Friedenbachs took Leo aside to show him a hidden spot on the roof that could conceal two people in a life-or-death emergency, Leo flushed with anger and told him either all would survive or none would survive. Fortunately, the group did not suffer the fate of Anne Frank and her family.

During their years of concealment it was Leo's strength and calm that was the glue that held the others together while the storm raged outside.

One such example of Leo's strength and faith occurred while his daughter Kitty was still living with them and when Leo, on top of a small pot-bellied coal stove, fashioned a matzah for Pesach. The unbleached flour grudgingly yielded a blackish and not very tasty product but it served well to remember the observance. What it lacked in gustatory excellence it made up in hope. The spirit and promise of the Pesach were alive and well that year. *"Bleib gesundt und munter, der Jud geht nicht unter."* (Stay healthy and be of good spirit, the Jew will not be beaten down.)

General Montgomery's British forces liberated Brussels on September 4, 1944. They had survived! As in Paris some weeks before there was joyous dancing in the streets. No nectar could match the savor of the air of freedom now breathed.

By 1947 Leo had built up a successful army surplus goods business in Brussels. He took in other survivors and helped them at material loss to himself. The Friedenbachs always shared their meager table with those less fortunate. Even though the horrors were behind them and their situation was steadily improving, Leo always kept handy a calendar with the date 1942 prominently circled. Whenever anyone would complain about a problem or some trivial disappointment, he would point silently to those numbers evoking the hellish days they had come through. No words were needed. The point was

Leo and Edith Friedenbach in La Hulpe, Belgium, August of 1947.

poignantly made. Matters were put back into a more rational perspective and the little bumps of daily life were hardly felt.

Leo Friedenbach was quiet and reserved by nature, a proud and highly principled man. Some wise observer of the human scene said that life is like a grindstone: whether it ground you down or polished you up depended on what you were made of. Leo refused to be ground down by the catastrophe. He refused to lose his head when all about him were losing theirs. A Viennese saying proclaims, *"Biegen, Nicht Brechen"* (bend, do not break). Leo did not break; he stood tall. In his personal and business dealings he was of an uncompromising integrity. His word was his bond and his promise was valid currency. He was a faithful husband, a loving father and grandfather. Because he was proud he often took less than he needed or could have gotten. His compassion and generosity made him give more than he could afford to give. Like the Israeli sabra, this native of Galicia's tough exterior belied a tender and feeling interior. He was an animal lover. He referred to his dog "Amos," a lab-retriever as his *kollege* (colleague). This world would be a better place if more were like him. He was a survivor.

Leo Friedenbach died July 21, 1988, in Norfolk, Virginia. ❖

Leo Friedenbach's daughter, Kitty Saks, has a story in this book.

Anonymity Increased Their Chances of Survival
ANNE FRIEDMAN

By Valerie Freeman Samsell

"You are the most beautiful daughters in all the world," Isaac Altenhaus whispered as he stroked his daughters long flowing hair.

For Anneke and Minneke, those wonderful carefree days of childhood would soon end, and only the memories of indescribable terror would endure.

Antwerp, Belgium was a peaceful metropolis where Gentiles and Jews lived side-by-side in friendship. The Altenhaus family enjoyed a quiet, happy life. Isaac Baruch Altenhaus, a custom tailor, was a good family provider, while Pepi, his devoted wife, took pride in her role as a "Jewish Mother." Their daughters Anneke and Minneke were happy children whose days were filled with childhood play.

On May 10, 1940, Germany invaded Belgium. Storm troopers goose-stepped robot-like through the streets of Antwerp, filling the hearts of its citizens with fear and despair.

Top photo - Isaac Baruch Altenhaus and his daughters, Minneke and Anneke.
Photo left - Isaac and Pepi Altenhaus 1928

Years before the invasion, Pepi felt the need to uproot her family and move them to America. Her already unbearable anxiety was constantly increasing because of the countless horror stories related by Jewish refugees fleeing Nazi persecution. Papa however, refused to leave because Uncle Oscar in America wrote only about hard times there. He reminded them with pride that Belgium had been good to them; they enjoyed prosperity, freedom, security.

Three weeks after the Nazis invaded Antwerp, Pepi once again sensed the urgency to leave Europe and this time convinced Isaac to flee. Within the hour, they packed everything they could carry, and set out on foot for France and freedom.

After several hours, they came to a schoolyard filled with hundreds of refugees. Some slept on filthy cobblestones while babies cried and

> "You are the most beautiful daughters in all the world," Isaac Altenhaus whispered.

women wept. Little Mina coughed all night and in the morning Pepi decided to return to their home in Antwerp. At least there she was surrounded by the security of her beloved home. After all, what could be worse than sleeping in schoolyards on cobblestones with hundreds of strangers?

For Anneke, ten years old, and Mina, seven, this was to be the first of a series of attempted escapes that would eventually lead to freedom.

Isaac took pride in his work as a custom tailor. He specialized in tailoring uniforms for the Antwerp Police Department. This specialization led the Nazis to insist on his manufacturing Nazi uniforms. Despite his dislike for the task, Isaac had no choice but to comply. At that time the Germans did not know he was Jewish.

Life went on as tension filled the city of Antwerp. Then in 1941, the harassment of Jewish citizens began in earnest. Jews were forced to identify themselves by wearing the yellow Star of David on their coats. Then came the closing of Jewish businesses, ordinances forbidding Jews in public places or public functions. These included the theater, parks, and even the trolley cars. A gathering of two or more Jews was considered a criminal offense as was being on the streets from 7 p.m. to 7 a.m. Finally, there was the deportation of Jewish men to what they presumed were "labor camps."

On a Wednesday afternoon in June, 1942, Isaac, then 44-years old, received a notice that he was to report to the railroad station in Antwerp for deportation to a work camp. Anneke, who was then 12, remembered that the father of a close schoolmate was a Nazi collaborator and in charge of the list of attendance at the station. It was a gamble but the family decided to hurry through the streets of Antwerp before the curfew was enacted, and ask the man to strike Isaac from the list. Isaac, Pepi and Anneke stood fearlessly in the

collaborator's home, pleading and crying for him to postpone Isaac's deportation.

"Go home," he said. "Don't worry, your name will not be called."

Luckily, Isaac and Pepi had money saved which could buy them a little more time. They were now convinced that they must leave their home and hide until the war was over.

In August of 1942, Isaac brought the bolts of cloth from his business over to the home of Janine Zurich, a school

Grandma Mindel, Pepi Altenhaus, Grandpa Beryl and Pepi's older brother, Oscar. Pepi's sister, Mary is standing.

Pepi and Anneke Altenhaus

chum of Anneke. An arrangement was then made to keep the goods there until someone could come for them.

The separation would be difficult, but there was no room for an entire family to hide. The girls went to live in the countryside and Isaac and Pepi stayed in the suburbs of Antwerp, hidden by friends.

The country was beautiful in August, but Anneke and Mina found it hard to adjust to a lifestyle so unfamiliar to them. They stayed with an elderly couple and played the part of Christian sisters who came to the country for reasons of poor health. Since Jews were forbidden to attend school, the couple felt that suspicions would be aroused if the girls were not enrolled in September when the school year began. Overcome with fear, they contacted Isaac and Pepi and arranged for the girls to go back to their parents in the suburbs. A family friend came to the country to bring Anneke and Mina to Antwerp. On the train ride back, Gestapo agents roamed the aisles demanding passports from

everyone. Miraculously, Anneke and Mina were passed by and their hearts then began to beat normally again.

Isaac and Pepi occupied one of four bedrooms on the second floor of their friend's home. An entrance foyer made up the entire first floor. The living room and kitchen were in the basement, and a small courtyard housed an opaque glass water closet with an open urinal nearby.

On a rainy October morning in 1942, three Nazi officers appeared at the front door. The Altenhaus family was gathered in the basement when their friend opened the door.

"Heil fraulein! We have orders to search your house," demanded the German officer. "It has been reported that your son is involved in the black market and is hiding goods in your home!"

"There is nothing here" the woman said, "but you are free to search the house."

As the Nazis went upstairs to investigate, the woman raced to the basement to warn the Altenhaus family.

"You must leave," she cried.

"Leave! Where will we go?" Isaac exclaimed.

"Anywhere! Just leave! Please!"

Her body was still shaking as she climbed the stairs to the bedrooms on the second floor, hoping to stall the soldiers.

Isaac had no time to think. He pushed his family into the courtyard and with little hesitation guided them into the water closet. They crowded together in a cohesive knot. Fear gripped their hearts. They died a thousand deaths as they envisioned the photograph of the old grandfather in his skull cap, so foolishly displayed on their dresser.

Upstairs the Nazis had opened the doors to three bedrooms and found nothing. Satisfied with this, they started to leave.

"I wish to use the toilet. Where is it?" a young soldier asked.

"Downstairs in the courtyard," the woman mumbled.

Pepi, Minneke, and Anneke Altenhaus, 1936.

Making his way to the courtyard, the Nazi stopped in front of the water closet. He was about to open it when he spotted the urinal. In a few minutes, the soldiers left empty-handed.

Frantic with fright, the woman told the Altenhauses that they must leave at once. In driving rain, suitcases in hand, the family began their weary journey back to their home in Antwerp.

Their house had been boarded up since August. It was now late October and the neighbors had given them up for dead. Better this way; anonymity increased their chances of survival. With no heat or electricity, only a kerosene lamp, the family set up housekeeping as best they could. Mrs. Carpentier, their trusted friend and lifeline to the outside world, brought food, bought with money that Isaac had saved. But this was not enough and Anneke would sneak through the darkened streets of Antwerp to secretly purchase food from the sympathetic grocer and dairyman. The danger of those excursions was intensified by the nightly street raids which were carried out by the Gestapo.

In their absence, the house next door to the Altenhaus family had been converted into a brothel. On occasion, a Nazi soldier would stumble down the street in a drunken stupor and mistakenly knock on the Altenhaus door, demanding to be let in. The terrified family would pray that each night would not be their last.

Every day was a struggle to survive. The uncertainty of the future created an atmosphere of anxiety and despair. Mrs. Carpentier often brought news of the war's developments that she learned from British Broadcasting reports. On a map of Europe and North Africa, Isaac

"You must leave," she cried. "Leave! Where will we go?" Isaac exclaimed. "Anywhere! Just leave! Please!"

would methodically mark the progress of the war. Strategically planning its end, he gave hope and encouragement to those he loved so dearly.

As the months went by, the money dwindled and hunger set in. They were forced to eat spoiled food. No one even noticed. Nothing mattered now. Their hunger was so devastating that there were times when they would drift in and out of consciousness.

When available, herring and sardines were their main staples. Isaac would often humor his family by asking, "Well, my darlings, how would you like your herring today?" With all they had been through they tried to maintain a sense of humor.

The food situation was a growing concern. With so little money left, the family decided to send Anneke over to the Zurich home to collect the bolts of cloth left earlier.

"I'm sorry Anneke," Mr. Zurich explained. "Your bolts of cloth were stolen by a house painter we hired some time ago. Now go home. There is nothing you or I can do!"

Mrs. Carpentier was outraged at the Zuriches' dishonesty. With Anneke in hand, she paid the family a visit.

"How dare you treat the Altenhaus family this way!" Mrs. Carpentier cried. "You must give them back their bolts of cloth so they will not starve! If you will not do this," she threatened, "I promise that my son, who is a police officer, will make it very difficult for your family!"

Anneke and Mrs. Carpentier went back to the Altenhaus home, not realizing that they were being followed by the Zurich family, newly ordained Nazi collaborators!

A week later, Anneke dreamt the Gestapo came for her family. In her dream she knew that they would never spend another night together.

The next day was the holiday of Erev Simchat Torah. This special day brought with it a ray of hope. It was a Tuesday in October, 1943, exactly one year since the Altenhaus family came back to their home to live in secrecy.

Anneke agonized over whether or not she should tell her parents about her dream. She didn't want to upset them, especially this day. Despite the fact that she needed someone with whom to share her fears and anxieties, she decided not to mention the dream.

Later that evening there was a banging on the door:

"*Mach auf Juden!* Open up Jews!" boomed a loud and terrifying voice.

Their hearts sank as panic gripped the family. Huddled together, their pulses beating rapidly, adrenaline pumped hot flushes through their bodies. They were trapped! There was no way out this time. Isaac, in shock, proceeded to answer the door.

"*Juden*," a Nazi collaborator yelled as he tried to switch on the hall lights. "You stupid Juden! Your lights are out because you do not pay your bill!"

Two storm troopers held Isaac while the collaborator pounced wildly on him, beating him into a bloody pulp.

"No! Please! Do not hurt my Papa! I beg you, please!" Anneke cried, tears streaming down her face.

"Shut up *Juden*," screamed the Nazi. "Go upstairs and collect your belongings. You all will be coming with us!"

Anneke, still trembling with fright, managed to walk up the stairs to her bedroom. She grabbed her bed pillow, hugging it tight, as though it was her only friend.

As they shoved the family into a large car, Anneke spotted the Zurich family standing on the other side of the street, gloating with satisfaction.

No one said a word as they rode through the blackened streets of Antwerp. The horror stories they had heard about were now becoming reality. Ironically, after all the years of anguish, of hiding and waiting, their capture brought with it a sense of relief. Suddenly the car stopped and a storm trooper dragged Anneke and Minneke out. They never saw their parents again.

The orphanage in which Anneke and Minneke were placed was under the auspices of HIAS (an organization established to aid displaced Jews). Of the 60 children who stayed there, 16 were waiting to be deported to Auschwitz. Anneke and Minneke were part of this group.

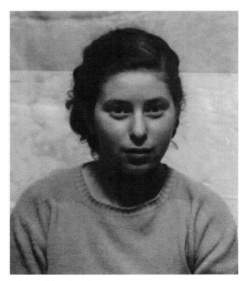

Anne Altenhaus

Mina Altenhaus

The orphanage in Lasne, in the province of Brabant.

The first week Anneke was there, she remained in shock, speaking to no one except Minneke. She cried continually, scarcely able to contain her grief. However, the necessity to be strong for Minneke's sake overrode her personal needs.

While at the orphanage, Anneke befriended Sonia, a girl her age. They shared their adolescent secrets and fantasies, and each became the family the other no longer had. In November, the orphanage prepared to close. The group of children who were brought there because of the war were to wait at the orphanage for deportation to Auschwitz. The others were to be taken to the Provence de Brabant, Belgium, where a Jewish sympathizer had offered his chateau to the orphans.

On the day they were to leave the White Brigade, a division of the Belgian Resistance, destroyed deportation orders for the 16 children scheduled to go to Auschwitz. They were now included in the move to Brabant.

The children were lined up by twos waiting for the train to Brabant when suddenly a woman's voice cried out, "Anneke! Anneke Altenhaus! Is that you? What are you doing here, Anneke?"

Anneke looked up and immediately spotted a Gentile friend of her mother's. Embarrassed and humiliated by her new lowly status, Anneke shamefully avoided the woman's eyes and hurried onto the train.

The chateau in Brabant was run like a kibbutz. The children performed their daily chores under a regimented schedule. They had been there only three weeks when Minneke became ill with scarlet fever and had to be hospitalized. Anneke became hysterical when they took her sister away, thinking she would never see her again. The separation was painful. Sonia and Minneke were all Anneke had left now and she missed her sister desperately. Forty days later, Minneke returned to the chateau pale and frightened, but cured.

Gestapo agents came to the chateau searching for children 16 and older to use as forced labor in work camps. Anneke trembled with fear as the Nazi lieutenant jerked the bed covers from her bed and snarled, "How old is this one?"

"She's only 14," the director answered.

"Very well," he replied and stomped out of the room.

1948 - "New American" girls, Mina and Anne

Anne and Tommy's Wedding, 1951

They later left with two unfortunate children that never returned.

Although the children were given food and shelter, they suffered a terrible sense of loss. Their families had been destroyed, and yet, they learned to adjust to their circumstances. They were survivors, "Children of the Holocaust."

In July of 1944, the director of the orphanage received a call that the Germans were panicking and picking up all Jewish children for execution. He immediately arranged for the children to be transferred to an institution for handicapped children.

The institution was filthy and it didn't take long for the children to become infested with lice. Anneke pleaded with them to let her keep her long braids.

"If you cut them off," she cried, "my papa will not recognize me when he comes to look for me after the war!" She won her case.

Three weeks later, the Americans invaded France and Belgium. In August of 1944, the Germans retreated. Belgium was liberated!

Within days the orphans made their way back to the chateau. There they found the once-elegant home completely vandalized, urine and feces everywhere, a souvenir of enraged Nazi soldiers who were thwarted in their plans to murder children.

In December of 1944, an American G.I. arrived at the orphanage carrying chocolates and oranges, looking for Anneke and Minneke. It was their cousin Barney from New York. At Antwerp City Hall, he found their dossier which included their present location. Uncle Oscar had asked him to find the girls and bring them back. Although Anneke still had hopes of finding her parents, she knew it was best if they went; arrangements began.

In the spring of 1945, Lisa, Sonia's mother, who had escaped from Auschwitz at the war's end, now appeared at the orphanage looking for her son and daughter.

"Mama, I want you to meet my friend Anneke Altenhaus!" Sonia exclaimed with pride.

"Anneke," Lisa wept, "I was with your parents in Antwerp waiting for

Anne's boys: Bobby, Barry, Bruce, and Brian Friedman

Anne's young men: Bobby, Brian, Bruce and Barry

deportation to Auschwitz. At Auschwitz they said, 'those who can work, go left. Those who can't, go right.' Your papa suffered from bronchitis and your mama wanted to be with him. They marched to the right. Anneke darling, those who went to the right were gassed."

Two weeks before they were to leave for America, Anneke was on her way to Antwerp to make the final arrangements for their trip. To her horror, the people who had betrayed her family were standing next to her on the trolley. No one said a word. Their faces turned white at the sight of Anneke who was too numb to cry out. The Zurich family quickly got off and disappeared.

Sonia took the girls to the boat. Anneke felt she was severing her roots because she was leaving her parents behind. Although she was told that they had died, a glimmer of hope still remained in her heart.

The new country was a difficult adjustment. For many years, recurring dreams of being chased by storm

troopers through Belgian streets made restful sleep impossible. Finally she understood she was safe in America.

In 1972, Anneke briefly left her husband and four sons to visit Sonia in Belgium. It was as though they were 16 again. Their friendship had lasted through the years.

Before Anneke's departure, they visited Brussels where a monument was erected in memory of the Jews who had died during the war. Isaac, Pepi and Sonia's father were listed alphabetically.

"My name should have been there," Anneke cried, as guilty tears ran down her cheeks.

"Anneke, don't cry," Sonia whispered. "We were blessed with the gift of 30 years of living."

Editor's note: That gift was 30 years old in 1972. Today 28 years later – the gift is 58 years old. And Anneke, now Mrs. Tommy Friedman and mother of four adult sons and six grandchildren, is "grateful for every moment of every day for the gift" that has enabled her to live to tell her story. ❖

The complete story of Anne Friedman can be found in her book, "My Name Is Anne, Too – A Tale of Survival in Nazi-Occupied Belgium," written by Anne Friedman.

The Friedman Family

Anne's newest grandchild, Ethan.

Herbert Friedman Photo by Susan Hirschbiel

Through the Kindness of Strangers HERBERT FRIEDMAN

By Wendy Juren Auerbach

There are many stories of rescue from the Holocaust and the story of the Kindertransport (Children's Transport), which saved thousands of Jewish refugee children from 1938-1939, is one of the brighter chapters in this period of dark history. Herbert Friedman was part of that transport of 10,000 children to England and this is his story.

HERBERT FRIEDMAN was born in Vienna, Austria on December 11, 1924. His parents had each immigrated separately to Austria from Radom, Poland. His father had come to Vienna during World War I to avoid conscription in the Polish Army and his mother, in search of a better way of life, arrived a short time after the war when she was only in her early 20's. Years later she would tell her son that "when she first arrived in Vienna, she thought she had arrived in heaven." The contrast between the life in Vienna and that which they had left behind in Poland seemed vast.

Herbert Friedman's parents met and married in Vienna, where his father designed women's shoes. The family lived in an apartment house near the

Danube, and Herbert, who also had an older brother and a younger sister, remembered having a normal childhood. Although the shadow of fascism had begun to creep across Germany into Austria, Herbert doesn't remember any overt acts of anti-Semitism as a child, but he admitted that it was definitely part of the culture.

"You might have a disagreement over one issue or another and someone would call you a dirty Jew or you might get into a fight as a child, … but we were still protected by the police, there were still laws to be obeyed. You were not afraid to walk the streets or go to the park." In the apartment building where the Friedmans lived, both Gentiles and Jews lived together as friendly neighbors.

This coexistence of Jew and Gentile seemed to be the way of life, especially during one extraordinary Friday evening in the winter of 1937. Herbert Friedman and two of his friends, one Jewish and one Gentile, were taking a stroll by the Danube when they noticed "something bobbing up and down in the water." They quickly realized that the object was a person, and without a moment's thought Herbert and one of his friends ran down the embankment, jumped into the cold churning river and rescued a young woman who they later found out was only 18 and attempting to commit suicide over an unhappy love affair. The third boy had run to get the police and an ambulance, which later

Nr. 287   Wien, Sonntag

Zwei Jungen retten eine Lebens-müde.

Der 13jährige Hauptschüler Herbert Friedmann (links) und der 15jährige Ernst Fleischer, die gemeinsam eine achtzehnjährige Lebensmüde aus dem Donaukanal gerettet haben.

Herb, on the left, and his friend appear in the newspaper for saving the life of a drowning woman.

took the woman to the hospital, while the police took Herbert and his friend Ernst back to the station. As Herbert and his friend were drying out, a newspaper reporter came to take a picture of the rescuers, but publicity was the last thing on Herbert's mind as he made his way back home. He was trying to figure out how he would explain where he had been to his mother.

Herbert arrived home quite a bit later than expected and very disheveled. Worried over not knowing where he had been, his mother naturally was

upset and chastised him soundly for having missed Friday night services with his father. When pressed to reveal the truth about his whereabouts he decided to leave out his tale of rescue and simply told her that he had been playing by the river and fell in. This of course unleashed another worried but loving tirade about playing by the river. Thoroughly exhausted, Herbert went to bed having put the photographer at the police station completely out of his mind.

It wasn't until the next day when the photo of Herbert and his friends appeared in the newspaper, that his parents, after being congratulated by several people, discovered what he had really been up to. Even as proud as they were, they still couldn't resist another lecture about recklessness. But little did anyone know that a bit of recklessness would come in handy very soon.

While only one mainstream newspaper had printed the picture of Herbert and Ernst, along with a description of the rescue, the Jewish press drew much attention to the event. In an era when many Jews were being characterized as cowards, they lauded the boys as heroes who had not given a thought as to whether the person they were saving was Jewish or not, and instead, had simply done the right thing. But the praise created animosity, because the Jewish press made a large point of reporting that "the lone Christian boy was the one who had run."

Within a few short months after this night of excitement by the Danube, the German Army marched into an exuberant Austria in March of 1938, and the lives of Herbert Friedman, his family and all Austrian Jews changed overnight. As Herbert remarked, "I went from saving a life one day to running for my life the next."

The Nazis wasted no time in enforcing their anti-Semitic rule. The brutal restrictions that had taken five years to hone in Germany were put in place literally overnight in Austria. Businesses were boycotted, causing many to shut down; parks and public areas were suddenly closed completely to Jews, and Jewish children were banned from going to public school. Many Austrian Jews hoped that this fearful period would pass, but they quickly realized that it would probably only grow worse. The Friedmans made efforts to leave the country, but getting out was extremely difficult. Restrictive immigration laws all over the world, including in the United States, made it virtually

impossible to leave Austria. The difficulty of securing an entry visa to any given country was also compounded by the difficulty of trying to acquire an exit visa from the Nazis. Herbert's mother wrote to a distant relative in America to try and secure affidavits for her husband and Herbert's older brother, sensing that they were in the most danger. At the time it was felt that men and older boys would be the most likely candidates to be arrested.

But within months of the *Anschluss* (the incorporation of Austria in to the Reich), the Germans tightened the noose even more. On the night of November 10, 1938, a terrible wave of "authorized" violence was unleashed against the Jews throughout Germany and Austria. Jewish shops were looted, all but one of the synagogues in Vienna was vandalized and burned to the ground, and many Jews were pulled from their homes and beaten. Thousands of men and boys were arrested and many lost their lives. The Germans claimed that *Kristallnacht* or "the night of the broken glass" was in retaliation for the murder of a German diplomat in Paris by a young Polish Jew, Hershel Greenspan, whose parents had been deported from Germany to Poland.

Herbert Friedman vividly remembers the day before *Kristallnacht*. "When we heard about Hershel Greenspan, we knew that things were going to be very dangerous, you just sensed it. And that very night there was a bang on the door.

"Your heart stops when you hear it." Two storm troopers had come looking for Herbert's older brother, but since he wasn't at home they debated whether or not to arrest Herbert instead. After his terrified mother spent several tense moments pleading with them not to take Herbert, they decided to come back later. When they had gone, Herbert's mother told him to run down to the street, find his brother and tell him not to come home. Herbert's mission was successful and his brother spent the night in safety at a friend's home.

But it was a busy night for Herbert and after warning his brother to not come home, his mother dispatched him to his uncle's house to warn him that the authorities were picking up men. The uncle managed to escape to his mother-in-law's house, but the SS suspected that he might be there instead of at his own home. As the Nazis were pounding on the door, Herbert's uncle quickly slipped under the kitchen table which had a very long tablecloth. Although his uncle's mother-in-law denied that he was there, the Nazis searched the whole apartment, but never looked under the kitchen table. They pounded on the kitchen table as he lay under it, demanded that his mother-in-law report him to the authorities if he showed up, and they left. Herbert's uncle always credited his nephew with saving his life. He later immigrated to Israel, but his wife and son were deported and did not survive.

The day after *Kristallnacht*, Herbert was on his way to the Kultusgemeinde, the governing authority for the Jewish community in Vienna, when he noticed a large group of people in a very cheerful mood standing around on the street. There were several storm troopers and a big truck parked in front of a mattress and bedding shop owned by a Jewish man, Mr. Springer. Herbert watched as the storm troopers loaded the contents of the shop into the truck, while the crowd continued to jeer and laugh and Mr. Springer stood by helplessly as the Nazis emptied his shop. When the truck had been loaded, Mr. Springer politely asked the storm trooper for a receipt. The storm trooper then turned to his audience on the street and with contempt announced, "The Jew wants a receipt." He then grabbed the terrified Springer by the collar, turned him around and gave him a hard kick in the rear which sent him flying onto the pavement. The storm trooper then said, "There Jew, there's your receipt." And the crowd went wild with laughter.

Even after almost 60 years, Herbert Friedman is still confounded by the speed at which the Austrians embraced Hitler. "Once Hitler came in, everybody suddenly seemed to be for the Nazis. It is unbelievable that so many people claimed to have secretly belonged to the Nazi party all along."

And while most Austrians embraced Hitler, some tried to weakly justify the treatment of the Jews. Herbert remembered hearing his neighbors saying, "Nothing is going to happen to you, we know you. You're good Jews. But the people across the street, those Jews, maybe they deserve what's happening to them. As young as I was, I wondered to myself if the people across the street were saying the same thing about us."

After *Kristallnacht*, Herbert decided that he must get out of Austria. His father and brother had received affidavits to leave the country, which they did in January of 1939. Herbert did not want to be left behind in such a hostile place and he often reflects on how at the tender age of 13 he worked up the nerve to act on this impulse to leave.

Because Herbert had made the news by saving the woman's life, the chief rabbi of Vienna, Rabbi David Taglicht was willing to meet with him when he asked for an appointment. Herbert asked him if he could help him to get out of the country. Herbert had applied for *Aliyah* at an earlier time, so Rabbi Taglicht helped him get an appointment at the Kultusgemeinde with the executive secretary, Dr. Lowenhertz.

"Today I wonder how could I go and see the chief rabbi of Vienna or the executive secretary of the Kultusgemeinde, and my folks knew nothing about it? At the time I was doing it on my own, out of fear, attempting to get out of the country. I just wanted out."

While Herbert was in the office talking to Dr. Lowenhertz, the executive secretary picked up the phone and called someone. He remembers hearing Dr. Lowenhertz saying something about a Kindertransport and when he put the phone down, Herbert asked him what the Kindertransport was. Dr. Lowenhertz explained that it was a project to transport 1000 children out of Austria. 800 were to go to England and 200 to Holland, but that they were still in negotiation with the Nazi authorities and did not yet know if they would allow it (the kindertransport). "And then he added, 'If you like, I'll put your name on the list.' I said to please include me, not knowing if anything would come of it."

After his meeting with Dr. Lowenhertz at the Kultusgemeinde, Herbert decided to pay a visit to the Palestine Office. While he was there, SS officers suddenly appeared and announced that men should step in to one room and women and children in to another. Even though he had had his Bar Mitzvah, Herbert decided to play it safe and stay with the women. He later learned that the men were taken to Dachau, while the women and children were detained for almost two hours and then released. After he was allowed to go, Herbert decided to warn any men approaching the office not to go in, knowing that they, too, would be arrested.

As he stood on the curb just in front of the Palestine Office, he would turn his head slightly and whisper to any men approaching the building "Gestapo, don't go in." What Herbert didn't realize was that a Nazi officer was standing behind the door of the office watching him. After noticing several men suddenly walking away, the SS officer called Herbert to come over to him, requesting to know what he had been telling all of these men. After repeated denials, the Nazi grew impatient and slapped Herbert across the face, knocking him down a short flight of steps. Herbert picked himself up and ran home, very relieved to have gotten away with only a bloody nose and in one piece, but to this day he hopes that what he did may have helped save a few men's lives.

Kristallnacht was a brutal wake up call to the world and helped to make the Kindertransport happen. In Great Britain, the British Jewish Refugee Committee, working with the Movement for the Care of Children from Germany, lobbied Prime Minister Neville Chamberlain to ease refugee restrictions in order to try and bring over as many children as quickly as possible. The British government agreed to let in an unspecified number of children from Germany, Austria, and Czechoslovakia, but with three stipulations.

The first was that no child could be older than 16 in order not to be seen as a threat to the British labor pool. The second condition was that no part of

the transport effort could be supported by any public funds and because they could not be dependent upon public support, the relief agencies had to guarantee the sum of 50 pounds (roughly $1,500 in today's currency) for each child. At the time this was more than the fare from Europe to the United States. And finally the children would only be granted temporary travel visas with the intention that Britain would only be a transit country for them.

This massive volunteer effort was mobilized quickly and the first transport left within three weeks of *Kristallnacht* and continued until the last two days before the war broke out. Herbert Friedman will forever have lasting gratitude to all of those who made the Kindertransport happen. He marvels at the fact that no one got paid, that all the donations were private and at the speed with which it was organized. In the end, 10,000 children from the age of two to 16 years were saved, but tragically nine out of ten children never saw their parents again.

Shortly after he had been put on the Kindertransport list, Herbert received a cable telling him that he had been chosen for the next transport.

At the Kultusgemeinde he was given a list of instructions as to what he could bring and told when the train would leave. He was also assigned the number 325, written on a small board, which he was to wear around his neck at all times during the trip. The list of what he

Editor's Note: The following poem was written by Herb Friedman's grandson, Aaron Friedman, when he was 14 years old. Aaron is the son of Mark and Ellen Friedman of Baltimore. The poem appeared in the October 30, 1998 issue of the Southeastern Virginia Jewish News.

HOLOCAUST POEM

Walking through the halls of the
  living dead
Dead in body
But alive through their stories,
That are repeated over and over.
   I reflect and realize
     What would happen if I was
      at the selection on the
      platform of Auschwitz?

I look strong
I might have been selected to live
And to toil endlessly
To prolong the hell that had
   engulfed the world and my life.
What of my family,
   My brothers and mother
    would almost certainly perish
    in the gas chambers
    And rot as ash in
     the crematorium.

My father might live,
But probably not.

   If this happened
   I would be alone
   Just as the souls
   Of the living dead.

by Aaron Friedman

could take was very limited and nothing could be brought that had not been formally inspected and turned in ahead of time. All possessions had to have been owned for at least one year and no money, jewelry, cameras or musical instruments were allowed. To defy the rules meant risking the chance to leave. Herbert remembers packing a few extra books, but because they were not on his packing list, they were taken by the authorities. Only a small amount of food was allowed for the trip. (Herbert Friedman held on to these original documents and several of them were featured in the documentary "Into the Arms of Strangers").

In Vienna, the authorities specified that each child could only be accompanied by one adult to the station and had to be dropped off at the foot of the steps leading to the railroad station. Herbert's mother accompanied him because at that time women were thought to be less at risk than Jewish men. No parent was allowed on to the platform, and as Herbert recalled, "There was a lot of crying and heart wrenching goodbyes. To this day, I remember how terrible it was. Even thinking about it now, I feel like crying." The transports left at night in order not to attract a lot of public attention. The train carrying Herbert Friedman left shortly after midnight on December 11, 1938, his 14th birthday.

As Herbert started his trip out of Vienna and through Germany, he felt very apprehensive. Right before the Dutch border, German storm troopers boarded the trains to double check papers and randomly search suitcases.

If everything was not in order, the child could be pulled from the train.

As Herbert Friedman remembers, some of the greatest heroes of the Kindertransport were the chaperones who accompanied the children. While they undertook their very brave journeys, their families were held hostage to insure that they would return once the children on the transport had been delivered. Though free momentarily, they were forced to return to an unknown fate. To this day, Herbert Friedman does not know what became of any of the adults who accompanied him out of Vienna.

After almost 48 hours, Herbert's train crossed the border into Holland. He remembered that "all hell broke loose on the train among the children. There was jubilation and cheering, and we

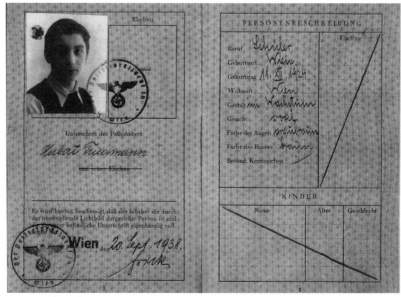

Herbert's travel visa used during transport to England.

— 112 —

yelled out 'Long live Holland!'" People from the Dutch Jewish refugee agency met us at the train and brought hot chocolate." But this was only the first leg of the trip. After the long train ride, Herbert boarded the ferry Prague and crossed the channel to England.

He was taken to a summer camp in Dovercourt at Lowestoft, which was right on the ocean. "The weather there was unbelievably cold. We had no heat and slept in cabins. I put on every bit of clothing that I had and I still froze. After the second night I gave up and just went into the communal dining hall where they had a fireplace. I spread a blanket out along with all the other kids and slept on the floor."

The relief of having escaped Nazi Germany soon turned to uncertainty about the immediate future, but as Herbert recalled, not all of the children had the same experience.

"For all of us, we're in a strange country. We don't have any relatives, we don't have anybody that we know, we don't speak the language. We had no idea what was going to happen to us."

Upon arrival many of the children were being picked up by volunteer foster parents, while others waited to be chosen. Herbert remembers that, "Many of the children were well treated, but some had a less pleasant experience. Most people wanted younger children or older girls, who were sometimes used as domestics or babysitters. Some boys

From the Gurs Camp he wrote in pure desperation, "Help me, I'm eating grass."

were put to work on farms, and some children were, unfortunately, abused." Teenage boys like himself were usually passed over and often slipped through the cracks of the system, moving from one place to another, ultimately ending up in group homes.

Herbert's chilly arrival was only the beginning of a challenging stay in England. For the first eight months of his stay in England, he lived in nine different locations. In September of 1939, along with about 30 other boys, he was finally settled in at the Kendra Hall School, in Croyden which had once been a private school for girls.

The school buildings were now vacant, having been evacuated because of the growing threat of war. There he got his first taste of an air raid alarm, although mercifully no bombs fell. While they were safe from the Nazis, some children of the Kindertransport were separated from their siblings. During this time, one of Herbert's friends, Loeble, who was also living at Kendra Hall School, asked Herbert to come and help him find his five-year-old sister who had

been placed in a convent nearly 70 kilometers away. After several attempts to visit her, they finally made it, but the small child did not recognize her heartbroken brother.

After spending only several days at Kendra Hall School, war broke out, and the Royal British Air Force needed the abandoned school to house troops. Herbert was moved to the Townley Castle School in London, which was vacant because the British students had been evacuated. Upon his arrival in London, Herbert was told that the refugee children's committee had run out of funds and that he needed to find work. He soon found a job as a delivery boy for a tailor on Oxford Street, earning one pound a week, most of which went to room, board and transportation. During this time, the German Air Force began its devastating blitz on London and Herbert remembered many tense moments.

While he was in England, Herbert corresponded with his mother and other relatives who pleaded with him to help them. At one point, Herbert wrote to the refugee committee who had brought him over, hoping to be placed with a family so that they would perhaps help his mother join him. He received a confused response asking how he had come to England, who was responsible for him, and whether he was Jewish or not. In the end, his mother was able to leave Vienna via Italy and make her way to Baltimore with his younger sister in late 1939.

But Herbert also remembers that some very painful correspondence came from one of his favorite uncles in which he wrote, "Since I (Herbert) was safe, it was now my obligation to save my uncle." Later, his uncle was arrested by Italian police for being illegally in the country. He was ordered to leave or else be deported to Germany. He illegally entered France where he was arrested again. From the Gurs Camp he wrote in pure desperation, "Help me, I'm eating grass." Years later this letter still haunts Herbert Friedman and he often wrestles with the perspective he has now versus what he might have realistically been able to do for his uncle in England in 1939 as a boy in a strange country with limited knowledge of English and few contacts.

In November of 1940 Herbert Friedman, through the kindness of strangers (Julia Strauss and Dr. Alvin C. Thalheimer) was able to leave and join his family in Baltimore, Maryland, but the transition wasn't easy. After having been on his own and out of school for three years, sudden immersion into high school and American culture was a shock after living in wartime England. In the end Herbert not only rose to the challenge, but also graduated from high school and was offered a scholarship to Loyola University in Baltimore. However, college had to be postponed when he was drafted into the United States Army and ironically sent to the Pacific in spite of his desire for service in Europe.

After the war, he attended the school of pharmacy at the University of Maryland, and later was recalled into the army during the Korean War, where he rose to the rank of first lieutenant. He and his wife Joyce settled in Norfolk in the early 1950's where they raised their three sons. The Friedmans now also have seven grandchildren and divide their time between homes in Norfolk and Baltimore.

Over the years, Herbert Friedman has been back several times to Austria and England. In 1988, to commemorate the 50th anniversary of *Kristallnacht* and to promote the "new Austria," he was invited back to Austria by the Austrian Government, along with a group of former Austrians, to visit their old homeland. The visit included a meeting with Kurt Waldheim, who was president at that time, and dinner at the palace. As a result of that visit to Austria, one year later he found himself along with his family at a reception at the Austrian Embassy in Washington,

D.C. to receive a gold medal for his rescue of the young woman from the Danube in 1937. And although he is very proud of that good deed, Herbert Friedman still views his short time on the curb in front of the Palestine Office, helping a few men escape the Gestapo as much more meaningful.

Every Holocaust survivor has a different story, and most of them share the painful loss of family and friends.

Although Herbert Friedman was one of the lucky members of the Kindertransport to be reunited with his immediate family, his entire family, with the exception of one uncle, all perished in the Holocaust. It is for them as much as for future generations that he continues to tell his story. ❖

Our Johnny in Israel
JAN FROHLICH

By Lynda Gonsenhauser

Jan Frohlich in Israel after WWII.

"I saw so many people die (in the camps) of hunger, and I was not able to help nobody (anyone).… But I always said, 'Never mind. Tomorrow is another day. We will pass over.'"

These are among the words left behind by Holocaust survivor Jan Frohlich who spent the last years of his life in the Tidewater area. Jan was born May 15, 1927 in Pqesek, Czechoslovakia. He died May 14, 1999 in Norfolk, Virginia, a day before his 72nd birthday. In between the beginning and the end of his life he tramped through the harsh grounds of the concentration camps and later as a free man through the lively streets of Israel, where he served the Israeli army as a paratrooper.

His journey began when Jan was approximately 13 years old and taken along with his brother and sisters to Gestapo headquarters in Prague and thrown into a cellar overnight. As the oldest, it was his responsibility to keep up the morale of his younger siblings. He remembers telling them: "We will

not cry. We will sing." And through the lonely night, "we sang with five voices," he said.

He was at first placed in Theresienstadt and later transported out of that camp to Auschwitz. "The minute you came to Auschwitz, you knew this was not Theresienstadt.… We survived the (worst) thing … not only the beatings. Beatings (were) not the only thing you can suffer.… But the food (hunger) and the way they behaved towards you. It's the same thing. Nobody can help you."

After the war and following his recuperating in Prague, he moved to Haifa and became a paratrooper,

Jan Frohlich - kneeling at left - with Israeli soldiers during the late 1940's.

fighting in Israel's war of 1948. He subsequently made 270 jumps for Israel both as an instructor and soldier. Since he had blond hair and blue eyes, he was nicknamed "Johnny" by his Israeli comrades, after the British paratroopers for he was told "you look exactly like them.... This is our Johnny in Israel."

His wife Delores remembers how proud he was to be an American citizen and that he hung American flags both on his front porch and back deck. When he was recuperating from a crane accident

which occurred in his backyard, Delores recalls that Jan said, "I must have nine lives. If Hitler couldn't kill me, nothing will." ❖

Jan Frohlich and his wife, Delores

He Stared Death In the Face
Charles Goldman

By Ora Baer Gerstl

Charles and Esther Goldman

> NINETY PERCENT OF POLISH JEWRY — THREE MILLION MEN, WOMEN, AND CHILDREN — WERE SYSTEMATICALLY EXTERMINATED BY THE NAZI WAR MACHINE BETWEEN 1939 AND 1945. SIX OF THE THREE MILLION WERE MEMBERS OF GOLDMAN'S IMMEDIATE FAMILY: HIS MOTHER, THREE OLDER BROTHERS, HIS FIRST WIFE AND INFANT DAUGHTER.

It's been said that life is a series of doors closing and new ones opening. For CHARLES GOLDMAN of Norfolk, the doors slammed in a particularly ruthless way, yet somehow he always found the courage to open new ones.

He was a three-pack-a-day smoker and had a lung removed. He spent 11 days in an intensive-care unit. The situation was touch and go.

His physician was astonished by his will to live. Charles Goldman recalled his words: "I never saw a patient with as much courage as you have," he said.

For Charles, the harrowing illness and subsequent hospitalization were a challenge that left him undaunted. He had stared death in the face many times before. And he had always emerged, scarred perhaps, but a survivor.

Ninety percent of Polish Jewry – three million men, women, and children – were systematically exterminated by the Nazi war machine between 1939 and 1945. Six of the three million were members of Charles' immediate family: his mother, three older brothers, his first wife and infant daughter.

Somehow, Charles survived poverty, enslavement, cold, starvation, filth and beatings. Throughout the ordeal he shared with the rest of European Jewry, Charles refused to allow himself the luxury of becoming demoralized.

"After the war, my brother (the only one to survive), who had fought with the

Polish partisans against the Nazis, was surprised I was alive. I said: 'Of course I'm alive. I've been fighting'."

Grenades and guns were not in his arsenal. His only weapon was a strong will.

"I always believed that things would get better. Every opportunity I saw to stay alive, I took. I didn't give in … I tried to encourage others to live … I have a friend in St. Louis who says that if not for my encouragement, he'd be dead."

Charles, a short, barrel-chested man, has lived in Norfolk with his wife and two sons since 1956. He met his second wife, Esther, a native of Sokoly, Poland, after her liberation from Auschwitz in 1945. With his cheerful *mien* and obliging manner, the bespectacled, silver-haired Charles very much fits the image of a retired grocery merchant. Which he is. In fact his thick Polish accent and the French and Yiddish expressions that pepper his speech offer the only clue as to his trials as a 20th century wandering Jew, a victim of Hitler's failed Final Solution.

The youngest of six children born to a textile manufacturer in Belzec, Poland, Chil Zyskind Alexander Goldman was 23 when the Nazis invaded his native land in 1939. He was employed at the time in the family textile business in Lodz, a large industrial city in central Poland. His family had already scattered. His mother and brothers were in Lublin and his sister was

attending dental school in France. His father had died three years earlier of complications resulting from diabetes and lung disease. There is admiration in his husky voice as Charles recalls his father's simple piety and iron will. A faded photograph of the family patriarch adorns the bookcase in Charles' study. It bears the likeness of a full-bearded Jew in a black frock coat and large skullcap. The man in the picture seems a million miles away from

> Grenades and guns were not in his arsenal. His only weapon was a strong will.

Charles' Meadowbrook Terrace home. He was part of the vanished world of the *shtetl*, one preserved chiefly through the photographs of Roman Vishniac.

When the war broke out, the rich and vibrant quality of *shtetl* life was still evident in Lodz, a city with 233,000 Jews. But in 1939, when Nazis captured the city and renamed it Litzmannstadt, all that began to change. The invaders immediately ordered the Jews to wear the yellow Star of David on the front and back of their clothing.

They overran the Jewish cemetery and smashed the headstones. Within months, they had herded the Jews into a two-square-mile ghetto and expropriated their businesses.

By January, 1940, the ghetto had been sealed off. Conditions for the 164,000 residents were severe.

"Seven to eight people were living in two room apartments," Charles said. "My wife and I shared two rooms with five other people from a different family."

The streets reeked with raw sewage. Food became an obsession.

"In the ghetto, there was special money, like food stamps. We had to pay for our electricity and food with this."

Monthly rations for a family of three consisted of about 1 kilogram (2.2 pounds) of bread, 4 liters (136 ounces) of milk, and 60 ounces of horsemeat.

"Sometimes we had rotten potatoes, rotten rutabagas or rotten watermelon, (in addition). People suffered from diarrhea because of all this rotten food."

The Nazis opened a clothing factory to manufacture uniforms for the German army. Charles' wife worked there as a seamstress, and like other factory workers, received a special bonus ration that included a bowl of soup each day. Charles described the soup as little pieces of potato in water, with some other vegetables added occasionally.

THE SHOWER

She held the child close to her breast
And did not look upon the rest
Who numbed had heard the cold
command:
"Disrobe and by the chamber stand ...
Remember where your clothes are
hung,
They must not carelessly be flung;
You'll need them when you're clean
and dry ..."
On leashes strained guard dogs
nearby;
Weary, hungry, yet proud unbowed,
Shtetl met Vienna in this crowd;
The learned, simple, rich, the poor,
From Cracow, Kovno, Rhineland,
Rhur;
Though nakedness they could not
hide,
They kept their dignity, their pride;
What had they done to know such
pain
Outside the shower with no drain?
She held the child close to her breast
And did not look upon the rest
But sweetly whispered words of love
Although brute guards did cruelly
shove,
Although she knew what was to be...
Death, not water, flowed with
Zyklon-B.

Abbott Saks

When the tide of the war began to turn against the Germans after their debacle at Stalingrad during the winter of 1942-43, the Nazis reduced the already meager rations of their captives.

As long as he could afford the inflated prices, Charles bought foodstuffs on the black market. After that, he foraged the fields for vegetables. Then his stomach shrank and he began to adjust to his grossly inadequate diet.

"People tried to steal food from other people's apartments.... I saw corpses on the street and in houses of those who died from starvation," he remembered.

Liquidation of the ghetto had begun in 1940 with the deportation of the mentally ill and retarded. In 1941, roundups of children under 12 and adults over 60 began.

Although Charles' regular job was to unload coal trains, he was forced to load the deportees into cattle cars.

A few days after the roundups were launched, the true nature of the Nazi "resettlement" plan became clear.

"I saw a sign in blood that one of the deportees had written in a train car." Auschwitz was the destination.

Infants were torn from their mothers as the trains were loaded.

"I'll never forget the mother I saw nursing her child. She did not want to let the child go. The Nazi guard raised his bayonet and cut off the breast and the baby with one blow. The mother died on the spot."

Punishment for violations of Nazi policy was swift and severe. Curfew in the ghetto extended from 8 p.m. until 6 a.m. Those who broke the curfew or strayed near the ghetto fence were shot. In 1942, the Nazis captured eight men and four women who attempted escape from Lodz. They were hanged publicly.

Charles had two volatile encounters with the Nazi authorities during his internment in the ghetto. These gave him a personal taste of the enemy's brutal methods.

The first occurred when he gave his brother's furniture and apartment to an officer in the SA (a Nazi paramilitary group) who had offered to spirit away Charles' sister-in-law and two nieces to safety in Lublin. When the Gestapo got wind of the plan, they interrogated Charles and ultimately arrested his accomplice in the SA.

The second time, Charles was not quite so lucky. Accused of hiding merchandise from his textile plant, which the Nazis had seized right after the invasion, Charles was arrested and held prisoner for a week and a half. His ordeal culminated in five lashes on his bare backside. In light of the Gestapo's reputation for brutality, Charles views the comparative leniency of his punishment as a miracle.

"I was very surprised they let me live," he confessed.

But the quality of that life rapidly deteriorated.

After their mass liquidation campaign, the Germans transformed the ghetto into a labor camp. In 1944, just two months before the Soviet forces liberated Lublin, a city to the south of Lodz, Charles' wife gave birth to their first child, a daughter.

"When she was three months old, they (the Germans) started liquidating the ghetto because Russia was advancing and the Germans were nervous."

Acting through Chaim Rumkowsky, the leader of the Jewish community whom they had co-opted, the Nazis began a massive propaganda campaign to speed up the final liquidation.

"Rumkowsky told us not to hide. He said we would be reunited with our families and we'd be happy."

Charles was not deceived. For two days, he and his family hid in a closet, hoping to escape deportation. On the third day, the baby began to cry, and they were discovered.

Charles and his family were seized and loaded aboard the next train bound for Auschwitz. Nazi efficiency drained the Lodz Ghetto of its remaining 70,000 inhabitants at the rate of 1,200 per day.

"We were packed 75 to a train car, like sardines," Charles said.

The train made several stops during the 15-hour journey. At each station, pleas for water would rise from the human cargo suffocating within the train. The Poles heard the cries, but ignored them.

"We were standing so that we could scarcely breathe. Some suffocated and died on the train. Some people tried to sit down and were trampled to death."

Those who survived the hellish train ride found no relief at their destination. At the gate to Auschwitz, a German soldier made selections. Ten percent were sent to the right. They went to work.

The rest were sent to the left: to the gas chambers.

Despite Charles' entreaties, his wife would not leave their baby.

"We said good-bye. I knew I'd never see her again. She went to the left; I, to the right. I still grieve, but knew life must go on."

After only 11 days in the Nazis' most infamous death camp, "I was sent to Hochenstain, a labor camp in Germany, to work in a plant where they manufactured turbo (props) for airplanes," Charles said.

Conditions in the all-male camp were better than he had expected.

"The Germans told us that our camp was being liquidated because the war would soon be over," Charles recalled. With the advance of the Russian forces, Jewish lives suddenly became valuable. The German guards realized that without the Jewish laborers as security, their own lives would be in danger. They feared Soviet retaliation for the 20 million Russians killed during the war. Consequently they began marching the men of Hochenstain toward the advancing American troops in the hope of finding clemency.

"The guards did not harass us too much." Some of the old guards even smuggled bread in for the inmates.

Watery soup, decayed sausage and black bread with pieces of wood in it constituted the staples of the camp diet.

Some 50 inmates, the only Hungarian Jews at the camp, were repulsed by the rotten food and refused to eat. They all died of starvation.

For seven months, Charles worked in Hochenstain. By April 1945, the Allies' noose was tightening around Germany, and Russian troops were camped only 12 miles from Berlin.

"The Germans told us that our camp was being liquidated because the war would soon be over," Charles recalled. With the advance of the Russian forces, Jewish lives suddenly became valuable. The German guards realized that without the Jewish laborers as security, their own lives would be in danger. They feared Soviet retaliation for the 20 million Russians killed during the war. Consequently they began marching the men of Hochenstain toward the advancing American troops in the hope of finding clemency.

The men marched at night and hid in barns and stables with the break of dawn.

Liberation proved anticlimactic. On May 1, 1945, a German officer told the men that Hitler was dead. He ordered them to remain in a stable.

An hour or two passed. The men heard nothing. They gingerly opened the stable door. No one was there. Their German guards had donned civilian clothes and fled. At Pilsen, in what is now Czechoslovakia, the weary group from Hochenstain met up with the American liberating forces led by Gen. Dwight Eisenhower.

"We took them to Buchenwald … There were still half alive people and many dead … in the crematoria. Eisenhower cried like a baby," Charles remembered.

No longer a prisoner, he returned to Lodz stripped of everything but his dignity and his dreams. He had dropped to half of his normal weight.

In Lodz, he was reunited with one brother, who had fought against the Nazis with the Polish partisans. He discovered the fate of his family. Two nieces had been raised in a convent and were still alive. Two brothers had been killed in the Majdanek concentration camp near Lublin. Another had died during the Nazi bombardment of Warsaw. His mother and nephew had been shot dead in the streets of Czestochowa just three days before liberation.

In November 1945, after a three-week courtship, Charles remarried. His 21-year-old bride, Esther, was also a veteran of Auschwitz. They remained in Lodz until 1946. But the Communists were consolidating their takeover of Poland,

Esther, Raymond, Daniel, and Chil in December 1956, celebrating their immigration.

and anti-Semitic attacks by the Polish national guard continued to erupt. The Goldmans had no desire to be victims again. Unable to immigrate to France legally, they falsified passports and slipped across the French border, settling in Metz, a city in the Alsace-Lorraine region.

Their two sons, Raymond and Daniel, were born there. Although they struggled to eke out a living in France, the Goldmans were unable to succeed. They applied for visas to the United States. In 1956, their request was granted, and with the help of HIAS (United Hebrew Sheltering and Immigrant Aid Society), they were resettled in Norfolk.

After the dressmaking factory that employed him went bankrupt, Charles began a successful new career as a grocery merchant.

In 1961, a federal judge in Norfolk granted him U.S. citizenship and gave him a new name, Charles. The judge told Charles that the new name would be easier for Americans to pronounce than Chil Zyskind Alexander.

Charles had a new identity and a new life. But he could not forget the past.

"In the summer of 1962, I went to the Norfolk police department to apply for a liquor license for my grocery. My wife was wearing a short-sleeved dress, and the captain asked her why she had written her phone number on her arm. 'This isn't my telephone number,' she

Charles Goldman

said. 'This is my number from Auschwitz.' The captain didn't know how to apologize," Charles remembered. The Holocaust is part of Charles' history, but it does not haunt him. He lives in the present and looks forward to the future. Now retired, he takes pride in the accomplishments of his two sons, Tidewater businessmen, and dotes on his five grandchildren.

"I want to live as long as I can and be happy. I want to be at my grandchildren's Bar and Bat Mitzvahs ... I don't think about why I survived. I can't bring back the dead and I don't dwell on it," he said.

While Charles is not given to brooding, he is pessimistic about the future of Jewish life in America. He is alarmed by the rate of intermarriage and

assimilation among American Jewry, and believes anti-Semitism remains a force to be reckoned with. In the late 1970s, he joined the Tidewater Survivors Club in an effort to focus attention on the dangers of anti-Semitism and stimulate the Jewish community to adopt a vigilant and activist stance in response to bigotry.

"There are not many of us (survivors) left. In 20 years, none of us will be left. Our children and grandchildren must never forget. If the (U.S.) government allows a Nazi organization to get by, it can happen here. (Nazism) started small in Germany, too. We never thought it could happen. We couldn't fight what we didn't know about.... No one cares about Jews. We have to care about ourselves. Our only hope is not to forget." ❖

Charles Goldman died October 20, 1986. His wife, Esther, (of blessed memory) has a story in this book.

Her Memories – a Panorama of Horrors
Esther Goldman

By Reba Karp

Esther signing copies of her book, **Feeling Guilty.**

Photo by Betsy Karotkin

ESTHER GOLDMAN is a survivor – a special individual with an indomitable spirit who managed to survive in the face of the hardest circumstances. She is among the dwindling number of Jewish people victimized by the Holocaust.

An attractive woman, who speaks positively, she is not unlike other women who are neat and well-dressed. The one obvious exception are the numbers she has tattooed on her left arm. She does not try to conceal them, for they are testimony that she, in fact, is a special person – a survivor of Hitler's "Final Solution."

She was born in Sokoly, Poland in 1924 – before half of the world went mad. Among her earliest recollections of her childhood are fear and a life punctuated by hiding, which began when her mother sent her each evening to the home of an elderly Jewish couple. Here, she would spend the night, hiding from the Germans "who pulled young Jewish girls from their homes and raped them and God knows what else," she said.

Later, she and other young Jewish people of her town, were to spend many long days working for the German army, making an inflammable product she describes as similar to charcoal briquettes. This was in 1939.

Then on the eve of Rosh Hashanah of 1940 or '41, the Germans had a new idea – they decided to burn down Jewish homes, and her family's was among them. She remembers a plane flying low over the town early one morning, her mother was baking bread. The plane, she feels, was a signal, for shortly thereafter, Jewish homes began to burn. Her family escaped out of the back door, and spent Rosh Hashanah eve hiding in a cemetery. In the morning when they returned to sift through the ashes of their house, they met some of their Jewish neighbors who had not managed to escape – their bodies littered the streets.

Temporary refuge was found with another Jewish family, and life for the Jews who were left in Sokoly trudged on. In 1942, they heard a rumor that the Jewish people were going to be sent away. "In the evening we decided to hide. The roads were not blocked and we hid in the forest. Those who did not leave … they were killed."

She remembers a night in the forest lit up from the fire of German rifles and German spotlights. In the confusion, she was separated from her family. "I was all alone. I saw a neighbor, I went up to him and asked if he would take me along with him." Esther's mother had tried to prepare her family of ten for this moment, for the ordeal of survival. Each child was given some of her jewelry which they were to exchange for help or food. In addition, Esther wore as many garments as possible, which she could shed to help ransom herself. An outer garment bought her the privilege of hiding with 16 other

"A New Year and Repentance" (Rosh Hashanah/Yom Kippur) by MaryAnne Katz

Jews in an underground excavation where potatoes had been previously stored.

"I'm scratching now," she said, "because I remember the lice … we were two weeks with lice and no water to bathe … 16 people in a little lousy grave. We were almost buried alive."

One night stands out in her mind now. "We heard footsteps, there were two children, one was my brother. How they found the place I don't know. He asked me if I had something left that mother had given me. I had a bracelet – I gave it to him."

Before he left she learned that her mother and other sisters and brothers

— 124 —

were dead. "My mother gave all she had to Christian people to save the two youngest. I later learned that they turned the children over to the Nazis," she added.

Jewish children grew up fast in Poland in those days and her younger brother, already wise in the battle of survival, told Esther that if she wanted to leave the "grave" she should go to the synagogue in the city where Jews who were captured had been herded. And when she could no longer stand being "buried alive" she took his advice. "The Germans came to the synagogue and locked us up at night in case anyone had any idea about escaping. It was the first time I was jail." The next morning they were taken by train to the ghetto in Bialystock.

At the ghetto she found two of her brothers, including the one who sought her in the forest. But it was not a happy family reunion for they were unable to live together. For awhile she eked out survival by working as a seamstress in a factory making military clothing for the Germans.

"Then early one morning, when I awoke there was no one in the house where I lived. I could hear screaming and shouting and Germans in the streets. Everyone was running to hide, it was everyone for himself. I didn't know what to do, no one wanted to take me," she said, remembering that she returned to the attic where she slept. A strange woman was there. She had a

bag of dried beans. "It was the only food we had." The woman's last name was Pincus. In their fear and need for someone else, they decided they would face what was before them as sisters.

Since they could not remain hiding forever, they eventually found themselves on a cattle train to Birkenau. "The doors were slammed … I don't recall how long we rode. We were so squeezed we couldn't turn around. Babies were laying dead … the stench."

Then the doors opened. A day not much unlike many other days - except that Mengele was there and giving orders. "One to the left, one to the right. I spotted my sister-in-law and I started to run towards her. I got hit on the head and was forced to the ground."

Then the organized torture of the German Third Reich began to unfold. The prisoners were ordered to undress and their heads and bodies shaved. She will never forget the humiliation, she said. They were given old clothes and forced into quarters already over-crowded – shoved into a dark room with the dead, the dying and those determined to survive. There was no place to lay, no wall to lean against,

scarcely any area to stand and no familiar object to touch for orientation. Just the darkness and the nameless. "We just survived that night." In the morning they were lined up for count, five in a row. It was a regular procedure. "If someone was missing we had to stand for hours until that person was accounted for."

Her block number was 15 and she remembers the terror vividly. The nights were dark and the light of day revealed those who had died during the night. The lucky ones had a blanket, those who didn't would try to steal one or wait and take it from those who died. Death was common. "We pulled them (the bodies) out in the morning … wagons would carry them away," she said.

"I worked out of the camp in the field. I had an old coat. I was told to reverse it and fill the front with rocks and debris. We reversed the procedure the next day." The march to the fields and back to camp was another exercise in survival. "The dogs killed those unable to march back to camp." The routine was basically the same for six days each week. Ironically they were not forced to "work" on Sunday. "I don't know why," she said.

Events pass through her memory as a panorama of horror. "The camp hospital was a dreaded place. Once you were in, you were lucky to come out alive…. It was a place you'd pray to God you'd die."

Then she remembers the "show place" for the Red Cross. Here, men, women and children and humane conditions were paraded in front of the Red Cross to dupe them.

"Then afterwards they made us dig graves ... they put the children inside and gave them toys to play with, poured something over them and burned them alive."

She was later transferred to Auschwitz where she was selected to work in an ammunition factory. "Conditions were a little better. If you made your quota, you got a slice of bread, a piece of margarine ... the bread was so dear."

Another memory. "There were no children in Auschwitz. One woman was pregnant. They let her have the baby, then killed her and took the infant to experiment on it."

In 1945 as the war drew to an end, they were forced to march to Ravensbruck. "God Almighty. We thought Birkenau and Auschwitz were bad. People dead, piled all over." Then from Ravensbruck they were transported deep into Germany where their work once more consisted of "silly things." Then early in May the routine suddenly changed. "They let us out one morning. There were carrots laying in the field. We shoved all we could into our clothes to have something to eat." Then later they were put into their blocks, which were locked from the outside." We were frightened. We looked out in the

evening. The guards were gone. We somehow managed to get out, but not before crying and screaming. We feared they were going to burn us to death."

Once out, they found they were alone. No Germans. They searched the soldiers' barracks They were empty. "We knew the Germans were running," she said. They broke into a warehouse for food and then returned to their blocks and barricaded the doors "and waited for someone to liberate us. We prayed to God ... isn't it strange that we still believed in God?"

But no one came, so they decided to march, thinking "the highway would take us someplace." By the time they reached a town, the German citizens were frightened and offered them no resistance. They went into a bakery and took the bread, and what they couldn't eat themselves, they destroyed so no one else could.

After more trials, the band of camp refugees were given a horse and wagon from a Russian officer and they set out again. "Where we were going, I don't

Esther and all of her family, 1990
From left to right top: Raymond, Judy, Esther, Todd, Susan and Daniel. Bottom: Tova, Lauren, Aaron, and Shannon

know." But since all roads must end somewhere, they eventually met Polish Jewish soldiers who took care of them, telling their officers that they had found lost relatives. Of course, Esther notes, the officers knew it was only a ploy so they could help the survivors.

Esther has lived in the Tidewater area since 1957 with her husband, Charles Goldman (of blessed memory), also a Holocaust survivor. They have two grown sons and five grandchildren. She feels her story must be told and doesn't like the idea that it may be shortened. "Can you imagine four years of life being told in a few hours?" she questions.

"Now at night when I sleep I am running, trying to hide my children. In my mind I go through more than you can put on paper.

"More hell I don't think anyone can endure. When I awaken in the morning and realize that I am still alive, I feel it is a miracle." ❖

Esther's husband, Charles, of blessed memory, has a story in this book. Esther's complete story can be found in her book, "Feeling Guilty – A Survivor's Story," by Esther Goldman and Barbara Brantley Bailey.

Esther Goldman died December 14, 2001, prior to the publication of this book.

Lauren, Todd and Tova

Photo right - Esther and Tova

Photo below - Esther and her grandson, Todd, light candles at Yom Hashoah

Photo by Betsy Karotkin

A Cast Off From a Society Which Had Gone Mad
STEFAN GRUNWALD

By Reba Karp

There are times when STEFAN GRUNWALD'S mind refuses to remember. It is during these rare intervals that he is aware that there are pieces of him left over, the ragged edges to his psyche that he has tried to discard. But they are part of him and won't let go.

He looks back now, and not in any attempt to overlook the past which could take its title from Rembaud's "Season in Hell," because for Grunwald it was a "Childhood in Hell."

It wasn't that he didn't have any toys, for they are not necessary for growth; it wasn't that he didn't have enough to eat, for obviously the human body has the capacity to survive on very little; it wasn't that he had no home, for any shelter could be considered a roof over one's head, nor was it the fact that he had no shoes, for he still had two feet.

What seems to bother him the most now, was that he had no dignity. As a cast off from a society which had gone mad, Stefan was a "Jew boy," and as such wasn't entitled to dignity.

Stefan Grunwald

Photo by Stephen Jay Photography

He was born in Berlin in 1933. His father was a psychiatrist, art expert and journalist. The latter would lead him to being tortured for writing anti-Nazi tracts and protecting political activists.

Before the attempted genocide, his family was intellectual and secure. He was named after a friend of his father's, Stefan Zweig, an Austrian writer, who committed suicide in Brazil with his wife in 1943. Grunwald attributes it to despair and inability to live in Brazil as the Nazis seemingly began to take over the world. "He was a writer out of order," in a world that had no order.

Grunwald's records show that his flight into his "hell" began in 1934. In order to avoid the Nazi vise which was closing in on all Jews, his parents moved in with his grandmother in upper Silesia, which at the time was on the Eastern border of Germany. "My grandparents owned the second largest cement factory in Germany. Their name was Loewe, it was my mother's family." When forced to run again, his grandmother Irma Loewe stayed behind to try and liquidate the family's holdings. "She stayed until it was too late." In 1941 she was transported to Buchenwald and his father, the liberal journalist, was condemned to death in absentia.

But Stefan and his parents had elected to run, to enter a race for survival that would take them to Vienna, to Italy, and finally a pseudo-haven in Switzerland. But while hop-scotching from one torturous experience to another, the one common denominator, beside the hunger and degradation, was the persecution simply because they were Jewish – and this persecution preceded the arrival of the Germans, from whom they managed to stay one step ahead.

From upper Silesia, Stefan and his mother stopped briefly in Vienna. His father had gone ahead to Italy. They planned to join him later, when he had made preparations for their arrival. But they could not wait for his preparations. In the middle of the night, there was a knock on the door. It was no longer safe for them in Vienna. They would have to leave immediately.

Stefan was only three, but images from that train ride return. His mother, Ruth, who looked Italian, kept speaking Italian to him. He was confused. She was extremely anxious and when any one opened the door to their compartment, she made herself look busy in an effort to conceal her inner turmoil.

In her haste to leave Vienna, she packed what she could. But in her hurry to be reunited with her husband, she left all her belongings on the train. Their search for housing was hampered by the alliance between Germany and Italy which had grown stronger. They settled in the city of Sestri-Levanti, in cramped quarters. Their goal was to eventually cross the border into Switzerland, and to this end, his father Michael made frequent trips back and forth, seeking

refuge for his family. Finally, he found lodging for the family in the home of a farmer where they hoped to "sit out the war." But the Swiss closed the border to legal refugees before they could leave.

Boxed in, they remained in Sestri until 1939, when they had to flee once again. This time it was to a refuge in the Italian mountains. But it was only a brief respite, for the Italian farmer who took them in became frightened for his own safety and put them out.

A gray automobile drives out of his past. He can still see it and hear his mother crying. The year was 1940 and the car was driven by the Gestapo who picked up his father and took him to Genoa, where he was questioned about the Italian resistance. After two days of interrogation and torture, his father returned, only to be taken away again.

Ten days later he was released, this time at the intervention of a very old Italian family, who had enough ties in Genoa to "put pressure on the Germans."

But there were strings attached to his release this time. The Germans wanted him to spy on the resistance. He had 11 days to make up his mind. His decision was immediate. Once more they fled, literally leaving everything behind.

A former educator (he taught at Old Dominion University in Norfolk, Virginia), Grunwald has a philosophical nature that is stoic, yet not severe enough to lack humor, for he distinguishes his life after Sestri as the time "when the bad things began," and perhaps all that came before could be by comparison, considered "good."

As the Germans moved nearer, they were placed in an Italian detention camp outside of Sondrio, where they were lodged in what appeared to be an empty apartment building, with no lights, no heat and no facilities. "We had to drag straw in for sleeping. There was no food, no water, no clothing and no communication with the outside." What food they had was begged from neighboring farmers, but their diet for the most part consisted of bark from trees, which they boiled for tea, and their days were spent foraging for twigs to burn for warmth.

Only the children were permitted outside the compound and this was to beg for food. However, Grunwald remembers that hunger was not his only adversary. Older Italian children thought him easy prey for their pent-up anger and frustrations and caught him and beat upon him.

The Allies enter Italy. *Photo by Hugo Horvath*

Begging for food and running from bigger and stronger peers are only torn fragments from his childhood. He witnessed suicides, heart attacks, death by starvation and disease and the weeping and shrieking of those going insane.

"These were people who before had never been in a hostile environment." Aside from the lack of physical necessities, there was the psychological torture of waiting. "The constant threat of being taken across the border to Germany. Some couldn't handle it any longer."

Grunwald dates his "liberation" from the detention camp in the spring of 1942. This, he attributes to his father's friendship with the Mayor of Milan, who arranged a short stay for them in a cold room above a railroad station. Then they moved to an abandoned apartment building in Colico, with no facilities and no window glass. The family survived on a meager salary his father made by teaching French, Italian and German. To supplement his father's income, "I started stealing."

It was 1942. School was only an illusion, for as soon as he walked into class, the teacher made excuses to send him elsewhere. "She was determined to keep me out of the classroom."

If life was cheap, it was also precious – and he and his parents were reminded of this when German soldiers fired into their apartment. "The Germans only left because they were sure they had killed us. We survived by lying flat on the floor. It's the psychological factors that stick in the mind," he said, explaining that although they were living in a community, they were totally isolated. By 1943, the Germans were in Colico and as a consequence, the Grunwalds were only permitted to be the living dead. "We had no food and we were living in a town where food was available. The Italians were hypocrites. We were the token Jews. Their intention was starvation. We were given no jobs … their technique was to kill us by starvation." At one time their diet consisted of stray dogs, cats and squirrels.

"I'd get up in the morning, starved. I began the day looking for food. I'd go to school, come home at noon and still no food; back to school and then back home to no food."

His father joined the resistance and as a consequence was told to leave the community. It was early 1943. "The police came to the door and said 'out!'" We were not allowed to take anything. We were told to be out of the community in a half hour.

"We wandered the mountain for an hour. … We found a cave. We ate chestnuts." Eventually they joined up with a multi-national band which had formed a mini-resistance, a band of displaced people.

"Now the weapons began to come in … the children stole them from German tanks and trucks." The Germans, at this time, had totally taken over the

The memory of that time is "hunger, hunger and cold. No school and, of course, total chaos."

adjoining countryside. "They went into the best houses, took over the railroad."

The memory of that time is "hunger, hunger and cold. No school and, of course, total chaos." Sleep was frequently interrupted by the warning, "The Germans are coming!" Then it was a mad scramble to get up in to the mountains to hide. When the threat subsided, they returned, upset by the police. "I had no peace, there was constant mental anguish. A child needs routine. You eat dogs and cats which is totally against the child. You become ready to lie. Reality and unreality are the same," he said.

Even friendships were illusions in reality. Real before the shot was fired;

a fragment from a nightmare afterwards. He remembers just such an incident. He had come down from the mountain with a friend to sabotage a German truck. A round of fire came at them. His friend was hit and fell at his feet as he started to run back up the mountain. More shots, shouts, a spotlight followed him. Two hours later as he lay exhausted, the cry "Germans!" forced him from his fitful sleep to run once more from the Germans. It was unreal.

Pressure from the German army increased during July and August of 1943. The refugees were forced to move deeper into the mountains to avoid being captured. "My parents started talking about leaving Italy. Suddenly there was money for a guide into Switzerland. They spent the night talking. Later the guide was shot. My father had already given him money."

In desperation they persisted. Another guide. Another set of instructions. Grunwald remembers them well. "We walked up the mountain. We were later picked up by an automobile … we weaved in and out of skirmishes with the Germans. We were dropped off at a stable. Down in the valley was a half frozen river, snow was on the ground. At 9:30 in the night, the guide signaled us to go down in the valley." Once in the valley, a German patrol came by and they were forced to jump into the cold river. "Funny, how you remember," he continued. "I can still see the German patrol walking by; I can hear them talk, see their weapons. I can still smell the smoke (from cigarettes) wafting over."

When the danger abated, they pulled themselves from the water. But another patrol came by and they were forced once more into the frigid water. My mother hurt herself and my father was having a kidney attack. The fear now was of being overheard."

Eventually they reached the barbed wire which separated Italy from Switzerland. The guide handed his father a pair of wire cutters and ran away. They were on their own now and there was no turning back. But there was more to getting through than cutting the wire, for the wires were laden with bells and any attempt to tamper with them would sound the bells and alert the Germans.

His father snipped the wire and they hurriedly crawled under, scratching and scrambling for safety as the now alerted Germans descended upon them. "We had to climb a steep hill. I have since been back and I don't see how we made it. My father got shot in the leg and my mother tried to pull him up the hill. At that point, the Swiss border guards intervened and helped pull him up. It was an incredible scene."

That was October 3, 1943. On October 6 or 7, the Swiss refused to assist any more escaping refugees. "We had a suitcase of meager belongings and as we scrambled up the hill, it opened up and all the contents fell out. We entered Switzerland with nothing."

His father was taken to a hospital and he and his mother to a schoolhouse. "I was given my first hot chocolate.… I can still smell it, feel that cup in my hands. We were given blankets, they were the first in a long time. We didn't see my father for five days. My mother and I were taken to a Swiss reception camp."

The war was not over for Grunwald. The brief sojourn in the schoolhouse was only the eye of his storm, for afterwards would dawn what he describes as "the worst period of my life as a Jew boy." What made him different? he questioned. He felt like everyone else.

"The underpinning is, you are experiencing being Jewish on the front line! Never has being a Jew come as close to me as then. Young people don't run any more. After liberation, for 20, 30 years all I did was run. Running in Jewish people is a pathological factor," he said, drawing from Joseph Roth, a Jewish writer. "The difference between fear and anxiety is for fear, you see the danger; anxiety is hidden. All I've been doing for the last 40 years is running."

Shortly after the schoolhouse encounter, his mind rebelled. It simply could not accept anymore cruelty because he was Jewish. "The most astonishing thing happened. I blanked out for three months. The next thing I realized I was in Basel. I don't remember getting there. I was living with a Swiss Christian doctor. He was a sympathizer

TO MY BABA

I met you only once; you were on flight from Europe to these shores.

Of the most precious things you took along were two white pillows with which you and your husband had started many years of marriage.
Aside from that I knew you not.

However, like echoes from the past through your daughter, Irma, and granddaughter, Ruth, my mother, come aspects of yourself that shaped my life in many ways: kindness and empathy; strength and conviction; a life centered in family, friends and children; good cheer and humor in times of hardship; caution in days of brightness.

A tough woman you must have been, because your lineage does reflect that down to me.

All those aspects, no doubt, will make survivors of my children, too.

Baba, Baba, no sweeter words we have except perhaps for Mama, Mama dear.

Stefan Grunwald

with the plight of the Jews. My mother and father were put in a Swiss detention camp."

Now when he rationalizes about the blackout, he feels it was not only related to the anxiety which preceded it, but also to the fact that for the first time in his life, he had been separated from his parents. "I had always been with my mother. Maybe I protected myself by going blank."

It was January, 1944. But for a child returning from a long sleep, it was meaningless. "The doctor and his wife had two children who had been killed two months apart. They were about my age. The wife kept their ashes in urns in a semi-darkened room with flowers. Periodically. I was expected to go in and pray. I did that once or twice and then refused."

His punishment was deprivation once again. "Here I was in a house with everything, but I was deprived. The good doctor was seldom home." Grunwald's days were spent trying to get back into the house, if he was out; or trying to get out, if he was inside.

"The biggest mistake the Swiss made was putting children into homes without first checking them out," he said.

But Grunwald must seek a balance and goes within his memories and finds more pleasant thoughts. Two families had treated him humanely; one was a curator of a museum who eventually

procured a job for his father and the other was a Swiss Jewish family.

A ragged edge of his memories protrudes as he recalls the complication and disorientation he experienced when he had the opportunity to visit his family in the detention camp. His mother was pregnant, there were no facilities and the diet was rudimentary. "It was depressing to be there." But he was ready for a new home. His stay

"*From my viewpoint, the Jews of America saved my life.*"

with the Swiss doctor was over, and his trip from the home of the doctor to the museum director was both physically and psychologically painful. The latter was caused by the badge he was wearing which labeled him, "Juden Kind," which he explains did not carry the same connotations as it did in Nazi Germany. Nevertheless, he tore it off.

The physical discomfort was caused by wearing shoes that were too small, too narrow and with holes in the bottom.

"I was in constant agony. I often called these shoes the 'concentration camp for my feet.' I had two choices, either wear the shoes or go barefoot." It was winter and the alternative was just as painful. "I had a pair of socks and it was full of holes."

His stay at the home of Herr Simonett, the museum director in Brugg, was a pleasant respite, but it did not last long as the Swiss families only committed themselves for limited periods.

He was next assigned to a family who had four children of their own, a period labeled, a "living hell." Conditions in their quarters were cramped, and the "mother was an absolute Hitler in terms of her attitude toward children," he said. Little things annoyed her, such as a child neglecting to wash his hands after going to the bathroom. "She would beat the hell out of you," Grunwald said.

It was winter of '44 - '45 and except for his stay with the Simonett family, he had missed the perimeters of even the most limited childhood. It was cold. He had to go to school without warm clothing. "I had to walk to school without decent shoes. I caught pneumonia. They let my father out of the detention camp to visit me. I told him all I wanted was to get to a warm place and stay with him." At this point, Grunwald had not even seen a doctor.

Later his condition grew more severe and he was finally taken to the hospital.

Now greatly concerned over his son's well-being, the elder Grunwald was able to get his son removed to another home, this time with a Jewish family, the Haarpuders, an older couple.

It was yet another pleasant respite from a childhood of running, fear and disorder. Then, in 1945 the Grunwalds managed to become a family again, and the three of them and Stefan's new brother, Thomas, moved into quarters at a hotel. His father was given a temporary job in the museum. But it was a long time before Grunwald could escape from the limitations of his childhood, for even as his life tried to normalize itself, he was reminded that he was a refugee and "a Jew boy." Among the most painful and persistent incidents throughout his childhood in Switzerland was the taunting by his schoolmates, encouraged by the children of the family whom he had lived with temporarily. Grunwald reasons that this was prompted by the anger they felt, "the certain shame and element of failure" attached to a refugee being removed from their home.

Then, too, until the war ended, they had to endure "the incredible fear and anxiety" of the constant threat of being extradited back to Germany. "You had to get permission to remain from one month to another."

Grunwald lived in Switzerland until 1953 when he came to New York. His father died in Switzerland in 1957; his mother, in 1967. He has two brothers living in Switzerland, one a psychologist and the other, a specialist in repairing antique clocks. Grunwald served in the U.S. Army from '54 - '56 and received his Ph.D. from the University of Colorado in 1965. In 1968 he was called to Norfolk by the chairman of Old Dominion University for a visiting professorship and stayed until 1979 when he left for a career as a publisher.

Today he puts his life in order as a former academician and as a publisher, for he is now seeking new ways to turn his suppressed anxiety and fears into creativity.

Caring for other Jews is important, for from a "totally screwed up beginning in New York," he was able to put things in order with the help of a family he calls "absolute Jews."

"They were the first people who took me in. Shabbat appealed to me. Suddenly I was made to feel like a *mensch*. It was an important factor in my life. I fell from some kind of hell into a Jewish cushion."

"From my viewpoint, the Jews of America saved my life." Nightmares are rare now; running away, flights of the past. From the hungry child with no shoes on the cold, cobblestone streets of Italy and Switzerland, he views himself as the emerging "*Yiddisha Mensch*," one who insists on human rights, dignity and security for himself as well as for others. ❖

"Shabbat Shalom" by MaryAnne Katz

Reprinted from Yom Hashoah supplement, April 1984, published by the United Jewish Federation of Tidewater.

DEVORAH GUTTERMAN is a small quiet woman. Her gentle outward appearance is in conflict with the turmoil within, for the memories of man's inhumanity to man are her constant companions, memories of atrocities which won't fade and diminish with the passing of time.

"Why?" she questions softly as she begins to recall the years she was forced to live under the sentence of death – from 1939 when war became imminent in Poland until the culmination of World War II in 1945.

Her experiences were uniquely horrible, for she was on the outside, looking into the barbed wires of the concentration camps, living on forged Polish papers which made every Pole her potential enemy. "When the Gestapo would walk by me, they weren't looking me in the face to see if they could detect any signs of my being Jewish. But not so with the Polish people," she said.

Before the war Devorah lived with her family in a small Polish village of Wislica. "My family was very religious. My father was a Chasid; 'davening' was the biggest honor to him," she said, explaining that her home was frequently the scene of happy religious activity. On Simchas Torah, the men would march in prayer with the Torahs from the shul to their home where food and merriment awaited them.

Her family was wealthy by the standards of the day, she recalls, dealing in

Forged Papers and Chutzpah Her Lifeline
Devorah Gutterman

By Reba Karp

Devorah Gutterman

Photo by Stephen Jay Photography

wholesale and retail leather goods. But they shared with those less fortunate.

"My father would lend money without interest," she said, explaining that it was the custom among the village poor to pick up their stipend of money from her father after Shabbat each week. With this money, they would bargain during the week, buying food and paying back other debts. Then on Friday night, just prior to Shabbat, they paid her father, with the loan cycle resuming again Saturday after Shabbat. The underlying reason behind what appears to be a complicated lending system was basically simple – "so the people would not feel they were recipients of charity," she said. (Maimonides' highest degree of charity is to aid the poor by giving them a loan or job so that they can adequately support themselves.)

Additionally, she recalls with special pride "pushkas" for many yeshivas bursting with coins in their home. "My mother knew when someone was sick in the village and would fill containers of food before each meal for those in need. These she would deliver before she sat down for her food."

Another memory, that of an old woman who was paralyzed and who was forced

to live with her impoverished daughter and grandchildren fills her thoughts. "My mother organized the neighbors to bring food to her family. Our day was Wednesday," she said, recalling how she would carry the basket to the family so that all could eat.

Devorah treasures these and similar memories of her family, rich in Jewish ritual and charity. Then other memories take over and she is forced to question why people so good and pious were allowed to suffer. "It seems so strange," she said. "It is as if I went to sleep surrounded by my large family and when I woke up five years later, there was no one left." (Her oldest brother, Pinchas, survived Auschwitz and moved to Australia.)

But it was not the sleep of relief. She experienced, rather, the nightmare of five years of the Holocaust.

She dates the beginning of her personal struggle with the war as occurring on Friday evening, September 1, 1939. At the time she was married and pregnant with her eldest daughter, Sheila, and living with her husband in Sosnowiec, where he owned and operated a flour mill. Since they were not far from the German border, by Saturday morning, everyone was in a panic … "burning papers and money they didn't want to fall into German hands." Fearful of an immediate attack from the Germans, they fled with other family members to Wislica to be with her parents. They tried to reach their destination by train,

but the tracks were hemmed in by the approaching war. "For miles and miles, nothing moved. We couldn't leave the train until daylight at which time we began to walk … We lost contact with some members of the family along the way. There were crowds of people running. We didn't know where we were running."

However, sanctuary was not to be found at Wislica. They discovered that Devorah's brothers and father had sought refuge in the village of Lublin. They followed them, hoping that the extra miles between them and the Germans would offer them relative safety.

It was not to be. "We never arrived in Lublin. We found out along the way that the Germans were already there and," her eyes grow misty, "we realized that we couldn't run away. We returned to Wislica."

The journey by foot from Sosnowiec to Wislica and toward Lublin and finally back to Wislica was a trial of survival and endurance. They were frequently without food and water. They slept outside and huddled together in the field. "Money was worthless," she said. That they survived at all was due to chance encounters with open Polish farms where they found raw potatoes and carrots in the fields. Other food the farmers hoarded for themselves.

After their return from their futile trek toward Lublin, they spent a few days in

Wislica, a time of fear and uncertainty." Although we had mixed feelings and fears and expected bad times, we didn't think there would be gas chambers."

And so the little band of refugees, armed with the indomitable Jewish spirit for survival, decided to return to Sosnowiec and the fate that awaited them there. They hired the services of a Polish farmer who took them halfway to their destination and then forced them out of his wagon.

"He threw us out … we had to walk the rest of the way," a journey made more difficult by the presence of her brother's two children. Once at Sosnowiec, they found their worst fears realized. The Germans had put locks on her husband's flour mill, and to remove them would have brought an immediate death sentence.

"They took everything. My husband's partner, who had remained behind, had managed to get out a couple of sacks of flour, which were like sacks of gold. We found a baker to make bread and we bartered for other food."

And then they waited – through the uncertainties of the day and the fears of the night – for their unknown future to catch up with them.

It did, in the form of a note posted several weeks later, that all Jewish men had to report to Gestapo headquarters. Black letters upon white paper spelling death. So they sought to escape once more.

"The *Judenrat* were on the watch for those seeking to get out of town." But the family had a plan. "I went first, giving prepared signs and signals to my husband and brother when I saw a member of the *Judenrat* approaching," she said.

Around each corner – fear; across each street – the enemy. To those seeing the young Jewish woman on the street, she was merely on an errand. At times she had to nod to those passing, hoping they could not detect her fearful

She views her life then as a series of knots tied together, each needing the one preceding it in order for it to be tied, and each part of her ragged lifeline to survival.

heartbeat, nor the frightened figures who followed close behind her.

"We made it to the train stop and boarded for Remdcin where the order for Jewish men to report to the Gestapo had not yet been issued," she recalled.

They sat huddled in fear. The train stopped at stations along the way and German soldiers boarded to give the brutal order: "Jews out!"

"The sound of his voice was so thunderous … I didn't just get up, I was picked up by the voice and forced out."

They walked the rest of the way and stayed with relatives in Remdcin until her husband and brother left for Wislica to join her parents once again.

Her destination – the only choice left – return to Sosnowiec. "How could I just leave everything? We were hoping that things would calm down and we could start life again."

However, that was not meant to be. As the war closed in on her in 1940, she rejoined her husband. "Life was very difficult, even though we always had enough to eat." Although it was a death sentence to do so, her family was still selling leather goods they had managed to hide. If the Poles who bought the merchandise wanted to report them, they all would have been shot. "The Jewish people were not only surrounded by German murderers, but by Polish murderers as well."

She views her life then as a series of knots tied together, each needing the one preceding it in order for it to be tied, and each a part of her ragged lifeline to survival. "There was no smartness involved – things just happened. I never knew what to do, but I had to do something – and by chance it often turned out to be right," she said.

"We lived in a shtetl which had been converted into a ghetto. Cross over the bridge and be shot, unless you had permission from the Gestapo. We lived in fear, subjected to searches and other humiliations."

Resignation, coupled with the Jewish determination to survive, settled in until 1942 when it became apparent that the Germans were systematically liquidating the ghettos. "Knowing our days were numbered, we planned ahead. My parents and husband were hidden underground by a farmer. Since I had a baby, it would have been virtually impossible to join them. Because I didn't look Jewish I was able to obtain forged Polish papers through the underground for myself and my baby." She became a woman without a past, present or future, seeking sanctuary and lodging at whatever door fate led her. Many doors opened and many doors closed, and for a short while she lived with a Jewish family in Dcialoseyce until the Germans started liquidating the Jews in the town for a second time.

She fled once more into uncertainties with only the address of a woman in Jedenjuw who "might be willing to help her." "I caught a train with my little girl, not knowing where I was going. It was toward the end of September. Winter started very early that year. The train was full. I was standing on the platform between two cars.

"It was cold. I asked permission to get my little girl in the doorway so she could be a little warmer. I was still on the outside. Someone recognized my voice, even in the dark, and threatened to turn me in to the Germans at the next stop. After all, I was Jewish and had no right to live."

The train continued on its journey into the dark. She held onto her child, unable to feel the motion of the train or the emerging winter cold … now only conscious of fear and the desire to live.

She quickly lost herself and her child in the crowd that departed from the train and wisely decided not to go into the train station, even though it would have offered her a buffer against the cold. "I remained outside until another train came. If I had gone into the station and the woman who threatened had seen me, I don't know what would have happened."

When she finally found her way to the house in Jedenjuw, the woman was hesitant about letting her in. Devorah edged closer to the door, lest it be closed. Where else had she to go?

"Miraculously there was another Jewish man hiding in the house and he pulled me in." But her sanctuary was to be short-lived, for she was to remain in the house for only a month before she was told she would have to leave. Forced out among uncaring strangers again, she moved in with another Polish farmer who was in need of money. "The farmer was poor; he sold me a loaf of bread and a bucket of potatoes." this was to last her for the month. "I didn't eat the bread. My baby needed nourishment."

Here she was fortunate enough to be befriended by the farmer's daughter who taught her Polish expressions, mannerisms and Catholic prayers. "How to behave if I had to go to church to save myself."

The daughter of the farmer was among the more educated Poles and tried to treat Devorah as a fellow human being and even offered her extra food, such as noodles with bacon grease. "I really wanted to eat it," she said. "But I could not eat the grease."

This respite from the outside ended abruptly as the Germans began to take a census among those living on the farms. "The family was afraid and I was told to leave." But the farmer's daughter had made a contribution toward her survival.

Once again she packed her simple belongings, took her child by the hand and stepped out into the unknown.

Since she was left with no other choice, she returned to Jedenjuw and found a room across the street from where the Jewish man, who had originally befriended her, now lived with other Jewish refugees. It was January, 1943. The temperature was around 15 degrees below zero and her unheated room had a window with two or three missing panes.

During the day she sought the warmth of the house across the street, with the other Jews waiting for the Gestapo to catch up with them. But at night she had to return to her own room in fear of a surprise "liquidation" raid on the house. Somehow many of these occurred at night, as if the Germans, themselves, were ashamed of their actions and sought anonymity of the dark.

Her room had been rented to her by a Polish doctor, who, subsequently, risked his life to register her in city hall as a Polish woman. Then, with her forged Polish papers and "chutzpah" she applied for an apartment as a Polish citizen. "I knew I couldn't stay where I was indefinitely for the neighbors could not help but see me leave the house each night and return to my room. We were living in what had formerly been a Jewish ghetto and was now occupied by other Poles."

Devorah was a woman alone in a hostile world. Everyone was her enemy. The Poles sought the Jews out and turned in those the Germans couldn't recognize.

Unknown faces in any Polish community aroused suspicion, and those who didn't speak perfect Polish were systematically turned in by their neighbors.

She lived in constant fear, on guard for any gestures which might arouse suspicion and was alert to signals of danger that would send her seeking another refuge. "Fortunately I spoke good Polish. I had to give the image of being a Pole.

"When you live in fear, your mind gets more active. The human mind gets strong from fear; it builds resistance to death. Yet, I was convinced that I wouldn't survive. My only prayer was that the bullet would come from behind."

Nonetheless, survival became the challenge, if only for the sake of her child. She obtained another apartment with her forged Polish papers and with the help of the American money she was systematically receiving from her parents who were still hiding in an underground shelter on a Polish farm. It was February, 1943 and another Jewish woman living on forged Polish

papers moved in with her. Her name was Marie, and although she offered Devorah companionship, she made it more difficult for them to blend in with the Poles, for she spoke very little Polish and was not familiar with their customs and traditions.

As a camouflage, she put crucifixes upon her apartment walls and went to church every Sunday. (Despite the hatred exhibited by the majority of Poles, she feels that every Jew who did survive, did so with the help from those who were more humane.) "There was much jealousy from the Poles, for many Jews before the war were considered wealthy. There was an old saying, 'The streets are Polish; but the buildings are Jewish.'"

She taught her daughter. Sheila, Catholic prayers and reared her as Catholic. "I put a cap tightly on her head to cover her dark curly hair … I went out as little as possible, mainly to church or to buy meager rations … I was pretending I was no different from the others in the neighborhood."

Her mind stretched beyond the day. "I had to think ahead, of what would happen to Sheila if I had to run. I couldn't go to my parents because I couldn't live in such a place with a small child." So, in preparation for an emergency, she rented a room in Kielce. It was not much. It was located in the area of a former ghetto. Water was running down the walls and those who lived in the area were the "lowest class of Poles." But in spite of its condition, it was to be a haven for her and her child.

She feels she is alive today because her parents managed to save some American money which they had hidden in the attic of their former home. It was later taken out of its hiding place by her brother, who, at great risk to himself, returned to the house and bargained with the Polish family living there. In exchange for the money, he told them where the family had hidden some leather goods.

"Of course they could have killed him and had both," she said.

The transfer of money from Devorah's parents to her was an elaborate and risky plan, but it worked. At regular intervals, her parents would send her an item of clothing with the farmer. Sewn into the garment would be a dollar or two, "which by Polish standards was worth a fortune." She would take the American money to a flour miller and exchange it for Polish money.

The American money the farmer brought kept Devorah alive and the Polish money she gave him before he returned to his farm, kept her parents alive. "If the farmer knew they had American money with them, he would have killed my family. It was very complicated and at any step along the way, all could be lost."

In thinking back she rationalizes now that this was another reason that she fought so hard to survive. She was her family's link to survival. "They depended upon me."

There was no laughter in Devorah's life; only tears and the absence of tears. At times when tears were not enough to relieve her suffering, she sought to inflict pain upon herself. Such was the case when the farmer brought her the news that her brother was dead. "I tore the skin from my face."

She learned a costly lesson, when in a moment of utter despair, she said *"oy vey"* out loud in a public situation. Shortly after the utterance, she saw someone walk quickly back to the house.

It wasn't long before she was visited by two Polish policemen. "I bluffed my way, acted calm. They still wanted to take away my forged Polish papers," she said. After they left, taking her papers with them, she asked help from a former Polish pharmacist. It was a desperate move – but surely the war would end soon – all she needed was a little more time.

My Mother

Like Jacob our father,
my mother Chasia ("God spares")
found a stone for lack of a pillow
as she too experienced flight
in a night of terror,
pursued by Edomites-Germans who
begrudged the survival of Jacob's
descendants.

But unlike Jacob she would not
return home, to vanquished Poland.
Yet the angels that promised to
sustain her were, no doubt, the ones
from his ladder who guided her
safely to the ancestral homeland.

Rabbi Israel Zoberman

He interceded for her before the police had time to check on the paper's authenticity and after a convincing argument, the papers were returned to her. "He told the police I was a very religious Catholic and since the next day was Easter Sunday, I would need the papers in order to go to church." (The papers were identification when being stopped by Gestapo or the Polish police. No one ventured out without them.)

Once again she was forced to flee, this time back to the woman who had taught her Polish habits. However, she was only allowed to stay there two or three days. But even 48 hours can seem like a lifetime to someone who has nowhere to go. In desperation she contacted other Jewish people whom she knew were in hiding and asked them for help. One suggested that she take her child and go to a health resort area in the mountains, for it was a region which attracted people from other countries who came seeking physical rejuvenation. He felt the international atmosphere would be conducive toward hiding them.

She walked away, trying to put things into perspective. Her thoughts were racing to keep pace with her pulse. How long had she been running? How much more could her body endure before the pressures of the uncertainties tore it apart?

First things first. She needed to get to the health resort in order to find a room before moving Sheila and the only route was a train from Crakow. She hesitated. It was a dangerous route.

In the morning she caught the train. When she arrived at her destination, everything was closed – like a resort area out-of-season. "My mind was racing. I had made the trip for nothing." Once again, the familiar problem. "Where to spend the night?"

She took a chance and approached a house. A young woman with a child answered the door. "I told her a story, about looking for a place to live with my sick child and that I needed a place to spend the evening. I was a good actress. I played with and hugged her child. I later put the child to sleep and helped her say prayers.

"The woman offered me a place to stay with Sheila. I told her I would be back. But I didn't return. I was afraid to be so far from my parents. I had the feeling I had to keep my family under my wing."

She had a lot to think about on her return trip to Crakow. How much farther had she to travel before she found peace? At the Jedrzejow train station she saw the same policeman who had visited her apartment and took away her identification papers earlier. Instinct dictated that she avoid another encounter. "I pressed myself up against the wall until he left and I stayed that way. I didn't know when he would return and I didn't know what to expect."

All was not lost, however. She still had her ace; the room she had rented months before in the ghetto in Kielce.

When they arrived, even its impoverished conditions seemed as a haven for the three refugees. They were off the streets. "I tried to improvise some furnishings – crosses, Jesus and Mary. I turned a tub upside down for a table, put a blanket over a board to make it look like a bed. We slept on the floor." It would have been dangerous for the neighbors to think they had arrived with nothing – it could only mean they were running away from something.

So they settled in their room of fear until another harmless incident made her vulnerable once more.

"Sheila was playing with some children. They asked her if she was Jewish. The child didn't even understand what was being asked and replied, 'yes.'"

It wasn't long afterwards that she was visited by two Polish policemen. She tried to play her part again, but this time they were more clever and interrogated her and Marie in separate rooms and then compared notes.

Discrepancies were obvious.

Then, what must have been a pre-planned scenario unfolded. Devorah and Marie were not the only ones playing roles. One left, on the pretense of getting cigarettes, and the other allowed himself to be "hurriedly" bribed.

"We had to flee again. But where? I had no other place to go. Where could you run with a young child?"

The only option left was to put Sheila in a Catholic children's home, an involved and dangerous process. "It was an unbelievable task." It required permission from the Gestapo, permission she dared not ask for. She fabricated a story. Her husband was a German war prisoner and she had to work in order to support herself and the child, and, in order to work, she needed someone to take care of her child.

She visited many children's homes during the next few days and remembers that her feet were swollen from walking. But the response was always the same. She had to have permission from the Gestapo.

"I continued to look until I found a small home which had only about 100 to 150 children."

"I told the nun that I was starving. I cried. I spent a long time talking to her, and when I finished she told me that she didn't have the strength to tell me 'no,' that she would take my daughter without the Gestapo's permission, even though they would kill her on the spot if they found out."

However, the nun made the agreement conditional. "It was temporary. I had to take Sheila out in about eight days."

She arrived at the home as planned, with Sheila's personal belongings in one hand and the child, in a new dress, holding on to the other. Sheila was then three years old.

Her heart was heavy, for leaving a child crying and begging not to be left, was difficult. But she had no other choice. Still bargaining for time, she returned to the home around a month later and told another story, that her husband's family was too poor to take them in. "I

> *"I kept thinking that if I had a little more time, the war would soon be over."*

kept thinking that if I had a little more time, the war would soon be over."

At night, as she lay in fear awaiting the knock on her door, her thoughts were with the child she had to leave. She thought of the poor conditions, the lack of food. Sheila's diet at the home consisted of a thin slice of bread and a cup of black coffee in the morning. The main meal was cabbage with water, and again for the evening fare, Sheila got another thin slice of bread and cup of black coffee.

She visited her – when she dared. "One day I found her sick, weak, with sores all over her body. I went out, with great risk, and bought her butter and eggs … I aroused suspicion and was asked to take Sheila out of the home.

"I begged for a couple more days."

At this time Devorah had managed to find a place for herself by being the outside connection for Jews hiding in a chimney on a Polish farm. She threatened to leave them without that "connection" unless they helped her find a place for her child. "I didn't know what I was going to do," she remembered.

By chance, one of the Jewish men had had some business dealings with the priest before the war. "He wrote to the priest, told him I was a Jewish woman who had married a Catholic before the war and had converted, that the child had been born Catholic. He told the priest that my husband was a prisoner and the child had been asked to leave the home due to overcrowded conditions. He told him we would both die of hunger if this was allowed to happen."

The letter ended with the man begging the priest to go to the home and intercede for her child. When the letter was finished, Devorah was entrusted with a dangerous mission. She delivered the letter to the priest in person. If he had desired, he could have turned them all in to the Gestapo.

But he chose to help them and spoke to the nuns about the child. The conditions were limited. She was to take Sheila out of the home in a month. This time Devorah felt a little more at ease with the limitations. She knew that since the priest had requested asylum for the child even if she did not return for Sheila in the specified time, no harm would come to her.

"After that, I didn't see Sheila until we were liberated."

Living in fear for so long had made Devorah strong, but she had to be in order to make the decisions and to take the chances that she risked. One such incident led her to be jailed as a result of sleeping in the back of a wagon. This was during the interval when Sheila was in the home and she could not return to her room after "bribing" the Polish policemen. She had not yet moved in as the outside connection with those hiding on the farm.

Her crime was not so much that she spent the night in a wagon, but the suspicion that she was Jewish. After being forced to endure interrogation by the Gestapo, who "ruled" that she did not "look" Jewish, she was nonetheless put in a Polish jail with other women for the night. It was an evening of mental torture and hell. Her "cell" mates were hardened Polish women off the streets, who, suspecting she was Jewish, subjected her to the most inhumane mental abuse.

Devorah lights a candle at Yom Hashoah.
Photo by Betsy Karotkin

In the morning after she was subsequently released she made the decision to return to the jail on the pretense of picking up a package she had left. Her real motive was to see the women once more.

She picked up her package and looked into the cell at the women who were still locked up. When she was certain that all had seen her, a free woman, she said "goodbye," turned and left the jail. "I had to show them I was alive. This was worth a risk to my life."

Finally, liberation came. It was a long awaited moment which fell short of her expectations.

In seeking out her mother and father, she found only an empty underground excavation. "Six months earlier I would have still had my parents – six months later I wouldn't be here," she explained. When she was liberated her arms and legs were covered with blood blisters from not eating.

Devorah's husband did not survive the Holocaust. She remarried and with her second husband had two daughters and a son, who is a physician.

When I asked Devorah if she still has faith in God, she admitted the question has haunted her thoughts. The philosopher, Emil Fackenheim, in an article on "Kristallnacht" provided her with an answer. He noted that if the contemporary Jew turns his back on his faith, denies that which his ancestors voluntarily died for, then ... "Hitler will have won this war from the grave." ❖

Devorah died on December 30, 2001.

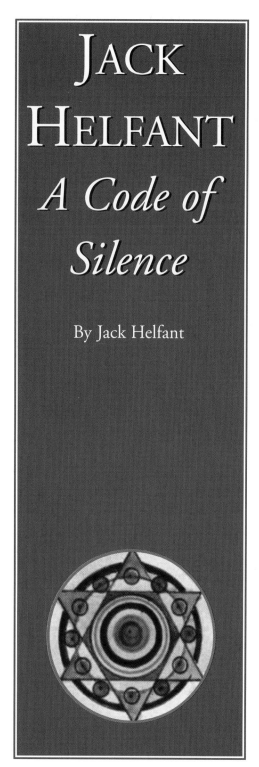

JACK HELFANT
A Code of Silence

By Jack Helfant

I was a T/4 (sergeant) with the 54th Signal Battalion, part of the 18th Airborne Corps. In April 1945, as the war in Europe was winding down, we were in a cleanup operation outside of Hagenau, Germany.

Four of us were called in to our C.O. and given instructions to proceed to a prisoner work camp and notify the occupants (prisoners) that the German guards had abandoned their camp and they were now free. We were told that the four of us were selected because we spoke several different languages in order to communicate with the prisoners. Mine were French and Yiddish. We were identified by the American flag on our left sleeves.

Entering the camp, it looked deserted; there were various types of buildings but no outside activity. Not knowing what would confront us, we entered the first building (actually one of a series of barracks). As we entered, we were faced with dozens of people clothed in striped uniforms; they were sitting, standing, lying down, kneeling and all of them were transfixed as if in an hypnotic trance. We then realized these were females of all ages. Initially we were not aware of the odor but later it became obvious – two of our guys had to step outside in order to catch their breath.

We spread out among them explaining, as best we could, that we were Americans (pointing to the flag) and they were no longer prisoners. They seemed to be totally in awe of us or completely dumbstruck by the change

We were identified by the American flag on our left sleeves.

Jack Helfant

Jack and his granddaughter, Jennifer.

Jack Helfant with some of his children and grandchildren, Bob Josephberg,
Joan Irvine, Jennifer Josephberg, Jaime Irvine, Rebecca Saunders and Sheila Josephberg.

in uniforms. None of us got any direct response; they were totally silent. As best we could, we explained to them that the civilian authorities would be there soon, relieve us and start the process for their freedom. Beyond the fixed hypnotized looks, the odor, the deplorable condition of the women, the four of us in patrolling the camp had seen sights that went beyond anything we saw in the war. It seemed to create a "code of silence" between us that remained with the four of us through December 1945 when we returned home. After we reported back to our commanding officer, he arranged tours for our battalion to view the prison.

To this day the horrible conditions we encountered remain mostly a blank; I still cannot bring many of the pictures back to my mind. ❖

American troops returning home, December of 1945, Norfolk, Virginia.

Photo by Hugo Horvath

Elie Wiesel writes in "One Generation After," a story of Just Men, an allegory, used to teach mankind the meaning of right and wrong, of good and evil. It is taken from the writings of the great Rabbis and many scholars share its simple wisdom in speeches, writings and conversations. I would like to tell you the story of one of the Just Men. "The Just Men" legend begins like this:

> *The Great Master was looking from the walls of Heaven to the Earth below. His face was sad, puzzled and angry. The angels surrounding the Great One were silent. What could have happened to create such an expression. No one moved. Finally, one angel came before the Great One and asked what was the matter. What was the cause of such emotion? Slowly, turning His face to the table of angels, the Great One spoke. "I created man so that life as we know it would have meaning, worth. I created man so that I could view the world and all of its goodness with happiness and contentment, knowing that all was well in my creation. Yet, today, when I look over the walls, I see nothing of the creature I made. I see only evil, hatred, violence and greed…. I see murder and avarice and hate…. I see destruction, and pollution and war … I see the innocents being murdered in the gas chambers created by man … I see nothing of the Good that I made … I will destroy the creation and begin again."*
>
> *All were silent. The world was doomed … but the smallest angel dared speak again. "But, Great Master, do you not see the good that is still there? Do you not see what is happening in Europe, even as we speak? Do you not see the Army of Patton, with the battalion of black soldiers sweeping into the chambers of horror and liberating the few that still have hope, life? Do you not see that evil is being destroyed even as we speak? That the evil that has run rampant for over 10 years is about to be conquered by the very thought of good and compassion that drove you to create man? Please, Great One, allow one more chance, take one more look … Do you not see?" …*
>
> *This is the story of Rev. Willie James Hilton, Liberator of Dachau and other camps. This is the story of all of the liberators who marched into the face of evil, and with good as their sword, vanquished the bad. Read and learn, read and honor. Read and never forget.*

The Legend of the Just
REVEREND WILLIE JAMES HILTON

By Barbara Brantley Bailey

WILLIE JAMES HILTON was born in Manning, South Carolina, on July 15, 1923. He was born into a poor, black family in a racist society, a society that showed little liberties to certain people, people of color. He began his walk to liberation on the day he was born, not knowing then that what he learned as he grew into a fine, young Black American, that the emotion he nurtured would carry him to the most racist place of all, that of Nazi Germany.

Because Willie's family was poor sharecroppers, people who didn't have much hope for a better future, Willie left at an early age of 15 years to try to find a better life. It was 1938 when he arrived in Hampton Roads, Virginia, determined to get an education and make a difference in his life and, unknowingly, the life of others less fortunate. When World War II broke out in Europe, Willie, like most Americans, didn't pay much attention to Hitler's armies as they conquered and destroyed. But, when Japan attacked the USA, Willie was upset. In May of

Rev. and Mrs. Willie James Hilton   *Photo by Betsy Karotkin*

1942, he was drafted out of Newport News, Virginia. America needed young, fighting men, and for once, color didn't matter.

Willie was inducted into Basic Training in Richmond, Virginia, and then sent to Wheeling, Georgia, to learn infantry skills that were needed to become a Combat Engineer. From Georgia, he was sent to Camp Shank, New York, finally ready to become what the U.S. Army deemed was a soldier, ready to fight. He disembarked from Camp Shank on June 5, 1943 and landed in France, joining with the 184th Battalion of Combat Engineers, under the leadership of Colonel Kellum.

This was a regiment of all Black soldiers, for in those days there were no such things as integrated groups of fighting men. Under Colonel Kellum's leadership, the 184th eventually merged with General George Patton's Third Army, somewhere in France and began joining the fight to push the Germans back into their own country. One of Willie's jobs included riding a tank with artillery firing power to protect the push of troops against the Germans.

Another of his jobs was to clear out mine fields with his bayonet. The mines had to be cleared so Patton's Third Army could keep pressure on the Germans and push them back to Berlin. Another job that the 184th group did was to build the first bridge across the Rhine, into the Rhineland. There were people dying all over the place because the Germans knew once a bridge was secured, Patton's army would come with full force.

Once the 184th made its way into Germany, the situation became worse. The Germans were defending their homeland, and after years of destroying others, they were about to get a taste of their own medicine. To quote Willie: "The Germans were mean, but we were meaner. When you captured a soldier, you had to keep your guard up, because he would drop his hand, draw a weapon you didn't know he had, and in a second, you would be a goner."

As the 184th moved deeper into Germany, the soldiers began to notice "this barb-wired place, with people who looked dead inside. The people were covered with lice, and sores, and had no human look. They were skeletons, walking around, most … not even moving. Some were close to buildings that were smoking, like they had been burned. They were starving to death. We learned they were Jews. We learned that they had been put in these places to kill, just to kill … ! They were not prisoners who were bad people, who had done crimes, they were just put there because they were Jews. We went inside the buildings that were left standing and saw horrible things … human heads in jars and skeletons in ovens. They were afraid of us, most of them had not seen a Black man, and they didn't know what we were going to do. They just sat there and stared at us.

"We found some Nazis and took them as prisoners. We couldn't believe what they had done. We were all Black men, and young, and all of us had seen some bad things in our lives in the U.S., but this was something that we had never seen. People being killed by the hundreds, by the thousands. There were dead bodies that looked like skeletons all over the place, and no children. They even killed the women. We saw women having babies in ditches and there was so much blood everywhere. What kind of people could do this? What kind of people would kill women in a war? And where were the children? We didn't see any. These Jews had no army to help them, to fight for them, so we did it. We couldn't stay and help for long, but we did what we could. We gave them some food, and some blankets and some soap. We tried to give them some medicine, but we didn't have much.

"The camp was named Dachau. And after that we saw more camps like this one, all so much alike, so much the same. Except the names. I can't remember all of the names. I wish I could remember. I fought the Germans even harder after that. I had seen some bad things against colored folks in the USA, but not like this. I couldn't believe that people could treat people so bad," he said.

As the 184th Battalion of Engineers moved towards Berlin, under the command of General George Patton, they saw more camps and did what they could to help. The most important thing became to win the war. But they treated the German soldiers they met with even more will to defeat them, to win.

Finally, on the orders of the European Commander, The Third Army stopped. We had reached Berlin, but were ordered out so the Russians could capture Berlin. "I was fortunate to have survived. I had seen things that no human should see. We got orders that our shells were falling on the Russians, so we pulled back," he added.

"I speak to groups and tell what I saw, what happened. A whole lot of things happened that aren't right, shouldn't have happened.... Sir, I know the truth, I was there!"

Willie James Hilton stayed in Germany and helped rebuild and relocate people after the fall of Europe. He was eventually sent to serve on the Pacific Front in Japan with the 133rd Battalion of Combat Engineers. He was in Okinawa when the bombs were dropped on Hiroshima and Nagasaki. He received an honorable discharge from the Army on January 18, 1946 and returned home to begin building a life, one that kept the promise of the Just Men.

The promise
"When the Great One saw that there were still honorable men and women trying to do the right thing, to teach justice and liberty and honor, He paused ... then He said ... I see, my little Angel, you are right. There ARE people who still care, who have honor and who fight injustice. I will refrain from my destruction as long as I see ONE "Just Man" on Earth, still working for the good of all. I will honor man, if he will honor Me by continuing to fight for all of humanity."
Reverend Willie James Hilton is one of these "Just Men." ❖

One of many bridges built by the Combat Engineers   *Photo by Hugo Horvath*

"You must be careful."

"Why?"

"They will get you. They are picking up people off the streets. Why do you have to go?"

"Don't worry, Daddy. I'll be fine."

Date and place: 1994, Norfolk, Virginia

Irving Igdal in Munich, 1946.

My father was IRVING IGDAL and he had been a self-employed grocer in Lambert's Point. Born in Shaki, Lithuania, he arrived in Norfolk in 1949. Prior to his death he had been retired for 20 years. His illness had

Irving Igdal   Photo by Betsy Karotkin

His Memories Consumed His Thoughts

Irving Igdal
Israel Igdalski

By Frieda Igdal

become noticeable during the late 1980s and as the disease of Alzheimer's progressed, my father seemed to spend more time in the ghetto and less time with us. There was no way for my mother, Ruth, and me to reason with him, so we would just assure him that all was well. When he was not verbalizing about his fears, he would collect little packets of food and other essentials to see us through hard times. In his mind's eye the time and place were the Kovno Ghetto in 1943.

Only five percent of Lithuanian Jewry survived the war. Most were destroyed in the three month span of July – September of 1941.

My father came from a large and vibrant family. The loss of them haunted him all the days of his life. Consequently, things were a little different when I was growing up. He would never tell me a fairy tale, so when I would ask Daddy to tell me a story, he would tell me a *Shakiah Misa* (a tale of his shtetl, Shaki).

Today I am thankful that I was obliged to listen to those tales, but at the time I longed for the stories that the American kids of my generation were being told. But, my father could not put his memories on a back shelf and they consumed his every thought. As the years passed, Shaki was always on his lips, and needless to say, in his heart. I was fortunate that, aside from the time before his death, the ghetto and camps were not the stories he shared with me. He always said that he was lucky, that someone was always looking out for him. He gave examples. There was the Nazi in Dachau who rubbed onions on his boils, a home remedy of sorts. There was the Gentile from his home

Irving Igdal's father, Alexander Igdalski.

Irving with family members before the war, most of whom perished in the Holocaust.

Chayna Igdalski (Irving Igdal's sister-in-law) and her daughter, Ruth. Chayna was shot during the "Death March." Her daughter, Ruth, was murdered in March 1944, during the Kinderaction in the ghetto.

The surviving Igdalski brothers after the war.

town who brought him news of his family and bread to the ghetto gates. He and his brother Dovid were never separated and remained side by side in the ghetto and at Dachau.

But he remembered vividly the screams of the mothers and fathers who had been out of the ghetto working and upon their return discovered that all the elderly and children had been taken away and killed. The wails of the mothers as all they had to hold onto were the shoes and clothes of their little ones echoed through his memories. Among the young victims were his seven-year-old niece and nephew (two first cousins) who reportedly went to their deaths, hand in hand.

Faigelkeh, my father's nanny, had married and had a family of her own. My father promised that as long as he had food, then Faigelkeh would not starve. But hunger was not what had killed her, for she and her family were murdered at the 9th fort in "The Great Action."

When the ghetto was liquidated, the survivors were taken to the Stutthof Kz Lager, where the men and women were separated, shaved, stripped-searched and thrown their uniforms. As the men were being taken away to Dachau, my dad spotted my mom, they were sweethearts, and screamed down, "If we live through this, wait for me!"

My father was lucky because at Dachau he was thrown a great warm coat that he managed to hold onto until the end of the war. When the war was nearing an end, madness reigned at Dachau. My uncle and father started walking. My father was very weak and he refused to walk any further. My uncle dragged him across a bridge and into the hands of Eisenhower's Army. The bridge was blown up as they crossed it.

My father was lucky. Many had it worse.

Despite his experiences in Dachau, it was the memories of his family that consumed him – he remembers his sister who came back from Israel so she could be with her father during the war. She was two months pregnant when she was forced to dig her own grave and

Irving Igdal and his daughter, Frieda.

Irving's Market, Norfolk, Virginia.

shot into it with her mother and sisters. The men of Shaki had been killed the same way two months before.

Other family memories were of his sister who was too weak to walk and was taken in a cart to her death, and of his two darling nieces who walked beside their mother's cart and died with her.

There was his sister who refused to turn her fur coat in to the Germans and she told them she would wear it until it was forcefully taken from her.

If the end is all the same, what the hell.

But it didn't begin that way for my father and his family as they had been very wealthy. My grandfather had a chain of stores specializing in fabrics and furs, consequently he was able to offer the best to his children. One uncle was a physician who was educated at the University of Bologna. One uncle had studied engineering in England. One aunt had studied piano in Switzerland and my father was heir to the business.

Hitler and Stalin had made a deal and the Baltic States fell victim. The Russians came in and nationalized all the businesses and as a consequence, many of the wealthy Jews were to be deported to Siberia. My grandfather, as well as others, bribed their way out of Siberia for his family and himself. Within days of their assigned time to have been transported to Siberia, the Nazis occupied Lithuania. I often wondered what would have happened

The Igdalski Family

if they had not bribed the communist officials, who would have survived Siberia? So many of the Baltic Jews were sent there.

And then there were the happy memories. My daddy traveled and knew many people who lived in Kovno. He would frequently talk about the beautiful Jewish lifestyle – Jewish theater and kosher bakeries and restaurants. Other memories included my father talking about winning some sort of dance contest in the 1930s in Czechoslovakia. My grandparents would go to Baden-Baden and Palanga to the baths on vacation.

But those memories were far away from the Holocaust and what ultimately happened to most of my father's family and the horror of their loss haunted him all the days of his life. ❖

Irving Igdal died in Norfolk in June of 1994. Irving's wife, Ruth Igdal, has a story in this book.

Irving Igdal, Mrs. Lida, Alex Bromberg, Szaja Lida, and Bluma Bromberg, (Ber Luftreiber in background) with other survivors in Washington D.C., 1983.

Ruth Igdal

Photo by Echard Wheeler

"We thought even the birds were afraid to come here ..."
Ruth Igdal – Survivor
Ruth Shapiro Igdalski

By Reba Karp

On June 21, 1941, RUTH SHAPIRO IGDAL left her home in Pokrojus, Lithuania to start a new job in Kovno, Lithuania. "I took the train Saturday evening, after Sabbath.

"It was a beautiful day," she said, perfect in every way to start a trip which would take her 400 miles from her native city. "It was a beautiful little city. My sister Anna had left six months before, I was going to join her. It was an easy feeling for me.

"Friends came to say goodbye. There was much laughter and crying," Ruth added, explaining that living in a small town had limited her possibilities of a job as a bookkeeper, as the Russians, who occupied the Baltic states at that time, gave the jobs to the poorer people.

Ruth adds that at the time, she did not feel threatened, despite the fact that the area was full of Jewish refugees fleeing from Hitler's advancing German troops. "The Jewish families took them in and gave them room and food. We loved them like brothers and sisters."

Ruth remembers she traveled through the night with other Jewish young men and women. It was a festive time. Not even her worst nightmares gave any indication of what lay before her.

She arrived in Kovno around 8 o'clock in the morning. Her sister and a friend, Rita Sands, also a survivor who died in Philadelphia in 2001, met her at the station. Their happy reunion was marred by the confusion of a town

Ruth's shtetl in Pokrojus, Lithuania

under siege. "I thought it was war maneuvers," she said. But the radio, when she arrived at her sister's apartment, broadcast the news that the Germans had crossed the border to Lithuania and that war had been declared between Russia and Germany.

As people in time of trial tend to do, they began to congregate and talk of the pending disaster and the options. "I wanted to go home, but there was no way to get home," she said. But when the radio announced that for every Lithuanian killed, 100 Jews would be murdered, they realized they were in danger.

"We planned to cross the border to Russia, 300 miles away." They packed what they could carry and set out on foot – a small group of Jews fearful for their lives – lost among the thousands that filled the roads as the air thundered with gun fire and the sky filled with fighter planes. After ten days on the march, buying food from neighboring families and sleeping where they could find shelter, they realized there was nowhere to go. The Germans had moved in around them.

Once more they huddled together and discussed their options. There was no other alternative but to return to Kovno. "It was a hard journey back," she explained, made all the more uncomfortable for the weary foot-travelers by the Lithuanians, who were now denying them food. What they did manage to get, they shared equally among themselves.

"It was terrible," Ruth continued. "There is no way to explain it." The trip to nowhere which had taken them ten days, took 14 days to return them to their uncertain fate. "Our shoes were taken away from us. We walked barefoot. We were getting weak. We didn't sleep at night. We cried, talked. We didn't understand what was happening.

"The roads were full of refugees. We had to step over dead bodies, those of men, women and children."

They returned to her sister's apartment, which looked like an oasis after their weary, futile journey. But it was only the eye of the storm. "Jewish people couldn't go out on the streets. There was killing, looting. We were scared to open the door." When, out of necessity they ventured out to get food, they were consistently pushed back to the end of the lines, physically abused.

"The Jewish men were scared to go out because they were picked up and carried away. We women took turns standing in the lines.

"One Sunday morning, my friend Shoshana and I went to stand in line. We were identified as being Jewish and were picked up." They were among hundreds who were pushed into another crowd and herded into a school already crowded with Jewish people. From that building they were taken to the "7th Fort," also crowded with frightened Jewish people.

Then the systematic killing of people began. "One woman screamed to go home to her baby who she had left alone. The more the people screamed, the more they were tortured," she said.

"We huddled together, planning to escape when it was dark … many were already dead, many were pretending to be dead. So Shoshana and I pretended to be dead."

Ruth lay still among the dying and dead. "I reached out and grabbed Shoshana, who had a club foot, and urged her to run.

"But she said, 'where?'"

It didn't matter where. Fear had become their ally and urged them on. Little by little they worked their way through the woods until they were once again on the road. And they continued to run, jumping into roadside ditches with the approach of passing cars.

"When we finally made it back to the apartment, we were told we were thought dead. They were sitting *shiva*. So many had been shot." Later, when there was no food in the city, they ventured out cautiously, pretending to be Lithuanians. "If you got away with it, you got food."

And so they existed, until the end of July when it was announced that all Jews had to move into the Ghetto Slabotka. "It was once a shtetl of middle class Jews. We had until August 15 to move in. The ghetto was closed the

Ruth Shapiro on a bridge in Lithuania. Anna, her sister, is seated on the rocks below next to her fiance who perished in the Holocaust.

next day. No one could come in and no one could go out."

Jewish committees were formed, these were the governing bodies who distributed the food, kept order. Ruth remembers the food – "horse meat, rotten potatoes." Although inside the Ghetto was overcrowded, makeshift and barely livable, it at least offered refuge against the hostile world waiting to annihilate them on the outside.

The first "call" was for lawyers and doctors. "These never returned. We

"We huddled together, planning to escape when it was dark … many were already dead, many were pretending to be dead. So Shoshana and I pretended to be dead."

were unaware of concentration camps. Then another group. It didn't return either," she added.

"Those young enough had to work. The Germans asked for specific laborers at the gate. These did manage to return after working all day," she said, explaining that in order for those not on work detail to survive, they had to sneak out with the laborers and come back in with the laborers. When the laborers were herded off to work, the others took different routes in search of food.

They learned to survive, to become invisible when necessary. They knew which groups were destined not to return and before the "call-up" they would hide in attics and basements "with the rats."

She remembers much and her thoughts overlap. Other unwanted memories surface. "The Germans locked the door to the hospital in the Ghetto and burned it down with the eight doctors, 15 nurses and 45 patients inside. They blamed it on typhus."

The Ghetto was divided into large and small divisions. The small Ghetto was liquidated in one week. They were taken to the fort and killed.

"On October 28, 1941, everyone, except the sick, were lined up and told to march between lines of SS officers … one group told to go to the left, one to the right … families were deliberately split … ten thousand were taken to the now empty small ghetto. On October

29 they were taken to the fort and instantly killed … just a mountain of bodies … some still alive and struggling to get away from the dead."

Feelings and emotions were all but extinguished, but not hope. "We had a hope, maybe some of the Jewish people would survive, many felt they would be the one to tell the story." And so they held on even as the Ghetto was systematically liquidated. They slept where they found themselves, five and six in a room, unheated. "It was so cold, we would tear the buildings down for wood."

By November, 1943, those still alive were taken outside the Ghetto to a camp, "another step toward total

Anna Shapiro (seated at right) with the little theater group from her village.

Ruth Shapiro and her siblings, Anna, Liebsa and Lionel, with their beloved pet, Bobek.

liquidation," she said. The camp consisted of barracks with three tiered wooden planks for beds. Work detail began at six in the morning, ended at eight in the night. The children, old and sick stayed behind.

On March 27, 1944, when the workers returned to camp, they discovered that the old and children had been taken away and killed. The parents began shrieking. A few children survived by hiding. In anguish the parents wanted to burn the barracks and throw themselves into the flames. "But, of course, after the hysteria subsided, they couldn't do it," she added.

"But in the end, they got everyone in some filthy corner to die. I remember as a young woman I had long beautiful hair. It was now full of lice and had to be cut."

"I cried … we are human beings!" She questioned whether that fact had been overlooked by the rest of the world.

Before they were moved once again, from Gifangen Lager Alextos, Ruth recalls that one of her friends escaped from the group and crept back into the now surfacely deserted ghetto. However, beneath the ground Jewish life scurried for existence. Bunkers were full of humanity trying hard to survive by eluding the Nazi vise which was closing in on them.

Here, again, the German murder machine was thorough. The solution was so simple. They bombed the underground shelters with everyone inside. No one escaped.

From the Gifangen Lager, Ruth and her sister, Anna, were moved to Poneves, where they became a part of a group of Jewish laborers building an airport. Conditions were barbaric. They were beaten with systemic regularity, forced to work hard, fed little and left to sleep out in the open, or if possible in nearby barns, which served to keep them in, more than the elements out.

Two months later, Ruth and her group were transported once again. This time to Shaulen, which was only 35 miles from her home. But all she could do was look over the horizon in the direction of where she spent her last happy moments. Home was so far

Clockwise: Anna, Lionel, Ruth and Liebsa

Liebsa and Ruth before the war.

away. Shaulen was a liquidated ghetto and except for the unquieted spirits of people deprived of their right to exist, all that remained were the lice, roaches and rats, which she said, "grew bigger and bigger each day."

The dehumanizing conditions were overbearing. What remained of her sensibilities recoiled from filth. She sacrificed her ration, of what was considered coffee, so that she could attempt to wash her hair. The dark residue was not so much an attempt to cleanse the hair as to ease the itching. Ruth cries and must stop. The memory of those conditions intrude upon her security even now.

"I can still hear the noise of a train as it stops ... only it is a thousand times worse."

The next stop was Germany, but as Ruth explains, "it was not so quick." Destination unknown, they were loaded into coal wagons, with the men separated from the women – 50 people into a wagon. The train stopped abruptly at the Lithuanian town of Tawrig. They huddled together, no longer able to comprehend fear even as the locks to their coal car were opened. The women were told to get out. "But, we had not anything to fear from anyone," she said, explaining that even death would have been anti-climactical. "We were taken to a very big room, it must have been a former store front. We were told to take off our clothes ... hundreds of Lithuanians surrounded the

window front and peered in at us. Then we were told to dress again. We were not ashamed. We were just like animals.

"But to this day, I still don't know why we were asked to do such a thing."

Later they learned their destination was Stutthof. They arrived late at night. It seemed so dark. Once more they were carted off as less than human from one group of cars and forced into others ... "how much they beat upon us. It was impossible to think of what they would do next," she said.

Once more she and her sister were behind barbed wire. She looked around her. There were thousands. "We looked from left to right. We couldn't believe what we saw." Now she rationalizes that Stutthof must have been the last stop for Jews from many different localities. These were the stalwart who had survived only to be waiting extermination.

The systemic separation of families began. The boys who had been isolated with their fathers were now torn away. "They begged to go with their fathers, they promised to do anything, if only they could go with them." Their pleas fell on deaf ears.

Even though the war was winding down, the Germans were still concerned with collecting valuables from the Jewish people. On the guise of delousing the women and giving them showers, they were told to remove their

Ruth and her sister, Liebsa, before the war.

clothes, drop all their personal belongings and move forward into a large room. Before entering they were asked to lift their arms in the air. At first Ruth thought this was part of the delousing procedure. But when she entered the large room and was forced upon a table for an internal examination in an attempt to remove valuables hidden inside her body, she knew it was only another Teutonic ritual – barbaric and brutal. Afterwards she looked out of the back door, and what at first appeared to be a huge mountain, but upon closer examination was seen as a huge pile of shoes – all that remained of those who had taken the shower of death.

Since she had nothing more to give the Germans, she was allowed to leave. The women formed a line and were issued makeshift shoes, a dress and a coat. "There was no concern as to fit … after the clothes we were taken to other barracks where we slept on planks piled four layers high … later we traded clothes with one another for a better fit."

For two days they lay upon bunks, with no food or contact with the outside world. On the third day the barracks were opened and the women were told to line up. Ruth remembers there were blocks and blocks of women. "And we stood the whole day in the sun." Just by digging in the sand with their feet they unearthed papers, photographs and other items of those who had stood earlier where they were now standing.

On the fourth day it was a repeat of the same, only they were given a little bowl with what was identified as food, but it looked like long pieces of grass. "Still to this day I don't know what it was." Later she was to pass a barrack which was identified as the hospital. "We saw two people carry out bodies, just sticks with head and feet. Then we knew what it was we had survived for."

The routine became monotonous. "People were just drying up … we were just waiting to die. We lost continuity of the days … we thought even the birds are afraid to come here … the only view was the sand and the sun."

Ruth and her new baby, Frieda Marlene

In August of 1944, there was a call for women to work. Everyone was anxious, it was a chance to get out, she said. However, since there were so many women it took a few days until they could even get to her and her sister.

Her new station was Stainort which she said was considered part of Stutthof.

"We got up with the light and stood in lines for count and then went to work … digging trenches for soldiers … we didn't have the strength to get past the sand … we had picks to break rocks. At noon we were given a bit of oatmeal and a thin slice of bread. We stayed in the heat and worked until dark. We slept in a tar paper hut-like enclosure … on straw. It was impossible to stand up … we had to sleep 50 women, close to one another, there was no space."

The morning revealed those who had died in the night or who were dying.

"They were gone by nightfall, when we returned," she said.

In December of 1944 she was in another work camp, in Rewodzik, which offered the same conditions. "The beatings … the madness," she said, recalling the woman who was shot in the head because she ran to get the potato she saw while working in the field.

Then on January 19, 1945, they were awakened earlier than usual. "We heard planes … the Germans were nervous, upset, the whole camp was taken out … we had to walk in the snow … those who turned their heads to look back, were shot." One was her sister-in-law Sofia Igdalski.

By night they had reached a village deserted by the Germans fleeing west from the Russians. Ruth and her sister plus four other women huddled in the top of a barn under straw for warmth. "The next day we knew we couldn't go on any further. We hid in the hay … the rest were carried away. We stayed there for three and half days with no food … we survived on icicles hanging from the roof."

At the end of the fourth day a group of Germans started to establish headquarters in the barn. The women could hear their voices from the loft and realized it would be only a few moments before they were detected.

"We were so weak we hardly looked at one another. But the Germans left

Szaja Lida, Simon Weisberg, Ruth Levenson, Frieda Horwitz, Annie Weisberg, Harry Bromberg, Esther Goldman, Frieda Igdal, Paula Bromberg, Faye Floch Lazarus, Sonia Floch, and Ethel Floch Weisman at the wedding of Ruth's daughter, Frieda.

suddenly. Then on the sixth day one of the women said she thought she heard a Russian song." The Russians were moving into the area. The date – January 25, 1945.

The group was lead by a Jewish general who offered them help. "We couldn't eat, we weighed only 65 to 70 pounds each … he rubbed our feet with cream … he took care of us for one week."

But their travail was not over. The first group of Russians were replaced by another group of Russians, these looking for women. So the six women fled and hid in the enclosure where the pigs and chickens were kept. "In the morning we looked out the window and saw they too were gone, so we went back into the house."

Finally they were transported by another group of soldiers to Grodna, Poland and moved in with other Jews who had come out of hiding.

"We wanted to go home … we had to register. We stood in line, but as we stood, some people who knew one of the women warned us in Yiddish, that if we stood in line we would be transported to Russia, to hard labor."

They were advised where to hide and were later taken to Jewish homes where they obtained false passports to send them further west. "We were not to talk on the train, we had to hide the fact that we were refugees," she said. As prearranged at Bialystock they were recognized by the way they were dressed and picked up by other Jewish people who helped them on their way. "We celebrated the first Passover since the war in Lublin … we felt those who met us … everybody was my sister and brother."

Since Ruth and her sister couldn't get to Israel because of Ruth's health, they became part of a network called the Brecha, an organization whose aim it was to help Jewish refugees. Then Ruth became ill from the pus which had settled in her shoulder from continual beatings. "I was told I wouldn't survive unless they amputated the arm."

But the third operation proved the diagnosis incorrect, and while she was recuperating in the hospital her sister, Anna, (Anna Burk of Norfolk, of blessed memory) came with the news that Ruth's husband, Irving was still alive. Ruth had married him earlier in the ghetto as a matter of convenience to elude early transportation. But it was just a paper wedding, she explained. The marriage of convenience was October 23, 1942. Their formal Jewish marriage was on December 10, 1945.

"I hadn't seen him since Stutthof where someone remembers him hollering behind barbed wire as we were led off, 'Wait for me.'"

The Igdals lived in Munich until they moved to America in 1949.

While recuperating in the hospital she remembered her aunt Mary Leibman's address in Boston as it was when her mother had corresponded with her before the war. She gave a letter to an American soldier who sent it through the Red Cross. "When my aunt got the letter she called my sister, Edith Klavans, who was living in Norfolk. Edith arrived in America on the last boat in 1939."

Ruth's lost family is ever on her mind. Perhaps it is because they disappeared so quickly. "While in the Kovno Ghetto we hoped that our family … had survived by escaping to the Russian border. We prayed for them."

This hope was dispelled by a gentile woman who had been married to a Jewish lawyer in Pokrojus. He was murdered by the Germans. Through her eyes, Ruth heard the story of how her family and other members of the community were killed.

"The Germans and Lithuanian hooligans … worked together. They ordered all the Jews from their homes, to line up with little food and water. And nothing else. They panicked … children crying and screaming … people asking, 'what is our sin? what have we done? Please God help, help' … God turned them down…."

"But I still believe in God. I still do … (even) under beatings with wooden sticks and guns."

The woman told Ruth that her family and the other Jews of the city were forced to stand for seven days without food and water, dying in the street.

"On the eighth day, they forced them at gunpoint to walk three kilometers to the forest at Morke Kalve, to dig their own graves … to put boards over the graves and to walk on them…."

"Then the Germans and the hooligans started to shoot … the children they threw into the grave alive."

Despite the pain of the Holocaust, Ruth has happier memories, which she cherishes. She remembers her father, Moshe Shapiro who died at 39. "He was a gentle man … he believed in the goodness of humanity. The happiest hours were spent Friday night with the family after shul … the beauty of the Sabbath (in Pokrojus) I will never forget." ❖

Ruth's husband, Irving, another Holocaust survivor, died in 1994. Her daughter, Frieda Marlene Igdal, a pharmacist, lives in Norfolk.

Ruth Igdal's sister, Anna, as well as her husband, Irving, and brother-in-law, Charles, have stories in this book.

Ruth and Anna with friends from their village in Lithuania who survived the Holocaust.

I paid a big price to be Jewish
BRUNYA JACOBS

By Paul Lankford

Brunya Jacobs

She lives alone in her room at the end of a hallway in a retirement home in Newport News. Her only surviving relative, her son, Abe, lives in Vermont and sends his mother money to supplement the $37 a month in reparations from the German government. Thirty-seven dollars a month the Germans pay her for the mother, the father, two brothers, and two sisters who died in a camp in Treblinka, Poland.

BRUNYA JACOBS would most likely have shared her family's fate had she not run away, against her mother's wishes, with Jacob Jacobs, the man she would later marry. She remembers the sound that caused her to flee: German soldier's boots on the floors and stairs of her home as they searched the houses of her Polish neighborhood for attractive young women to take into prostitution. Hiding in a wardrobe upstairs in her home that night, Brunya knew that her world and her entire way of life had irrevocably changed. She knew that escape was her only chance.

Though Brunya and Jacob did escape to Russia, where they married and managed to survive under increasingly harsh conditions for three years, they could not avoid the Germans indefinitely. While Brunya worked in a bakery near Stalingrad and her husband dug bunkers for the Russian army somewhere out in the country, the Nazis invaded Russia. Brunya fled a second time, but this flight would end in her capture and internment in a labor camp in Muhldorf, Germany. It was a forced

labor camp, not a death camp like Dachau or Auschwitz, where Hitler carried out his campaign to exterminate the Jewish people. Brunya slept on wooden slats and spent most of her days moving piles of bricks from one place to another.

"I went from 125 pounds to 90 pounds," Brunya says. "We drank water, not much food. My body got swollen up. I could barely function. But I was thinking that people who got weak and couldn't do nothing – they would be killed. So I kept working." She survived until American soldiers liberated the camp in 1945.

Brunya and her sons, Samuel and Abe.

Brunya (right) and her mother, Rebecca.

tried forgetting the sights and sounds of the war years. But the memories remained, and the losses continued. After her husband Jacob died, Brunya moved to Newport News to be with Samuel. Two years later, Samuel died of cancer.

Today, Brunya keeps the curtains pulled across the only window in her room. She no longer wants to see the view outside her window. But it is the view from an interior window, the window of her mind and her memory that Brunya Jacobs can never ignore. Today, alone at 84, she sees and remembers the past only too clearly and too painfully. "I paid a big price to be Jewish," Brunya says. "That is my story." And it is a story that Brunya Jacobs must share with those who will listen. ❖

Brunya and her son, Samuel.

Brunya never saw her parents and siblings again, but she did find Jacob in Poland after the war. They moved to a refugee camp Allied forces had set up in Germany where they lived for three years and had two sons. In 1950, President Truman arranged for a large group of refugees to immigrate to the United States.

"Truman let me into this country on New Year's Day in 1950," Brunya says. She and her family started a new life in Syracuse, New York. She met other Holocaust survivors there, and found out that her family probably died in a death camp in Treblinka, Poland.

Like other survivors, Brunya focused on raising her sons, Abe and Samuel, and

NIGHTMARE ODYSSEY
Rosalia Kats Kaplan

By Ginny Sealey Bobby

When ROSALIA KATS KAPLAN was a little girl in Nazi-occupied Holland, she thought wearing the required yellow Star of David made her special, set her apart from the other children in her neighborhood.

She found out the hard way that the cherished adornment worn by Jews for centuries with great pride, came with new responsibilities.

"In the beginning I thought it was fun. … I got to wear a star that made me different from all the other kids," she said. "But I soon realized that this wasn't because I was special, but because someone thought I was bad."

Known by her family and friends as "Lia," Kaplan was seven years old when the Nazi army invaded Holland in 1940. She was introduced to the atrocities of war at an age when most children are playing with dolls and learning their alphabet.

"It is very hard for young children to understand what is going on around them," said Kaplan.

Rosalia Kats Kaplan

She remembers her first confrontation with the Holocaust – the result of an innocent, but child-like defiance. "My mother once knitted me a dress and I was so proud that I wanted my grandmother to see it. I ran out of the house before my mother could sew the star on the dress. While walking to my grandmother's house, a member of the Nazi council picked me up and took me to the German headquarters," she said. "He wanted to know where my star was and I told him that I was not going to put a star on my new dress. He made me scrub bicycles for two weeks and refused when my father offered to take my place.

"He said I was the one caught not wearing the star so it was my lesson to learn."

Kaplan, who lives in the Kempsville section of Virginia Beach with her husband, Abe, now believes that talking about her childhood experiences may serve to not only educate the community, but reduce the recurrent nightmares she still has about the war.

"I didn't want to talk about it for a long time…. I just wanted to forget that it happened and get on with my life," Kaplan said. "But the nightmares won't let me forget … and now I dream that it is my children who are having to go through what I did."

The mother of three and grandmother, Kaplan speaks with a soft Dutch lilt. Only her dark eyes, creased at the corners, reveal the deep brooding of one who has experienced great heartbreak and pain.

"I get really depressed sometimes … at times I feel cheated in some way … cheated of my childhood." On the advice of her doctors, Lia had the concentration camp identification numbers, tattooed on her forearm, removed. She admitted that constantly looking at the numbers only served to push her further into depression.

Rosalia was born in 1933 to Abraham ("Ami") and Esther Kats. She was the youngest of two children; her brother Max was 4 years her senior. A quiet, robust man, Ami worked in architectural design where he blue-printed the interior layout of department stores and factories. Lia remembers her early childhood as being happy, filled with toys and friends. Only the adults seemed worried about the war.

Lia recalled that her mother seemed to become more and more high-strung and anxious as the war drew closer. Then one morning, Lia was grabbed from her bed and told by her parents to put on as many clothes as she could wear. They were all going away for awhile. Her flight into the night of the Holocaust had begun.

"Nothing was explained to me … my mother just screamed that I should go and not ask questions. My grandmother was the only person to explain what was happening," she said.

Her grandmother was the center of Lia's world. She adored her grandmother

Rosalia and her brother, Max.

and only agreed to go quietly because "Oma" had assured her everything would be fine.

Kaplan was separated from her family and taken to the home of a local police officer and his young wife. To protect themselves and Lia, the couple had her sleep in a hollowed out section of their dining room wall. Alone and confused, Kaplan remembers crying almost continuously until the couple decided that they could no longer hide her. "My grandmother came and took me back to her house," she explained. "Oma told me that my parents had gone away and she was the only family that I had." Kaplan and her grandmother remained in the vacant

house for only a few days before the local members of the Nazi network discovered the two frightened Jews.

The night they raided the house is the source of constant nightmares for the Holocaust survivor, who believes she will never recover from the feelings of guilt for sacrificing her grandmother's life.

"I will never forget the way my grandmother gave her life to save me," she said. "As the soldiers burst through the front door, my Oma pushed me down the back steps and told me to run and don't stop. She was blocking the doorway to give me a head start before they started after me. And that is the last time I saw her, standing there so strong and brave. She came out of hiding for me and died for me. I hid in the graveyard that night and slept behind a huge tombstone."

From that night in 1941, seven-year-old Rosalia Kats began her nightmare odyssey of survival. "In that type of situation, you grow up fast. You become wise."

It was at this time that she realized that her uncle was a member of the Dutch underground resistance movement, a group responsible for her survival as well as thousands of others who survived.

"While I was being hidden by the underground, I stayed in 25 'underground' homes. Some of the people who hid me were good but there

Esther and Abraham Kats

Lia's paternal grandmother, Anna Kats, who sacrificed her own life to save Lia.

She said that she was so hungry that she once broke through the kitchen window of a Nazi encampment during the night to steal food. Driven by hunger pains, she stuck her hand in a boiling pot to grab a fistful of peas. She remembers that the skin peeled off her scalded hand but can only recall the momentary relief from the pain in her stomach.

"I became wild … some kind of animal running the streets, afraid of being picked up by the Germans. I would do anything to survive."

Kaplan tries to remember what she relied on at such an early age to survive. "I don't know what it was inside me that took care of me in those situations. I didn't trust any adults…. I thought my parents had left me. I remember one time soldiers finally caught up with me and from three different sides began shooting at me," she whispered. "Somehow I knew not to run away in a straight line but to zig-zag as I ran down the street. To this day I don't know what it was that kept me alive."

were others who took advantage of a little girl."

At one home, she remembers the Nazis suspected that she was being hidden. The family that she was staying with had hidden her in a small boat on the river among tall river grass. From that vantage point, Kaplan watched as the soldiers set the house on fire in hopes that she was hiding in the walls. She was forced to stay in the boat for nearly two weeks before underground members came to her rescue. She doesn't know how she survived it.

"Something in me told me not to get out of the boat. The river was being watched; and from where I was, I could see the patrols looking for me," she said. "There were some wild ducks who had built their nests in the reeds where I was hiding. After I had been out there for about four days, I became desperate. I ate the raw duck eggs and drank the river water."

Another time she remembers staying with a man who was so poor himself that all they had to eat was tulip bulbs, dandelions and sugar beets.

"The tulip bulbs tasted like garlic or onions and the dandelions had a real spinach-like taste. These were the staples of my diet for a long time."

Then, when it became all the more dangerous for Kaplan to remain in the town, even in hiding, the underground moved her to nearby Friesland. There, she became involved with several underground activities including a stint as a courier of illegal communications. Since outside communications was restricted, the underground printed a newspaper that detailed the evening broadcasts of the BBC. Kaplan distributed the newspaper. "I was so little and so quick that they chose me to run from house to house slipping the newspapers under the doors of each house." She recalls that she once helped smuggle counterfeit ration cards to a fighter pilot shot down near Friesland.

"When you are a child, you don't think about danger; you just do it because you want to or you are told to do it. It's like when you crossed the street without looking … a child's mind doesn't grasp the danger of a situation," she said.

While her work with the underground may have saved lives, her exploits jeopardized her own existence. The Nazis were aware that Kaplan was working with the underground and targeted her for immediate capture. "They wanted to find me because they thought being a child I would betray all those people who had helped to save me."

Although she was living under the assumed name "Lisje Franken," the Germans discovered her identity and put out a reward for anyone who

captured her. Kaplan can now sympathize with the townspeople who turned her over to the Germans. "Everybody was ravaged by the war. All of Holland was starving … the Jews were not the only ones who suffered. I guess those who turned me in were doing it to save themselves but everyone ended up in the German labor camps anyway."

Kaplan remembers the stay in the jails before being deported as the hardest part of her survival. Determined to put an end to the underground, the Germans attempted to force Kaplan to confess everything she knew about its activities. Although she was repeatedly beaten, and psychologically abused, she would not give the names of the people who had hidden her. "I have to admit that I really didn't know all the names

Rachel (Shellie) and her mother, Rosalina, Rosalia's aunt and maternal grandmother

Mauritz, Shellie's son, and Rosje and Greta, Shellie's twin daughters. All three children were killed during the Holocaust.

of those people and because they moved at night I oftentimes didn't know where I was when I was moved," she said. "One thing I did know was that they could beat me forever and I would not have told them what I did know."

In December, 1944, Kaplan was deported to Auschwitz. She remained there until the allies liberated the camp in April, 1945. While in the camp, Kaplan faced one of her greatest challenges; she was chosen to be part of a medical experimentation. As a means of preventing the adolescent girls from menstruating, camp doctors forced them to ingest camphor – the chemical used in moth flakes.

"I was never expected to have children and when I did become pregnant the doctors all thought I would not survive," she said. "But I proved them wrong because I wanted to have something of my own to love and to love me back."

Kaplan is a true survivor. When she was rescued from the camp, she was 12 years old and weighed 36 pounds. She was weakened by severe malnutrition and dehydration and she was suffering with a skin disease she contracted from the filthy living conditions.

Although Kaplan's memories of the camp are sometimes distorted and vague, she has not forgotten the day she was liberated.

"I can still see the soldiers rushing the camp gates. There were only a few

Rosalia Kats as a child before World War II.

thousand people left who were not moved out of the camp as the Allies moved closer. One soldier picked me up and put me on his shoulders and ran around the camp with me clinging to his head. Another soldier gave me a chocolate bar and biscuits."

From the camp, Kaplan was taken to a hospital orphanage for homeless, abandoned and displaced children. Although Lia endured the rigors of three years in hiding and seven months in a concentration camp, neither her parents or her bother were forced into a camp. While she was recuperating from the trauma of her experience, the Red Cross located Kaplan's mother and reunited the two.

"When I first saw my mother I didn't think she was my mother. I wouldn't go to her…. I wouldn't let her touch me. I thought my mother was dead. Then I wanted to know why she never came for me, why she didn't take me with her when she took my brother. These were the questions of a sick and rejected child."

Andy, Rosalia and Abraham Kaplan

Following the War, Kaplan's parents were divorced, an event she blames on the Holocaust. "They had grown apart … and both felt some of the responsibility for what the war had done to our family. I suppose they could have been talking about divorce even before the war. I would have never known."

Kaplan feels that her mother was a hard woman to understand. She and her mother eventually resumed a tense but consistent communication. Her mother died in February, 2000.

Nowadays Kaplan prefers to focus on the joy her family brings her. Her son, Ronnie, lives in Lynchburg with her only grandchild, Sylvia, who she adores. Kaplan's only daughter, Lisa, and her husband, Steve, live in San Antonio, Texas.

As Mrs. Kaplan reflects on her love for her family, she thinks about the many families who aided and sheltered her. "More than thirty families risked their lives. They put themselves in tremendous danger to help and protect me. These people should not be forgotten." ❖

Lisa Kaplan, Rosalia's daughter

Ronnie Kaplan, Rosalia's oldest son

Rosalia's granddaughter, Sylvia Ashley Kaplan

Rosalia's brother, Max and mother, Esther.

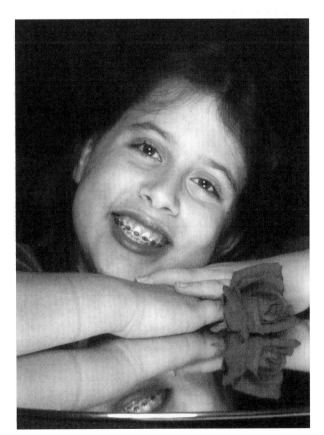

David Katz   *Photo by Sam Katz*

Testimony: On The Run from Nazis
DAVID KATZ

By David Katz

Editor's Note: The following article was written by Holocaust survivor, David Katz, of Chesapeake, Virginia, highlighting some of his experiences during World War II as he struggled to survive. It is taken from a longer autobiography, which he has dedicated in memory of his parents who perished in Auschwitz in 1942. He is married to local artist MaryAnne Katz whose art has appeared in the *Southeastern Virginia News*, *Renewal Magazine*, and this book.

I was born in Leipzig, Germany on February 12, 1930, to Abraham and Regina Wolkowitz (nee Jedlitzki). Leipzig at that time was the musical capital of Europe, the home to famous composers such as Bach, Mendelssohn, Schumann, Wagner, Teleman and numerous others during at least part of their creative lives. This musical climate was well suited to my parents' lifestyle since both were professional musicians who graduated from the Leipzig Conservatory of Music, my mother a concert pianist and teacher, and my father a well-rounded musician, who was proficient on several instruments. He was also a conductor, arranger and composer.

My parents started my musical education when I was about four years old, my mother on piano, and my father on the violin. My musical education continued until 1938, when it was interrupted for reasons, which will soon become apparent.

From the time of my birth we lived in a large apartment with my maternal grandparents at 49 Nordstrasse in Leipzig. As far back as I can remember, music was a constant companion in our home. My parents both gave private lessons, and at least once a week, musician friends would join my parents in the performance of chamber music. Since those events always took place after my bedtime, I would quietly sneak out of my bed and open the door, so that I could better hear those beautiful sounds.

In 1933, Adolph Hitler became Chancellor of Germany, and with that event began the persecution of Jews in Germany. That country was in the throes of a serious depression, with unemployment at an all-time high. Hitler convinced the German populace that the Jews were at the root of all their problems. From that time on, life for the Jews became progressively worse.

Even after the beginning of the Nazi regime, Jewish religious life continued to be practiced in our home. My parents made sure that I received a proper Jewish education, and we attended services regularly at the Leipzig synagogue, which was an absolutely magnificent structure. Shabbat was always celebrated in our home. My grandmother or my mother would light the candles, after which my grandfather chanted the Kiddush.

My Aunt Golda and Uncle Leo lived one block away from us at 41

"A New Year and Repentance"
(Rosh Hashanah/Yom Kippur) by
MaryAnne Katz

Nordstrasse. From the time of my birth, my life was fully intertwined with them and their children, my cousins Marichen (Mary), Wolfgang (Billy), Hella (Helen), and Renee. David was born later, in the United States. Wolfgang and I would go to school together, and not a day would go by that we would not be accosted by German youths that insulted us with racial slurs and would throw sticks or stones at us.

Starting in 1936, life for the Jews became more and more unbearable, and my parents started proceedings to enable us to immigrate to the United States. In 1937, we made our way to

The Hague, Holland, with just a few belongings and my father's favorite violin. The Germans did not allow the Jews to remove anything of value from the country, so we were lucky to get at least one of his precious instruments out of Germany. While waiting in The Hague for our final emigration papers, my mother became homesick for her parents, and so we left Holland and returned to Leipzig. That decision turned out to be the gravest mistake of our lives.

The pogroms against the Jews in Germany began the evening of November 9, 1938. That evening, known as *Kristallnacht* (night of broken glass), began when roving gangs of Nazis, instigated by Hitler's propaganda machinery, smashed the storefronts of Jewish merchants and looted their stores. At the same time, all the synagogues in Germany were set ablaze and burned down.

The next morning, two Gestapo agents (secret police) accompanied by SS guards (elite military) with drawn guns pounded on our door. Since my grandparents held Polish passports, they were given one hour to each pack one suitcase, and were then taken to the railroad station and deported to Poland. We knew that it would only be a matter of days or perhaps even hours, before they would return for my parents and me, so we had to find a place for us to hide until such time as we could find a way out of the country.

David Katz and photos of his mother, Regina, and his father, Abraham Wollkowitz.

It was strictly forbidden for Germans to protect Jews, and anyone found to be harboring Jews, was immediately sent to a concentration camp, and ultimately to their death. That same fate also awaited Catholic priests who dared speak out against the inhuman treatment of Jews. As a result, it was just about impossible to find a safe haven anywhere in the country. My father had a good friend, a musician and a Catholic, who risked his own life and gave us refuge in his home until we were able to flee from Germany.

In December, 1938, my father was able to be smuggled out of Germany, and he made his way to Brussels, Belgium. My mother and I followed in February, 1939, making our way to the border by train. Then, it took whatever money we had left in the world to pay a smuggler who walked us into Belgium through fields and forests so as not to be detected by the German border guards. Finally, we were reunited with my father in Brussels and to safety at last. Little did we know then what the future held for us.

My aunt and uncle and their children had taken refuge in the Polish embassy in Leipzig, and through a circuitous route that took them to Switzerland and Italy, were able to make their way to the United States before the war engulfed all of Europe.

We left Germany leaving all our worldly belongings behind, but our life in Brussels was a happy one. We lived in a small two room apartment at 102 Rue des Plantes, and my father was able to find jobs here and there playing the piano or violin, so that we were able to sustain our lives reasonably well. I went to a public school near our home, and learned to speak French and Flemish, both of which I learned to speak fluently within a very short time.

It looked as though we would be able to put our lives back together again when in May, 1940, we awoke to the sound of wailing sirens and of aerial warfare above our heads. Germany had attacked Belgium, and we knew that it would only be a matter of days before that small country would fall. Once again, we packed our meager belongings and fled from the rapidly advancing German army. This time to France.

None of us had any passports, so we had to get into France illegally. My father crossed into France first, and was immediately arrested and sent to a labor camp. By the time my mother and I left Brussels, the Germans had breached the Maginot line (the French defenses against invasion) and had started the invasion of France. My mother and I left Brussels by train, and the trip to France turned into a nightmare. The entire trip was stop-and-go between German bombings and shellings, and exchanges of machine gun and artillery fire between the French and German armies.

By then, Germany had made big advances into northern France, including Paris, and the French president, Marechal Philipe Petain, the hero of the Battle of Verdun during World War I, capitulated. Hitler agreed to leave the southern half of France in French hands while they occupied the north, an agreement on which he later reneged when he occupied the entire country.

My mother and I were held in a farm compound surrounded by a tall stone wall topped with barbed wire and embedded with broken glass shards. Our sleeping facilities consisted of a bale of hay in the horse stables. Many a night I awoke screaming with huge rats climbing all over my body. About two weeks after our arrest, we were taken by train to the city of Mende, to be delivered to the concentration camp "Rieuxcros." Our first sight of the camp was most traumatic. Row upon row of wooden barracks surrounded by barbed wire fences, with armed guards patrolling the perimeter. Rieuxcros was a camp for women and children. My father was interned in another camp about three hundred miles away.

Inside the barracks were rows of wooden bunks, two high, and we slept packed like sardines, with only a straw mattress and a rough horse blanket for bedding. The sanitary facilities were located in a wooden barrack in the center of the camp, and consisted of trenches along one wall, over which were some long wooden planks with a round hole about every two feet or so, with a small partition between them.

By that time, my uncle and aunt and their children were settled in Buffalo, New York, and with the help of some friends and relatives who were American citizens, they sent us the affidavits necessary for us to immigrate to the United States. Once again it seemed as though all hope was not lost.

David and MaryAnne's Wedding.

The United States government had strict immigration laws at that time that allowed only a certain number of immigrants to enter the country every month. So, while waiting for our number to come up, we were shipped to another camp, closer to the embarkation port of Marseille. This time, we were reunited with my father at Les Milles, a camp near the city of Aix en Provence. Les Milles was located in an old brick factory. Most of the windows had been broken, and the dampness was unbearable. It seemed as though we were always wet. We were still surrounded by high barbed wire fences and armed guards, and the food was no better than the previous camps. However, with what we thought was our eventual departure for the "golden land," our spirits were kept high, and we were willing to put up with just about anything.

While waiting at Les Milles, disaster struck once again. On December 7, 1941, the Japanese attacked Pearl Harbor. This event erased all our hopes of ever being able to get out of Europe.

With the United States at war with Japan, and its entry into the war with Germany, we were shipped to another camp, Rivesaltes, near the Spanish border. The situation there was even worse than the other camps, with the arrival of warmer weather. Sanitary facilities were totally lacking, and mosquitoes spread diseases such as malaria and typhus throughout the camp. The lack of proper medications made this problem even worse. The Vichy government cooperated with the Germans in rounding up all the Jews in France for deportation to camps in Eastern Europe.

Within hours, the camp authorities ordered all of us to pack up whatever meager belongings we still had, and to await transportation. I was then 12 years old, and the O.S.E. (Oeuvre de Secour aux Enfants), an immigrant aid society, managed to convince the French authorities to remove the children from the camp in order to prevent their deportation. At this point, nothing was known about the death camps and the systematic mass murders being perpetrated against millions of people in those camps. Everyone thought that they were being shipped to a labor camp in order to work in a munitions factory.

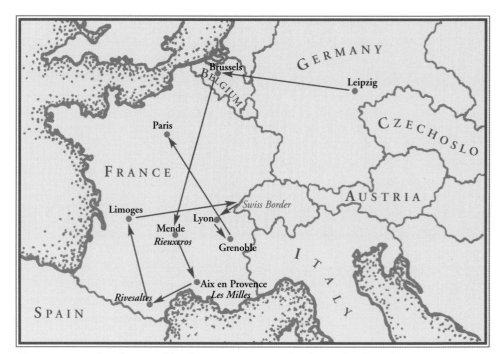

From 1939 until 1945, David lived in continuous travel seeking safety from the Nazi regime.

After I and the other children in the camp were rescued by the O.S.E., we were taken to an orphanage near the city of Limoges. Although life at the orphanage was strictly regimented, we were well taken care of. The food was satisfactory, and we were getting some medical attention. Also, we were getting some sort of education from an instructor. As a few of the boys including me were nearing age 13, a rabbi was brought in from Limoges to prepare us for our Bar Mitzvah. It seems ironic that, in spite of all the hardships we had endured, we never abandoned our Jewish heritage. Of course, the absence of my parents was utmost in my mind, and not a day went by that I did not cry myself to sleep.

The Bar Mitzvah ceremony was held in a makeshift sanctuary in the basement of a demolished house in Limoges, with five of us boys as the celebrants.

One morning we heard the roar of motorcycles and trucks approaching the orphanage, and I had a strong feeling that we were also on the verge of being deported. Rumors to that effect had been circulating for several days. Before I even knew if the Germans were really coming for us, I and another boy my age, managed to jump out of a window and make our escape just as the Germans neared the area. At that moment, a truck hauling garbage drove by, and we both jumped on the back of that truck. I got off several miles down the road when I felt that I was far enough away from German patrols so as not to be discovered.

Here I was, 13 years old, alone and without a penny, scared to death in unfamiliar territory, not being able to trust anyone lest they be German collaborators. I remember my parents and other adults in the camps saying that if only they could get to Switzerland, a neutral country, we would be safe. So, I made my way all across France, walking, and sometimes catching a short ride on the back of a farmer's hay wagon, traveling mostly at night for fear of being seen by German soldiers. After I had made my way all the way across France to the Alps and the Swiss border, I found it impossible to get into Switzerland. The German army had machine gun nests set up at every mountain pass. After numerous attempts during the next few days, nearly frozen to death, and near starvation, I gave up any hope of getting to my destination.

I next found myself in the city of Lyon. Shortly after arriving there, while walking down a narrow side street, I noticed a shabbily dressed man walking in front of me. Every once in a while he shot furtive glances at me to see if I was still following him. When he made his way into the basement of an old apartment building, I followed him in, and was surprised to see about 20 foreign speaking men and women hiding in that damp basement that had

become their home. Their fear made me decide that it would be too difficult to hide in such a large city with its large German presence. Thus, I made my way further south, to the city of Grenoble.

Grenoble, also being a large city, had a large German garrison, and because of my fear of being caught, I felt no safer there than in Lyon. A member of the maquis, the French resistance movement, told me that they had a large contingent in a nearby mountain village, and that I might be safer there. With much apprehension, I made my way to the village of Villard de Lans, a picturesque village nestled high in the French Alps. There I was told that the Catholic priest in the village was a strong supporter of the resistance movement and that I could confide in him.

My first step was to see Monsieur le Cure. He immediately sent his housekeeper to get me some fresh clothes and shoes, and that evening, I had the first real meal in years. I also had comfortable sleeping quarters in the church, and slept in a real bed. One thing that the Priest told me, will forever stick in my mind, "The Germans have taken away your parents and all you owned, but the one thing they will never be able to take away from you is your Jewish heritage."

After a while, the Germans became suspicious of the priest's clandestine activities, and he could no longer risk

hiding me. He knew an elderly farmer in the village, who needed help on his farm. I worked for that farmer in exchange for room and board.

While working on the farm, I befriended the leader of one of the resistance groups in the area, and from that time on, I became a member of the maquis, although I continued to work on the farm. I changed my name to Daniel Dupont, and was able to obtain forged documents bearing that name. I also became the youngest member of the group. Barely 14 years old, I became their courier, and it was my duty to relay messages between the various groups of maquis in that area. Two-way radios could not be used, as the Germans could easily spot their position. It was on one such mission, that all of a sudden, I found myself surrounded by about a dozen German soldiers shouting "Hande hoch" (hands up) and motioning for me to raise my hands.

They spoke no French, and I could not admit to speak German, since that surely would have given away my identity. However, since I understood every word they were saying, I realized that they were going to take me to Gestapo headquarters for questioning. As they were marching me back to the village at gunpoint, we were fired upon by some of the maquis, and during the ensuing confusion, I was able to escape, and make my way hastily back to the farm. After that, every time the

Germans made their way to the village, I would go into the woods to rejoin the members of the French resistance, since that seemed to be the safest hiding place. Since we could not light any fires, as they could easily have been detected by the German patrols, our meals consisted of raw horse meat, and raw eggs, which we punctured with a nail at both ends, and then sucked out.

A few months later, the end of the war was in sight. The Allied forces had landed in Normandy, and the Free French Forces under General De Gaulle and the American Army invaded southern France from North Africa. During all those years, I was unable to contact my uncle and aunt in Buffalo, but I still remembered their address. When I met an American Army chaplain in Villard de Lans, I asked him to please get in touch with them. He wrote them, advising them that he had located me, and that I was safe and sound after much suffering.

Following the German surrender, I made my way to Paris. I was housed in an orphanage in Montmorency, a suburb of Paris. I met a wonderful Jewish woman, a well-known French composer, and she took me under her wing. I took piano and composition lessons from Madame Aaron-Cohen, and practically lived in her home. The year was 1945, I was 15 years old, and had seen and suffered enough to last a hundred lifetimes.

After my arrival in Paris, I contacted the International Red Cross and some other organizations in order to find the whereabouts of my parents. After a few weeks, they notified me that my parents were transported to Auschwitz, Poland, in 1942, and that they were murdered in the gas chambers. I also was notified that my grandparents were murdered in the Warsaw ghetto.

I was finally able to contact my family in Buffalo, and they put the wheels in motion to enable me to immigrate to the United States. Waiting for what seemed an eternity, I was finally able to leave Europe.

I arrived in the United States on the SS Desirade, a converted freighter, on April 16, 1946, to join the wonderful uncle

and aunt who raised me as one of their own, and the brothers and sisters I never had. ❖

David and MaryAnne Katz's grandchildren, Jennifer and Arden

David, MaryAnne and their children, Gina, Avery, Samuel and Sarah.

— 176 —

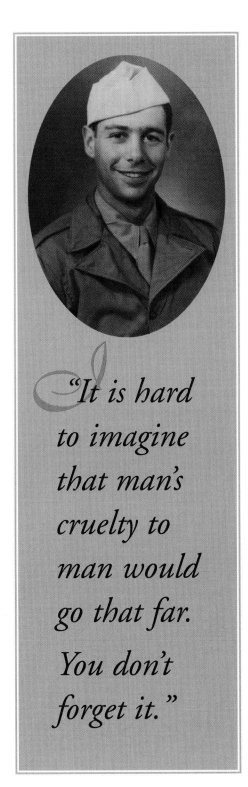

"*It is hard to imagine that man's cruelty to man would go that far. You don't forget it.*"

Norman Kozak

Images — forever imprinted in his mind

By Moira Wright Bodner

The memory of the stench of Dachau has stayed with NORMAN KOZAK for more than fifty years.

"The smell was horrible," remembers Kozak. "Anyone within 10 or 15 miles had to smell it when the wind shifted."

As a 19-year-old-Army medical technician, Kozak entered Dachau a couple of days after its liberation. The images of what he encountered there are forever imprinted in his mind.

These include piles of bodies in front of ovens and living survivors so thin it seemed as if he was looking through them.

"How could people survive at all in those conditions?" he asks.

Only in recent years has Kozak felt comfortable talking about the ten days he spent in Dachau providing assistance to the survivors. It is hard for him to recount the experience without crying. Kozak has shared his experiences at Dachau with his children because he thinks it is important that they know what he saw. When he was a teacher at Deep Creek High School, Kozak also gave talks to the students about his experience at Dachau. But after three years he found it too difficult emotionally and discontinued the talks.

Kozak was one of five Jews in his 200 man unit. Although they were upset about what they discovered at Dachau they didn't talk about it among themselves. Kozak remembers that one of them took pictures, but he hasn't seen or heard from any of his former Army buddies since they left Dachau.

The 56 intervening years have only made the horror of Dachau worse for Kozak. "It is hard to imagine that man's cruelty to man would go that far. You don't forget it." ❖

Norman Kozak at his home in the Tidewater area.

Elizabeth Lacher
Finding Goodness in Everything

By Kitty Wolf

ELIZABETH LACHER was born in Budapest in 1917. She was the oldest of four children, three girls and one boy. Her early years were very pleasant, growing up in a loving, middle class family. As a young adult she helped her father with his handbag manufacturing business.

She married in 1938. She and her new husband began their own box manufacturing business. They were doing quite well when the first signs of the war began to reach them. Elizabeth's husband was sent to a work camp in 1940. For the next two years he was in and out of work camps until 1942 when he was sent to Russia where he was killed in a deliberate explosion. At home, the Germans had reached Budapest. Their businesses were confiscated. Elizabeth's business was allowed to continue because it had begun making boxes for the Germans. She had to give ownership to her non-Jewish foreman but she was allowed to continue working.

Elizabeth and her second husband, Lester.

Elizabeth and Lester

Things only got worse for the Jews. Jewish houses were ordered to have yellow stars on them and soon everyone had to move into designated homes. The men were all taken to labor camps. Elizabeth moved in with her mother, sisters and other female relatives in a very small apartment. The Jews began to be taken away. First Elizabeth was arrested and taken to a field where she managed to slip away. Then she was arrested again. She left Budapest in 1944, not to return again for 40 years. She was transported to Dachau and from there to several other camps by foot and by "cattle car" ending up at Bergen-Belsen where she was liberated in 1945 at the end of the war.

While she was convalescing in a hospital in Sweden, the International Red Cross interviewed her and took down information about her relatives and friends. They were able to help her discover that her parents and two siblings survived. The International Red Cross helped her locate and contact them. They also located her late husband's family in the United States.

This is where the story she wants to tell begins. The Lacher family, friends of Elizabeth's family in Budapest, had immigrated to America in 1938. They were looking at the Red Cross lists and saw Elizabeth's name. One of the sons, Lester, had been quite interested in Elizabeth before she had chosen to marry someone else. This young man and his mother wrote letters to Elizabeth encouraging her to join them in the USA. At first she turned down their generous offer. She was planning to go home to be with her family. The Lachers persisted, sending her a first class steamship ticket! That "luxury" after all she had been through, was very tempting – so off she went to the USA. Who knew what could happen?

After only a few weeks, she knew this was the man for her. They were married shortly thereafter and had a long, happy marriage and a son, Frank.

After her husband died, Elizabeth moved to Chesapeake, to be near her son and his family. She has two wonderful grandchildren, Michael and Michelle.

Through all of her life Elizabeth has been a caring person with a wonderful attitude – always looking at the bright side and finding goodness in everything. The Portsmouth community is fortunate to have her as a member, where she spends her time volunteering to help others. She participates in Meals on Wheels and helps in the public school library. For the past 15 years she has been a volunteer at Portsmouth United Religious School where she teaches about the Holocaust, runs the Israeli stamp collection program and helps out in the library. Although she came to this community through misfortune she has never complained or felt sorry for herself. She has truly enriched the lives of others through her fortitude and beautiful nature. ❖

Elizabeth Lacher

One Step Ahead of the Germans
Szaja Lida — Survivor

By Reba Karp

Szaja Lida

Photo by Stephen Jay Photography

"It's hard to believe in God," Holocaust survivor SZAJA LIDA said, wondering where the divine presence was when the Jews were victimized by the Germans.

Then he pauses and explains the "other side of the coin." The Jews gave the civilized world its civilized life, he adds, noting that the Bible is still revered and Hitler's *Mein Kampf* is now only an example of unrestrained demagoguery.

Szaja's odyssey through the horrors of the Third Reich is one which took him from Krakow, Poland in 1939 to work camps, concentration camps, ammunition factories and finally to liberation in 1945. His exploits were that of a survivor, one determined to endure in spite of the odds and live to spit in the face of the devil.

The war touched Szaja and his family in 1939. He was 26 years old. "The Germans attacked at midnight," he remembers. "And everyone able to run, ran. We didn't know where we were going, we were just running." After three days his mother and younger sister couldn't run any more and returned home. Szaja and his brother-in-law continued to search for sanctuary as the situation was more threatening for Jewish men.

They were on the move for seven days and during that time could not find any water, for the wells had run dry due to the demands of thousands of people running from an unknown fate. "We were able to buy food … no one was concerned about who was Jewish then," he said.

While on the run, he was introduced to the specter of death. At one point a German plane gunned down the helpless civilians. He was not on the road at the time. It would be the first of many narrow escapes and he would learn to survive.

Later, when conscripted off the road by German soldiers to help construct a road adjacent to a bridge, he learned another fact of aggression. The Jewish people of Poland had no legal rights, and as such were subjected to stop and search and seizure of all personal property and money. He would also learn to outwit the Germans.

After the road was finished and the Germans released him, he realized that he had no place to run and he began his weary trek back to Krakow. When he reached home, he found his family still alive, despite the fact that each house had some dead. Before the war the Lida family owned a factory where underwear was produced. The Germans took over the business and later closed it down entirely.

Although there were no ghettos in Poland between the two wars, the Jews still lived together in specific com munities which made it easier for the Germans in the beginning. He recalls one morning when their homes were searched by 25 or 30 German soldiers, "two or three in every home," he noted

for he has a mind for details. "We didn't know what they wanted, they knocked you down if you asked." The attack on the defenseless Jewish community was for search and seizure of valuables. The Lidas were prepared, despite the uncertainty of the event, and had placed German marks in a nightstand within easy search "so they would look no further."

They had outwitted the Germans. Some of their neighbors were not so lucky. Many had nothing for the Germans and were subsequently abused and humiliated.

One of the first overt acts of anti-Semitism was the forced wearing of the Star of David. Later the Jewish people were not supposed to use any mode of transportation, and still later they were restricted from walking on the sidewalk. "Those who disobeyed, were caught and beaten," he said.

Eventually, restrictions prohibited the Jews from leaving town which was necessary in order to trade for food as Polish currency had become devaluated. Established ghettos designed to hold 10,000 were filled to 60,000.

During 1941- 42, Szaja and other young men worked for the Germans, loading grain, drying out wetlands. "The SS officers could not believe Jews could do such good work," he said, adding that despite hard work "everyday someone was dragged home, beaten."

In view of the encroaching hostility and constant threat to their family, the Lidas got permission to leave Krakow and return to the small town where their grandparents had lived. "I rented a one room apartment. I was lucky I got it … and we loaded everything we could in a truck and left."

He describes the move as one being "from hell to paradise," for the Krakow German headquarters had outlawed the Jewish people. They were no longer recognized as human beings and could be killed without explanation. They spent the winter of '42 - '43 in the small town which, before the war, had about 100 Jews, and now held close to 600 Jewish people who fled from the sealing of ghettos and a sure "death sentence" to other Polish cities.

While living in the shtetl, Szaja became a member of the *Judenrat*, those of the Jewish community who acted as the intermediaries between the people and the Germans. He was at the headquarters when the news arrived that all Jews were to be assembled on the streets at 7 o'clock on a Monday morning. It was Sunday night. The order was delivered by SS officers carrying two slips of paper. One was the notice for every Jew to be ready to leave; and the other was a note asking for extortion money – money to be used for transportation, feeding of the soldiers and for the use of "tools" – bullets to shoot the Jews. "And we had to pay for it," he remembers.

There was no way out and no way in, and yet the Lidas outwitted the Nazis again. Szaja hid his family Sunday night in a neighbor's pile of hay. In the morning, he took his place with the Judenrein and watched helplessly as they first carted off the elderly to a cemetery where they were shot and dumped into already prepared graves. Then the rest were loaded on wagons and taken to the railroad station 20 kilometers away for the journey to Auschwitz.

Finally, the Germans searched the homes for those too sick to leave. It was quick and methodical. Those

found were shot. Szaja and other *Judenrat* were given the job of taking the bodies to the cemetery and digging graves for them. He glanced sadly over the graves of the elderly shot earlier. "The dirt was still moving – 24 hours later," he said, unable to hold back his emotions. They buried the dead as ordered and said kaddish out of respect.

"[It was] years ago and it seems like it is happening now." His eyes are full of tears.

A new dimension in the battle for survival began for Szaja and his family. He took them food each night until he thought it safe for them to return to their home. Others who had hidden also returned, and just before the Germans were to remove those remaining, the Lidas hid again – this time in the attic of a Polish farmer. This sanctuary only lasted eight days, until the farmer noted that he had found a place where they could live in peace until the end of the war.

"He left us in the middle of a field in the frost, cold … "

They knocked on neighboring doors, begging help. "All we received were

curses," he said. Legally they were supposed to be dead, for all that had lived in the shtetl were gone. Their entire world had become hostile. Exposed to the cold and with no food, they decided they would go to Krakow and take their chances in the ghetto. In order to assure a better chance at reaching their destination, the family separated on the train. Szaja was sitting near a Jewish woman and her two children when the Germans caught them, and took them off the train and shot them. He was overlooked, but his heart was heavy; another young Jewish woman and her children were dead.

Since he was a young man and would be shot upon entering the ghetto, he parted with his family and moved through the hostile elements of Krakow. "Every step my life was in danger. No Jews were allowed to live outside." He found his way to a work camp where he saw two of his friends and with their help moved in with the workers, avoiding the regular entrance channels where all valuables were taken away.

The workers were given only 500 calories of food a day, but his valuables managed to "buy" additional food for his friends and himself. These friends are still alive living in Tennessee, he said. Although he caught typhus and nearly died, he was given a chance to recuperate by the Austrian camp official, interested in lowering the number of those who died in his camp or who became too ill to work and were subsequently shot.

In the winter of '43, the surviving workers were loaded on trains for a seven hour trip to an ammunition factory. Since he knew his life depended upon having something to sell, in exchange for food, he changed clothes with another worker who was dressed in little more than rags – and once more outwitted the Germans, who, disdainful of his clothes, did not thoroughly search him.

Conditions at the factory were inhumane. One camp produced chemicals to make mines, which turned the workers' skin and hair yellow. "No one lived longer than a month. There was so much hunger … some wore paper bag clothes, shoes … and the warehouse was full of clothes from the Jewish dead."

Food consisted of a plate of dirty water. "If someone found a piece of potato, the whole camp knew." And because of the conditions, the number of workers never exceeded 2,500, despite the fact that they brought in 500 new workers each month. No one was shot. They died of starvation.

Szaja was assigned to loading heavy empty shells from a train en route to the factory. The shells weighed between 80 and 90 pounds and were beyond his physical ability to carry. After several weeks, "I knew I would not make it," he said, explaining that the procedure was to carry the shells over one shoulder. "They wore through my heavy overcoat, jacket and shirt to the shoulder" … which had become bruised and bloodied.

He had to gain time and sought a way to survive and found the weak link – the Polish manager the Germans had put in charge. An alcoholic, Szaja offered him money for a quart of vodka if he would find him another place to work. The man agreed and he was assigned to loading smaller, empty shells into the factory for others to fill, a job which kept him one step ahead of the specter of death.

He was determined to stay a step ahead and looked for ways to do so. Since he had been a candy maker before the war, he put his best effort forward and got someone to smuggle him in some sugar, poppy seed and other ingredients needed to make candy. Then he

The Pond At Birkenau

In winter's somberness
the pond at Birkenau
submerged with human remains,
contemplates the liberating spring
when blossoming flowers
will bring to mind
what was plucked
before its time,
that no snow
could ever hide.

Rabbi Israel Zoberman

bartered with someone in the camp to make the necessary utensils "and I made seven pounds of candy that first time," he said, explaining that he got two young boys to sell it through the camp. "If the Germans found out, they would have killed me," he added.

The scenario reads like the script from a tense prison escape movie, for when the Germans made their systematic search of the blocks, he was prepared. All ingredients and equipment went out a window until the search was over. Szaja is an example of the indomitable Jewish spirit, for despite conditions, he never lost his pride. He adds, "I made good candy and every day."

With the money earned from the candy, he bought clothes and food for a cousin who had arrived in camp shortly after him. "And she survived," he said proudly.

Szaja may not have had any more money than others in the beginning, but he was innovative and managed to outwit his captors when he was searched. He remembers one particular day. He had some money with him, for it was the day he was to pay for candy ingredients. A Ukrainian decided to search him. As was the procedure, all prisoners carried their eating utensils with them for their meager rations. His was a small bucket with a handle, and as he held his hands up as ordered, he wrapped his paper currency around the handle and inside the palm of his hand. The Ukrainian never thought to look

Szaja Lida and his wife, Ruth

into his hand, he just made sure there was nothing in the bucket or in his clothes.

Cut off from communications, the only clues as to what was happening in the outside world were events surrounding the camp. A signal that the war was going badly for the Germans occurred in April, 1944, when work crews were forced into the forests to exhume and burn the bodies of workers previously killed. "The stench was overpowering," he remembers. The work crews never returned.

Before the camp was closed in June '44, a breakout was planned. He held back, despite the fact that the camp was buzzing with intrigue. Two of his friends decided to join the escapees. He warned them against it, reminding them

that the woods were infested with Germans. Each ten feet of forest contained either Germans or ammunition. I asked them, "Do you think we can break through?"

His friends went as far as the fence and then decided to return. Half of the camp escaped that night. They cut the wire fence and by 7 or 8 a.m. that next morning, the Germans had already caught 100 of them. "All were caught except two … and all were shot in front of us" he said.

Before the camp was closed "selections" were made. "Those with nothing to wear were considered the weakest" and were subsequently shot. He remembers a mother begging for the life of her small daughter. The SS officer responded by shooting both of them. He remembers another horror. As those who had been selected to be shot were being led away, they begged, not for their lives, but for a piece of bread, their hunger was so intense.

The next day, he found himself on a train for Buchenwald. Each prisoner received a half loaf of bread, a little margarine and marmalade. There were about 100 in each train car, "and hardly room to stand." By the time the train reached its destination, after picking up more prisoners along the way, there were 3,000 human souls on board. Once unloaded they were confronted by four crematoriums and the stench of burning human flesh.

As they waited to be admitted to the camp, few thought they would survive, for they had to wait under the ominous threat and smoke and stench of the crematorium.

However, Szaja held on to a fragment of hope, feeling that if the Germans wanted them dead, they would not have gone through all the trouble of transporting them to Buchenwald. He tried to bolster the spirits of those around him.

He was right, but once into the admitting quarters, he was finally forced to part with his remaining item of value, a piece of gold chain. He still tried to think ahead. He divided what was left among his friends and pushed his share into a piece of soap, which he stuffed into his boots.

After quarantine, the workers were sent to a village near Berlin to work in an ammunition factory producing anti-tank grenades. They worked on two shifts – 12 hours each. The food he describes as being "too much to die and not enough to live."

There were acts of courage – and desperation at this camp as the war began to wind down. One involved a boy who had been badly beaten by a German who threatened to kill him if he didn't show up for work the next day. Of course, it would have been impossible, he said, so out of desperation, the boy started a fire in the factory.

"None came out alive. All was destroyed."

But in less than three months, the plant was rebuilt, with the help of the cruel Hitler Youth Corps. The months dragged on and close to April the

factory was closed forever. In typical German Teutonic fashion, the prisoners were ordered to clean up the factory so that the approaching Russians would find it in order! Each prisoner was given a pack of cigarettes for his labor … the first Szaja had had in three years.

Once more he was shoved on a train, this time the destination was Theresenstadt. Except for a half loaf of bread and a stick of margarine, they had no food for days and no water. Incredibly, before he left he was given back his old clothes and the boots with the soap and piece of gold chain!

The Germans were losing and the tracks were heavy with traffic, forcing the train to stop every 20 minutes. "People started to die … we didn't know what to do with the bodies … we lined them up around the edges and used them as pillows."

Finally, they reached a large station where cars were loaded with rutabagas, the first and only food they had had in days. The dead were carried away in borrowed horses and wagons, and the prisoners were expected to bury them. "We were so weak we couldn't dig more than two feet a day."

After eight or nine more days of a diet restricted to rutabagas, more began to die. Once more the Germans stopped the train and borrowed shovels and wagons to bury the dead. The soldiers did not seem to care. Szaja estimates that he was on the train for 24 days before they arrived at Theresenstadt, where they found the German guards had disappeared. The camp was left to operate on its own.

Getting enough food was a problem, and as he walked through the camp he noticed a group of people who were in special enclosures. These were the converts … Jews of and from intermarriages with Germans. He climbed over the fence and approached an elderly woman who asked him to help her move her belongings in exchange for old bread, obviously rations she had stored away. Other elderly women also asked his help and "by night I had my belly full and … three bags of bread," which he threw over the fence and shared with those who had continued to sit in the barracks because "they couldn't find anything to eat."

Liberation was a little less than they expected, it consisted merely of a Russian who was passing through who opened the gates and told them they were free. "Later the Red Cross came and disinfected us, bathed us and weighed us." After two weeks of eating the bread shared by the elderly *mishlings*, Szaja weighed 66 pounds. His weight at the beginning of the war was 170 pounds.

Liberation was not without its irony. Before the Red Cross arrived, some of the prisoners had pillaged nearby towns for food. Szaja warned them to eat only staples such as bread, potatoes, rice –

that their systems would be unable to tolerate rich foods. Those who did not heed his warnings developed dysentery and died. "Hundreds … thousands died this way. The streets were filled with human waste and people lying in the waste … half the camp died after liberation."

The joy of liberation was further marred for Szaja who remembers the busses sent by countries to pick up its citizens. "But none came from Poland. Our hearts were broken, everything was lost." Later he returned to his home and it was "like going back to a cemetery. We were told to leave," he said.

"I asked myself, did it pay to be left over? I left and never returned." ❖

Szaja died July 25, 1999. His wife, Ruth, also a Holocaust survivor, and their daughter, Anna Lida Karp, live in Norfolk. The Lida's only granddaughter, Rachelle, lives in Florida.

Ruth and Anna Lida

Szaja, Rachelle, Anna and Ruth Lida

— 186 —

Speaking for Those Who Cannot Speak for Themselves
HANNS LOEWENBACH

By Reba Karp

HANNS LOEWENBACH begins the story of his wartime experiences by explaining that his travails began with "the bad luck of being born in Germany in 1915."

Hanns' father was away at the time of his birth, a soldier in the German Army during World War I between 1914 and 1918. Hanns explains that about 100,000 German Jews fought for Germany and 12,000 died.

"Germany had lost the war and the scapegoat for loosing the war were the International Jews, according to the disappointed nationalist German population. No wonder that I experienced the hate against the Jews when I was 9 years old in 1924."

The incident he recalled was the event of a birthday party of a friend who had invited him "only to show his new comrades that he had broken his friendship with me by beating me up." This was but one incident of anti-Semitism that he encountered through school.

"Even one of my history teachers explained in class that the reason that Germany had lost the war was partly

Hanns Loewenbach

Photo by Echard Wheeler

the fault of the Jews … I was looking forward to finishing school and going to college. But, in 1933 when I almost finished school, Hitler became the Reich Chancellor and one of his first laws against the Jews was that they were not allowed to enter the university. So in this moment all my dreams were shattered."

His survival route took him from his home in Berlin to a rather shaky port in Shanghai.

He remembers that his father was "one of the first Jews" taken forcibly out of their homes. The Gestapo arrested his father, Louis, while he was having dinner with his family. This was in 1934 and as a German businessman in partnership with two others, one a Protestant and the other, Catholic, in a thriving business, he was asked to sign away all his rights to his partners. Since he refused, he was transported to Buchenwald and later taken to Dachau.

The only information that the family heard concerning his whereabouts came months later when a radio news commentator reported that his father, Louis Loewenbach, had been caught trying to leave Germany and "get money out of the country into Holland."

Since the Loewenbach family knew Louis was being held in a concentration camp, they realized that the report was not possible, that it was only propaganda released by the Third Reich

Hanns sharing his story with students in the Tidewater area. Photo by Susan Hirschbiel

to further their systematic destruction of the German Jewish citizens. However, it was not always possible to convince other Jews that what they were hearing was not so, for as Loewenbach explains: "They had to first experience the injustice for themselves."

These were the days of paradoxes and on July 1, 1935, despite his Jewish background and arrest of his father, Loewenbach was called to serve in the German military. One of the questions they asked him was if he wanted to be a soldier.

"I told them, 'no'," and explained this rejection of the German military was due to a particular vicious news report in which Goebbels referred to "Jews as lice."

"At 20 you are very brave," he adds. The recruiting officer shrugged his shoulders at the offense, for it was too early for even the Germans to take Hitler seriously. So having refused military service, Loewenbach, without the support of his family business, worked as a salesman for another Jewish merchant; his mother, Meta, also without funds from her husband's business, was forced to rent rooms in the family's former ten-room home.

Although times were erratic, all went reasonably well until two months after the Olympic games in Berlin in October, 1936 when he was picked up with other young Jewish men and put in the back of a truck: destination SS Headquarters and, possibly, a concentration camp. Remembering how his father had been taken forcefully from his home never to return, Loewenbach jumped from the truck near Alexander Platz in Berlin, a place as busy as Times Square, New York City, "and from that moment on I was living illegally.–.every day in another place," he recalls. Fortunately for him, he had joined a Zionist Movement in Germany in 1925, and through his association with the organization, became acquainted with a Jewish woman who helped feed him and keep him alive.

"I felt the safest on a train or street car," he adds, "for everyone was going somewhere." The fear he experienced at this time was so instilled in him that it

Approximately 20,000 Jewish refugees found safe haven in Shanghai. Limited movement and wartime deprivation made life difficult in the "Shanghai Ghetto." Although they did not suffer the daily terrors of their fellow Jews trapped in Europe, their life in Shanghai has been described using the Yiddish expression, "shond khay," (a shame of a life).

followed him even into freedom and shaped his responses to normal situations. In 1978 when he was in the hospital for tests prior to heart surgery and the doctor woke him up to give him tests, he was gripped by fear and "ran out of the room."

Understand, he continued, in Germany, "I was not living under normal conditions. I felt like a deer and it was open hunting season." He began sleeping in places with two exits, if the Germans entered by one, he would have an escape exit through the other.

"Actually I slept with one eye open and I still sleep the same way."

Eventually he tried to escape. "I swam two miles to Denmark and was turned back by the Danish. I had to swim two miles back. I was given the choice of being taken to the border and turned in and delivered to the Gestapo or to swim back." It was only after the Germans marched into Denmark that they openly sought to help their Jews, he adds.

"We were all alone. We are still alone! We should never forget that," he adds emphatically. Once back on German soil, he was on the brink of giving up, for "how long can you run?" he questions. "But it is unbelievable how life can work," he adds, explaining that he was sitting on a park bench in Berlin, pondering his next move when he was approached by a tall Gestapo agent, who called him by name. When

he looked up it was into the eyes of a former schoolmate from Luebeck. But instead of the cold calculating eyes of a Jew-hating German, he could clearly see that his former friend was happy to see him. "He asked me, 'What are you doing here, Hanns? Don't you know what we have planned for the Jews?' For that moment, I ceased being a Jew.

"I answered him, 'I would leave if I could.'"

His former schoolmate was in a position to help and offered to do so, providing Hanns could get a photograph for a passport. Even though it seemed like a miracle, Hanns felt helpless, for he wondered if his friend would meet him to help him or turn him in. "In his uniform, my schoolmate became an enemy." After he obtained his photo at an *automate*, his immediate thoughts were of his mother. What would happen to her if he did manage to escape? These were his immediate questions. The date was November 7, 1938. Two nights later, November 9, 1938, *Kristallnacht*, he found himself on the streets of Nazi Germany where he witnessed the destruction of synagogues and Jewish business. "That evening I had not made arrangements on where to sleep and I was on the streets when the trucks with the SS came and threw fire bombs into synagogues. A few minutes later came the fire brigades, not to put fires out, but to make sure it would not spread to other houses.

"Then they threw stones in Jewish shops and tossed the merchandise out on the streets, pulled the Jewish men out and marched them to police headquarters. Later they were taken to concentration camps … that night all over Germany and Austria the same thing was happening."

The agony of the moment was further intensified the next day when the Jewish residents, those who survived and were not deported to the camps, were charged one billion marks to clean up after the destruction.

He felt helpless, angry and frightened. "I knew at any moment I would be discovered. Now I needed to go somewhere." With the passport he had obtained with his friend's help and financial help from the Zionist organization of his youth, he bought a train ticket for Italy. "Brave or not, I had to do something," he explains. Once in Rome, he sought the assistance of the Jewish community and learned that the only place open for him was Shanghai. With their financial assistance, he also managed to get both his mother and father out of Germany. Those were the days, he explains, when money could get Jews even out of concentration camps if they had somewhere to go. "Hitler," he adds, "kept saying, 'take the Jews, what are you complaining about? Take them!'"

Although life in Shanghai was hard and full of privations, it was still life. At first, the refugees were fed by

Hanns and his wife, Jutta
Photo by Susan Hirschbiel

contributions of already-established Jews living in Shanghai. These were Sephardic Jews, originally from Baghdad, who were very well established in the country.

Later, outside funds, which were sent for the refugees to two *yeshivot* in Shanghai, were their only source of financial assistance. These funds, from the Joint Distribution Committee (JDC), helped to feed the refugees. Since funds were limited, immigration was also limited. Many wanted to enter, but funds were lacking to support a larger population. Those who adapted quickly to their new environment learned how to supplement their meager rations. Loewenbach was one of them. "I learned to speak Chinese very quickly. I was 23-24 years old at the time. I went into the country in a rickshaw and bought chicken eggs. My mother sold them to restaurants, etc."

Since he had learned to design and make hats while in Germany, with $20 he also opened a hat shop. When all their resources were pooled, "we could just eat and drink," he explains. Those who had made it to Shanghai were in far better shape than those who were unable to escape, and they were grateful. But despite the fact that they were granted asylum in Shanghai, they lived constantly under a threat of starvation. From December 1942, Pearl Harbor, the Germans and Japanese were allies, he explains, and the Japanese were, subsequently, ordered by the Germans to eliminate the Jews. Gas chambers were built. But no Jews were gassed. "The emperor left it up to the army; the army to the navy and the navy turned it back to the emperor."

In 1946, after the war ended, his mother died in Shanghai; his father, three months later, went to live with his sister, Alice, in Sweden, who had managed to escape there during the war. He stayed with her until 1950. His father then moved to Germany to work on his restitution and died there in 1954. In 1947, Loewenbach moved to America with his first wife, Ruth, whom he married in Shanghai. He lived and worked in New York until Ruth died. Lowenbach married his second wife, Jutta, in 1960, in Berlin, during one of his trips back to Germany.

Until he heard Elie Wiesel speak at a Holocaust gathering, he did not talk about his experiences during the war, nor did he want to talk about them. He did not even want to share the agony of those years with his children. Loewenbach has three children, a daughter by his first wife, Ruth Miriam Becker of Virginia Beach; and two with his second wife, a son Ben Loewenbach, a biomedical engineer, living in Erie, Pennsylvania, and daughter Dr. Gail Loewenbach, who married Richard Sobel.

Today, Hanns feels it is imperative for those who witnessed the Holocaust to speak up and tell their story. This is especially important in the light that there are those who deny the Holocaust ever happened, that six million Jews perished.

Hanns states, "The six million should not be forgotten … I feel I must speak for those who cannot speak for themselves." ❖

The Loewenbach family: back row - Richard, Dean, Hanns, Ben, and Steven. Front row - Alan, Gail, Haley, Jutta, Miriam, and Rachel. Hanns' grandson, David, is not in this photo.

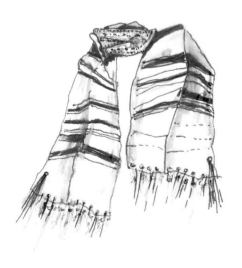

Hanns lights a candle at the community Holocaust Commemoration.

Liberation: Kaddish Begins

REVEREND BER LUFTRIEBER

By Reba Karp

Editor's Note: The following are but two incidents – fragments from a tapestry of horror – which occurred during the internment of Rev. Ber Luftrieber, former President of the Holocaust Survivors Club of Tidewater. The incidents came to my attention while viewing a video tape which he made with Laurel Vlock several years ago. The pain on Ber's face; the suffering in his voice prompted me to explore these incidents further. I sensed the agony between the lines, that which was not said, that which was too much for him to verbalize. In his own words, "each day in the camps, was like a whole book." Ber Luftrieber was a private person. Very quiet, almost courtly. Ber and his wife, Rosa, also a survivor and both of blessed memory, have one son, and grandchildren living in Israel.

BER LUFTRIEBER is a proud man who bears his memories sparingly and with dignity. They are a blur of pain which began on November 15, 1939 when he was forced inside the walls of the Warsaw Ghetto. If liberation was an anodyne for the pain, it was a narcotic he rejected until many years later.

Liberation caught him off guard. His mind responded to the stimulant that here was freedom; but his soul rejected the notion, for too many had died – too horribly. As Ber explained: "I was liberated in Vienna…. I felt that I am by myself, in a desert. I looked at the world like a desert. I felt like Noah when he left the Ark after The Flood. Only he had his family with him."

Perhaps his vision of the barren wasteland was appropriate, for he

Reverend Ber Luftrieber

Photo by Stephen Jay Photography

questions why so many who knew the conditions in the camps never "lifted a finger to help." Consequently, he explains, when he first saw a Russian soldier and realized that he could walk free in the streets, he also realized that "I am not the same."

Appropriately, he has selected his liberation date to say *Yahrzeit* for those of his family who were murdered. The actual dates are but dust underfoot in the deserted camps.

The ghetto closed in on him and his wife and a daughter, who was born in 1936. His parents were the first of his family to be taken away to Treblinka, found after "hiding in the attic of a home." The house was a makeshift construction, overcrowded, burdened with suffering. The attic was an extension of that overcrowding and suffering. But, it was the only shelter the aging Luftriebers could find in the inhumanely overcrowded ghetto.

"Many didn't have a place to stay. They used to stay in the public places, like the schools and synagogues." He was lucky, for when he arrived, his brother-in-law was already there and offered him shelter. Fearful, because they were older and subjected to immediate transportation, his parents sought refuge in the attic until discovered, and dragged away and stuffed onto a wagon to be transported to death.

He could only stand by and watch. The voices, the bleating of those who knew

My child was then six years old. She didn't need any comfort. She knew. The children knew already … she didn't cry.

they were about to perish, are like sounds he encountered but weeks ago.

He and his wife and daughter were deported after the uprising which started in April 1943. There was nowhere to hide. The Germans had torched the buildings, forcing the Jews into the open. "We went into the streets. All the buildings in Warsaw were tall buildings, big buildings. We went through the streets, the pieces were hot from the fires. I don't know why they didn't shoot us. Maybe they were lazy …

"The next day they loaded us on freight cars. We couldn't raise a finger, a hand, so tight it was. My child was then six-years-old. She didn't need any comfort. She knew. The children knew already … she didn't cry.

"The next day we arrived at Majdaneck. We thought, relieved, at least not Treblinka, because Treblinka we already knew they had no working place. It was straight to the gas chamber….

"There were the Germans with the dogs with the hollering, screaming, beatings." Then a few days later, the selections began with the women and the children. "They grabbed them, they chased them with the dogs." It was the last time he saw his wife and child. "I didn't feel all the time … after the liberation I felt, then I start to feel again," he said.

"… There was no day they didn't kill some people. We didn't have any hope

… Nothing. The people were like animals without thinking. Take cattle to slaughter … it was day to day…."

And then Ber encounters a memory which makes the mind explode. His brother-in-law had a pair of *tefillin*, so precious, so irreplaceable – connections to sanity, lifelines to God. One day the *tefillin* were discovered by the Germans while they were working outside the camp.

The prisoners knew something was wrong as they stood in line to get their soup and there was no soup. As they waited, his brother-in-law was dragged before them, rope around his neck, naked, his body already swollen from beatings. "They took him to the gallows … they put him there to stand … But they didn't hang him. We had an order that everyone of us had to hit him … not too fast."

They waited and they shuffled, each in his turn, to strike the defenseless human being. No one was excused.

"When he fell … they opened his mouth and poured water into it, and they kept it up until … they couldn't pour any more water in …

"… Later we davened *Mincha*. I said *Kaddish*…. I don't know what hell is like, but it was worse." ❖

Rosa Luftrieber lights a remembrance candle

The Set of Tefillin

The set of Tefillin in my bag
on a Polish pilgrimage
evokes martyred ancestors
who donned them with hearts
Turned heavenward.
I wonder of God's words' fate,
did they ascend with their
earthly custodians?

Rabbi Israel Zoberman

Living by Her Wits and False Identity Papers

Janine May-Levine

By Reba Karp

An office in back of a closet and a bell that rang to warn her of impending danger were part of JANINE MAY-LEVINE'S survival mechanism during World War II.

"I still have nightmares. Whenever I hear a noise at night, I jump. The Gestapo is still there. You never leave it behind you," she explains.

Such an atmosphere and fears were far removed from her comfortable childhood. "As a young girl, I was happy go lucky. At the end of the war, I was a nervous wreck. I was a different person," she adds. While growing up, Janine remembers that her family was wealthy and lived on a large piece of property in the central part of France, which they shared with her aunt, uncle and grandparents. She had two brothers and two sisters.

Janine's family home.

The first signs that things were going to change occurred when the Jewish people had to register with the police. "I was about 16 or 17," she recalls. "But my father said, don't worry about it. They are not going to bother us. They are looking for foreigners. Nothing will

Photo left - Janine's father

Photo above - Janine and her first husband, David Roiter

Photo right - David Roiter

happen to us. Let's do the right thing." She attributes this optimism to the fact that the family was ninth generation French.

The "right thing" her father mentioned was followed by Jews being compelled to sew yellow stars on their clothing. Since those that wore the star were among the first being picked up by the Germans, this time Janine and her family did not follow orders. And if the townspeople noticed they were not following orders, Janine adds, "no one in the community said anything."

The rumble of war and its discomforts continued to move closer and "when I was 20, my father lost his business and

we moved to Paris to a furnished apartment." By then Janine was married to her first husband who was in the French army. "His name was David Roiter. He would come to my house often. I was 17 when we got engaged. Because of the war we got married so we could see each other more often."

Since apartments in war-torn Paris were hard to find, the young couple at first lived with her husband's parents. They eventually moved into their own apartment. Food was scarce. "You had to use coupons and stand in long lines," Janine says.

If there was any time for the newlyweds to enjoy their time together, it was short

lived after "Hitler invaded France and took half of it," Janine remembers.

The full intent of Hitler's plans didn't become evident to Janine until they "came and picked up my husband. It was only the second or third time they had picked up Jews," she explains. "They picked him up from our apartment at six o'clock in the morning. They came even though we weren't listed as living there. They also took my husband's father … it was the last time I saw my husband and I never saw my father-in-law again, either. We were told that the Jews were being shipped to Germany to work. Five years later I found out that my husband had been

shot by German soldiers in a concentration camp."

Now all alone with limited food and freedom, she once again went to live with her mother-in-law. "She was happy to see me because she was alone also." Three months later, the Germans started picking up women and children. "I told my mother-in-law that we should leave, but she didn't want to. She was afraid her husband and son would not be able to find her when they were released."

So Janine left alone, on a bike with a small suitcase. "I told my mother-in-law that I would be back in the morning for the rest of my things. When I returned the next day the manager of the building was waiting for me. He told me that they had picked

up my mother-in-law…. I never saw her again. Five years later I found out that she died in the gas chamber of a concentration camp."

Janine, who was living on her wits and false identity papers at the time, was working for a company that sold farm equipment and large machinery. Since her employer took frequent business trips to Switzerland, it became apparent to the workers that he could pass on important messages to the American Embassy there. "We were at the mercy of being picked up anyway and we wanted to do something constructive."

So a system was devised in which they reported, in invisible ink on the back of envelopes carried into Switzerland by her boss, pertinent information which they felt would be of help to the Allied troops.

All movements were carefully scrutinized by the Germans and eventually a few of the letters fell into their possession. "The SS had a sample of my handwriting," and they knew "I was keeping books in the office," she informs. "However, (for just such an emergency) there was a second set of books … by another person in the office. So when the SS came looking for me and the books they were shown, the handwriting didn't match."

The visit from the SS triggered the safety procedure that they had planned for just such an emergency. "My boss rang a bell (to my office) and I locked

my office door. The SS asked to search the (entire) office and my boss said 'okay'," she explains, adding that when they got to the closet door and found it locked, they questioned what was behind it, they were told it was just an office supply closet.

When her boss offered to give the Germans a key to the door, hoping to catch them off guard, "They said 'no' and left the office," Janine says, recalling how she heard the dangerous conversation from behind her locked door. "In those minutes, you don't even think," she says, recalling the fear.

"My boss saved my life that day," she adds. Her trials were not over, for the Germans left a soldier outside the office for two days and two nights to see if Janine would return.

Since she was already in the office, all she had to do was wait until the guard was lifted and she could escape.

"My boss said I could not stay any longer because it was too dangerous. So that's when I left and I had to find a way to get past the demarcation line." Although she had false papers, since she was already under suspicion, she could not go to the police and ask for permission to travel to the south of France.

She had to find other means of transportation. "I rode on the back of a truck for four hours in the middle of the night. The truck stopped and I was told to go into the woods and wait for a person who would be whistling a certain tune and only then could I show myself. I waited about two hours in the woods for the person," she says. Once she met up with her guide, the rest of the way was a treacherous route by foot, during which she had to crawl across a field and into a ditch and wait until she was told to jump across the road.

Across the road was free France and once on the other side of the road, the Germans couldn't touch you, she adds. It was a long ordeal that took days. "Later I learned that my guide was killed on his way back."

Two weeks after she entered free France, the German occupation arrived. She remembers the day well. "I stood at the curb watching them come in. I cried." But since she had false identity papers, she was able to get another job and kept moving. It was not a happy time. "I witnessed the German soldiers picking up Jewish families and taking babies and children from their mothers. The mothers were put in one truck and the babies in another. One German soldier refused to take a baby from its mother and was shot and killed by his superior officer."

Still living on her wits and trying to stay one step ahead of the Germans, Janine eventually went back to Paris and got a job as a secretary. Afraid to remain, she decided to leave Paris once again and started her journey with a cousin who had transportation. Later, her cousin let her off at a train station which was

packed with French soldiers, refugees and wounded people. While waiting, the station was bombed by the Germans and the French soldiers saved her life. She was only 16 kilometers from where her parents lived and had no way to contact them.

After France was liberated she got a job as an interpreter for the U.S. Army, where she eventually met an American soldier who would become her second husband. She later moved with him to America and had one child.

Now 81 years old and a resident of Virginia Beach, Virginia, she enjoys reading, knitting and walking. Despite her pleasant life and surroundings, the Holocaust and all its dangers are still strong memories. "I wouldn't have the nerve to live through that again. In those days you only thought about survival and how to out think and outwit the Germans." ❖

Kevin, Janine's grandson

Janine and her daughter, Nadine.

His Survival a Series of Miracles
ABE OKUN

By Karen Yeulovea Stout

Abe Okun   *Photo by Stephen Jay Photography*

At 68, ABE OKUN looks like the father that he is. It is remarkable that a man with his history would appear so youthful. Another trait which is immediately recognizable is his confidence. His bearing is one from which success emanates.

Neatly dressed in a dark blue suit his soft spoken manner aids him in telling the story which is so hard to tell. He speaks with a rich European accent. His English is not always perfect, but he expresses himself eloquently. His words are more than adequate in telling his story.

His sister died in a concentration camp with the rest of his family; only Abe and his brother, both of whom had avoided being transported to a camp, survived. Perhaps their experience was almost as devastating.

Prior to 1940, Abe and his family owned and operated a leather factory in Bialystock, Poland. "It was a nice life," remembers Abe. "Bialystock was an industrial town … a prosperous city. We had everything. After the war, it became no-man's land, no Jews. When Hitler came, he put together 120,000 (Jews) from all the surroundings. A family of ten or 12 lived in one room. Every couple of weeks they made 'selections,' at four or five o'clock in the morning, anybody they could get hold of. They said they took them to work camps, but actually they took them to Auschwitz or Majdanek, to be gassed. We knew what to expect from them (the Nazis), what the end would be."

Abe and his family, however, were prepared. Abe reasoned that the best place for them to hide would be under the house where they lived. So he, his brothers and two friends built a bunker under their home.

"Everyone did according to their way of thinking," Abe said. "A lot of them tried to make bunkers, but after the war, my bunker was one of three left (in Bialystock). A lot of people went to the woods." Abe and his family knew it would be "impossible to make it in the woods when the cold … (came)." The cold, however, would be the least of their troubles.

In 1940 the Germans came to Bialy-stock and took the Jews away in the middle of the night. Abe terms these raids on human beings, "actions." The last was in August of 1943 when the Germans grabbed 2,500 people, put them in a large synagogue, dropped grenades and burned everyone inside. "Bialystock was liquidated," he said.

But it was in 1940, after the "first action," that Abe and his family moved underground into a bunker under the house. The Germans came and turned everything upside down in the house, he remembers. "But they couldn't find us."

Since survival meant staying ahead of the Germans, Abe and his family decided to build another bunker, this one where they could hold out much longer. "We found the Jewish gymnasium. It was empty by then. We decided to build a bunker underneath that … (would) last for six months. We didn't think the war … (would) last longer."

The bunker was about 8 feet by12 feet and a little under six feet deep. "On top was the crawl space," Abe said. "We had to leave a yard of ground on top in case they came searching for us." They built bunk beds for Abe, his family and two friends. However, only two would survive.

"When they started to evacuate and kill everyone in town, we got into the bunker," Abe said. They were nine difficult days, for the water they had prepared leaked out from the wooden barrels into the ground. "We had no

water left…. We drank water from a spoon," he said, "in order to make the water last longer.

"The Germans searched every building to see if Jews were hiding. They went from room to room, and knocked out a big hole with a long iron and (stuck) the pick into the ground, to see if there were any bunkers underneath," he said.

Then they made the "Little Ghetto." The Germans picked Jewish people and told them to make their own government (Judenrat). They were responsible to the police and to bring Jews to the Germans. In 1943, when they took away 90,000 Jews from the "Little Ghetto," they left the Judenrat, the police and the working class. The "working class" were those Jewish people who were able to perform manual labor. Abe said, "They put them in that building where I had my bunker."

In order to learn what was going on above the bunker, Abe left by his secret door. While out, with the chutzpah of a man determined to survive, he made latkes to send under the house.

When Abe returned to the bunker, he told those hidden what he had learned, that the Germans were preparing to

clean out the ghetto. The rumor was that they were going to remove the last of the Jews – the *Judenrat* and the workers.

"It was hard to take," Abe said, but he was determined to remain in the bunker until the end. "I was sure I (would) come through it, not knowing how or why."

Perhaps Abe's mother had had a premonition of her son's ultimate survival in a dream she had while hiding in the bunker. "She said 'I went to a wedding. We were all dressed up, dancing and music was playing,'" he remembered.

"After Hitler had his speech, on Pesach (Passover) 1939, he promised that he would have all the Jews killed (by) next Pesach. If any one (Jew) will be alive, he will bow for them. That was the reason to … live."

So Abe's decision was to remain in hiding. His brother and two friends decided to stay with him. The four of them had the resolve, "We have built the bunker and we will live in the bunker. We will make it."

The rest of his family, however, decided to take their chances on the outside, which was unfortunate as it turned out. "But they had enough of the life in the grave," Abe said.

"The next day they picked everyone up, put them on the train…. We found out later they went to Auschwitz. They got

killed with all the rest, burned, killed, burned! We stayed in that bunker for another 11 months."

During the 11 months, the building, which housed the bunker was used for many purposes. They brought in the Jews from the small towns. They packed them in that building … two weeks later, they pulled them all out and sent them to the gas chambers. Eventually the building was converted into a hospital. "The headquarters of the Germans was in the hospital. We heard the soldiers walking by and even saw them." During the time of the "Little Ghetto," the *Judenrat* had turned the building into an orphanage. "We could hear and see through the hole, we could see the faces of the nurses, the doctors and the children … and hear at night the screams when the Germans picked out the girls to have relations with and then kill them. We could see it through the holes! When they (the Jewish doctors and nurses) went along with the kids, they thought that would be their passport to life. (But) they were killed, as we found out later. After being there, maybe a month, they pulled them all out together and sent them away. Nobody knew where they went. We thought maybe they would live."

His sister's four-year-old child was there. Abe has heard conflicting stories concerning the child's fate. One was that the children made it to Switzerland. Another, that they were sent to a camp

Abe and his family, however, were prepared. Abe reasoned that the best place for them to hide would be under the house where they lived. So he, his brothers and two friends built a bunker under their home.

"to a crematorium, where they were all burned, the doctors, nurses and children. I hope still that maybe the child was sent away to Israel or someplace else and is still alive. But there is no way to find out," Abe said.

No matter what was happening to the world around them, they had to go on. Obtaining water for survival was playing the odds against that survival, however. "We were trying to gather water from the rain, bring it back to the bunker … we saw a bunker on the other side of the street. We couldn't figure out how they could get water, so we went to them to see if they had water." The people he found were hiding in a small cellar, under a burned house. There were 12 of them, crammed into small quarters.

"If they wanted to eat, there was no way to get by one another. Only at night, to stretch their legs, could they get out." They had water which they got from a well about three blocks away, but didn't have anything to eat. "We decided we would trade. We had some flour and peas and they would bring us water." They planned to make the exchange the next night. "We went to look for them. There was nobody there." The Germans had gotten to them first, he said solemnly.

Outsmarting the Germans was part and parcel of survival and when the Germans renovated the building into a hospital, it gave them easier access to water. The Germans turned on the water in the building, and Abe and his companions drilled a hole into the pipe with a drill they got from a dentist. It was just a small hole, Abe said, but it was enough to supply them with water through a hose which they had the forethought to stash in the bunker, for just such an emergency.

Abe notes that when the hole first went into the pipe, there was a whistling sound made due to the water pressure in the pipes. Overhead, the Germans were sleeping. "Somehow I closed the little hole with my finger and put some plastic around it."

With the water came the opportunity to clean themselves. After their initial bathing, they discovered they were full of lice. "The only way we could get rid of these things was to wash ourselves in kerosene." But that offered only a temporary respite, for as soon as they changed into clean shirts, the lice returned. "The only way … (was) to go in the same shirt, soaked in kerosene."

Abe and his family had "prepared as much" kerosene as they could, for when the electricity was cut off, the kerosene in a small lamp provided light for a couple of hours, to use for reading. One particular book comes to mind. "Today it would be an antique," Abe said. "It is the story of an old, retired postmaster who gets together, everyday, with a former storekeeper and … tells what he sees for the future. He talked about Hitler, who would get so big that he will try to take over the world." The book predicted the whole war, month by month, until the end. The postmaster saw the Second World War. "He predicted everything. It came out exactly." According to the book the war was to be over in 1945. Hitler would be at the top of the mountain, from which he would fall and "get hit so hard that he would not be able to get up. And that's exactly the way it went," Abe laughed.

Reading that particular book helped Abe and his brother plan for what was ahead. Instead of thinking that the war would be over in six months, they altered their outlook and planned for a longer duration, trying to stretch their food so it would last. "We had other books, too, but that was one that I remember well."

Besides reading, they had few ways of entertaining themselves. "We made friends with a rat … he was our mascot. When he came running in the bunker to look for food, we caught him and put him in a suitcase. We held him there until he started to smell." Abe laughed, "We had to let him out."

Since there was little to do to keep the mind active, their sleep patterns changed. "We were like babies, sleeping four hours and four hours up," Abe said.

Likewise, their eating habits changed. During their stay in the bunker they ate only raw peas and flour. "We had half a glass (of peas) for 24 hours, to chew on, raw," Abe said. However distasteful this may seem, it was a rather lucky coincidence or "miracle" as Abe would call it, that the peas were eaten raw.

After liberation, when they visited a doctor, he asked them what they ate. "We told him raw peas," Abe said, explaining that the doctor told them that they were lucky that they had no way to cook it. Cooked, the peas would have lost some of the vitamins; eaten

"I have seen more miracles in my life than in the history of the world."

raw, they not only provided the full benefit of the vitamins, but gave their teeth something to chew on.

And so, a whole series of "miracles" unfolded before him. Recalling each, Abe seemed to find a little joy, smiling or laughing at an otherwise unhappy review of memories. "What I have seen in that bunker, I have seen miracles that nobody could explain." Abe explained further, "They (the Germans) had a way

of sniffing out the bunkers. I was lucky; they didn't get hold of my bunker," Abe said, explaining another miracle – this one regarding the entrance to his bunker. "We heard the Germans and the *Judenrat* (trying) to find the Jewish people who were hiding." He quickly crawled out and put a piece of plywood over the hole. He stayed out long enough to observe their procedure. They were going from one room to the other, knocking out a piece of flooring and then looking underneath. It was a big building, maybe 20 rooms downstairs, and then upstairs. "When they came close to the room where I had my bunker, maybe 15 or 20 Germans, I decided to hold that board because standing on it would have opened it … I felt this German standing on the door. I was laying underneath, holding it, and hoping … They knocked out a hole, and looked into it. I saw them standing on top and heard them talking. After an hour of strenuous waiting … they left.

"At night, when everybody was gone, I decided to go and take a look … I saw the holes they made in every room." When he reached the room where his bunker was concealed, he sat down with amazement, for another miracle had happened. "I saw a hole three-quarters drilled out, but the one who drilled the holes didn't go through. He pulled out the drill, went over about a foot away and drilled four holes into the other board," Abe said, explaining that if the German had continued drilling in one

spot, with one knock with the iron, the board would have jumped out. "They would have found the entrance." Abe likes to think that, perhaps, the man who drilled the hole realized there was a bunker underneath and purposely ignored it. But even so, it was a miracle that there were Gentiles who helped Jewish people during the Holocaust, considering the consequences they would face if they were caught.

"We had one Pole … We trusted him to buy some bread. He didn't know where we were, we didn't want to let him know. We went three miles from our bunker to the other end of town, to see what he could get for us, because we ran out of supplies after three months. We gave him whatever we had, and he bought us supplies. His wife did not want to. The Germans used to walk by his house. I was there, one time, she started to scream, 'I'm going to call the Germans in.' He knocked her down. He had a conscience. That was the difference from one person to another."

Abe remembers another incident suggesting an element of conscience. One of the Germans who was in charge of pulling people from their homes in the ghetto for transportation to concentration camps, suffered a heart attack. "He couldn't take it. So, you have one German who had something for feeling."

From the vantage point of being able to look back on events, Abe reasons that the Germans had been thoroughly

Anticipating the arrival of Russian Troops.   *Photo by Hugo Horvath*

brainwashed and that the process started when they were very young. "The children were the ones to throw stones and scream *schmutzig Juden* (dirty Jew)."

The Polish people were brainwashed, also, and because they sympathized with the German cause so completely, the crematoriums were built in Poland. Other people would not have cooperated so easily, he reasons. "For every Jew on the street, (the Poles) used to get ten pounds of sugar. They could recognize a Jew more than the Germans … The Poles were the ones who were catching Jews, in order to get something to eat," Abe said.

After six months of living in the bunker, the two men who were with Abe and his brother could not take it any longer.

"One at a time they went out to see if, maybe, they could get to the woods. They got caught. After we were liberated, we saw, in the jail, on the wall, written in blood (a message), 'To the brothers Okun, if they will be alive: See that you will avenge for our lives.'"

Abe and his brother never took revenge. Their health was poor due to the years of deprivation. At 5 feet, 10 inches, Abe Okun estimated his weight upon liberation to be 70 pounds. "We started to eat. We got sick, like all the others. Everything we could get our hands on, we ate," Abe recalled.

The last bombardment was in 1945. The hospital had abandoned the building. "We knew something had happened," Abe said. "We listened,

through the hole, in the crawl space, and heard the singing of the Russian soldiers. We went out of the bunker to see what was going on. The Russian soldiers stopped us and asked, 'Who are you, and where did you come from?' They wanted to arrest us because we didn't have … (papers) with us. We told them that we came out of a bunker and they didn't believe us. The officer said he wanted to go and see if we are telling the truth. So, we went and showed him where the bunker was. He got halfway under the floor, crawling, and decided not to go anymore," Abe said.

Abe Okun met his first wife, Sabina Miller, in 1945. During the war, she had worked in an ammunition factory in Auschwitz. "She was one who took part in blowing up the crematorium." Three girls were hanged for it, but when it was her turn to fall from the gallows, fate intervened. The order was out to evacuate the camp because the Russians were approaching.

Despite the fact that the war was over, it hadn't ended for the Jews who were still in Poland. The Polish Fighters for Independence took over where Hitler left off and tried to rid the country of the remaining Jews. Abe recalls one Pole saying with pride while holding up a photograph of a young Jewish couple, "I married this couple a week ago and the next day, I buried them." The girl in the photograph had been in Auschwitz with his wife. "When she

How can we prevent it from happening again? "Educate, educate, educate," Abe simply stated. That one word, repeated three times for emphasis.

recognized her, we decided to get out of Bialystock.... That gave us the push to run away," Abe said.

They made their way to an American refugee camp in Austria, where they could eat, drink and stay until transported elsewhere. But they remained there for four years until his brother went to Australia. Then, a couple months later, Abe and his wife were brought by the Jewish community to Norfolk, Virginia. In 1962, his wife died from Multiple Sclerosis.

Abe does not like to be reminded of the Holocaust. He explains, "I am putting it out of my mind … not feeding my soul … putting it in a drawer and keeping the drawer closed, most of the time, I try to talk very little about my experience." Abe feels that talking about his life would make everyone "miserable," especially his children. "It will come their time to know. They will be able to read and to see. They are starting to ask questions. I answer them, but I calm it down to a shorter version.… "

Since he remembers the past in detail, he is understandably bitter. "It's a miracle, but if I would have to go through it again … I would rather to go out and kill the first Nazis and then let them kill me. My life is happy, it's beautiful, but I don't think a person should struggle and suffer that much in order to … later breathe and enjoy life," he stated sadly.

Yet, as he mentions frequently, he continues to believe in luck, miracles and God. Luck? "The way luck puts your path in life, I was happy to go along on the path I was chosen to."

Miracles? "I have seen more miracles in my life than in the history of the world."

God? "There is no question, I believe in God, but I put it in a different perspective. I say it is a wonderful way to raise children, to bring them up to be good people."

How can we prevent it from happening again? "Educate, educate, educate," Abe simply stated. That one word, repeated three times for emphasis. ❖

Reprinted from Yom Hashoah supplement, April 1984, published by the United Jewish Federation of Tidewater.

Editor's note: Abe remarried in 1972 and had three children. Abe died on August 7, 1985.

ALLEN ORNDORFF
The Importance of Telling Their Story
By Moira Wright Bodner

Liberators of the U.S. Seventh Army are cheered as they enter the Dachau concentration camp. *Dachau, Germany, April, 30, 1945.   Photo by S. Blau*
National Archives, Washington, D.C., courtesy of the United States Holocaust Memorial Museum

Allen Orndorff

"You put the horrible stuff out of your mind," says ALLEN ORNDORFF, a Christian liberator, as he attempted to explain his reaction to being at Dachau shortly after its liberation.

For many years, Orndorff did not talk about what he encountered at Dachau. Now, over half a century later, he is a volunteer at the War Memorial Museum in Newport News, Virginia, and shares with visitors his memories of Dachau.

As a high school senior in Winchester, Virginia, Orndorff volunteered for the Army the day after Pearl Harbor. He was attached to the 101st Airborne Division when it was sent to Dachau. He was shocked, as were his Army buddies, at what they found. He remembers there wasn't much talk then among them about the overwhelming human suffering they had encountered.

Orndorff speaks about Dachau because he feels it is important for people to know the truth of what happened. "In almost every group I've spoken to in six years as a volunteer, there is a kid who raises her hand and questions the Holocaust," says Orndorff.

Orndoff, who was wounded three times in 32 months of combat has three Purple Hearts. He tells Museum visitors about being at a railroad terminal where corpses were stacked three feet deep in boxcars. He recounts the horror of liberating a camp where women inmates were subjected to brutal medical experiments, exposing them to heavy doses of radiation.

The helplessness of the victims has stayed with Orndorff during the years. "Those people were someone's wife, mother, sister. Their memory deserves our telling their story," he says. ❖

Mr. and Mrs. Reed, Irving Althaus, and Mr. and Mrs. Orndorff attend Yom Hashoah ceremony in Newport News, Virginia, 2001.

German citizens evacuate as American troops enter their city.
Photo by Hugo Horvath

"Those people were someone's wife, mother, sister. Their memory deserves our telling their story."

Henry Zvi Perkiel
THE SATCHEL

By Henry Zvi Perkiel

This particular episode from my past, which I am writing about in my memoir, I chose because it is unique and one of a kind. It happened about half a century ago when I was going through the Holocaust experience during World War II. My name is HENRY ZVI PERKIEL. I was born and lived in Warsaw, Poland, with my parents and two brothers. We had a very full and comfortable life, attending private school, etc.

As the war progressed, our whole family was confined and incarcerated in the Warsaw Ghetto. We were forced to abandon our home, where we lived almost a lifetime, in minutes. My mother and ten-year-old brother got separated from us and I never saw them again. As we were being transported in cattle cars from the inhuman, bloody

Umschlag Platz (transfer point) in Warsaw to camp Majdanek, my father and older brother vanished. I will never be able again, in my lifetime, to see, to hug or to touch my mother, my father and my youngest brother. They were

Since childhood I have carried this special will to survive and live with perfection, purity, honesty and fairness. I hope my story will reach this particular German guard from the past.

gone forever. My oldest brother did survive and is living in New York, with his wife.

At a very young age I was lonely, homeless, without parents and did not know yet what hardship, suffering, pain and hunger I would still have to undergo. Majdanek was just the beginning of more misery, cruelty and hell to come. Its function was to take part in the extermination of Jews and other nationalities. It had a double barbed-wire fence, electrically charged, and many watch towers. Majdanek also had seven gas chambers and some gallows.

One morning, after roll call *(apel)* and plenty of tiring and futile exercise until exhaustion, the Germans selected many inmates, myself included, and put us on a freight train on the way to Auschwitz.

At Auschwitz we received numbers tattooed on the left arm. Mine was 128195. I was thrown into a large water tank by two SS guards while they were giggling, and when I tried to get out, they beat on my fingertips. The same day we left on foot to Buna, which was a sub-camp of Auschwitz. I worked there mainly as a painter for a German firm, I.G. Farben. I was assigned to a painters' work detachment: Maler Commando Number 118 with our German prisoner-orderly Kapo Arthur, an exceptionally nice, good-natured person.

I was still in Buna when I found myself in a barrack hospital with an adjacent little crematorium. After some of my good teeth were pulled out without any tranquilizer, an SS inspection team came in and looked at my chart in the doctor's presence who, I had a feeling, wanted to protect me.

Near the end of the war, the Germans began evacuating many camps because of the advancing Russian troops. Masses of prisoners were moved out from Camp Buna (Monowitz) where I was, and sent on long-distance death marches in which the prisoners suffered heavy losses.

It was very cold and snowing. We were dressed very lightly and had no food or water. The following unusual and rare occurrence happened while we were on the death march from Camp Buna, and involved one of the many German soldiers whose function was to guard

the wide and long columns of prisoners walking towards their unknown destiny. Many hundreds of exhausted, sick and starving prisoners died on the way. I was walking first in the row which was closest to the forest.

Suddenly, unexpectedly, unheard of in those times, one of the German guards who was walking alongside, approached me, the prisoner, the nobody, the so-called enemy of the Third Reich, out of thousands of prisoners, and whispered into my ears that he did not feel well and would like me to hold his military satchel. I was shocked and practically speechless with disbelief. I accepted his request without any hesitation.

Immediately I strapped it over my head in front of my chest to keep it safe.

Since I was starving and knew that if I did not put any food in my stomach I might die, I made a decision to search the satchel for food, only.

But, before I did that, I switched my place and pushed myself deep inside the marching prisoners so as not to be recognized by the guard in case he returned. Only then I started to search the satchel for food and found bread and triangle-shaped cheeses. From sheer desperation I could not resist and started to devour some of the food and enjoyed it immensely, adding energy to my deteriorating condition.

At the same time, I had to be very careful not to cause the slightest suspicion among the starving prisoners who would attack me instantly for the

life-saving food. In the satchel were also personal belongings, such as utensils, silverware, shaving equipment, etc., of which I started to dispose, one by one, so as not to be detected. I did this by throwing them down into the falling snow. I also got rid of the empty satchel. Then I took a deep breath and started to feel more optimistic, but I was still concerned about the outcome of the deadly game.

Darkness came and we kept walking all night in deep snow and freezing temperatures. Then the morning came and, from nowhere, the biggest fright of my life: The German guard who gave me his satchel was looking for me with another guard on a three-wheeled motorcycle, screaming and calling in German: Where is the young fellow *(junge kerl)* to whom I gave my satchel? The deadly search continued for many hours, nonstop.

For me it was, and continues to be, a lifetime nightmare. For the time being I had survived a very dangerous cat-and-mouse ordeal. The next day, however, I felt a tremendous jolt to my body; the impact of what had happened shook me up so much that I thought I had been shot. Soon after that ordeal, I began to comprehend how precious life really is, that there won't be another one. I felt strong and protected from evil. I was no longer frightened. My thinking changed from being a loser to the more positive attitude that I WILL SURVIVE!

Henry Perkiel

Soon we entered a huge brick dwelling with a very large hall and all kinds of machinery and equipment. I was sure that this was the end of us. It looked like a real gas chamber with all those protruding chimneys; I started to think of escaping. But, luckily, always having hope that life is worthwhile, I slept through the night, sitting up. And when dawn came we were on the march again until we reached an open grassy field. Some of the prisoners ate the grass and dead human flesh while waiting to be picked up by cattle cars without any roof or cover on the way to Buchenwald and then to Therezienstadt.

The snow, which was falling into the cars was, for a while, our food and nourishment. In Therezienstadt I contracted the dreadful disease typhus and spent time in a makeshift hospital. While lying in the hospital bed, I suddenly heard screaming, shouting and the mingling of many voices. I picked

myself up and when I came closer to the window, my heart almost stopped. I became aware that people were yelling and crying from disbelief that the war was over.

I was liberated by the incoming Russian troops who took over the camp, Therezienstadt. I was stripped, washed and scrubbed with hard brushes by Russian women soldiers. At that time, being liberated and simultaneously cured of my disease, meant I was born the second time. I became a new person, believing it was my natural instinct to survive.

Since childhood I have carried this special will to survive and live with perfection, purity, honesty and fairness. I hope my story will reach this particular German guard from the past, now of age, hopefully still alive like I am still alive. Perhaps because of his blessed bread and cheeses I survived the war, and the young guard survived, too. It was a meal of a lifetime. This unusual, remarkable and rare occurrence gave me the enormous and wonderful strength and stamina with the endurance to live. This is why I hope that he and I will, one day, meet again.

I don't understand why the German guard trusted me with his satchel rather than one of his comrades. This is my biggest puzzle and always will be. ❖

Perkiel, a retired jeweler and Holocaust survivor, was a former resident of the Tidewater area.

SHE WAS ON SCHINDLER'S LIST
Anna Perl

By Fred Kirsch

Anna Perl with her grandson, Josh, and her daughter, Sonia.

Editor's Note: the following article appeared in *The Virginian Pilot*, January 21, 1994. It is reprinted with permission. Anna Perl died March 11, 1997.

She was barely 20 years old and working in the laundry room at Plaszow concentration camp in Poland. By day, she'd wash the piles and piles of bloody sheets that were dumped through the doors.

By night, she slept on a thin mattress in the barracks, her arms wrapped around her sister, Erna, wondering in the darkness if tomorrow would be the day they killed her.

Then one day, in the spring of 1943, a small Jewish man in a suit came to the laundry.

"We need ten women to work in the factory," he said, looking around, stopping at the young woman with the bright eyes that somehow still flickered with life.

"What is your name?"

"Anna Duklawer."

He wrote it down. Next to the others:

Rosner.

Dresner.

Horowitz.

Stagel.

Scharf.

Pefferberg.

Hirsch.

Anna Duklawer was on Schindler's list.

Today, ANNA DUKLAWER PERL sits in the living room of the small Virginia Beach, Virginia, house she shares with her daughter, Sonia Cohen's family and three of her ten grandchildren.

Anna is 71 now. Her face is creased with time, and the letters Kz, a German abbreviation for "concentration camp," burned into her left forearm a half century ago, have faded into a dull blue-grey.

"I don't know why I was chosen that day," she says. "It's a question I've asked myself hundreds and hundreds of times. Why me? Why was I chosen to live?"

Anna Duklawer was one of the 1,100 Jews spared from certain death by

Top photo - Julius and Sophia Duklawer, Anna's parents.

Middle photo - The Duklawer Family. Anna is far right.

Photo right - Anna's family on vacation before the war.

Photo far right - Anna and her cousin, Herman, in Poland after the war.

working in German industrialist Oskar Schindler's enamel ware factory during the Holocaust.

For almost five decades, she never said much about the horrors of Plaszow or the salvation of becoming, as she puts it, "one of Schindler's Jews." She rarely mentioned it to her friends. To her husband. To her family.

"I kept it inside," she says. "I didn't want my family to go through it, too. I

Photo left - Anna and her husband, John Perl, after the war, 1948. Anna was pregnant with Sonia at the time.

Photo below - John, Paul, Julius, Sonia, and Anna Perl, 1952.

Photo bottom right - John, Sonia, and Anna.

just told them that, without a man named Oskar Schindler, I wouldn't be here. But I never told them the whole story.

"But now, with the movie.... "

With Steven Spielberg's "Schindler's List" being hailed as the movie of the year and perhaps the finest Holocaust film of all time, Anna Duklawer Perl, a shy woman who quietly raised three children and worked as a seamstress, finds that everyone wants to hear her story.

She has been Hillary Rodham Clinton's guest at the White House. She has been interviewed by newspapers as far away as Florida. She has been on local TV. She has been quoted in *Newsweek*. And at a special screening of "Schindler's List" at Pembroke Mall in Virginia Beach, she was the guest speaker.

"When I first heard of the film, I didn't know if I wanted to see it," says Anna, who saw the movie in November during a viewing at the American Holocaust Museum in Washington attended by President and Mrs. Clinton and Spielberg.

"But I knew I had to. It was so powerful, so moving. People ask me, 'Did it really happen that way? Was it really like that?'

"That's the way it was. Only the concentration camp was worse."

Anna Duklawer was living in the ski resort town of Zakopane, high in the mountains of Poland, in 1939 when the Nazis loaded the townspeople into trucks and resettled them in a four-block by four-block ghetto in Krakow.

"It was so beautiful in the mountains," she said. "But the Nazis didn't want Jews living in a place that was so beautiful. That could not be."

In Krakow, the Duklawer family – father, mother, Anna, brother Morris and sister – were herded into a one-room apartment.

"Morris was about 14, and he was blond and blue-eyed," she says. "He looked like a Christian. We told him to escape out of the ghetto to the German side and get his freedom. Somehow he could survive."

He did, but one day he came back. "He said he missed us too much," says Anna. "When the Nazis found him,

Anna, Tali, and Josh, 1995

they beat and dragged him off to a truck.

Anna's mother ran after her only son and climbed onto the truck.

"We didn't say anything. We knew. We were never going to see them again."

Anna's grandchildren

Anna's grandchildren and family members celebrate her 70th birthday at her home in Virginia Beach, Virginia.

Anna Perl with Hillary Clinton, Laurie Perl (Anna's daughter-in-law), and Laurie's mother.

In 1942, the truck came for the Jews still in the Krakow ghetto and took Anna, her father and her sister to Plaszow and its mad commandant, Amon Goeth.

At Plaszow, Anna was assigned to the laundry, where she was beaten regularly. "For no reason. You'd just be beaten.

"Goeth was a monster. He was much worse than in the movie. He had moods and we all lived in fear of them. Many times I saw him just shoot people who didn't say the right thing."

One day, Goeth hanged a friend of Anna's.

"He didn't like the fact that my friend had once been rich. Just like in the movie, he used to stand up there on the balcony of his palace and shoot us. I didn't hate him because I was too busy being afraid. Fear was the biggest emotion. You never knew what was going to happen there."

She was at Plaszow for several months when her name was added to Schindler's list.

"Yes, we had heard of this Schindler," she says. "That things were better. But I had never seen him. I didn't know where I was going to, but I knew it couldn't be worse."

At first, Anna did not want to go and leave her sister.

"But she begged me. She said, 'Go. With Schindler, there is life. You must go.'"

At Schindler's enamel ware factory, she alternated her time between making pots and pans and working in the kitchen preparing meals.

"It was humane," she says. "It wasn't easy. There was never enough to eat, and there were guards everywhere. But not one of us was ever harmed."

"He'd make the rounds. He was like in the movie. Very handsome. A ladies' man. He'd always had a beautiful girl with him. And he had this huge ring. We used to say you could see him coming from the light of his ring.

"He was a good man. You could tell that. I think maybe in the beginning he was more interested in the money and saw us a cheap labor. Yes, maybe that was so. But I think Schindler and us grew together. And in the end, he gave away all his money. It was common knowledge he was bribing the Germans right and left."

The scariest moment of all for Anna came in 1944 when Plaszow was closed down and its prisoners ticketed to Auschwitz, where Jews were being killed at the rate of 10,000 a day.

"Schindler would have to give us back to Goeth. And that would be the end."

But Schindler bribed Goeth and purchased his employees from the commandant, under the pretext of relocating his factory to Czechoslovakia and converting it to a munitions plant "absolutely essential to the war effort."

*Anna Perl with Steven Spielberg, the producer of **Schindler's List** and Mrs. Schindler, seated at right.*

The Schindler Jews were released in two train loads, one carrying the men, the other the women.

The women's train was routed to Auschwitz by mistake.

"Before they even opened the doors, I could smell the bodies and hair that were being burned in the ovens. I knew something had gone terribly wrong.

"They cut our hair real short and sent us to the shower. Our only hope was Schindler would find us."

The next day Anna and a group of women were being herded off toward the showers again when she heard a voice.

"What are you doing with these people? These are my people."

"Schindler," says Anna.

Until the liberation, Anna worked at the Czechoslovakian factory making "fake ammunition. At least that's what the others said. They said none of it worked."

When the war ended, Anna Duklawer went back to the village in the mountains. Every day for months, she'd go to the community center in town and ask anyone she hadn't seen the day before about her family.

One day she heard about her father.

"He had a bad infection and he couldn't work, so they poisoned him," she says. "It was only days before the Russians came."

And then she heard about her sister.

"Someone told me they put her on a boat with about 300 other young girls and took it out and sank it in the Baltic Sea. It was near the end, and they were trying to kill as many Jews as they could."

Soon after, Anna met John Perl, an attorney from Czechoslovakia, who had escaped the Germans with forged papers.

"He said, 'You have no one. Why don't you come with me?'"

They were married 44 years before he died nearly five years ago. Their two sons, Paul and Julius, are electrical engineers. Sonia, named after Anna's mother, is a nutritionist. Julius was named after Anna's father.

"My mother always raised us with the belief that the dishes could wait," Sonia says. "She always had time for us. She might not have directly told us about her life, but we learned from her that life is precious."

Like many of Schindler's Jews, Anna felt a strong desire to live in Israel and moved there with the family in 1965.

Over the years, she'd hear bits of news about Oskar Schindler from others on "The List."

He was in Europe. He was in Argentina. Another business failed. He was still drinking hard and with the ladies. He had fallen into debt, and they were raising money for him. A tree was planted in his honor on Jerusalem's Avenue of the Righteous. He had moved to Israel.

In 1966, Anna heard there was to be a reunion of the survivors from Schindler's list in Tel Aviv, Israel. She took Sonia with her and rode the bus from Beersheva for four hours.

"It was one of the most emotional moments I've ever seen," says Sonia. "When she walked into the room, everyone yelled, 'Anna, Anna,' and hugged her. Everyone knew her. She had told me that people would not remember her, that she was just a young girl then and very quiet. I guess she wasn't so quiet."

Anna and her husband – the children followed later – immigrated to the United States in the late '60s to help care for relatives who were ill. The family ended up staying. Until she retired five years ago, she worked as a seamstress for LaVogue, Miller and Rhoads and other department stores.

She doesn't remember the exact day, but it was sometime in 1974 when he heard that Oskar Schindler had died.

"I think a little bit of all of us died, too," she says, with the afternoon winter sun filtering across the living room and falling on her. "But you go on, because that is what we are. Survivors."

And now, with the making of "Schindler's List," she finds Oskar Schindler alive again. And she finds herself talking about and sharing a part of her life that was locked inside of her for so long.

"It's good we have the movie," she says. "I was afraid of the wounds it would open. But it has healed some, too."

And maybe Anna Duklawer Perl knows the answer to the question she's asked all these years: Why was she on Schindler's list?

"I guess," she says, looking around the living room at her daughter and grandchildren, who number among the 6,000 descendants of the Jews on Shindler's life, "God wanted me to pass life on." ❖

Today is one year ago since my Grandma Anna died.

Her name was Anna Perl. She helped me do things that I couldn't do yet. She played with me. She talked to me a lot and she listened to me. She let me watch her TV. Grandma Anna taught me to play chess. When we played hide and go seek, she found the best places to hide. She hid in the closet, the only way I could find her was a piece of her orange rope that was sticking out of the door.

We planted flowers together in the front of the house and since I like flowers, so I planted a spider plant at home.

Grandma Anna was 74 years old. To me she wasn't old at all.

My grandma waiting for me after school

My Special Grandmother

Dedicated to: Anna Perl 1922-1997
By Josh Cohen March 11, 1998

This essay was written when Josh was six years old. It was entered in a competition for children sponsored by Channel 15, WHRO

My grandmother was invited to the White House to tell the President's wife the story about a good man named Oskar Shindler who saved her life and if he wouldn't, I wouldn't be alive. She was a Holocost surviver. Grandma said that I was her best friend and that I was making her feel happy. She always was waiting for me in the window when my school bus arrived. She said that every day 12:00 she looked at the clock on the wall and thought that she had still four hours to wait for me to come home from school and that was too long for her.

My grandmother Anna said that when I walked to the door her heart was pounding from happiness to see me again.

Adele and Warren Reed

We speak to prove that it did happen ...
ADELE AND WARREN REED

By Rachel Zoberman

They risked their lives to help others. They did not let anything stand in their way while they fought for the rights of others.

ADELE AND WARREN REED are examples of true heroes. Their actions during a time of utter destruction and hatred show us that even in the darkest of times, the human spirit can shine through to shed light and goodness.

At the young age of 22, Adele did not let fear deter her from her beliefs. As an Austrian and devout Catholic, she was very much against the actions of Hitler and the Germans. When a good "friend" reported her for making political statements against Germany, the Gestapo was waiting for her at 6 a.m. the next morning. They took her from her job at the Steel Works and imprisoned her at the city jail. At the courthouse, Adele was then given an ultimatum, either join a pro-German group such as the SS or SA, a women's association group, or be sent to a wartime women's concentration camp. Adele refused to join and was sent to Ravensbrook. "I refused to belong. I wanted to be Austrian," explains Adele.

Adele spent two years in the camp. "It was a nightmare. I smelled death," she says. Day-to-day life was brutal; Adele experienced horrific conditions that will forever be etched in her mind. Six to eight people shared a bed; talking was forbidden. They were often forced to do manual labor as early as 2 a.m., constantly threatened by officers and dogs. The women were starved each day, given only soup and a piece of bread. One memory that Adele will never be able to forget is being forced to remove the clothes of the victims from the gas chambers.

How was anyone able to survive these inhumane times? "You had to have faith. I made up my mind that I was going to be a survivor. And I asked God for help," says Adele. Adele had hope, hope that people would care and be willing to help. People did … like her husband-to-be, Warren Reed, who was a liberator with the United States Army.

Warren grew up in West Virginia. At 22, under the command of General Patton, he went across France and Germany through the Rhineland. In Germany, he witnessed first-hand the horrors within the concentration camp,

Ohrdruf Nord. From the outside, Warren said, the camp looked like a college campus. That was until they saw 37 dead bodies in the courtyard. "We were all in shock. Death was something we had seen as infantry men, but nothing like this," says Warren. "Everyone was in a daze. Some got sick, and some just stood and shook their heads." Warren says they had no idea of the degree of inhumanity, and as soon as they arrived there was no doubt in their minds why they were there. They saw the mass graveyards; they saw the Germans' attempt to get rid of the evidence by burning the bodies. Warren has photographs of these horrific sights. Ohrdruf Nord was the first camp found by the Western armies and the only one visited by Eisenhower.

Warren was sent back to the U.S. after the war and was discharged from the army. He chose to reenlist and worked as a constabulary military policeman with the Austrian police at Camp McCauley in Linz, Austria. It was here on September 16, 1948 that he met Adele. When Warren moved to work in Germany, Adele joined him and they were married on December 5, 1953. The following April they moved to the United States.

Warren's army career took them back and forth between the U.S. and Europe. In 1972, they settled in Newport News, Virginia, where they live today near their daughter, Roena, and her husband Robert.

At age 79, the horrors of the Holocaust are still clearly engraved in their minds. The Reeds realize the importance of educating others on what happened so such a nightmare will never occur again. They speak at local schools and to student groups at the Virginia War Museum. Adele says that sometimes she is uncertain whether to go, but when she arrives she know it is worthwhile. "When we speak, you can hear a pin drop. The children are interested and it makes me feel good. I am so glad when I go."

The Reeds say that being able to open up and share their experiences makes life a little bit easier. They find comfort in talking to each other as well.

They have learned first-hand how quickly genocide and destruction can occur. "A few people let it happen and the majority went along with it. They were willing to listen to anything they thought would make life better," says Warren. He urges the world to be careful and to never let such a thing happen again. "People shouldn't get too complacent because it could happen again."

"We speak to prove to people that it did happen, and they are wrong if they don't believe us," says Adele.

The Reeds will continue to share their story and do their part to make sure that history never repeats itself. ❖

Pianist's Life Is a Lesson In Survival
GEORGI RIABIKOFF

By Michael Futch

Georgi Riabikoff

Editor's Note: the following article appeared in *The Fayetteville Observer*, July 21, 1995. It is reprinted with permission of *The Fayetteville Observer*.

Half a a century later GEORGI RIABIKOFF still feels the pain in his fingers when he plays.

A Russian concert pianist by age four, he was captured and tortured as a teenager by the German secret police for helping Jewish families in Kiev, Russia, hide and escape death during World War II. Hitler's Gestapo broke his arms, crushed his fingers and drove hot spikes through his palms to try to get him to betray the persecuted people in hiding.

Riabikoff was living in Kiev with his Russian Orthodox family. German Nazis singled out the child prodigy for torture when it was discovered he was a fine boy pianist.

"'If you would not tell us where they are,' they said, 'you would not play again.' I knew I could not tell them," he said. "They first started to put my hands and fingers in steel doors and started to crack them. They broke my arms. They used these tortures for a long time. After they knew they couldn't break me, I was ready to die."

Riabikoff said he was "just like a skeleton" when he was rescued from the Berlin Buch concentration camp experimental hospital by British and American troops in 1945, toward the end of the war. It appeared that his promising musical career was over. His great-uncle was the Russian composer

Rachmaninoff, and his grandfather had studied with Franz Liszt, the Hungarian composer.

Remarkably, he regained the use of his hands and continued his musical career, first playing for American and British troops. Later, he would perform for five U.S. presidents, King George VI, Winston Churchill, and for Luci Johnson's White House wedding.

"It's inconceivable that anybody could recover that much facility after having gone through that. The main thing is he plays music that nobody else plays even. There is no musician alive with the technique he has," said McKellar Israel, a friend of Riabikoff's and a music teacher at Sandhills Community College in Pinehurst.

At the time of the interview, Riabikoff was scheduled to perform a Sunday afternoon concert at Sandhills Community College's 699-seat Owens Auditorium. He played the college ten times before. The program is part of the college's "Remembering Heroes" series honoring veterans of World War II on the 50th anniversary of the end of the war in Europe.

LIFE AND DEATH

He estimates that he helped save the lives of about 300 people during the Nazi occupation of Kiev. They hid in fear in secret tunnels under the Black Forest outside Kiev. As luck would have it, Riabikoff met the man who was in charge of building the underground passages during World War I, and when the Nazis closed in on the city, he told Riabikoff that people could be saved in the forest.

"We are all human. In certain times, when there is life and death all around you," Riabikoff said, "you wish to do something. To help people."

Following his liberation, Riabikoff nearly lost his hands. His status as a concert pianist was known, and the young man was brought to the attention of British Field Marshal Bernard Montgomery and Gen. Dwight D. Eisenhower, then commander of Allied Forces in Europe. They wanted to help him.

"They brought in the best surgeons from London and New York. When they saw my hands," Riabikoff recalled, "they said, 'Forget it. You'll never be able to play 'Chopsticks.' They said they would have to amputate my hands immediately or I would die from blood poisoning."

With a desire to play again, Riabikoff would have no part of that. He thought of the people, including his own father, who had given their lives so that he could live and perform.

"People said it was like a miracle," Riabikoff said by telephone from his home in Virginia Beach, Virginia. "I still have never fully recovered. I still have pain when I play. I can tolerate it, but I can still feel it. Therefore, I have more expression and feeling to give to people, the purity and feeling and inspiration of the human element."

… Riabikoff started playing piano at about 2-1/2, and he was the youngest person ever accepted to Kiev Conservatory. Riabikoff studied in the European conservatories with Russian composer and pianist Sergei Prokofiev.

Following the war, he graduated from the Music Academy of Detmold, studied with Walter Gieseking and Conrad Hansen, and played concerts in Europe.

He came to this country with his mother in 1949. His father had been burned alive in front of them following an unsuccessful escape from Berlin Buch. Riabikoff called it "the worst concentration camp in Germany. They used people like guinea pigs. It was one of the most secret places and not as well known.

"I dream often about it, but not as often as I used to," he said. "Sometimes it's hard to believe. It's hard to explain to people who were not there about going through that nightmare." ❖

"There have been two days of my life that were both unimaginable and unforgettable," says Rocco Russo, a WWII veteran and non-Jewish liberator. The first was D-Day June 6, 1944 in Normandy; the second was Liberation Day at Dachau Concentration Camp.

ROCCO L. RUSSO
I can testify to the monstrous cruelty of the Nazi regime that we defeated.

By Lisa Richmon

In a speech delivered for Yom Hashoah, at Norfolk's Temple Israel, Russo describes how the related events were seared into his brain as two of the most horrifying days he has known in 76 years.

"I firmly believe the second day could not be accomplished without the first, and I would not change it for anything," says Russo. "I was there for the beginning of freedom in Europe and the world, and I can testify to the monstrous cruelty of the Nazi regime that we defeated. I was a personal witness to the unspeakable horror that Nazi Germany visited upon the inmates of the Dachau Concentration Camp."

Rocco Russo lived in Norfolk, Virginia, and graduated from Holy Trinity High School in June, 1943. One month later he was inducted into the Army and left Norfolk for basic infantry training. In February, 1944, he was on his way to Europe to serve with F Company of the 116th Infantry. Young and green, the men were informed that they would be landing in the First Wave in the coming invasion of France on Omaha Beach. Their colonel detected a slight hesitation and told them, "if you are thinking of a way to get out of this outfit, forget it because there is no way." "Actually, we were eager to fight those Germans," say Russo. "We wouldn't have had it any other way."

When F Company 116th Infantry 29th Division shipped off to England, Russo was assigned to barracks where he quickly made two good friends. "They took me in hand," he says. "They shared their food packages from home and became like family to me."

On Sundays while attending mass, two additional men befriended Russo. Tony Vardaro was a skilled rifle squad leader, Russo's senior of seven years and

Rocco Russo   Photo by Susan Hirschbiel

someone he respected. "I knew Tony and I became close," says Russo, recalling the angst-ridden night before landing on Omaha Beach. "Tony was depressed and I stayed with him. He showed me a picture of his young son, Tom, and wife, Mary. Tony feared he'd be killed on the beach and never see his son again." Tom was only eight months

American troops headed to the front lines – the blade attached to the jeep was used to sever wires.
Photo by Hugo Horvath

42nd infantry division, when they liberated Dachau Concentration Camp on April 29, 1945.

"I always thought I knew what I was fighting for," says Russo. "I wasn't raised with guns but I'd seen evil up close and would do anything to stop it. I remember going into Berchesgarten very quickly after it had been captured. All I could think was that I was close to my goal, which was to personally shoot Adolph Hitler. But Hitler was apparently in Berlin. I didn't see Hitler but figured at least we were beating the hell out of all of the Germans and I fully expected to get home safe and sound, which was my other goal."

Before Dachau, Russo had good reason to think he'd seen the worst there was to see. After all he was part of the Allied Forces' first successful landing on the European Continent since it had been captured by the Third Reich. He was an original member of the Omaha Beach scene later depicted by actors in the first 25 stomach-turning minutes of the movie *Saving Private Ryan.* "What I'd seen was terrible enough landing on Omaha Beach; fighting in the hedgerows; dikes in Normandy." The sweetness of victory and bitter taste of defeat was still fresh for Russo.

"On that night, our colonel interrupted dinner and said, 'in case you don't know why you're fighting this war I'm going to take you and show you.' I thought I knew. But never in God's world was I prepared for what I saw in Dachau."

old when Tony left for overseas." In France, Tony and I used to look for each other at the end of each day. Ironically, Tony made it through Normandy, however our buddy Sergeant John Cooney was the first soldier I saw dead on D-Day."

Beginning on D-Day and for the first 25 days of combat, Russo's original landing group got smaller and smaller. A staggering number were dead or wounded. It was considered a tenuous victory, gaining a foothold in Europe for the first time since it was captured by the Third Reich. The victory was expanded each day after that.

On July 11, before Russo's unit shoved off to St. Lo to continue fighting the Germans, they suffered 110 out of 160 casualties. Two months after D-Day, on August 4, 1944, Russo was seriously wounded in the stomach and eventually left the continent. At the time of his

injury, only three men remained from the original assault group.

"In the course of a few days, I lost three of my best friends." The next day after arriving in St. Lo, a friend of mine came to tell me that Tony had been killed. This was a terrible time for me and I couldn't help going to see his body lying back one hedgerow. I cried when I saw him sitting dead under a tree where he had been hit by a shell. I made a promise to myself that someday I would tell his son what a great soldier and friend his father was." Fifty years later, in 1994, Russo kept his promise and tracked down Tony's family in Pennsylvania and New Jersey.

When he returned to the continent in January of 1945, Russo was assigned to the 108th Artillery Group, headquarters group. He became a radio man relaying firing instructions from spotters to the gun operators. He was backing up the

The soldiers piled into two trucks and headed toward the village of Dachau and the Concentration Camp just outside of town. The next moments were unforgettable:

"I smelled it long before I saw it."

"When we got within about a mile of the camp, the stench was unbearable. Mind you, I was accustomed to the smell of war, to the acrid smell of cordite and decaying animals. But that was nothing compared to this. We pulled up in front of the huge iron gates of Dachau, topped with the monstrous golden eagle ornament of the Third Reich. A sergeant from the 42nd met us there and told us what they had found when they entered the camp. He said this was a concentration camp used to exterminate Jews and other political prisoners. This was my first encounter with a concentration camp.

"We walked through the gates of Dachau and walked into hell. He did not have to tell us that the terrible stench was from dead bodies. There were more bodies than I could have imagined. We went through the gate and walked about one block up the hard road, turned right and crossed a bridge over a canal. Before crossing the canal we saw a dead Kraut lying on the pavement. His face and head were destroyed by some of the GIs who were outraged by the number of human beings murdered.

"It was a good thing for the Germans that we had not seen this *before* we

started fighting the war in Normandy. I don't think any of us could have controlled ourselves. We would have killed them on sight and never taken a German prisoner.

"We walked into the compound and arrived at a building that had a huge plate glass window from the floor to the ceiling and the ceiling was extremely high. The room looked like a shower room and was almost completely full of dead women, children and men who were completely nude, having thought they were going to take a shower. The bodies were skin and bones and discarded in a way that I didn't even think the Germans were capable of. We went inside the building where the bodies were continuing to be cremated to prevent the possibility of spreading disease. The doors of the furnaces were open and I could see the bones just melting away. Believe me, it was awful to see my buddies killed. But this was worse because it was *huge numbers* of innocent human beings."

Later, Russo visited some of the prisoners who were still alive and being treated by American medics. "I will never forget how they greeted us. Even though most of their families had been completely wiped out, they could not stop thanking us for liberating them. We went back to our own camp. When we arrived and chow was available, I don't believe two people ate a bite. Seeing dead bodies was not new to us but these people were murdered after being tortured beyond imagination. I didn't know what a concentration camp

"They have asked me to preserve for them the memories of a part of history in which I was a participant. Not to glorify war, but to try to record and respect the pain, the suffering, the fear, the anguish and the occasional laughter and bond of friendship. To those who argue the existence of the Holocaust or its unspeakable magnitude, I would love to look them in the face and tell what I saw. And then I'd ask them what they ever did for their country."

— 225 —

was before, but I will always be grateful to the colonel for taking us to see this part of the Holocaust. I will never forget what I saw with my own eyes on that day," he said.

"We liberated 32,000 people. Had we gotten there two days sooner maybe we would have liberated 64,000. But if we were there only two days later, they probably would have all been killed by those cruel Nazi bastards."

"On May 7, six days after liberation, I received a call on my radio 'ceasefire on the 15th corps front. The Germans have surrendered and the war is over in Europe. Do not fire unless fired upon.'"

"There is a popular song which says of memory, 'what's too painful to remember, we simply choose to forget.'" But according to Russo, we cannot do

that with the Holocaust. "Memory is a tricky and sometimes transient thing. Some things are burned into our memories with the impact of a branding iron. My memory of that day is vivid in horror. I know that there are many things just too overwhelming to be accepted."

Of many lessons learned, Russo has seen how prejudice and hate can poison the soul. In Germany these destructive forces robbed the world of an entire section of humanity. Though he was turned against Germany, he believes that what he saw caused him to have greater compassion. "I don't feel prejudice to other groups and have tried to help minorities when I could."

During close to three years of service, Russo received many medals including the Purple Heart, Combat Infantry Badge, Bronze Star, Good Conduct

Medal, WWII Victory Ribbon, and American Field of Service Ribbon. The prestigious Presidential Unit Citation was presented to the entire 116th regiment. Russo was also a recipient of the ETO (European Theatre of Operation) ribbon with four battle stars and a bronze arrowhead.

Russo knows with great conviction what he was fighting for. He acknowledges that after all the excruciating stories told, there are still Holocaust deniers who say it's a Jewish conspiracy. It's one reason why, at the insistence of his children, he wrote his memoirs. "They have asked me to preserve for them the memories of a part of history in which I was a participant. Not to glorify war, but to try to record and respect the pain, the suffering, the fear, the anguish and the occasional laughter and bond of friendship. To those who argue the existence of the Holocaust or its unspeakable magnitude, I would love to look them in the face and tell what I saw. And then I'd ask them what they ever did for their country." ❖

Rocco Russo passed away in January of 2001. His wife, Mary, lit the Righteous Gentile candle at Yom Hashoah, 2001, in his memory and in memory of all who helped others during the Holocaust.

American troops headed home to the USA   *Photo by Hugo Horvath*

A STORY OF COURAGE, CUNNING AND INTRIGUE
Kitty Saks

By Reba Karp

Kitty Saks   *Photo by Echard Wheeler*

This is a story which might not have been written if three desperate Jews had not bribed officials in Brussels, Belgium in 1940 to be put on the list of those scheduled to leave for America early in May of that year.

The threesome took the place of Edith and Leo Friedenbach and their daughter Kitty. As a consequence, the Friedenbachs were put on another list. Their new date of departure was May 15, 1940. The Germans marched in on May 10, 1940.

The Friedenbachs' story is one of courage, cunning and intrigue, made possible only because, unlike the Poles, the Belgians, as a rule, were not overly anti-Semitic. As Kitty Friedenbach Saks says today, "They (Belgians) would help their fellow human beings, although there were some who lacked that human respect."

Kitty's story begins when she traces her family's anguish with World War II back to 1938. At that time it became apparent that with the approach of the

Kitty Saks

Germans, the Jewish population would be in jeopardy. Kitty was born in Vienna, where she lived with her parents and grandparents. Her father was a fruit merchant; her grandfather, a retired jeweler. "My mother was a musician and piano teacher. We lived with my grandparents in a very nice apartment overlooking the Danube Canal," she said.

Memories of the apartment are overshadowed with bitterness. The home she remembers so fondly was "confiscated" by an officer in the Wehrmacht. "He walked into my grandparents' apartment … on a Shabbat evening. He looked around and liked what he saw. He liked the apartment, the furnishings, the view.

I remember my grandmother had just lit the Shabbat candles and we were ready to sit down to dinner.

"He told my grandparents that he would personally see that they were resettled in another apartment. What choice did they have?"

Shortly after that "intrusion," Kitty and her parents began their elaborate attempts to get over the border into Belgium. Her grandparents decided to stay behind because her grandfather was a veteran of the Austrian army in World War I. He thought that perhaps it would afford them some protection, that they would be able to live in Vienna. "Of course, that proved to be untrue," she added. Her grandparents were among the first to perish in experiments with gas in trucks.

Leo Friedenbach crossed the border first, but not because he put his life before that of his family. "We knew that they took the men first and dispatched them to labor camps. I believe Buchenwald was at that time under construction."

The procedure to leave Vienna before the Germans entered Austria was elaborate. It was made possible for Kitty and her family by the fact they had cousins in Norfolk, Virginia, Harry and Margie Coplon. "My father stood in line many, many nights just to get to the authorities, to have his name put on the list so that we would be able to leave Vienna, all of us.

"However, the doors were always slammed just before he got to the front of the line."

The alternative route across the border was to hire a guide and take risks. "What choice did we have?" she asks.

During those predawn days of the concentration camps, word among desperate men traveled quickly and through dangerous routes. Mercenaries willing to help those wishing to escape would gather in Aachen, a small town on the border, at the Schloss Hotel. There, for a price, refugees could buy their attempt to cross the border to Belgium or France, countries yet unoccupied by the Germans.

Her father made it on the first try and sent word for Kitty and her mother to follow. "We left in March of 1939 and made it to Aachen and to the famous Schloss Hotel." The trip from Vienna to Aachen was only the beginning of seven nerve-wracking attempts to cross the border – a woman, alone, with a small child.

"Once we were spotted by searchlights and turned back. On another try, the guide on the Belgian side failed to appear at the appointed time and place," she said, explaining that the effort was a joint one which had to be coordinated on both sides. "Still on another occasion, and after being caught and detained at the check point building, we were stripped and searched. This was a painful embarrassment to my mother, who was a very proper person. She was even more upset that I, a six-year-old, was so treated." This time they were turned back due to some irregularity in their papers and also because a fellow refugee was remembered from a previous attempt to cross the border. The fellow refugee was detained and "we never saw him again." At that point, Belgium seemed a far and distant place to Kitty's mother, who as a woman, was more vulnerable to the vicissitudes of the guides and border patrol.

They tried again, this time with a woman as their guide. Her plan was to pretend that they were heading for a picnic near the border. But that attempt proved to be another bitter disappointment, for just as they had convinced the guards of their "innocent" intentions another voice called out "Halt!" – and added sarcastically, *Sie wollen uber die grune grenze* (You want to go over to the green, i.e., beautiful, yearned-for border). Yes they did … but it was back to Aachen and the Schloss Hotel!

"'Here comes Friedenbach with the kid,' still rings in my ears," she added. "It was becoming a joke."

Time was working against them. The money and valuables they had brought with them from Vienna were all but gone. "We planned ahead for just such an emergency," Kitty said. "My mother phoned my grandparents who wired money. The prearranged code was

'tante ist sehr krank.'" ("Auntie is very sick," which told Kitty's grandparents that they didn't make it; send money.)

The days at the Schloss Hotel were full of intrigue, as desperate men and women maneuvered and bargained with guides. Although only six years old at the time, Kitty sensed the enormity of the situation. Alone with her mother much of the time, she could feel the fear. "We had no choice but to keep trying. We knew the alternative. Crossing the border was a great risk to all – including the guides."

"It would be dangerous to all if they were discovered hiding a Jewish child, for the Germans would kill everyone…."

It was understandable, she reasons, as she recalls their last and successful attempt. "My mother noticed that the guide had been drinking heavily. She voiced doubts about his ability to get us across in his condition. His response was that only in *this* condition *could* he do the job."

It was a cold April night in the woods between Aachen and the Belgium border. On a previous crossing in January, a child had frozen to death. "They rubbed and massaged me all night long, giving me what warmth they could."

Once across the border, in Eupen-Malmedy, the exhausted party was given warmth and breakfast at a prearranged farm house where they were joined by another group fleeing the Nazis. They

Kitty Saks at her Solemn Communion in 1944.

left by train for Brussels where they were joined by her father. They had a few moments of joy at the reunion; but it was sobered by the thoughts of their next great effort – getting to America, an attempt which was thwarted by another's bargaining with the officials.

The Germans marched in. Soon after, a law was passed that no Jewish child could attend school. Unaware, Kitty and her friend, Mela, displaying their compulsory big yellow star, walked into class. "Much to our shock when we entered, the teacher asked us what we were doing in school. We were allowed to remain for the day, but we had to sit behind the stove." That was the last day Kitty attended a public school in Belgium.

"My physical education teacher at that time was a woman by the name of Femande Henrard. She was a saint,

"My physical education teacher at that time was a woman by the name of Femande Henrard. She was a saint, a true heroine of the war. At great risk to herself she saved hundreds of Jewish children by placing them in convents."

a true heroine of the war. At great risk to herself she saved hundreds of Jewish children by placing them in convents. She saw me one day running an errand for my parents. She stopped me with the warning: 'Don't you know that it is dangerous for you to be walking the streets with your star? They (Germans) will pick you up and then your parents will be picked up.' She told me she had a plan, for my parents to come to see her."

That night they met with Mademoiselle Henrard and she explained her plan to place Kitty in a convent school as a Catholic under an assumed name. "Of course my father objected at first, but later he gave me his last 50 francs to save me. There was no other way." (Kitty's parents were expected to pay a stipend to the convent for the room and board.) "This was minimal," she added, explaining that once when her parents did not have the money, her mother gave the school her gold wedding band.

"I was 9 years old at the time and it sounded exciting," Kitty said. It was easier said than done, for Mademoiselle Henrard had to try several convent schools before she could find a place for Kitty.

"The nuns explained their reluctance. It would be dangerous to all if they were discovered hiding a Jewish child. The Germans would kill everyone connected with the school – Catholic children as well as the nuns." With each try, Kitty would accompany Mademoiselle

Henrard to the different schools. Since she was allowed to return to her parents after each thwarted attempt, she viewed it as a grand play.

Mademoiselle Henrard still persisted, as she did for many Jewish families. Finally, Paridaens, a convent in Louvain, a Catholic Boarding elementary-secondary school, accepted her. She was enrolled under the assumed name of Rosette Nizole, deceased niece of a priest. "It was necessary for my parents to sign a document giving permission for the school to give me Catholic training and to baptize me. Not to partake in religious instruction and activities would have quickly aroused suspicion."

It was a momentous day in her life and memories still echo through her mind as distinctly as the bell which rang to open the convent door. "We were ushered into a gigantic waiting room. When the doors banged shut, I knew I would not be back with my parents that night."

The new friends, new name and new identity were not as formidable as the new surroundings which were so foreign to her Jewish upbringing. Crucifixes in place of menorahs, Latin liturgies in place of *davening* Hebrew; she was a long way from home. "I cried myself to sleep that night."

Kitty learned the sacraments and was secretly baptized "under great cere-mony" in a side chapel. One of the sisters who knew about it made Kitty a white dress for the occasion. "I understood why it was necessary, that my parents had to sign to save me. I also knew that I was Jewish and I was proud of my heritage. After being baptized and learning my catechism backward and forward, I continued to say 'Sh'ma,' the traditional Jewish prayer of faith, privately every night in secret."

In order to succeed, Mademoiselle Henrard had to think of everything. Small details were important, one slip could alert the Germans and endanger them all. During holidays and vacations, when the Catholic girls went home, Kitty was placed in orphanages for she could no longer return safely to her parents. The orphanages were in great contrast to the convent school. Conditions were poor – hunger, malnutrition, cold and disease. "One summer vacation I was taken to Institut St. Charles in the Ardennes, where there were several other Jewish children. One of our daily chores was to pick worms out of the mattress stuffing. It was not my favorite activity."

She managed to survive each "vacation," to return to Paridaens, which by comparison seemed a paradise. Although Kitty's parents did not know where she was, she was kept informed of their general condition by Mademoiselle Henrard or her associate, who one day told her that the Gestapo had visited the building where her parents were hiding, but that they were okay.

*W*ildflowers

by Abbott Saks

*A rumbling breaks upon the
  morn serene
And engine's whistle wails
  beneath the sky;
Bucolic peace pervades this
  Polish scene
As lone and lovely country-
  side roll by …
A farmer's child looks up but
  cannot say
What lies beyond the rails,
  that final bend;
Head bowed, his father turns
  his face away
As cattle cars lurch on and
  eastward wend …
Young and old, the lame and
  whole these wagons bear,
Both poor and proud will
  know a common fate;
Their lot, nightmarish hunger,
  thirst to share,
For schedules must be kept,
  THESE trains must not be
  late …*

*A mother seeks to soothe her
  infant's cry
Amid the moans of those from
  lands afar,
And all along the way they
  wonder why
And where go they who wear
  the yellow star …
Beside the tracks the bright
  wildflowers bloom
And peaceful brooks a rustic
  idyll seem,
But day grows dark, and now
  Satanic doom …
The wagons screech and stop
  … at Oswiecim*

— 231 —

Photo above and below - Kitty, Leo and Edith Friedenbach after the war in Ostende, Belgium, 1946

Kitty later learned that it was only a capricious twist of fate which had spared her parents. The much frightened Friedenbachs heard the Gestapo enter the building from their small quarters on the fourth floor. Her father was in bed at the time, a bed supported by heavy springs which groaned and loudly creaked with every turn of the body. The Gestapo got as far as the fourth floor, pulling people out as they progressed. They stopped in front of her parents' door. It was only held closed by a small latch. They pounded and the latch strained.

Forced, out of fear, to remain perfectly still on the bed, his eyes warned Kitty's mother across the room not to move. They remained frozen in fear, daring not to breathe, as the Germans banged once more with their boots against the door. The fragile lock held again. At this moment, the landlady downstairs shouted up at the Germans that the people living in the apartment were Austrians with work permits who were out working. This sounded reasonable and reluctantly they left.

Kitty reasons now that they did not persist because of this and the fact that they already had a carload of helpless humans.

Before the Gestapo returned, and they did, her parents sought refuge in another apartment building. It was later learned that the Jews picked up in the building had been sold out by Belgians for 50 francs each. "They lost 150 francs because I wasn't there and my parents escaped."

When Kitty learned of the near disaster she begged permission to go see her parents in their new hiding place. At first, for her safety, she was refused. But she persisted. Finally, they relented and Henrard's assistant, Mademoiselle Esther, took her as far as one block from her parent's quarters.

"I had to go the last stretch alone." It seemed like such a long block. The surroundings were new and she felt so small and alone. Although only about 10 years old at the time, she had maturity beyond her years. Jewish children were forced to grow up fast in Europe. She ran into what she terms "potential disaster," for just outside her parents' building, she met one of her old girl friends. "Her parents were known Nazi sympathizers and she knew, of course, that I was Jewish. We greeted each other with 'bonjour' and I entered. An awful scenario flashed through my mind of all of us being denounced; the Gestapo seizing us and deporting us to some unknown but suspected horror."

"But nothing happened. Did she say something to her parents? Or did she just dismiss it from her mind as a casual meeting? I'll never know."

Once Kitty's parents were settled in their new hiding place, they were determined to be prepared for such surprise visits from the Gestapo. Her father devised a hiding place by partitioning off part of the room, which had a slanting roof, and covering it with wallpaper, the same pattern as was on

Sister Marie Victoire, Kitty and Sister Marie Dominique at the Paridaens Convent in Belgium, 1955

the other walls of the room. The opening for ventilation was under the bed, which was up against the false wall. The wallpaper was carefully chosen to give the room a larger appearance so no one would suspect the presence of a false wall, she said. Fortunately, they never had to use the room.

Her parents managed to stay alive while in hiding by making cigarettes for a German Jew who had a Gentile spouse. Tobacco was distributed to the Jews in hiding, who had special machines to make the cigarettes. They were also provided with boxes to package the finished products, which were later sold on the Black Market to the German Wehrmacht.

Kitty explained there was little profit in it for the Jews in hiding, who out of necessity had become cheap labor. Once more her father's ingenuity provided him with a little extra sustenance. He devised a way to cut down on the tobacco used by putting loose particles in the center and packing it firmer on the ends. The saved tobacco was used to make extra packs for his own sale later. These were distributed, espionage fashion, to a man who had a special knock and special code.

"Of course it was not a large amount, but enough to make ends meet for a couple days here and there. It was never enough, my parents always ran out of food; then there was the cold and the unsanitary conditions and the lack of

freedom. They could not be seen on the streets. But they managed to survive."

Kitty was transferred from convent to convent; from orphanage to orphanage – each with stories of its own. She remembers one shift, during Christmas vacation, when she was being introduced to the girls at a Malines orphanage in Belgium, she almost encountered disaster, and only quick thinking on her part helped her avoid it. There was another girl at the orphanage with the same name, Rosette Nizole.

"Quickly, I changed mine, I said my name was Laurant, which satisfied them, but I had to do some very fast thinking. Actually, my experiences in all the Catholic institutions was like being in a play where you had to make up your own words, your own part as you went along. There was just no other way."

She had to remember to speak French, not German and was once put on trial by her peers when she spoke a few German words in her sleep. "I thought fast again. I told them I had a German aunt who used to visit and that I learned a few words from her."

Toward the end of the war, Kitty had to be perceptive to all nuances, to take nothing at face value. Mademoiselle Henrard and her associates had placed so many children that a lack of continuity was developing. "She must have found it hard to keep up with all

of us. Of course she couldn't keep any written records."

Conditions at orphanages grew steadily worse. In a particular one, the girls all had severe skin infections, which was due in part, no doubt, to the fact that they were bathed only every two weeks. The procedure was to bathe 12 children in one bath water – outside. When she

> *"Actually, my experiences in all the Catholic institutions was like being in a play where you had to make up your own words, your own part as you went along. There was just no other way."*

could endure no more, she went up to one of the Catholic sisters and implored her to let her be number five instead of number ten.

Mademoiselle Henrard later took her out of that particular orphanage. "I must have been her pet. She found another place for me, three blocks from my parents. They did not know where I was, but I knew where they were. She placed me with the Sisters of Charity of St. Vincent de Paul," Kitty remembers.

*The Saks' daugher, Tonie, and her husband,
Frank Wilkins*

*Mary Lou and David Saks, the parents
of Elliot and Adam*

"Mademoiselle Esther used to visit my father to see how he was and he would beg her to tell him where I was. She would answer him with '*Pas loin*,' which means 'not far,' but she would not tell him where."

In the early days of September, 1944, the British troops entered Brussels. They could hear the guns all night. "The morning of September 4, 1944 at 9 o'clock, the doors swung open and one of the sisters came in and told us we were liberated. The unbelievable nightmare had ended. I can still hear the joyful words of one of the Catholic sisters: '*Mes enfants, nous sommes liberees* – my children, we are liberated.'"

"I asked permission to go to my parents, who I knew weren't far away. The Mother Superior told me I would have to wait until they contacted Mademoiselle Henrard and someone came to pick me up. Meanwhile, they dressed us so we could go see the British troops. When I returned, I learned that my parents had been at the convent looking for me."

"They packed a little bag for me to go to Mademoiselle Henrard, who was also only a short distance away. When I arrived at her home, she kissed me and said, 'Good luck. You know how to get home.'"

"I ran across the cobblestone streets all the way to my parents' apartment. I knocked on the door. I yelled! I screamed!"

"My mother looked out of the window and cried: 'Kitty! Kitty!'"

"I had come home to stay."

Kitty later learned that Mademoiselle Henrard had been picked up earlier by the Germans and questioned about her activities. "But she never revealed one name, never!" Kitty corresponded with Mademoiselle Henrard until her death. Understandably, Kitty would like to see Mademoiselle Henrard's name among those honored on the Avenue of the Righteous in Israel. "I will also carry with me, in fondest memory and deepest gratitude, the names of four nuns who cared for me during the most

trying time of my life. Sister Marie Bernadette, Sister Marie Loyola, Sister Marie Dominique and Sister Marie Michael."

Kitty is married to Abbott Saks, Adjunct Associate Professor at Old Dominion University. They have two children, David, who is a physician and Antonie, the Regional Visual Director for North Carolina Furniture Company. She and Abbott have two grandsons, Elliot and Adam. ❖

Kitty's father, Leo Friedenbach, has a story in this book.

Elliot and Adam Saks

Kitty and Abbott Saks

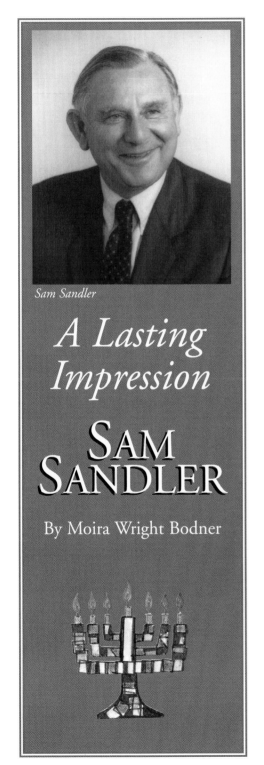

Sam Sandler

A Lasting Impression

SAM SANDLER

By Moira Wright Bodner

A 13-year-old boy, full of spunk and determination, made a lasting impression upon SAM SANDLER, when, as a young GI, he visited Buchenwald shortly after its liberation.

"I've often wondered what became of that boy," says Sandler, who served in the 184th AAA Gun Battalion, an Air Corp anti-aircraft unit of the 9th Defense Command.

The youngster, who had been at Buchenwald for several years, gave Sandler a tour of the death camp. The gas works and the crematoriums "horrified" him.

Sandler, a past President of the United Jewish Federation of Tidewater, was only 22 and "could never think of something like that in my wildest dreams. I wasn't prepared for what I saw," he says.

It wasn't until about a year later that the full impact of what Sandler encountered at Buchenwald hit him.

Understanding what he had seen was intensely emotional for Sandler. "I just can't understand how people could do something like that," he says.

Although he doesn't know the name of the 13-year-old boy he met at Buchenwald, to Sandler the boy represents the triumph of the human spirit.

"He was so full of life, in the midst of such horror," recalls Sandler. ❖

Sam Sandler died in August, 1996. Sam's wife, Reba, died May, 1997.

Sandler family being honored at the Hebrew Academy of Tidewater. Back row: Steve, Toni, Wesley, Reba, Sam, Sheri, Annie, and Art. Front row: Mitchell, Katie, Eva, Jessica, Dylan, Leyla, and Max.

And Edye Makes Six
HANNA SCHROB

By Lisa Richmon

HANNA SCHROB is one of the lucky ones. Her immediate family of six survived. She was not quite seven years old when the Gestapo knocked on the door for Hanna's mother and father, two brothers and newborn sister. Together, and apart, the Spielmans endured internment camps, the daily threat of extermination and years of degradation before returning to freedom. Amazingly, Hanna's post-war life, with its tumultuous beginning was not only restored to normal as a child in New Jersey; she became joyful in her roles as wife, mother, sister and friend to many around the world.

When Hanna's mother, Helen, was three, Hanna's grandparents longed for the old country and moved from New York to Germany. Years later, Helen Hudes met and married Alexander Spielman, an Austrian salesman. In 1932, Alexander and Helen, then living in Essen, Germany, gave birth to their first child, Bernard. This was around the same time Hitler started gaining power in Germany. Along with Hanna's aunts and uncles, Helen and Alexander

Hanna Schrob lights memorial candle at Yom Hashoah observance.   *Photo by Ed Karotkin*

Spielman saw the danger in Germany and moved across the border to Maastricht, Holland where they believed they would be safe. Here in Maastricht, Hanna and her two siblings were born.

"Our life in Maastricht was very normal and very happy," recalls Hanna. "My mother wanted for nothing. My father had a very lucrative eyeglass import business and we lived in a beautiful home. Then as danger loomed throughout Europe, my aunts and uncles were able to sail to the United States. Before they departed, they tried to convince my parents to leave with them. At that time, my father was a disbeliever who didn't think that Hitler would come into Holland.

Unfortunately, by the time we were packed and ready to leave, the 'last ship' departed before we could board."

During this time, people all over Europe would take great risks to help in whatever way they could: food, shelter, information and continuing the education of the children. "But there were those who couldn't be trusted, who would turn you in if given the chance," says Hanna, "out of fear, or with the hope of gaining some benefit from the Nazis." Hanna's mother was pregnant when she and her family became trapped in an increasingly bleak situation. A generous neighbor offered to store the valuables that had been crated for the Spielmans' departure and transported their belongings over the roof of the house so nobody could see what they were doing. Because these neighbors were Gentile, they had reason to believe they could help and promised Hanna's parents they could recover the belongings after the war, if they survived. "If not for their courageous help," says Hanna pointing to a beloved tea service and candelabra, "we would have nothing but each other to connect us to our past."

In 1940, Hitler conquered Holland, proving Hannah's father wrong. The only way to continue the education of the children was in private by Jewish teachers. During an air raid with bombs and sirens in the background, Hanna's mother went into labor with her fourth child. At the hospital, the nurse and doctors were frantically getting other patients down into the basement, leaving Helen alone to deliver her baby. Six weeks after the birth of Edye, the Nazis knocked on their door and took them away. Off to a living hell went two adults, three children, an infant and some suitcases.

"Imagine what you would choose, from all your possessions, to squeeze into a few small bags. Ours was not a difficult decision; it was diapers, clothing and items for survival. The Nazis pushed us onto a truck and we were taken to a jail where we slept on hay, and my mother stayed up all night beating off the rats."

Holland was one of the first European countries to provide refuge for Jews escaping Hitler's regime. There were wooden barracks constructed in Westerbork intended to house the many Jews awaiting permanent residence in Holland. But Hitler had fences raised around this temporary refuge, and it became a transition camp for his prisoners. "After a few days in the jail, we were transported to Westerbork to await transport to an extermination camp. Each time we were scheduled on a transport for the extermination camp, the train was so tightly packed, we had to wait for the next one. Because my mother was an American citizen, we were spared extermination, not once, but many times," Hanna remembers.

In Westerbork, conditions were sub-standard for adults and worse for an infant. Because of poor nourishment, Helen lost her milk and could no longer nourish Edye. They slept on baby's diapers to dry them out. The facilities consisted merely of long barracks for collective elimination. This was intentionally unsanitary, dehumanizing and not isolated. Hanna learned that the Nazi's meticulous record keeping was second only to their fanatical methods of cruelty.

Things got dramatically worse when, after six months, Alexander Spielman was separated from his entire family. All but Alexander were transported to Liebenau, an internment camp in Germany. "As we left my father behind, my mother said she would never see him again. From Liebenau we were transported to Vitel, an internment camp in France."

One of Hanna's most terrifying memories of Vitel involves a baby carriage. "Someone gave my mother an old beat-up carriage, and one day she suggested I take the baby for a walk. While on our walk, there was an air raid. Planes started flying and bombs were going off. I was on a rubble-covered road, rushing to get back to my mother when the baby carriage tipped over and Edye rolled out. I scooped her in my arms as fast as I could, turned the carriage and pulled it all the way back. Without a second to spare, we reached the door where they pulled us in and locked the doors. I can see the whole thing like it happened yesterday."

Hanna also remembers routine examinations for head lice that were performed there. The punishment, if lice were found, was having your head shaved. "It was my mother's worst nightmare that my long thick ponytails would be shaved off and I'd be bald. She found a woman – a dentist – who sprayed me with everything imaginable, including heavy-duty Lysol. When it was my turn to be examined, there were no lice found."

After almost two years of being separated from her father, Hanna witnessed a miracle. Of the many transports that had been coming into Vitel, from different prison camps around Europe, Hanna stared in disbelief when her father emerged. Alexander was escorting a blind man and was the very last man to arrive on the very last transport to Vitel. Hanna's mother, who believed she would never see her father again, screamed first and fainted with surprise!

"It was a beautiful sight when the American jeeps and tanks started rolling in to liberate the camp. I remember an American soldier who came over the fence and gave me some carrots and white bread. Then I went running to my mother to show her, 'look what I have for Edye!'

"From Vitel they were shipped to La Bourboule, placed in a hotel and deliced and prepared for orientation to life as free people. Helen's American citizenship was instrumental in getting them passage on the *Thomas H. Barry* battleship, though they were sworn to

Alice Cahana, guest speaker and Holocaust survivor at Yom Hashoah, 1999, with Hanna Schrob.

secrecy not to disclose the name of the ship until after the war ended.

"The voyage was a wonderful experience," says Hanna. "I remember things like sitting on the beds and talking to wounded soldiers who were in such bad shape, but still had so much to give. So different from what we had experienced the past two years! The voyage to Boston was long, ending after six weeks."

Upon arriving they were greeted with doughnuts and hot chocolate by the American Red Cross. "Then we got on a train to New York City, where we had a very emotional reunion with our relatives who were waiting for us to arrive. It was December 25, 1944, and the entire city was illuminated for the holidays. We'd heard stories about America being paved in gold, but this was more spectacular than anything I could imagine."

At first, the Spielman family was separated to live with different relatives, until they were reunited in their own home in Orange, New Jersey. There, they had some difficult adjustment to make. Although things were normal growing up, Hanna saw the war's effect on her father. He had been very successful in Europe, but the business he had before the war didn't fare well for him in the U.S. He went to work for his relatives in the liquor business.

At home, there was great concern for Edye, who arrived in America severely undernourished, needing special care.

The Spielmans' perseverance on her behalf paid off and she became stronger and healthy. The extra attention focused on Edye never caused sibling rivalry but only made Hanna closer to her baby sister.

After high school, Hanna met and married Herb Schrob. "We had an exciting life," says Hanna. "He showed me the world and that helped me develop the self-esteem I never had." At home, Hanna and Herb were loving parents to four children; Michelle, Amy, David and Alan.

On their tenth wedding anniversary, Hanna and Herb moved overseas with their three children to Breda, Holland. There, Herb would oversee a factory being built by his then employer, Joe Foster of Foster-Grant. Herb and Hanna befriended many Jews during their four years there. At the time, the Jews had no place to worship and were trying to re-establish a temple that was destroyed by the bombings, and the government couldn't subsidize the project as no funds were available.

On a visit back to the states, Herb and Hanna did a lot of legwork to raise money but came up with nothing. When Joe Foster found out what they were trying to do, he told Herb to tell them he would provide the funds needed to rebuild what was lost. "This was one of the highlights of our life," says Hanna. "It meant so much to Herb and me to help give them a place to pray again!" Joe Foster was a philanthropist who never talked about

what he did for others. It wasn't until the eulogy at his funeral, that Hanna and Herb learned that the creation of a Temple, with his namesake, was the most treasured in a long list of endowments. After Beth Foster was built, Joe Foster sent Hanna and Herb to Breda to attend the dedication.

"In spite of all of its troubles, America is the best country in the world," says Hanna. "I travel all over and when I come back to American soil, I feel so intensely proud to be an American. I plan to go into the schools and tell my story. My hope is that the children will realize how lucky they are to be in a free country. I'm searching for a way to inspire them to think first, without just following the crowd; to know what's right and stand up for it."

Hanna has moved to South Florida to be near her brother and sister. Bernie, a rabbi, Edye, a mother of two, and Hanna each created their own loving families in different parts of the country. Though they are very close and see each other on holidays, they haven't lived in the same city for 50 years. Says Hanna, looking ahead, "we have a beautiful relationship that we need to continue. We need to be together." ❖

"I feel so intensely proud to be an American."

The Memory Never Leaves
EDDIE SHAMES

By Moira Wright Bodner

Eddie Shames   *Photo by Perry Deglandon*

EDDIE SHAMES never talks about what he saw as one of the first American officers to enter Dachau, but "sees it every night when I go to sleep."

Shames was with the Office of Strategic Services, attached to the 506th Parachute Infantry with the 101st Airborne Division, when his commanding officer sent him to Dachau as an observer. The previous year, when he was 20, he had received a battle field commission at Normandy.

"I can't believe what I saw. How human beings could treat other human beings that way is unbelievable," says Shames, an Army Colonel.

He doesn't talk about Dachau to anyone, not even his wife and two sons. When he visits Israel he doesn't go to Yad Vashem. "It is too painful. I've seen enough. I don't want to relive that stuff."

A direct, outspoken man, Shames has no tolerance for anti-Semitism of any type. Although 50 years have passed, his feelings against those who perpetrated the Holocaust are intensely unforgiving. His wife's family in Lithuania perished, with only her mother and aunt surviving.

"The horror of Dachau never leaves," says Shames. ❖

From the Shadow of the Holocaust
FRANK SHATZ

By William T. Walker

One day in 1944, FRANK SHATZ undertook the most unusual assignment of his life. It seemed simple enough: he was to deliver a heavy suitcase to a luxurious villa in Budapest, Hungary.

Frank soon learned, however, that the suitcase contained gold, and its recipient was none other than Nazi SS Col. Adolf Eichmann, who was organizing the deportation of Jews to death camps.

In a role worthy of Oskar Schindler, Frank Shatz was delivering part of a $1 million ransom so that the Nazis would permit 3,000 Hungarian Jews to go to Switzerland, rather than to Auschwitz.

Today, Shatz plays down the danger of his mission. He recalls arriving at the villa, catching a glimpse of the cadaverous Eichmann, being relieved of the suitcase and going on his way.

But the mission was far from simple – or safe. In fact, it was decidedly dangerous. Shatz, himself a Jew, had just escaped from a Nazi slave-labor group; fascist thugs roamed the streets hunting Jews; and Allied bombers

Frank Shatz

Courtesy of the College of William & Mary

regularly dropped heavy loads of munitions on Budapest. Despite the danger, Shatz took the risk to help save Jews from the gas chambers.

In many ways, the act set a life-long pattern for the remarkable Holocaust survivor. Despite years of hardship – or perhaps, because of them – Frank Shatz has developed a strong commitment to good deeds. One of the primary beneficiaries is the College of William and Mary.

Frank's philanthropy is based on a simple proposition: "Having survived the horrors of living under the Nazis and the Communists, I believe that the best investment one can make for the future is to provide financial support for the education of young people," he said. "To my mind, a world view based on

"It is my feeling that you owe something to the world because you were saved so many times by miracles. I am just attempting to pay that debt."

solid knowledge is the best safeguard against the dangers of revisiting the horrors of the past."

As a Jewish resident of Central Europe in the 20th century, Frank is well acquainted with horror. A native of Parkan, Czechoslovakia (now Slovakia), Frank learned of the Nazi threat when refugees from Germany began to come through the town, but he thought that he was protected by his father's status as a national World War I hero. The chimera of protection evaporated in 1944, when Frank and other young Jews were sent to Romania as slave-laborers to help build a railroad line over the rugged Carpathian Mountains.

"We were treated just like animals. If we dropped a rail and crushed someone's leg, the Nazis would shoot him. He no longer had value to them," Shatz said. "All we had to eat was thin soup and a few kilos of bread."

Later that year, the Soviets began to push the Nazis and their work crews back toward Budapest. One day, as Allied bombers flew overhead, the laborers were ordered to hide in a cornfield. Later, Frank narrowly evaded the guards when they rounded up the laborers, and he made his way to Budapest.

"I had very little chance of surviving," Shatz recalled. "I had no place to stay, no food, no papers. Fascist gangs were questioning suspicious persons. Miraculously, I ran into a Jewish friend

from my hometown, and he took me to one of the 'safe houses' established by Swedish diplomat Raoul Wallenberg. A few days later I joined the Zionist underground and was provided false identity papers."

Until the Red Army conquered Budapest in January of 1945, Shatz helped the underground save Jewish lives, while dodging death almost every day. Once he escaped by a hair's breadth, when bombs destroyed his apartment only five minutes before he arrived.

After the fighting ended, Shatz first worked as a translator for the Soviets, and then became a correspondent in Prague, where two things forever changed his life. First, he met Jarka, his future wife. "It was the best thing that ever happened to me," he said.

Second, he read *The Anatomy of Peace*, a book by Hungarian journalist Emery Reves. Inspired by Reves' vision of world peace through universal law, Shatz believed that the book could be an antidote to the hatred that was once again welling up, as the Communists installed a system every bit as repressive as that of the Nazis. Recognizing the warning signs, Frank and Jarka Shatz began to take those small steps of mental defiance that eventually led to active participation in the anti-Communist underground.

"Resistance to oppression had become a habit," Shatz explained. "We couldn't sit idly by. I was a journalist, and I used my ability to move around freely to arrange escapes for those in danger. As a result, Jarka and I became the hunted species. After the secret police arrested and interrogated me, the underground told us to leave the country."

In 1954 the couple made a hair-raising escape through the Iron Curtain to the West, with only the clothes on their backs and one small piece of hand luggage. In the bag, without her husband's knowledge, Jarka had placed *The Anatomy of Peace.*

Eventually the Shatzes immigrated to the United States, where he founded a highly successful leather company in Lake Placid, New York.

"During our first return trip to Europe, I decided to pay my respects to the one man who had so profoundly influenced my outlook on world events by devising a concrete plan for peace. Reves agreed to see me for ten minutes. The visit lasted three hours. Our meetings in the ensuing years became routine," Shatz said.

As the relationship between Frank and Jarka Shatz and Emery Reves and his wife, Wendy, grew, Frank began to take steps to advance Reves' vision. In Lake Placid, he founded the Council on Foreign Policy and the Olympic People-for-People Program. When the couple bought a home in Williamsburg, Virginia, Frank Shatz looked for other opportunities to extend Reves' vision.

One soon appeared.

"Emery Reves had died in 1981, and Wendy was determined to create a memorial that would reflect his vision of world peace based on universal law. But she was at a loss to find the right vehicle," Shatz recalled. "She wrote us a letter asking for assistance. By coincidence, or maybe fate, the very same day her letter arrived, The College of William and Mary announced its intention to establish a world-class center for international studies. This turned out to be the decisive factor in our decision to recommend that Wendy select the college as the recipient of a $3 million endowment."

Building on Wendy Reves' gift, Frank and Jarka Shatz established a $1 million bequest to fund a diplomat-in-residence. Moreover, they encouraged others to make gifts that have established a peace program in the center, a writer's festival, a Swem Library endowment, student scholarships, and a professorship and lecture series in English.

"Frank and Jarka Shatz give not only of their resources, but they give of themselves," said James A. Bill, founding Director of the Reves Center for International Studies and now professor of government. Working with Shatz, Bill planned the center's effort to restart the stalled Middle East peace process in 1997.

"There were some dark and discouraging nights as we tried to persuade Israel, Palestine and Syria to send senior representatives. But Frank was there

with us, urging us to keep plugging away," Bill said. "Eventually the Israeli Ambassador to the United Nations, the Palestinian Liberation Organization's Washington representative, and the Syrian Ambassador to the U.S. all came together in one room. Through his inspiration, Frank enabled us to give a gentle nudge to the peace process and realize Wendy Reves' aspirations to memorialize her husband."

Sometimes, Shatz's willingness to give to W&M and its students can be painful. For several years he has delivered wrenching talks to Prof. David Holmes' freshman seminar on World War II.

"It is critical for our young people to have the experience of speaking with someone who lived through the Holocaust. Frank's presentations on his experiences are legendary," Holmes said.

As difficult as these sessions are, for Shatz they're part of a grand plan. As he reminisces about his many narrow escapes in the 1940s and '50s, he sums it up in typical understatement: "It is my feeling that you owe something to the world because you were saved so many times by miracles. I am just attempting to pay that debt." ❖

No Time to Mourn
SHALOM STEINBACH

As told to Eric Berryman

Shalom Steinbach   *Photo by Stephen Jay Photography*

We came from Kovno (Kaunas), the old provincial capital of Lithuania. My father, Zvi Yitchock and my mother Feigel, owned a haberdashery at 17 Vilnagasse and we lived at 57 Grodner Gasse, near the Niemen River. By modern American standards ours was a large family. I am the oldest (1920), followed by Ephraim (1923), Leibke (1924), Miriam (1929) and little brother Michele (1933). Kovno had a large Jewish population in those prewar years, some 30% of the over-all citizenry, and of course we lived in a completely Jewish neighborhood. Schools, newspapers, or organizations – what you will – were all Jewish.

There was little contact with the Lithuanians. Although we got along pretty well, they were in no sense an intimate part of our lives. Yiddish was the spoken language and the schools also taught Hebrew. My brothers were especially fine students. Lithuanian was used with the general population, but most people could not speak it fluently. In any case, a Jew was always recognizable by his accent, even if he had lived and moved for years among Gentiles.

The rush of modernity had not yet reached this little country. Trams were still pulled by horses, and there were no traffic lights. As a small child I thought the only person in the whole country who owned a car was the president of the republic. Horses and wagons remained the prevailing mode of transportation throughout my youth. Whatever increase in the number of cars there was, in later years, they could still be counted on the fingers of your hands. The shtetl also had electricity in later years, perhaps no more than one or two bulbs for one or two rooms with kerosene for supplemental light. No electrical outlets, just bulbs – charges were determined by the number of light bulbs.

Despite such apparent inconveniences, we lived a full life. For recreation there was a great deal of walking. We hiked everywhere, it seems to me now: through the woods outside the city, in the hills and along the river banks. In summer on Saturday nights, especially moonlit ones, we would go rowing and sing songs to the music of mandolins. Summers were spent on my paternal grandfather's farm in Grinkishok. The shtetl was still very real in my time, though slowly fading to extinction, and my Zayde's place was about as typical as they ever got. It provided a popular retreat for our family.

Lithuania was considered to be a nice country to live in. There were no luxuries, but most people made a living.

Nevertheless, in the late 1930s my father decided to leave and establish a home and business for us in America in 1938 on a tourist visa. The war separated us and my father died in America in 1945. As any history of the region will show, none of the Baltic states were spared the influence of fascism. It was in the air; you could not put a finger on it but somehow the environment had turned poisonously hostile. As a 12 or 13-year-old, I remember playing in the shtetl with a neighbor's boy when, completely out of the blue, he turned and told me, "I like you, you are a nice guy, but when Hitler comes I'll be the first to cut your throat."

After graduation from gymnasium, my ambition was to settle in Palestine, but by then the gates had closed to us everywhere.

War began in Kovno early on a Sunday morning. I returned late from seeing a rousing Russian propaganda film (Lithuania was incorporated in the USSR in 1940) and simply fell in bed, dead to the world. Not long afterwards, a blinding flash and monumental explosion threw me on the floor. My weariness was such that after inspecting the sky from my window and noting a puzzlingly clear night, I went back to bed dimly aware of continuing but distant rumbles. At 7 o'clock I looked once more and saw Russian trucks forming convoys across the river. There were hundreds of them all crammed

with people and not all soldiers. I realized there were many women and children. They were evacuating their families and going mighty fast. The streets below were full of bewildered civilians.

From about 4 a.m., when the concussion of what turned out to be the German bombardment of the airfield knocked me out of bed, the radio played only music and songs. At 10 o'clock they finally announced that Hitler had betrayed the pact. America, Britain and France were with us and together we shall triumph, they proclaimed. Suddenly the capitalist countries were our allies.

There followed an intense but highly amateurish consultation among family members and friends on what our best course should be, and it was decided that the men, especially the young men, must leave immediately. Women and children will remain. After all, what can they do to women and children? Men, on the other hand, are vulnerable to forced conscription, work brigades and who knows what other sort of danger and abuse. Some elected to remain. Among them was my Uncle Mashe. "Why run?" he decides, "Why should I run after death? Let it find me here, I am staying at home." Ephraim, Leibke and I were joined by our friends. All of us packed just enough necessities to fill two suitcases apiece.

Since the Germans were coming from the southwest, we decided our path lay in a northeasterly direction, through Jonava and Wilcomir towards Russia. Our instinct told us to run away from the front. In any case, what did we know of the Baltic coast and boats? It was my decision. Of the seven, only I survived.

We could see Russian soldiers pulling back singly, not in organized groups but looking over their shoulders and running with their rifles in their hands. By the time we walked three or four blocks it was quite clear that there could be no progress with so many suitcases. Before reaching the highway we stopped at my aunt's house and left the big ones, with a cheery "I'll be back." In fact, at the start our plan was to go entirely by bicycle, but we failed to get one for each of us. In any case, we soon discovered that the road was too crowded to ride on and, besides, how can you put a suitcase on a bicycle?

So we walked, with our four or five bicycles and our small suitcases until we were hot and tired and threw away the bicycles. Then we threw away the suitcases. Most people walked, some – the lucky ones – rode on horses and wagons with their possessions piled high. After 25 or 30 miles we reached Jonava, the little shtetl where my mother had been born and raised. There, at the Vilija River Bridge, thousands of people were stranded. It was already late evening on Monday.

"They mined the bridge," a friend told me, "and they're going to blow it up."

Shalom Steinbach's brother, Michele, age five.

Some of the people had been there staring across the river for hours. "It's not a big river," I told them, "it's not the Brooklyn Bridge. It will take no more than three minutes to cross. Let's go." The seven of us started running and suddenly the whole multitude followed. Shortly after we crossed, it blew up. The bridge really blew up! It was a moment of happiness for us. Now we were beyond the reach of the Germans. It was already dark, and we were very tired.

A nearby barn promised shelter for the night, a good sleep and a fresh start in the morning. We had barely locked ourselves inside when the peace was shattered by hard banging and loud Russian voices demanding to be let in.

"We are Jews," I called out. Under the circumstances Russian soldiers did not suspect a Jew to be an enemy.

Surprisingly, the officer replied, "I am also a Jew." He continued with the news, "You are in an extremely bad position here. This is 'No Man's Land'; our trenches are close and there's going to be a fight in the morning." To aid a safe departure he gave us the password that led us safely through Russian lines.

Thousands of refugees, some robbed by partisans, clogged the road. Russians riding trucks, young women nursing their babies, discarded property strewn everywhere, the dead and the dying and no time to mourn. Forward was life. The German planes attacked, strafing soldiers and refugees without discrimination. Efforts to find shelter in the ditches were almost worthless. People in the open had no cover at all, and death spread. My brothers and our companions survived the attack, a fact we interpreted as an omen that we were destined to remain alive.

We walked another day and a night, getting whatever food and water we could from farmers along the way. Water was especially scarce. A few gave it to us, most chased us away. The Lithuanian underground was already well organized to harm Jews, and many farmers were threatened if they helped us. Lithuanian soldiers now changed into partisans and exercised their heroism by attacking any Jews they found.

Ten kilometers from Wilcomir we heard explosions and saw people streaming back. The Germans were already in town, having dropped paratroopers from Memel. All our efforts were for nothing. Here, believing ourselves to be well behind the lines and at least a day ahead of the advancing German army, we were trapped. Latvia's border and safety was a myth. This new animal, the Blitzkrieg, could not be outrun. Bullets and explosions surrounded us; by chance, we found shelter in a potato cellar moments before the farmer closed the doors. Others, not so fortunate, screamed to be let in but were denied. The place was full of frightened and despairing Jews. When the fighting stopped, the farmer gave us all some white cheese and milk and pushed us out. Unwillingly – there was nowhere to go, nowhere to run.

While others were determined to return home, I still felt some hope of escape and suggested that our group go off the road and head east, straight through the woods. We saw men running in the uniform of Lithuanian police and followed them. After all, they were officials and must know where safety could be found. Abruptly they stopped, threw off the uniforms and put on civilian clothes. I was totally astonished. Here were the policemen and now they were Lithuanian patriots by the simple act of changing their clothes. We could not do that. We were different. How could it be so simple? For us it was a matter of life and death, and for them it was a change of wardrobe. To this day that scene has not left me.

Shortly afterwards we decided to go home. Leibke, sadly, became seriously ill, too sick to attempt the road back. A farmer allowed us to sleep in his barn but when it came time to leave and I tried to carry Leibke, I totally lacked the strength. We pleaded for compassion and the farmer agreed to permit him to stay in the barn another night. The rest of us must go. Partisans wielding clubs on horseback came screaming and chased us to the edge of the village. We felt this would be our last walk. Talking Lithuanian between ourselves and led by those of our number who had more of an Aryan look about them, we found the road. The first Germans we saw ignored us. What beauty and power they represented. They projected strength we could almost smell.

Shalom's family, June 1938.

Once, as I walked the road, a knot of people appeared at a great distance. Partisans? Germans? Trouble? "Don't worry," said the old man, "they are Jews."

"How do you know?" I asked. "I see people coming from far away. They are only silhouettes, too distant to identify." He replied, "They are Jews. Can't you see the way they walk with bowed heads?"

Towards evening the traffic thinned and a man directed us to a nearby farm where about 200 Jews, awaiting the opportunity to return home, were being housed and fed. The farmer was a man of great character and unfailing generosity. War had eliminated his markets. So all the products of his harvest and labors were placed at our disposal. Couples and the infirm were guests in his house, and the young and single – boys and girls together – found accommodation in a clean barn, full of sweet smelling hay. Suddenly and unexpectedly and for the briefest of moments, there was talk and laughter in a safe place. I related our experiences, especially Leibke's plight. Unanimously they urged us to immediately return for him, and bring him to this place. At dawn Ephraim and I departed.

After getting lost and being redirected we found Leibke still in his barn. His fever was terribly high and he would not walk. With great difficulty and for the sum of 300 rubles, we persuaded a farmer to take us as far as Jonava. On the move at last, we pretended to sleep with our faces covered to hide our Jewishness.

Not far down the road a soldier stopped the farmer, motions Ephraim and me to get off then orders the wagon to proceed. It was a work detail to clear telephone lines, cut by the retreating Russians. Entreaties did not move him, so we worked at a great pace. Just as suddenly, the German tells us to leave, to run. He was silent to our profuse thanks. Neither Ephraim nor I possessed the strength to catch up with the wagon. I ran, on that late summer day, until the clothes were glued to my body. In desperation, we hired a couple of boys to chase after it, and marveled at their speed.

On our return to the generous farmer's place, our group decided to split up. Leibke was far too ill to attempt the journey home and it was agreed that I should remain with him there until he recovered.

All of them, Ephraim and the four friends, were picked up on the outskirts of Kovno by partisans and shot. The slaughter of Jews (mostly men and adolescent boys) by Lithuanians during those first few weeks of war seemed even to surprise the Germans. They were the ones who finally put a stop to it.

Our farmer came under relentless pressure from anti-Semites to rid his property of Jews. Threats on his person and property ultimately made it impossible for Leibke and me to remain. This farmer was a fine man, his memory has not dimmed with the years.

Once, as I walked the road, a knot of people appeared at a great distance. Partisans? Germans? Trouble? "Don't worry," said the old man, "they are Jews."

"How do you know?" I asked. "I see people coming from far away. They are only silhouettes, too distant to identify." He replied, "They are Jews. Can't you see the way they walk with bowed heads?"

Leibke and I delayed our entry into Kovno by two or three days, after gentiles warned us that the city was a slaughter house. Finally, too exhausted to care, we were arrested by a couple of unarmed teenagers. We were so naive then, that when they asked if we were Jews, we did not deny it.

We spent one night in a crowded cell, and early the following morning we were lined up and marched across the bridge. First stop was the Fort, an old Tsarist place where we heard a lot of shooting. After standing in line and having all personal effects confiscated, they marched us once more, this time to the Gelye Turme (Yellow Jail), where we were packed 50 to a cell.

Some of the faces were familiar. I recognized people who had been arrested by the Russians for Zionist activities. Another, a well-known man, lightened the atmosphere with his pronouncement that, "My doctor insists I take different pills everyday – this pill and this pill and this pill. He assures me I cannot hope to live without them. Now I do not eat, I do not drink and I do not take any pills and I am still alive! If I get home, I shall never take another pill again."

We were distracted by a German officer who announced: "We are not here to hurt anyone. We have stopped the killing. If you are not communist you can go free."

They called my name, and I answered.

Their curiosity seemed easily satisfied: name, occupation, political affiliation, and so on. I stressed the family business and its related capitalist associations. I was then returned to my cell and my brother was called. He did not return. I was among the first several hundred to be released, and asked about Leibke. The officials gave perfunctory assurances and when I persisted they became angry and ordered me out.

At home the atmosphere was tense and gloomy. From the first bombardment my mother began to withdraw into a shocked stillness, though she asked about Ephraim and Leibke. There was nothing to say. If Leibke and I had stayed in the country another day or two, perhaps we might not have been detained at all. If the group had stayed together, Ephraim would also have returned. If, if, if.

For a few days, the Germans introduced a semblance of order. They posted signs warning that looters would be shot, and issued ration cards. With care we could even manage to sneak into shul on occasion.

Shortly thereafter, a neighbor came running to say he had seen a group of prisoners loading furniture right off Vilnagasse, and thought he recognized Leibke among them. I ran to see for myself, and sure enough in a gang of about 30 men, there was my brother barefoot and looking pale. A single Lithuanian guard stood watching on a street full of curious onlookers, relatives, and plain passersby. "They took my shoes away," he told me, "but I still have the money you gave me."

It haunts me still why I failed to say, "Jump off the truck and run!" What could one clumsy looking guard with his rifle have done in such a crowded setting? How primitive, how naive, how foolishly law-abiding we were. The man said we can't, and we obeyed. Even those prisoners who carried furniture from inside the houses dutifully returned to the truck. Leibke disappeared from our lives on that day.

At home, I pieced together some of what occurred after our departure, when Lithuanians searched the houses and arrested every man and boy. In the *shtetlach* virtually everyone was massacred immediately. In one brief moment my grandfather, uncle, cousins, and friends had ceased to exist. By an amazing show of fortitude our own house was not raided because the struz (caretaker) stood at the entrance and denied that Jews lived there. Later, it was here on Grodnergasse overlooking the river, that the Gestapo established its headquarters.

All radios were forbidden to us. When men began to be pulled away from ration lines, only women could venture out. The first decree was published about August 1st: all Jews must remove themselves to the Slobodka district of Kovno, where a ghetto would be erected. Slobodka, site of an old and distinguished Yeshiva, was to be our prison for almost three years.

In fact there were two ghettos, the Large and the Small, divided by a major road and connected by a foot bridge. Somehow my mother was able to organize a place for us on the outskirts of the Large one. I think she exchanged homes with a Gentile acquaintance. For those who were not so fortunate, there was the Jewish Committee who acted as a housing referral agency. We took whatever possessions we could from our home and business. Peasants around the city heard of the decree and hired their wagons out for exorbitant rates. The Germans restrained Lithuanians from molesting us en route. At the store, some old customers realized an unprecedented opportunity to get whatever they could for nothing, "You might as well give it away, they won't let you keep it."

Our new apartment consisted of one room and a kitchen, and for five months we shared it with another woman and her two children. Compared to what came later, it was actually paradise.

In the ghetto we were not permitted mail or allowed to earn money, and lived solely by barter and trade. After barbed wire was strung and the ghetto closed, the Jewish Labor Department was tasked to organize daily work forces. All who registered got a piece of bread and a tiny ration of margarine. More importantly, on the work force we got out of the ghetto and could sell or exchange things from our bodies. A shirt, scarf, pair of socks or shoes – whatever one could manage to carry without alerting attention – became the new currency. By this time, all Jews were required to wear the yellow badge.

Among the earliest of German deceptions was a special appeal, advertising important work for 500 well-educated and intelligent young men. We never knew what to evade, so it was that I almost joined a friend and volunteered, declining only at the last moment for fear of leaving my family without protection. I watched as the 500 marched off, my friend smiling and calling out, "See you later." Of course they never returned. As best as I could explain it, the rationale was that they did not want educated men at all. They wanted ordinary men who could be used for manual labor. The others were potentially dangerous and needed to be dispatched quickly.

When winter came we heated the two rooms at first by burning our furniture, then we tore away the garden fences. I would collect scraps on the work force, and hide them in my clothing. Working by the railroad, on one occasion, I managed to claim a complete railroad sleeper; here was wood to cook and heat from for a week.

It was painfully heavy and we were marched a long way on that day. At the ghetto entrance they took it away. We survived by pure chance at times and we grew to be quickwitted and tried to be stoic, but too often death came with random suddenness.

When the Germans decided that the strategically important road that ran through the two Slobodka Ghettos could no longer be divided, all the Little Ghetto residents – several thousand people of all ages – were assembled in the square. Lithuanians marched them away into the country, and shot them all.

According to German rules, all ghettos in Europe were to be eliminated, only concentration camps could exist. By definition a ghetto had the young and the old, women and children, and more or less resembled a normal community. Concentration camps, on the other hand, were official places of hard labor suitable only for men. Nazis liked their packages neat, and so it was that Slobodka Ghetto became ICZ Kaunas

(Concentration Camp Kovno). Nothing changed, we still lived in the same houses and did the same things. There were no barracks or morning head counts or any of the regimens I was to endure later in Dachau. Our existence went on as before, except that our alertness was constantly being refined as the German tempo for liquidation increased.

Their principal machine for reducing the population was the "Special Action." Actions were always mounted against certain identifiable categories of people. For example, one Action was targeted against the old (a beard could qualify one as being "old," and many orthodox young men were rounded up), and another focused on the young. The Children's Action was the worst. It was a horror that blisters dreams. With the pretext that all children would be taken to a *kinderheim*, the ghetto was surrounded and all exits sealed. Everyone was to stay at home. Ukrainians accompanied by a few German supervisors went from house to house collecting children of every age. From my window lookout I watched the soldiers going into the houses. I saw the running and heard the screams as doors were kicked in and mothers and their children dragged into the open. One woman who refused to let go had her child torn from her hand, and to get at the other one they set a police dog loose to attack her. In her panic the woman dropped a child about two years old, who was snatched up instantly and flung on the tuck. In some instances they shot the mothers out of hand.

My family hid. In fact I had become part of an organization that built a most elaborate *maline* (secret bunker). It was so ingeniously constructed and well supplied with food and fresh water (from a well), we could have hidden there in safety for a year or more. An electrician had even hooked up light tapped from the main so cleverly it defied detection.

Once an Action was concluded, survivors of targeted groups generally had to be hidden, although there was never any consistent policy even in that. If a child was seen, for example, he was more often than not ignored. The Action was officially over, children no longer officially existed and that was that.

A peculiar Action, if it can be called that, concerned the order for all our police to report for inspection. To a man they were trucked away and for a few days we had no ghetto police at all. Then several of them returned, with an account of what had happened to our Chief of Police Levine, who was known to all as "DeGaulle." He was a tall, redheaded man whose strength of character and leadership qualities earned him the nickname.

Photo by permission of the U.S. Holocaust Memorial Museum.

DeGaulle was the best, and he had been accused by the Germans of betraying his duties, of being a traitor, of no less than being a leader of the ghetto underground. They said he planned the building of *malines* and, worse, of actually assisting in their construction. Furthermore, he was charged with organizing Jewish Partisans and helping them escape. To save his life, Levine was ordered to reveal all that he knew. He refused and was burned alive as a lesson to the other police. The new Chief of Police was a very strict man, whom people avoided.

At about this time, as the Russians were approaching, it was decided to finally liquidate the whole ghetto. They decreed that everyone must assemble immediately, and to enforce the order, Ukrainians went from house to house gathering up the people. Our destination was announced as being a work camp in Germany. The end was near but we were not ready yet for meek surrender; we had our *maline*. Slobodka was, I think, the last ghetto to exist in Europe. Some of the credit for that is due to the *Judenrat* who, apparently, persuaded local German authorities either not to liquidate totally or, failing that, to proceed slowly in implementation of their directives.

German Kommandant Gecke (who became known to us as the "Murderer in White Gloves"), evidently played along and postponed the liquidation, claiming essential war work required

our continued existence. That may account for our three-year tenure there, long after similar creations had perished. In any event, Gecke's superiors must have become suspicious, because he disappeared – ordered to the Russian Front, it was rumored. Then the trains came and the Ukrainian soldiers and again, those who resisted were shot. This time the victims' riddled bodies were publicly displayed.

We hid in the *maline*, but since the time of the Kinder Action it was no longer much of a secret. Most of the other *malines* were quite primitive, perhaps a closet or under the bed, or a little artificial partition somewhere. These they had no trouble finding. Our clever hiding place had one definite weakness: too many people joined the group.

As much as they searched, using dogs and posting round-the-clock guards, we stayed hidden. The new Chief of Police was assigned the task and we were told in no uncertain terms that the *maline* had to be revealed and abandoned. They guaranteed not to use reprisals against us. Well, we gave it up. In the morning the Gestapo looked and exclaimed, *"Ach mein Gott! was die Juden alles gemacht haben."* By war's end maybe, one hundred people had managed to hide successfully. One hundred people out of a population that numbered close to 40,000.

After the *maline* was surrendered we began building another one, but on a smaller scale. We managed to complete

it just before the call for the ghetto's final liquidation. It was a pretty good *maline*, one in which we could survive for a few days even if they bombed the place. By coincidence, our building had been constructed under a new code that required a concrete bomb shelter. The entrance was from outside via trap doors. We got rid of the doors and made a small opening through shelving in the kitchen and in a normal search it was unlikely to be found. A second, very small maline, was built in the attic. This time there was no electricity and water had to be stored in barrels.

We heard them searching and shouting. They would come in the house, knocking on the floor and walls and probing with their picks. Each time three or four of them in their heavy boots shouting, *"Raus! Raus! Raus!"* Eventually one tires of hiding like that, not knowing what was going on outside. Unexpected people came pleading for shelter: a Jewish gate guard and his mother, the director of a bank and even the Chief of Police asked, "Do you have room for me?"

I was stunned. "You? You?" was as much as I could stammer.

"We're all in the same boat," he says. "No more politics."

They all joined us. What could I do? If these people are fugitives then it must mean that there is no more structure, that the end is near. However, the Germans did return to shout and probe all over again. On their third visit (even knowledge of this *maline* had leaked out), one of the soldiers discovered the entrance. Inside, we remained absolutely quiet. I could see the soldiers but they could not see us. One of them fetched a flashlight, *"Raus! Raus! Alle raus."* No one moved. *"In einer minute wergfen wir eine Handgranate runter. Eine minute!"*

I was the first. Going up a short ladder my head was precisely level with their boots. *"Los! Los! Los!"* They treated us roughly, but more or less kindly. I think these must have been regular combat troops on their way through the area, in retreat from the Russians. They were not the SS we were used to. All I carried was a wallet full of pictures, and my clothing consisted of a pair of pants tucked into stolen German army boots. My shirt was inadvertently left in the maline, on that hot summer day. Those who sheltered in the attic were not found, but they probably died anyway when the house was destroyed. Every house in Slobodka Ghetto was dynamited after its liquidation.

We all came out to the street and they marched us to the square, the last to be discovered, the last transport from Kovno. At the gathering place we joined another 200 or so others, surrounded by machine guns manned by Lithuanians, Ukrainians and Germans. I wanted to run, but there were too many guns. We failed to escape when there were only two or

Profanation

By Abbott Saks

Goethe, immortal master of the German tongue,
Once walked these wooded ways and breathed the Sylvan air that bore and nurtured noblest thought;
Soaring poetry of pine, and spruce and fir, shaded solitudes where woodland spirits stir,
Where sweet trills and warbled symphonies greet the golden dawn,
Idyllic grace of stately stag and gentle doe and fawn
This Teutonic treasure of rich and verdant harmonies;
Then fell the hellish night of dread and doom,
A stygian darkness deep and never dreamed, man was murd'rous beast where once man's brilliance beamed
And hoary name that once with pride could glory claim,
Will now live with eternal shame,
For Goethe walked the ways of Buchenwald.

three soldiers herding thousands and now there were too many guards. We marched off four to a row, thickly surrounded by German soldiers. Along the way I told Michele to remember my uncle's address in New York, I made him repeat it until it was memorized. If Michele remained alive he would at

least have one reference to a place of safety. He tried to step away from the column, but the soldiers pushed him back in line.

We reached the tracks after a long march, and saw the rows of freight trains awaiting us. They ushered us aboard without violence, 50 or 60 people per car. It was easy for me to escape then, unnoticed I merely jumped off and hid behind a pile of nearby logs. But when I looked back and saw my mother, sister and brother on the train looking back at me, I gave it up and returned to them. After a long delay the train departed, with guards posted on top of each car. We passed the time with friends who once ran a successful restaurant. Other people threw out little notes asking for help from partisans we knew were already operating in the countryside. It was hoped they would blow up the tracks and bridges and stop this evacuation of Jews.

We crossed into Germany, stopping at Koenigsberg in East Prussia where they allowed us to have some water. I admired the beautiful city. The Germans paid no notice, this was like any other train. After a few hours we left, stopping again in Stutthof, near Danzig, where they again left us alone for a long time. Then they announced that all women and children must leave the train, the men had to stay.

We debated: Should Michele stay with me? Maybe they only mean infants, he obviously wasn't an infant. It was decided that Michele would be safer with me. He simply did not get off the train with my mother and sister. There was no more to it than that; we were being so rushed there was not even time to say goodbye.

The train continued, stopping here and there in various cities. Kovno was the biggest place in Lithuania but this was my first glimpse of truly modern cities. At the stations we halted in, some people brought us bread – if the guards did not chase them away first. At last we reached our destination, *"Alle raus!"* It was Lager I, Dachau, and consisted of no more than a broad field surrounded by barbed wire and guard towers. No barracks, nothing but heaps of earth indicating preliminary signs of construction. We slept on bare ground. On the following day we were told to take everything off except our under-wear. My most valuable possessions were some money and my boots. I buried them in one of the heaps of dirt.

After a perfunctory shower we were issued a suit of blue and white striped pajama – like ticking and a pair of wooden shoes. We could keep our belts. For shelter they provided heavy carton structures, like round booths made of cardboard that were not unlike igloos. There were 15 in each box. Then they took our names, recorded where we came from, assigned a work place and gave us each a number engraved on a little metal triangle. No more yellow star, from now on we answered only by the number. On about the second day they also issued us a little canteen which was worn on the belt. Our first meal was a watery barley soup, but it tasted good.

While Michele stayed behind, I went to work at a Baustelle over an hour's march away. It was a big construction site deep in the woods (and thus naturally camouflaged), where thousands of people were digging, mixing cement and carrying planks. Besides ourselves there were Polish volunteers who worked for wages, lived in regular barracks and wore civilian clothes. We worked from dawn to dark, 12 to 15 hours a day. I think our daily ration was 200 grams of bread and the barley soup.

After two days of marching in wooden shoes my feet were bloody. People who became ill fell away and died. There was no one to complain to and no medical attention. Without relief I could not go another day, so I was determined to retrieve the old boots. A few prisoners had been assigned to the stocks of old clothing, and as always somebody knew somebody who was able to exchange his wooden shoes for a pair of old leather ones. Of course they did not get their old shoes. The point was they got shoes with quasi-official permission and could be seen wearing them. I had to be especially careful with my boots because if they were German army stock, they were something no one in Dachau had a right to wear. I disguised their appearance with smeared mud and wore them under my pants. It was like having a new life, sheer heaven. Those boots saved me, and I wore them until liberation. I also took my *tefillin,* which

I put on every morning before dawn. Whether it was done according to law or not, under the circumstances it was the best I could do. No one ever searched me, so I was lucky to keep my *tefillin* and the pictures. The money was no good anyway, and stayed in the dirt pile.

Lager 1 had a population of about 2,000 by now, including a few unexpected women who were put to work in the kitchen. The paradox was overwhelming; failure to obey orders resulted in being shot, yet at other times if you did not follow orders it turned out to be an advantage that saved your life. We felt certain that once they discovered the women and children who did not leave the trains in Stutthof, they would be killed. Instead, the women worked in the most enviable place in all of Dachau – the kitchen.

Those who had a female relative there were able to survive better because they could get an extra piece of bread, or some other food, once in a while.

The announcement came that all children must report for placement with a Jewish kapo who had been designated to look after them. There were only about ten or 15 children at this point, and they promised a school and care and safety in a *kinderheim* away from the work camp. I had grave doubts about this *kinderheim* yet you never knew. Here they insisted that women would be shot if they remained on the train and now after having passed

themselves off as men and been discovered. they were at work in the kitchen. Maybe there really was a *kinderheim*. I hesitated for a couple of days, debating the question back and forth and finally decided to bring Michele in. After he left I felt great pain and asked the kapos to return him, but of course they refused. It was a terrible mistake to give my brother up, to let him go. The time was late summer, 1944, and Michele was ten years old.

The SS replaced the regular soldiers who had brought us. Beatings, hangings, long hours of waiting in line, being counted became the norm. *"Appel! Appel!"* countings and beatings and hardly any food. It turned cold and when it rained, the water would flow under the cardboard walls of our boxes. At night we froze to the ground and had to break the ice to get up for the 4 a.m. roll call.

A good-natured guard was a rarity, a day without harassment and beatings was a miracle. Hours of hard labor were followed by hours of standing in line in the darkness. "Stand straight!" "Don't move!" "Turn this way!" "Inspection!" Kicks and blows and at last the line for soup. The soup was the high point of our lives. Afterwards there might even be time to visit another box and talk for a while.

As winter progressed they decided to build permanent barracks for us. We began by digging a big ditch, about four

feet deep and ten feet long, and covered it with a single frame roof. There were no other walls. When a person walked down into the ditch there were, on either side at ground level, a series of boards placed flush on the dirt. That was where we slept, some 25 to 50 people divided on each side. The roof was covered with earth, for insulation. In the coldest part of winter they gave us a little stove into which we fed bits of scrap wood. There was no chimney, so the smoke would fill the room. That inconvenience notwithstanding, it was a vast improvement over the cardboard box.

I never took my clothes off, it was too cold and I was afraid of having them stolen. But once, when we worked near the rail tracks, near one of those water towers used to replenish steam engine boilers, I saw the hose spilling fresh water and felt an irresistible need to wash myself. It was ice cold but I took my clothes off and stood under that spill rejoicing in the clean water.

As time went on, we started to suffer from lice. Lice were everywhere, and they were the biggest I have seen. Thereafter, when we awoke in the mornings, the dead were all around us in the barracks. Outside the Lager was a kind of morgue where the bodies would be piled up. I helped carry some of these, they were very light, just skeletons. On one occasion I was piling bodies up on a heap that was already too high, when the whole lot came

Americans entering Germany. *Photo by Hugo Horvath*

down on top of me. There were no emotions, it was just a daily chore, just a routine we had to follow. The original group of prisoners was diminishing quickly. Young people, boys, fell away. We worked shifts, day and night, and sometimes it happened that as we were readying to return, they would require that we work the next shift. My job was mixing cement in warm water to keep it from freezing, to build an underground factory that had walls several meters thick, deep in the ground. The roof of the place was domed, and looked a little like the Virginia Beach Convention and Exhibit Center. It was supposedly for the aircraft industry, to replace the factories bombed out by the Allies.

Lager 1 had an infirmary and one of the quickest lessons we learned was that no one was ever treated there. Once or twice a week, if the patient failed to get out, they came and carried him to the main lager and he was cremated. It made for little incentive to be sick, so people died in the barracks or outside. Working in the fields one day I picked and ate some berries. They were large and dark and looked like blueberries or cherries. The German supervisor warned us not to touch them, but we thought he wasn't telling the truth. I began to feel dizzy and could not see or hear and my body was paralyzed. I lay all day, along with the two others who had also eaten the berries. When it came time to return, the German improvised a wagon for us and they pulled us in.

On the third day I was the only one left alive and managed to get out of the infirmary just before they cleared it. I was young and strong and, as I have indicated, did not suffer as much as some of the others because of the lack of food. I also managed not to burn away too much energy on the job, but to apply just enough effort to go unnoticed. Even though the hunger pains were constant, I never felt I would pass out or collapse.

I knew they were trying to work us to death. I also knew that paper was a good insulator, and we had practically no clothes except the pajamas. Working on the cement mixer one day I stole an empty cement bag and cut holes for head and arms and wore it like a vest. What a difference it made! But I was scared stiff. This was sabotage and if detected, they would publicly hang me in the camp. Then I calmed down and rationalized and decided that if asked, my response would be to say I had only taken a damaged bag. My face and body was encrusted with cement. After liberation when I was able to take a bath, the color of my skin scared me. It looked dead.

Winter was the worst time. We stood for an hour and more at 4 o'clock in the morning, with snow up to our knees at times. I was so glad I had those boots. An attack of what appeared to be rheumatism laid me low for a few days, then it went away as suddenly as it had come. At nights, when we had an hour or so of free time, there would be gatherings in the barracks. They were illegal, but the debates and lectures, no matter how futile, served to relieve the burden of our days.

We also had a Jewish orchestra in the Lager, all of them survivors of the Slobodka Ghetto. As musicians they were treated a little better than the rest of us, and would play once in a while for the Germans. They actually gave a concert for the entire camp. It is difficult to imagine a more grotesque phenomenon. Everyone was free to attend, prisoners in the back, Germans in front, and there in Kz Dachau the Slobodka orchestra played music. It was such a contradiction, and it was not the only cultural event.

They brought in some Czech actors from Buchenwald, a whole troupe of them, who staged a play. A play with actors and singers! Their selection was a satire, a production that actually demeaned the Germans. Perhaps it meant that the war was coming to an end, in any case I was amazed at their courage.

I do not know if any of them survived after their brave display. I never saw them again. Whether they were brought in just for the show or actually eliminated I cannot say.

The food ration was reduced to 50 or 100 grams, and the bread came with green mold. I asked my father's cousin, a doctor from Kovno, whether it was safe to eat. He replied, "according to all medical training, that bread is poison.

A German master mechanic, a friendly man who once in a while dropped a piece of bread for me to pick up, let his newspaper fall as if by accident. The headline was "Abendland in Gefahr," Germany's western borders were in danger.

But people eat it and they do not die. Maybe under these circumstances it's better to eat."

The cold and long hours of labor put such a physical and mental strain on me, I volunteered for an announced need for electricians. I had always managed not to be sent out. In all the Ghetto Actions, and the work camp details, I had always managed to survive. Now I was desperate enough to risk the call, my ingrained fear of volunteering for something and never coming back notwithstanding.

An electrical engineer from Kovno assured me it would be all right, and he was quite aware that I had no training at all in anything electrical. Most of the volunteers were like me. But he promised to teach us enough to get by. His father was also in the camp, a big man I remembered from Kovno, with a big stomach (a Kovno sign of prosperity). Now he was just folds of skin.

Wonder of wonders, they marched us to Lager and assigned us to wooden barracks, three or four to a room, not

50. Every person had a separate place to sleep, on a straw mattress, actual straw and not a board. And to top it all, we each got a blanket. We worked in the Lager stringing wire on poles, I even got a set of spike irons and looked remarkably professional. They also gave us better food. We had heard of Eisenhower's second front and knew the war was ending. Here I was sitting in a warm barracks, wrapped in a blanket eating a piece of bread and downing hot sweet coffee with milk and thought, "I have it so good, why must it end now?" Amazing how the mind works.

After the main job was completed, we became Lager electricians. That meant I would shake the wires a little and if the lights failed to come on, called the engineer. After two months or so, we were sent back to Lager I, but I retained my electrician's standing, and life continued to be slightly better. I would walk around and troubleshoot with my spike irons, looking very official and armed with a ready-made explanation in case a guard or kapo asked questions. In this way I had the opportunity to circulate through the workplace and meet a variety of people, some of whom had been there for five years.

Precious possessions would often be entrusted to the Poles, in their permanent barracks. After hanging onto my wallet and pictures for so long, I left them there as well. At that time a typhus epidemic broke out and a curfew was imposed. All prisoners had to get typhus shots, not to protect them, but to spare the Germans. I dreaded getting that shot. The medic was an SS man who used the same needle for everyone. However, there would be no ration unless you first passed by this man. I did without my food that day.

By the time I returned to the Poles' barracks, all of our possessions were scattered and lost. When the Germans announced the quarantine, the Poles ransacked everything we had left with them. They were looking for money, and in their greed tore up the few things we had left to treasure, including all my family pictures.

A German master mechanic, a friendly man who once in a while dropped a piece of bread for me to pick up, let his newspaper fall as if by accident. The headline was *"Abendland in Gefahr,"* Germany's western borders were in danger. The first Germany city, Aachen, had fallen to the Americans. We had lived with feelings and promises of liberation for a long time, and it never materialized. We heard that Hitler was shot and thought it was all over. Instead, it was worse than ever. So even though good news came from the front, there was also the feeling that we would not survive. Only as time went on was there a heightened awareness.

One day the camp closed and we were told to prepare for evacuation to the Tyrol, where the Germans planned on continuing the war. My decision was to hold back as long as I could. I was not

leaving, even when they declared their intention to blow up the camp, I was going to stick it out.

Whenever they chased people to the main gate, I held back. Finally, I was among the few who remained from the old camp prisoners. When a friend wanted to cut his way through the wire with a pair of cutters he had made, I still held back. The guard towers looked empty and there were no more lights, but I was still afraid. We selected an alternate hiding place; he lowered himself down the latrine and I inserted myself into one of the huge piles of bodies. And there we hid until the last group had departed for the trains. The Americans then bombarded the trains, and they all came back. Night came, and the Americans bombed again. Shrapnel flew across the camp, one shell falling on a barracks and setting it on fire but no one moved. It was beautiful music to us, like a celebration. The feelings we had were eerie, we were all soon to be transported into another world. Perhaps this was what Jews felt when chased by the Egyptians and the Red Sea parted.

At 5 a.m. the Commandant came to the gate and called out that he wants to talk with the Lager's senior prisoner. My physician cousin came forward, and a few others, too. They gathered by the gate and the German Kommandant in his immaculate uniform told us, "The Americans are near and will probably come to the camp by tomorrow." He

suggested that no one leave because the retreating Germans could harm us. He hoped, and these were his words, "that Americans will treat us fairly and not worse than we have been treated by the Germans."

Keep calm, he says. If we want something or have questions, we should come to him. We yelled "Bread!" and he replied *"Jawohl."* Two-wheeled wagons, the ones we transported bodies with, were brought and loaded with bread. Before it could be distributed, Russian prisoners attacked us and grabbed whatever they could. One of them bit me on the hand, to get my piece of bread. In all the terror of the camp, none of us ever acted in this fashion. Complete anarchy threatened.

Then we heard American tanks. It was about 10 o'clock, April 23, 1945. A fine spring day. Suddenly everyone stormed the gates.

Shalom was a resident of Norfolk until the '90's when he moved with his family to Israel, where he later died. ❖

Editor's Note: This story is an edited transcript of interviews with Shalom Steinbach, who at the time was President of the Tidewater Survivor's Club. These interviews were conducted in 1984 by Lt. Cmdr. Eric Berryman over a series of months and included many meetings between the two men. At the time of the meetings, Eric was Deputy Chief of Public Information for Supreme Allied Command Atlantic.

Innocence Lost - Lessons Learned
Ethel Sternberg

By Eric Allan Futterman

If there's one thing that's abundantly clear about ETHEL STERNBERG, it is her insistence, that children – no matter how innocent their view of the world – understand the truth, as soon as possible.

The truth, according to Ethel, may be difficult but it will set them free.

This age-old philosophy runs deeply through Ethel's life as she gives a tour of the small synagogue she and her late husband founded in Williamsburg, Virginia, in 1958 with five other families. The building is small, but elegant. Clean, ornate, and comfortable. A place where worship is performed in comfort and children are given stern lectures about prejudice, political involvement and oftentimes their very first lesson on the harsh realities of the Holocaust.

Speaking slowly and methodically in her German accent, this gentle woman with a shock of white running down the middle of an otherwise deeply black and full hairline, explains the rationale, if one can call it that, that Hitler and the Nazis used to determined who lived and who died, who was to be given a life of privilege and who will lose all rights.

"And I'm talking to the kids and I say, Just imagine if all the blue-eyed, blond (haired) kids are on this side and all the dark-eyed (and dark-haired kids) on that side and a guy comes in and says, 'I don't like those blond kids, I want to get rid of these blond kids.' And that's all there is to it.'"

It is quite interesting that Ethel uses that bit of misdirection; choosing the blond-haired, blue-eyed kids – the very symbol of Arian superiority that Hitler claimed would lead the world – to demonstrate who could be the victims of prejudice. In many ways, it explains the sheer absurdity of the whole experience.

Ethel was swept up in the absurd life of bigotry, like so many other German children of the early 1930s as Adolf Hitler and his Nazis began the steady march of bigotry with simple laws dealing with lifestyle and business.

"I had a very normal childhood," Ethel says. "Born in 1924, I lived in a Gentile neighborhood. My parents' business was there. They were in the food business, owning two retail stores.

"The whole street was full of people who worked for the government at the railroad. They had a big income. (The

Germans) were wonderful people to do business with. I had friends, children. We played soccer with the boys, the girls with dolls and everything.

"The first thing (Hitler) did was forbid people who worked for the government to buy food from Jews … eat with them or be friendly with them. With that of course, business went down. My parents had to close the store to move into another neighborhood. I lost all my friends."

It takes a few moments for an adult to remember the pain that can embody a child who has lost all her friends. But for the little German girl who cared mostly about playing soccer on one day, then losing her friends the next, Ethel was only experiencing the genesis of her anguish.

Ethel likes to show visitors a photo-graph of her father taken shortly after World War I. She was proud of her father, as was her entire family. He fought bravely for Germany, for the Fatherland, in that conflict and was wounded in battle. Ultimately he died from his wounds, making him nothing less than a hero to Germany. That pride, that sacrifice for his country added a layer of naiveté to Ethel's family as Hitler's Holocaust began to take shape.

When they had a chance to leave, they did not. "My mother thought my father died for the Fatherland … so they certainly wouldn't do anything to us."

That sense of hope and innocence lasted even through the government-controlled mob action of 1938, later dubbed *Kristallnacht*. It was a night symbolic for what was to come for Europe's Jewish population. Thugs ran through Jewish neighborhoods and business districts and smashed windows, burned synagogues and vandalized homes and businesses.

Ethel subtly shakes her head from the very clear memory. "It's indescribable. There was glass all over, piles of (ashes) where there was fire, where they burned books and glass. It really was a crystal night. A terrible sight to see."

This was a turning point. Ethel's mother decided she could not count on her husband's honorable service to the German people in World War I for security. She arranged passports and visas on the black market to send Ethel and her brother to Spain.

While there, they received three letters from their mother, the last of which was filled with optimism, hope and ultimately, a tragically misguided trust of the German government.

Ethel closes her eyes for just a moment, perhaps rereading the handwritten note as a child whose last moments of innocence were about to be shattered.

Ethel deals with her lost innocence by giving children and adults lectures about a kind of cynicism she believes keeps America alive. It's not a cynicism filled with anger or inherent distrust of our leaders. Instead it's one that says, you can only be comfortable with your government's actions and motivations if you are involved in its daily mechanisms.

"In October or the end of September she wrote and said, 'isn't this wonderful? They sent us a letter saying we're going to be sent to this wonderful place where bombs don't fall. Nice and safe! And that she'll write us as soon as she gets there....'"

Ethel pauses to allow her visitor to realize the impact of that statement. The truth to Ethel's mother was embodied in her husband's service to her country, in her country's ultimate honor, saving innocent people from destruction.

It wasn't until more than fifty years after the end of the war that truth ultimately came to Ethel Sternberg.

"I wrote to the government in Hamburg where I was born. They sent me this wonderful book. Gives the name of 6,000 Jews that have been killed from this city alone. On the first page was my mother's name ... she was sent to a concentration camp and killed the same day she got there. They killed widows and young people first, even the widows of German soldiers who had died defending their country."

Ethel deals with her lost innocence by giving children and adults lectures about a kind of cynicism she believes keeps America alive. It's not a cynicism filled with anger or inherent distrust of our leaders. Instead it's one that says, you can only be comfortable with your government's actions and motivations if you are involved in its daily mechanisms.

"You don't get politically involved and let everybody talk you into something. It can happen so easily. It was something I needed strongly to tell the kids."

Year after year, from one decade to the next, however, Ethel watches young boys and girls become men and women through their Bar and Bat Mitzvahs, through their Jewish education and their American experience. She may have lost her innocence as a child during the Holocaust, but Ethel Sternberg did not, ultimately, lose. It is a message she proclaims to Hitler proudly, whenever she can.

"And you didn't defeat us. For all the many years that we Jews have been surviving ... not only the Holocaust but other things ... we still are on top of it. ... Thank God." ❖

My Child Is My Life

A Holocaust Story of a Mother and Her Infant in the Warsaw Ghetto
Excerpts From the Memoirs of Halina Sternlicht

By Ludwig Sternlicht, M.D.

… Nineteen-forty in the Warsaw Ghetto was still bearable. We had enough to eat and I shared my food with my friend Stella. She was a beautiful blonde with a wonderful character. We were beginning to witness many disturbing scenes as the Germans were deporting Jews from other towns into the ghetto. The streets were filled with people dressed in rags, hungry and with emaciated faces.

I became pregnant, but my heart grew heavy. Emotionally I wanted a baby, but my mind said, "no." On September 7, 1941 my son Ludvish (Ludwig) was born. My husband Juziek was ecstatic and shouted with joy, "I have a son. I have a son."

However, the Germans became much more restrictive and oppressive. First they closed the ghetto (October 1941), then they issued an order, under the penalty of death, to surrender all our jewelry and other luxury items. Since more and more displaced people were arriving in the Warsaw ghetto, the conditions deteriorated to such a degree that I did not leave my apartment at all.

The streets were filled with many hungry children who looked prematurely old and every day hundreds of people died of starvation and Typhus fever. Our stockpile of food was becoming exhausted and in order to buy smuggled food, we had to pay exorbitant prices. But I still shared my food with Stella and her father until our supplies hit the bottom and my husband forbade me to give any food away. He was afraid I would not have

Halina Sternlicht
Born 1918
Died 1996

Ludwig Sternlicht
Bytom, Poland, 1945

enough to eat and I was nursing Ludvish. But, I could not swallow a bite knowing that Stella was hungry and I, therefore, shared my portion with her, hiding it from my husband.

Meanwhile, the Jewish community wanted Juziek to become a textile buyer for the Germans and offered him an apartment on the Aryan side. But, he did not want to work for the Germans and told them, "I will rather remain with one shirt on my back, but have a clean conscience."

We lived on 76 Zhelaznaya Street. The Germans continued to make the ghetto smaller. They began partial deportation to the camps. We got orders to move to Novolipski Street, to Schultz's Fur Workshop. We were forced laborers and considered ourselves very lucky, because Juziek in 1936 had business dealings with him and knew him personally. When we moved to his shop, Schulz gave us "iron papers," which indicated that we were under his protection. Juziek placed great faith in that. He believed that nothing would happen to him. So he worked and I took care of our baby.

Unfortunately, this was short lived. One day we found out that a "aktion," a selection for deportation to death camps was planned for the following day. As women and children were usually the first to be selected, Juziek made a small shelter for me and Ludvish in the shop. The next day the Germans came. I pleaded with Juziek to hide with us

Devorah and Nachum Hirsch Maurueber,
Ludwig's paternal grandparents
circa 1900, Stanislawow, Poland

because I did not believe in the "iron papers." But he did not listen to me and left with his "iron papers." That was the last time I saw him. He was taken together with all the others who worked with him. Where? I do not know.

I hid with Ludvish in the shelter, where another woman with her daughter had forced their way. The shelter was very small, not to be noticeable, just room enough for one person. Probably due to lack of air, Ludvish cried the whole time. There are no words to describe my mental state. I was sure that at any moment the Germans would find and shoot the both of us. I put a gag in my baby's mouth to keep him from crying loudly, and I held him in such a way that he would not suffocate. I sat like that for a few hours and when my nerves could not take it any longer, I left the shelter.

As soon as we came out into the fresh air, Ludvish stopped crying. I nursed him and he immediately fell asleep. In

the meantime I learned that the Germans had been to Schultz's shop and since everyone had already been taken away, they spent only a few minutes looking around and then left. Luckily they did not find us.

I deluded myself that Juziek was taken to a work camp. Then I went looking for him, but of course, it was in vein. I was almost picked up myself and that is when my real suffering began. I got Juziek's job, but I did not know what to do with the baby since he was "illegal" in the ghetto. I found a dirty apartment that I was only able to reach by stepping through feces and assumed that the Germans would not go there and that Ludvish would be safe from them.

There was one broken bed where we slept together. During the day he stayed there alone with no one to look after him. When, occasionally, I would steal out of the shop during the day to check on him, I would frequently find him on the cold floor covered with blood as he had fallen out of the bed. Ludvish caught cold and developed bronchitis and diarrhea. He became dehydrated. It was a miracle that I saved him by running to the Aryan side and finding a nurse who gave him a saline solution injection which helped his body fill out a little bit. He was extremely undernourished because I did not have sufficient milk in my breasts as I was living off watered down soup and poor quality bread.

There were moments when I thought I was insane, but when I looked into my baby's beautiful pleading eyes and read "mommy save me," I would run like crazy everyday to get him a green apple and a carrot. Stella, my friends, worked for Toebbens (a food shop) and risked her own life bringing me an egg, a potato and carrot for Ludvish.

Life became intolerable. My job was to wash by hand thick sheepskin jackets that were sent from the front covered with blood. I remember once being beaten on my back with a leather whip which left swollen welts for weeks. My lungs hurt beyond endurance. But who could think about the pain when deportation and death were constantly hanging over our heads. Eventually an order was issued that every mother had to surrender her children; supposedly to

transfer them to better locations. Almost all the mothers obeyed, but I did not. I did not believe what the Germans told us. I knew that the children were being sent away to die. I shall never forget the desperate faces of the children taken away from their mothers and their anguished cries. This was when I realized that I had to cross over to the Aryan side, that I could not go on living in this manner.

I discussed it with Stella who said, "You have courage. You will survive." Others discouraged me by saying, "You are dark haired and Ludvish looks sick and 100 percent Jewish. The Poles will denounce you and kill you." I delayed making a decision as conditions in the ghetto grew worse from day to day. The food was so horrible that I could not even put it in my mouth. To help

swallow it, I would imagine I was eating meat, sausage and other food delicacies. But I forced myself to eat as I continued to nurse Ludvish.

I began to swell from malnutrition and became unable to wash the eight coats which were compulsory. Each time I could not complete my job, I was punished. My supervisor was a real sadist; I was beaten and once they pulled out a healthy tooth. There was talk about liquidation of the ghetto. After a particularly terrible night, in the morning we got orders to register on Mylna Street and then return to the workshops. As Ludvish was "illegal," I decided to go by myself and I left him in the shop. As I arrived on Mylna Street, I found out there was not any registration. Without wasting any time I ran back to Ludvish thinking that, maybe, I would be able to cross over to the other side. To my horror I saw the whole street filled with SS men with machine guns. I was panicky, out of my mind with worry. I had to get to my baby. There was no way I could accept the thought that Ludvish would die there alone. I did not know what to do, but I knew that somehow I had to get through.

I approached a column of SS men and looked for a face I could turn to for help. I knew I could be shot on the spot, but my intuition told me to turn to one particular SS man. Luckily, he was not aware that I had no right to have a child in the ghetto, or that all the

Halina, Ludwig and Manus Sternlicht, Munich, 1950-51

children had been taken away from their parents long ago. I used the highest degree of my courage and turned to the one I had selected and said, "I beg you, please help me! I have left my child asleep in the shop when I went to register. You probably also have a family and you know what it means to be a mother. As long as I live I will remember you with the greatest admiration. My life is in your hands because my child is my life."

He did not think long, looked at me and said, "Come show me where is your child." My heart was beating like a hammer. I did not know what he was going to do with me. However, he did have pity and helped me remove Ludvish from the prohibited zone. I returned to Mylna Street where the people from Novolipski Street were gathered. I told myself, "what will happen, will happen." I entered an apartment belonging to a family that had been deported to a death camp. Here the people waited for "selection." It was a miracle that I got there with my baby and now I waited for a second miracle.

I had some some Phenobarbital with me so I kept Ludvish asleep. This lasted for two or three days. It seemed like an eternity. Then my name was called. I was young and still able to work and had the right to remain in the shop. But what could I do with my baby? Without thinking I grabbed the tablecloth from a table, put Ludvish to sleep and placed him on the tablecloth. Then I tied it like it was a bundle of food. On top I put some canned food which I luckily found in the apartment and carried it on my back.

Ukranians were leading us back to Novolipski Street. On the way I heard a child cry. Another mother who had been carrying her child in the same manner was discovered and the child was immediately stabbed to death and the mother was shot on the spot. No one can imagine my horror and how petrified I was. It was a miracle that I had survived this "aktion." I don't know how I made it to the shelter. What I witnessed was too much for me and as soon as I arrived there, I fainted. When I woke up, I began planning to cross over to the Aryan side. I approached the guards and told them I needed medication for my child. I spoke so convincingly and sounded so self-assured that they believed me. They let me through and I walked to Aryan Warsaw.

I went to my friend Jurek's apartment. He was an Aryan who my husband and I dealt with in the ghetto. He gave me the address of his cousins who lived in Warsaw on Sadiba Offizerski and I moved in with Jadwiga and her sister. In order to survive outside the ghetto, I needed a *kennkarte* (identification card). I found out which German administrative office they were being issued from and, without money, was able to get an official *kennkarte* with the Aryan identity of Halina Sczepanska. Soon after there was a killing of several German officers in this section, apparently by the Polish underground. The Germans took revenge and bombarded the area all night. I felt the situation was becoming too dangerous and took my bundle and Ludvish in my arms and ran away. We started walking to Piaczesno. We had no place to sleep, but luckily I found a harvested field with a few overlooked potatoes. We ate them and I fell asleep with Ludvish on my stomach.

On the road to Piaczesno, I met an Ukrainian man who told me I could live in his house. Later from the dirt and hunger, Ludvish got sick and developed pustules on his face so badly that all I could see were his eyes. No Polish doctor would tend him because we were Jewish. Since my baby was sick, I had no choice but to go to a German hospital. In order to gain entrance, I approached one of the guards and told him I had a rendezvous with one of the doctors. Somehow I convinced him and he let me into the hospital. I walked the corridors and found one that I liked and explained that my child's face was covered with pustules. He gave me a pass and told me to return with Ludvish.

His name was Dr. Drees. He gave Ludvish a series of injections and an ointment for me to apply to the pustules. When Ludvish slowly began to improve, I asked him if he could find me some work in the hospital. Although he suggested the pharmacy, I told him that I would prefer working the kitchen because that would give me food for myself, my child and for the man who gave me shelter. I began working the next day and was given two assistants. The Germans were pleased and told me they had never tasted such good food.

Later, one of the Ukrainians I was living with became sick and required medication. I was ordered to steal it from the pharmacy otherwise they would expose me as a Jew. I had no choice and was caught and arrested a put in jail. Dr. Drees visited me. He was furious and could not believe what I had done. I asked him: "What would you do if your life and your child's life were threatened?" When he realized

why I was forced into this situation, he had me released and I returned to work.

Soon thereafter the Russians began approaching from the eastern front and the Germans began to flee from the hospital. I went into hiding. The Russian Army became our liberators as World War ll came to an end.

After the war, I worked for the UNRRA, United Nations Relief and Rehabilitation Administration in Katowice, Poland. I later found my sister, Sima and we decided to cross illegally into the American zone. We lived in a DP camp (Displaced Persons) in Landsberg, West Germany.

I met my second husband Manus Sternlicht who was a survivor of the Dachau Concentration Camp at an engagement party in Munich and we

were married in 1950. My husband, Manus, Ludwig and I immigrated to New York in 1952. I worked as a pharmacist for the City of New York and retired in 1978. My husband died in December, 1990 and I remained in New York until 1995 when I moved to Virginia Beach to live with my son Ludvish and his family. Never in my wildest dreams would I have believed I would live to see my son become a physician and that I would have a wonderful daughter, Ruth and four loving grandchildren. ❖

Halina Sternlicht died on April 22, 1996. Significant events in her life were inscribed on her tombstone in the B'nai Israel Cemetary, Norfolk.

(Ludwig Sternlicht - I married my wife Ruth Kappel in 1975. Both of her parents were Holocaust survivors. We have four children - Nachama Yosifa, Aliza Yehudit, Hillel Zvi, and Naomi Masada. I practice hematology and oncology with three partners at Cancer Specialists of Tidewater in Virginia Beach and Chesapeake.

(I want to thank Judy Katz for translating my mother's memoirs from Polish to English, my wife Ruth, and children for assisting me to condense the story and Reba Karp for her guidance.)

The Sternlicht Family - Aliza, Hillel, Naomi, Ruth, Ludwig and Nachama
Photo by Don Monteaux

He is 84 today in the year 2002. But, Private First Class (Serial #6900134) THOMAS WARRINGTON SR. was only 27 years old in the spring of 1945 when he entered the concentration camp with his U.S. Army unit in the German village of Buchenwald.

What he witnessed that day has stayed with him. "I still see it sometimes at night."

His unit, the Sixth Armored Division, ninth Infantry Battalion, Headquarter Company, Machine Gun Platoon, under the command of General Grow, "rode in on April, 1945. You can't imagine what a terrible thing this was ... piles of bodies, emaciated prisoners in striped uniforms."

When his unit moved on he was left behind to guard the German soldiers, some of whom were members of the SS unit. "My sergeant gave me a sub machine gun we called a 'grease gun.'" Warrington said. He also had the dual responsibility of guarding the Germans on one side and watching over the now liberated prisoners on the other side.

He remembers that there were all kinds of people incarcerated and that they were elated to be free.

It was a lot for the young American to grapple with; he could not accept the inhuman conditions he found at the camp. "Anyone who would set up a concentration camp had to be sub human. I would have refused to be part of it. It was surprising to me that as far

What a Terrible Thing This Was
THOMAS WARRINGTON, SR.

By Richard Marten and Reba Karp

Thomas Warrington, Sr.

as we had advanced in civilization that something like this could go on."

PFC Warrington was also surprised by the neat appearance of the German soldiers who were now his prisoners, some of whom were from the infamous SS, "who were hated by everyone, including their own soldiers." These were the Germans who killed without regard to life, or as Warrington explains, "soldiers who shot out of hand."

"They looked at us (the American soldiers) with contempt. I was dusty, I hadn't shaved; they were immaculate." But despite their arrogance, he was the victor and they were the vanquished. On that day, despite his appearance, "I could have been God."

The Germans' lack of respect for human life during World War II disturbs him, for he was brought up in the Methodist Church and as a Christian believes everyone should be treated humanely and that "everyone deserves a trial." He carried over this concern for his fellow man even to a wounded German soldier who was later dropped off by Jeep into his care. "He was an old man and frightened to death," he said, adding that he offered him what medical care was available.

The next day they marched the prisoners to a compound where they would be watched by the military police. "We were approached by a German military vehicle under the white flag of truce with the

At long last the American troops arrive. *Photo by Hugo Horvath*

Burgomeister (mayor) of the City of Jena who wanted our protection," he said explaining that the city was full of SS men "ready to fight to the bitter end."

As they marched into the city they passed a military hospital and Warrington remembers that some of the German patients were looking out of the windows. He recalls that he was wearing dark goggles that day and carrying a machine gun. Twenty-five years later as he was having his kitchen remodeled, he had a conversation with the man doing the job and discovered that he had been one of the patients in the hospital in Jena that day and was one of those looking out the windows as they passed by.

"He said he remembered me because I was wearing the goggles and carrying the machine gun."

Although Warrington did not personally see it, he heard from fellow soldiers at the Buchenwald camp that the infamous "Bitch of Buchenwald," a female member of the SS, did actually process a lamp shade made of human skin.*

"It was a terrible day for me," Warrington said. The memory of standing watch over the prisoners for 24 hours over a half century ago will be forever seared into his memory. "They (the Germans) believed they were super men. If they had any conscience, they had to live with it the rest of their lives."

As he says now, "I'll take it with me into the next world."❖

*There is historical controversy about whether the Nazis actually used human skin for such purposes.

He Remembers the Day
ARON WEINTRAUB

By Reba Karp

Aron Weintraub

Photo by Echard Wheeler

The German army marched into Lodz, Poland on September 6, 1939 and Holocaust survivor ARON WEINTRAUB well remembers that day. He also remembers that prior to that invasion, the President of Poland spoke on radio and encouraged his populace with the words: "… even a button on our uniforms we will not give up to the Germans."

Six days later the Germans came in and took the entire country.

It was those invading marching steps that pushed him from his gentle childhood as the youngest of six children born in a Chasidic Polish family onto the harsh streets of reality.

Early memories consist of taking dough to the bakery every Friday to be baked into challah for Shabbat. This was so that his family could avoid any cooking or activity that might overlap into Shabbat. He also remembers the pot of cholent which was placed over a flame Friday to cook all night so his family would have a hot meal after *davening* in shul Saturday morning.

Early on in their lives, Aron's father owned a furniture store. Later, the family branched off into making sweaters. "The company was called the Sweater Maker and eventually the whole family worked in this trade. My brothers and sisters were able to complete their educations but the Germans interrupted mine in 1939 when I was about 16," he said.

Even before the Germans, anti-Semitism was all around him. He recalls one incident of Catholic youth walking down the streets in the spring. "I was wearing a black coat and Jewish cap. The Catholics grabbed my hat. I didn't know I was supposed to take off my hat ... the next time the Catholics had a march, I hid until they passed," he said, explaining that "some of the Polish people would say to Jews, 'you don't belong in Poland, you belong in Palestine.'"

Aron's parents would attempt to explain anti-Semitism away. "They would say, 'You are Jewish and one of the chosen people and they are not'.... They couldn't give a good explanation."

Even as the threat of annihilation moved closer with Hitler's ascent to power in Germany in 1933, Aron's family rejected the idea of escape. "They believed that they should wait and see what happens. Their religious orientation was to wait for the Messiah. Once the Germans arrived, there were no options."

Before the Ghetto closed, Aron remembers that two of his brothers wanted to leave for Palestine. One of his brothers had met Menachem Begin when he visited Lodz earlier as a member of the Jewish organization, Betar, so he was instilled with the spirit of Zionism. "My mother was against it because she said when the Messiah comes, we will all go to Israel. The Messiah never came."

Anti-Semitism grew more intense when the German-Jews began to pour into Poland, seeking refuge from Hitler in 1934-35. As a reaction to the arrival of Jewish refugees, "sometimes when you walked down the street you would get beat up by the Poles."

Then the area the Weintraubs lived in was converted into a ghetto. "We had a break," he said, "we were already there and didn't have to look for a place to live." They opened their home to relatives who lived outside the area. "Food was rationed," he said. And he had to be careful while on the streets for fear of being picked up by the Germans and forced to work for them.

"You would have to do the work with no questions asked. One time I was picked up and I had to clean stables." Sometimes he was fed afterwards. Other times he was not.

A couple weeks before the ghetto closed, on a day referred to as "Bloody Thursday," Aron had an experience with German authority that put a scare in both him and his family. He had left the area designated to become the ghetto and was on the way to the home of his uncle who had lived outside the ghetto. His uncle, who had been wealthy, was afraid the Germans would eventually take him away and he wanted to escape and Aron was to try and salvage some of his personal belongings. He never made it to the house. Aron was picked up along with several hundred other Jews, taken to a former

> "We knew if they saw my mother they would take her, so to save her we took her to the place we dumped our trash and hid her in the trash."

Polish army barrack, and held for "ransom," a system by which upon getting their names, the Germans would go to the Jewish homes and demand compensation for their release. After he gave his name, Aron realized that he had put his family at risk. His brother was getting married on Friday and if the SS arrived with their demands during the ceremony, his entire family would be killed.

So thinking fast, as the Germans were releasing a group of young children, he "played dumb" and slipped out with them. Luck was with him, for as he hit the street, he saw a Jewish man with his horse and buggy and asked for a ride home.

Although he may have momentarily frightened his family by knocking on the door and interrupting the wedding, they were happy to see him. As Aron explains, his family were aware that he had been picked up with other young people and they were worried about his safety, but what could they do? "They were used to it," Aron explained.

Aron had become a "marked" young man, for his name had been placed on a wanted list. This was a small price to pay. He later learned that some of the Jews picked up that day never came home.

Not long after that episode, the ghetto was closed with barbed wire. Jews could no longer get out. Despite their imposed limitations, his Chasidic family continued to observe their daily rituals, one being the *minyan*, even though it was forbidden. "If the Germans caught you, you were taken away." So the family devised a plan. The place for worship was rotated among ten or 12 families, and while the adults prayed, a child stayed downstairs on guard. "If we saw anything suspicious, we would yell upstairs, 'throw down the key,'" Aron remembers.

What followed was the systematic liquidation of the ghetto. "The SS would go block by block, gathering everyone on the streets for selection. My mother's legs were swollen and she couldn't walk very well . . . she may have had cancer. We knew if they saw my mother they would take her, so to save her we took her to the place we dumped our trash and hid her in the trash."

That was only a delay to what was inevitable. In late June, 1944, the ghetto was liquidated. "There was no way out," he said. Aron, his mother and one brother, Shmule gave themselves up and were taken to Auschwitz-Birkenau in a train box car, a trip that took two or three days. There was no food and it was so crowded that the prisoners had to stand up all the time. "It was a horror." When the box car doors finally opened they were greeted by a travesty of reality, obviously an effort to subdue the pained prisoners, of music playing.

Their original thoughts upon hearing the music was that where they were, "can't be that bad." When they reached their final destination and his mother was immediately taken away, they realized differently. "That was the last time I saw her."

Later he and his brother were deloused and tattooed. It was the last time Aron saw Shmule. His number was 8587; his brother, Shmule, who died in Auschwitz, was 8586.

Aron was assigned work and taken to a camp where he labored as a carpenter, fixing trains and working for German civilians. "It was a blessing. The German civilians treated me good … if you did your job good." However, if not, and the civilians reported you to the SS, "you can figure out what the next step was," Aron said.

"When they would call for Jews I decided I wouldn't go. I would lay with the dead people and pretend to be dead. This saved my life."

"We were fed black bread and black coffee in the morning; at lunch we got soup … they would wake us up around 4:30 by ringing a bell to count us … then we would get dressed and worked for ten to 12 hours."

Later, Aron volunteered to help serve soup to his fellow prisoners, noting that the original "server" was too lazy to scoop down to the bottom of the pot. "What was left over belonged to me," he said. And this was good, for it gave him something to barter with. "Sometimes I would trade the soup for bread, shoes or clothes."

Aron and his brother, Shmule, were separated by camps about a mile apart and although he could not see him, Aron knew where his brother was and arranged to have some food smuggled

Aron after liberation in a sanitorium outside Munich.

into him. The soup, which was prepared in Aron's camp was transported to his brother's camp by a wagon pulled by the prisoners. So that his brother would have some extra food, Aron would slip bread to a man who knew his brother with instructions to give it to him.

"In return I would give him extra soup," Aron said. After the war, that same man met Aron's brother, Tyve, and told him he remembered Aron's acts of kindness and credited him with saving his life "because I gave him extra soup."

As the war was ending, the camps began to be liquidated, and he later learned it was during a forced march that his brother, Shmule, died. Aron remembers it was winter when his camp was liquidated and that there was snow on the ground. "As we marched we would hold each other up," he said recalling that one man in the line began dragging behind and the guards shot him in the back. "To keep up the march, we locked arms with the next person."

What followed was sleeping in stables and daily selections which determined who should live and who should die. "This went on for three to four days," he said, explaining that he knew the war was ending and he was determined to see it. "When they would call for Jews I decided I wouldn't go. I would lay with the dead people and pretend to be dead. This saved my life."

Aron remembers the exact day of his liberation. He was in Buchenwald. It was Tuesday, April 11, 1945, and he weighed only about 80 or 90 pounds at the time. "We saw the guard come down. We thought they were changing guards, but another guard didn't go up into the observation tower … then we saw tanks going by." Rumors of the war ending spread quickly through the camp. As the day passed, they learned the tanks belonged to Americans. "They treated us good. Later they gave us all kinds of food and we got sick because we weren't used to this kind of food … We couldn't communicate at first because we did not speak English." Among his liberators, he remembers one was a very tall, black man and one was a shorter white man. "You could see tears in their eyes."

Buchenwald contained many nationalities and political prisoners. Among those liberated with Aron were Elie Wiesel, Leon Blum, the Prime Minister of France, and some Catholic priests. Over the years, Aron and Elie Wiesel have kept in touch and Aron was in Washington with him at the dedication of the Holocaust Museum.

Angered by the condition of the prisoners, the Americans later brought in the townspeople from the surrounding areas to see what their soldiers had done. Those forced to be witnesses responded by saying they were unaware of the atrocities, but Aron remembers the American soldiers saying that the United States was 7,000, 8,000 miles away and the Americans knew what was going on in Germany. How could they say they did not know if they only lived a short distance from the scene?

The camps were eventually turned into camps for displaced persons. Rabbis and medical care were provided. Eventually he found himself in Lansberg, Germany. It may have been *beshert* for him to be at that particular place at that time, for one afternoon someone came up to him and touched him on his back. When he turned he found a familiar face! It was his brother's cousin by marriage. "She told me my brother Tyve and my sister Luba were still alive!" She also told him that his brother knew he had survived because he found his name on a Red Cross list of survivors. Interestingly, Aron had held onto the belief that his brother, Tyve, had survived. "Until I heard he was dead, I assumed he was alive."

Now it was up to them to find each other again, and the thought that raced through Aron's mind that day was how was he going to get to him.

Several weeks later when he was feeling stronger the opportunity presented itself and he went back to Poland to find his brother. "Trains were free for us then," he said, explaining that he was joined by several other survivors and on the way they were stopped by Russian soldiers. "We told them we were there looking for relatives and that we weren't spies." They also showed them the tattoos on their arms – and then they were allowed to continue on their way.

Since he had no idea where his brother was living, Aron followed the only clue he had – a restaurant where he was told his brother frequently visited. "He showed up a little later," Aron said. After they had time to exchange stories they went looking for Luba, who was living in a village on the Russian border. Although only three of the six children in his family had survived, it was a time for rejoicing. His father, Baruch, had died in the ghetto and his mother, Esther Perl, in the concentration camp.

Aided by the Haganah, Aron helped get his brother, his sister, her ex-sister-in-law, as well as other Jews, out of Poland and into Czechoslovakia and Germany by paying Russian soldiers to drive them. His brother made his way to the Island of Cyprus and eventually Palestine/Israel where he lived until he died in the early '90s. Luba made her way to Canada where she lived until she died four years ago.

The war had taken its toll on Aron and he later learned he had pleurisy and was placed in a Gautting sanitarium for eight to nine months in order to recover.

Although he didn't think he would get permission to enter the United States because he had been in a sanitarium, he applied and to his surprise, he received a visa. With the help of the Joint Distribution Committee, he came to America in 1949 and was met by Justine Nusbaum who worked with the Red Cross and had arranged for his arrival and a place to stay.

His first job was working for Broudy Kantor, filling vending machines. "I didn't like it too much because I had to drive and because of the language barrier. Broudy Kantor found me a job with Norfolk News Agency and I worked there until I retired."

Aron lives with his wife, Louiza, also a Holocaust survivor, in Virginia Beach, Virginia. They have two sons, one grandson, and one granddaughter. ❖

Aron's wife, Louiza, has a story in this book.

Aron lights a memorial candle.

You Never Knew What Would Happen
LOUIZA WEINTRAUB

By Reba Karp

Louiza Weintraub

Photo by Echard Wheeler

LOUIZA HALFON WEINTRAUB'S childhood in Salonika, Greece began on a positive note. "I was always a happy child. It was a happy household. I was blessed to have an older sister, Liana."

Her mother, Henriette, was French, her father, Leon, Greek, and they were married in 1932. "There was no anti-Semitism that I could detect. Jewish people lived peacefully with non-Jews."

This was until the Germans came. Then everything began to change for the Halfon family.

"I was approximately six years old when the war started. I became more aware of the war around 1942 because the Germans would constantly harass my father." Because he was Jewish they would pick him up and take him to Gestapo headquarters. That was when her mother, who was Catholic, would go and get him released. Louiza feels that picking him up and then releasing him was part of a plan to intimidate. "They made you aware that they were there. You never knew what would happen the next day."

Several distressing memories remain and she is willing to share one in particular. Her father had been picked up earlier and she recalls waiting for his release with her sister outside of Gestapo headquarters and watching a man attempting to cross the street. "The man tripped and fell and a German car ran over him," she remembers. But unlike times of civility, instead of stopping to offer help, the car continued on its way. Luckily, she remembers, the man was able to get up and walk away on his own. Aside from her father's harassment, "this was my first experience with the Germans" and a preview of things to come.

The family tried to stay one step ahead of the Germans by moving from place to place, hoping the Germans would lose track of them. "We were constantly looking for a place more safe," Louiza adds.

Luckily for the Halfons, the townspeople tried to help. "There was one friend, his name was Mr. Papathakis … he had a shop like my father where he fixed cars," and he offered them shelter in rooms in his basement.

"He always knew where the Germans were because he would listen to what people would say. In 1943, Mr. Papathakis came to my dad and told him things didn't look good. 'You are going to have to go into hiding,' he said." That was when he offered the family the use of his basement. "We stayed in his basement for almost a year. We would only come out at night after Mr. Papathakis gave the signal." Understandably such confinement was hard on Louiza and her sister so to help pass the time, "my dad invented games for us to play."

One consisted of blocks of wood covered with cloth which they used for playing hopscotch. The cloth-covered

Before the war in 1938 - Henrietta, Leon, Liana (five) and Louiza (two).

Photo above - Louiza's parents in 1970.

Photo left - Louiza after the war.

wood was to absorb any possible sounds which could originate when the blocks were thrown in the process of playing the game. "We had to be silent."

Another pastime was a game of fantasy that she and her sister would play in order to brighten their day. Louiza would describe a dress she would like to have. "My sister didn't forget," she said, explaining that after the war her sister became very adept in sewing. When Louiza least expected it, Liana made the dress Louiza had described while they were hiding in the basement and surprised her with it.

Food was scarce but their benefactor tried to provide as best as he could for their needs. It wasn't enough. Louiza recalls the time when he brought them a sack of beans. Her mother prepared the beans and her parents gave their portion to the girls. "I could see by the look on my mother's face that she was hungry, but we were my parent's priority."

Despite help from friends, the German vise was closing in on them, particularly for her father who was Jewish. In order to protect his family he left. "It was three to four months before we knew my father was still alive."

Louiza and her sister were also in danger, so her mother moved with them into a hotel. "We slept all the time. We couldn't leave the hotel. We were always hungry and crying." To make life easier for her children, her mother took them to an orphanage run by the Catholic church. "The nuns were wonderful to us," she says, "even though they knew we were Jewish. Everything they gave to the other orphans, they gave to us. We slept side by side on cots. At night, we would cry for our mom and dad."

Since the orphanage was next to Gestapo headquarters, the nuns became afraid of the consequences if they were discovered harboring Jewish children.

"We were at an age where children confided with other children and they were afraid that we would tell someone that we were Jewish."

Once again Louiza was moved for her safety because the nuns were afraid to keep both the girls. She went to live with a woman Louiza describes as a "righteous Gentile" who took Louiza into her home. The woman's brother, however, became very ill and she couldn't care for Louiza any longer. Louiza still maintains a friendship with this woman. "Mrs. Despina Henrick now lives in Montreal, Canada. I still see her and talk to her."

Faced with finding a safe place for Louiza, her mother, in desperation, took Louiza back to the orphanage hoping they would make an exception, which they did. The circumstances had become even more dangerous. "When I got back to the orphanage there was another set of Jewish girls there." Due to the close proximity of the orphanage and church to the German head-quarters, the nuns decided to convert the girls in order to protect them. Louiza does not feel that it violated their faith for she believes it was done to save their lives. (After the war her mother converted to Judaism and Louiza converted back when she was 12 years old.)

One chilling memory connected with those days keeps surfacing. "My sister had a beautiful voice and on Christmas Eve, she was selected to sing 'Ave

Maria,' accompanied by a German officer on the organ and one on the violin. The church was full of German officers in their uniforms. Today, I can't hear Perry Como or any other person sing the song without becoming emotional. I usually call my sister."

During this time her father was hiding in Albania and in 1944, near the end of the war, he returned to Salonika. "My father looked very thin and tired. We were told he was very ill."

Things were not over for the Jews. "They were putting Jews on trains. My mom and dad took us out of the orphanage. We went back to live in the basement of Mr. Papathakis. We were there for two days and the Germans came and took us away around 4 a.m." It was a time of panic when you reach for familiar items to take with you, she explains. "I remember the color of the blanket I took with me. It was red and the first thing I grabbed." She also remembers that she kept that same blanket with her until she left Greece after the war.

What followed was an all-night vigil at the train station awaiting their rather uncertain fate. The scene still fills her with more questions than there are answers. What happened was totally unexpected as there were many Jewish families at the station that night huddled together in silent desperation. Towards morning, the Halfon family was singled out and taken away. "How were the Germans able to pick them out

Louiza and Aron at their son, Eric's wedding

from all of the other family groups?" she questions. "And why us?" she wonders.

From the train station they were taken to German headquarters next to the orphanage and forced to wait in line on the sidewalk until a German soldier came up to them. He motioned for her father to follow him. Her father took Louiza's hand and told her mother and sister to stay where they were. The German soldier lead them into the building, where another officer interrogated her father. After establishing that her father repaired trucks for a living, the officer beckoned Louiza to come forward. "My father held my hand tightly."

When asked to come to him the second time, she reluctantly let go of her father's hand. "I sat on his lap. The officer told me he had a daughter at home just like me."

The inexplicable happened. The German officer told Louiza's father to take his family and go home. He gave Louiza's father a pass so he could reopen his shop and repair German cars and trucks. This was with the understanding that should he engage in any acts of sabotage, the family would pay with their lives.

Another scene flashes across her mind. The family rushed away from Gestapo headquarters. "My father said, 'hurry up, don't walk.' I remember looking at the other people on the street, feeling guilty."

They returned to the apartment they had abandoned earlier. It had been looted. "When the neighbors discovered we had returned, one by one they began to return our possessions."

The Halfon family was still not out of danger. Her father, who had been charged with repairing German trucks, discovered that this was not an easy task. Most of his workers wanted to sabotage the German vehicles. "It became too much for my father ... so he closed the shop and went to stay in Mr. Papathakis basement. It was not long after that the war ended." She adds, "My father told us, 'You are Jewish!' when he learned the war was over."

In 1955 the Halfon family moved to America. "About a month after moving to Norfolk, I met my husband (Aron) and a year later we were married." The Weintraubs have two married sons, Bernie and Eric, and two grandchildren. She is still close to her sister. Her father died about ten years ago, her mother, 13 years ago.

A few summers ago, Louiza, her sister, Liana, and Mrs. Despina Henrick, the woman who cared for her briefly during the war, went back to Greece to find some of the old landmarks. Everything had either changed or was gone.

One thing that constantly remains with her when she thinks back to those years is her recurring feelings of guilt. "So many died," she says remembering the night at Gestapo headquarters when she and her father were allowed to walk away.

"It is something you always carry with you." ❖

Louiza's husband, Aron, has a story in this book.

Bernie with Alexis

Photo below - Eric and his son, Evan Michael

Their Lives Would Never Be The Same
ABRAHAM AND HAZEL WILKOMER

By Paula Alperin

HAZEL WILKOMER was born Raizel Amluski on October 5, 1924 in Biala-Vaka, Poland (about ten miles from Vilna). Her first seventeen years were spent peacefully and happily on a tiny farm with her father, Meyer Laib, who was the proprietor of a small grocery store and bakery, her mother, Rivil, and her sister, Chipa, who was two-and-one-half years older than she. Raizel was a popular girl with many friends and she was well educated for a young girl at that time and place. She attended school, read the Hebrew prayers fluently and she became a skilled seamstress.

When the Germans invaded Poland, life as Raizel knew it, would never be the same. She and her family were sent to a labor camp in Biala-Vaka, which they called "The Torf." There she was forced to carry heavy lumber into a factory, where it was processed into compost. It was during this time that she met and married her first husband, a handsome boy from her hometown named Jonas Gurewicz.

In August, 1941, the Jews of Biala-Vaka were transported to the Vilna Ghetto

Hazel and Abraham Wilkomer

where Raizel, a teenager, was forced to labor for the Porabanic Airport digging ditches and trenches. In September, Raizel, her parents and sister managed to escape. Jonas did not go with them. Mother and daughters took refuge in the attic of a trusted non-Jewish neighbor in Biala-Vaka while Meyer went to their farm in hopes of salvaging their cow, some bread and coats for the family. About a block and a half from his home, Meyer was accosted by several Nazis who questioned him. Upon finding out where he was going and why, they informed him that he would not be hungry and would not need a coat. They proceeded to execute him with a bullet, shooting him dead on the spot. It was the first day of Rosh Hashana, 1941. The Nazis then set out to find the rest of the family. When the kindly neighbor saw them approaching, she warned Rivil and the children who fled to another neighbor in hopes of recovering a sewing machine that they had left for safekeeping. They were hoping it could be sold for cash or bartered for bread. Upon reaching this neighbor's house, the son-in-law who answered the door refused to give them the machine and told them that if they ever came back he would call the Gestapo.

Shortly after that they were captured and the girls were separated from their mother. One of only two survivors of Raizel's 52 cousins gave an account of what happened to Rivil. In 1943 she was marched off to Ponar along with her cousin's mother who was Rivil's sister. There, a pit was dug by the

Jewish male captives. Everyone was forced to disrobe and their valuables confiscated. They were made to line up at the edge of the pit and shot in turn and they fell into the pit on top of one another, forming a massive pile of sprawling, bloodied bodies. Raizel never saw her mother again.

They live with only their memories.

In May 1943, Raizel was sent to Klooga, in Estonia, by train. Inside the cattle car, she was horrified to see that the previous occupants had scribbled in blood, the words "don't forget us." In Klooga, Raizel worked in a warehouse where she made cinder blocks which she was forced to carry outdoors to dry. She was also made to cut lumber with an electric saw which she was forced to carry on her shoulders into a warehouse for processing.

In 1944, Raizel was sent to Stutthof in Danzig where she labored at Arbeit-lager-Rusasch and Zucklau (Shucar) on a railroad track. She used a four foot long handled tool with a hammer-like device on one end and a metal point on

the other to force small stones under the wooden slats to reinforce it. This was back-breaking work for a young girl and she was beaten regularly by German female guards who used a whip until she bled. In a twist of fate, it was here that Raizel was reunited with her, sister, Chipa and Jonas' mother, Mary, who was a great source of strength and stability to her. But none of them knew where Jonas was.

On March 10, 1945, they were finally liberated by the Russians. They tried desperately to locate Jonas through a Red Cross hospital in Stutthof, but their efforts failed. In time, they would come to realize that Jonas was lost to them forever. The three women, along with two others from the camp, left on foot to begin their grueling journey toward whatever was left of home. For weeks they walked the terrain, exhausted and weak from hunger. They managed to find an abandoned horse and wagon which Raizel hooked up. The women climbed into the wagon, grateful to let the horse pull them. Eventually they came across an abandoned farmhouse where they remained for two weeks to rest and regain their strength.

They were discovered by a Russian woman who fed them with what little she had; mostly cabbage. When all of the women became ill, they thought it was probably from the food and when they had all recovered, except for Chipa, it was decided that they must move on. The other women, however, became impatient with Chipa's inability to keep up with them. When they reached the town of Wlawa in Poland, Raizel immediately took Chipa to a makeshift hospital while the others continued on by train. Raizel visited Chipa every day but her sister was not eating and was becoming weaker. One day Chipa asked Raizel to get some sugar for her coffee. There were few luxuries available, but Raizel managed to beg a little sugar. When she tried to give the coffee to Chipa, she couldn't drink it. Raizel began to cry because she knew her sister wouldn't live. Chipa told her, "don't cry my sister, this is my destiny." The last time Raizel saw Chipa, her head was shaved and her body covered over. She was dead.

After several months, Raizel arrived in Warsaw. Having lost everyone she had ever loved and feeling totally alone, she tried frantically to find Mary. She finally located her in Warsaw through an intermediary. She could hardly wait to see her and went to the address she was given. Raizel was crushed when Mary, her mother-in-law, who had since remarried, said she could stay only a few days and suggested she move on to Lodz. Mary, who had been so protective of her, who had always encouraged her to stay by her side, was now rejecting her. She felt totally alone again. Mary asked Raizel to go down to the market to buy some salt which she needed in order to prepare their dinner. Half-heartedly, Raizel did this.

In an ironic twist of fate, a man named Abraham Wilkomer happened to be in the market and heard Raizel speaking the dialect of his hometown. He asked Raizel where she was from. She told him Vilna. He asked her what street. She told him Stephegas, which was really her cousin's address in Vilna. Raizal actually lived in a shtetl near Vilna but went to Vilna several times a week with her mother to pick up supplies for their grocery store. Raizel remembered him from Vilna because he was so handsome and quite a good dancer. Abraham asked Raizel if there were any other people here from Vilna. Raizel answered yes and took him back to Mary's apartment, who was also excited to see someone she knew. She ran to Abraham, calling him "Abrashia," her pet name for him. Throughout the time that Raizel was married to Jonas and for the many months when they continued to hope they would find him again, Mary would not allow another man to even speak to Raizel. Now Mary was ready to sanction a friendship between Raizel and this man, Abraham from Vilna.

Abraham had been married and had a child, a little girl, in Vilna. The family had fared well. Abraham was a successful tanner by trade and his wife had successfully invested in gold. When the Nazis invaded and the situation became critical, Abraham made a decision to leave Poland. For sometime, he had begged his wife to go with him but she wanted to stay to protect her investments and she would not let him take the child. He agonized over her decision. He went to his father whom he very much admired for advice. His father could only answer, "It must be your decision my son." In the end, he took his wife and daughter to the "safety" of his father's home. His little girl asked, "Daddy, where are you taking me?" He couldn't answer her. He could only bring himself to sing with her a little Yiddish song that he had taught her. Abraham was able to get on the last train from Vilna. With him were his brother-in-law (his sister's husband) and his six-year-old nephew. His wife and child remained in Vilna. He would try many times in the coming years to locate them, but he would never see them again. Abraham, his brother-in-law and nephew fled to Russia where the two men fought in the Polish Army. The little boy was separated from them and Abraham came to believe he had been taken to an orphanage in Uveckistan.

Meanwhile in Vilna, Jews were being rounded up. Six people had managed to escape. In retribution, the Nazis put signs on the backs of 60 other Jews and took them off to Ponar to be executed. Among them was a cousin of Raizel's, her cousin's husband and their two little girls. The Nazis picked up the two beautiful children by their long hair and threw them into the truck. Also taken was Abraham's sister, Shaina, the wife of this brother-in-law with whom he had fled. Shaina had been caught trying to escape to get milk for her baby. She was taken to Ponar, shot twice in the chest and left for dead. But she was not dead. She laid in the pit until long after silence fell, then clawed her way out from under the bodies that had fallen on top of her. She managed to drag herself to the home of Abraham's in-laws who were neighbors of Raizel's family. Raizel saw Shaina with the gunshot wounds and was there when the doctor came to dress them. Shaina survived somehow but it was only a temporary reprieve because she was recaptured, taken away and never heard from again.

During this time, Abraham suffered severe frostbite of his feet from the biting snow and cold after his shoes had worn out. In 1945, he was severely wounded at Bitgush. The Nazis pulled him up by his hair while he played dead. The Nazis laughed, hailing "another dead Jew" and they left him there in the snow. When discovered by the Allies, they rushed him to a hospital, certain they would have to amputate his leg because of the frostbite and the severity of the wound. A huge chunk was missing, but Abraham adamantly refused to let them take his leg. Miraculously, he recovered and though the leg never looked the same, he had full use of it during his lifetime.

Abraham had tried to trace his nephew. He thought he had seen him once, at a train station. He had called to him but the boy ran away, probably afraid, Abraham thought, of being sent to another orphanage. The boy was never found. In addition to his nephew, his wife and daughter and his other relatives, Abraham had been part of a close-knit family of eight siblings who worshiped their parents and adored each other. By the end of the war, Abraham had lost every member of his family Abraham came to Warsaw with a

Anne

A poem written in memory of Anne Frank by Abbott Saks

You blossomed in the darkest night
Of dungeon depths in attic's height;
Without, a monstrous sea of hate,
Within, bright hope to face blind fate;
Thoughtful, gentle, sweet-faced flower
Hidden in your secret tower;
When all the others breathed despair
They persevered for you were there;
They lived the years of isolation
Through your strength and inspiration;
You dreamed the dreams of yearning youth,
Of life's adventure, love and truth
And all you wrote your soul imparts …
You wrote forever on our hearts.
What madness man had given birth,
A cultured beast now stalked the earth
And bathed in blood the innocent
With brutal craft by Satan lent;
But you held fast to faith in man
And saw through darkness light, a plan …
You saw the rose and not the thorn,
A heart like yours is seldom born;
But for a piece of silver paid,
Another martyr would be made
And up the steps the storm drew nigh,
the dreaded green clad polizei …
To live your dreams would be denied,
you shared your bread the day you died;
Bergen-Belsen had its towers,
From them never blossomed flowers.

soldier, whom he had met in the hospital while recovering. When he met Raizel again on that fateful day in Warsaw, he had no idea what had become of his family. When she was able to tell him what she knew, he was disheartened but grateful to her because she was the first link he had to his home since the war.

Abraham and Raizel eventually ended up in Germany in a displaced persons camp called Lamperdien, where they were married. Their two older children, sons, Oscar and Michael, were both born in Germany. Having no other living relatives that they knew of, and no sponsors to help them begin a new life, the family continued to be shuffled from one DP camp to another. Finally in 1951, under the sponsorship of the Jewish Family Service of Norfolk, Virginia, Abraham, Raizel and the boys embarked from Bremerhaven on an American Army transport, the General Sturgis, for yet another journey. This time, to the United States. When they disembarked in New York and were processed at Ellis Island, their excitement turned to disappointment as they experienced another setback. Both boys, who were very ill with measles had to be quarantined in a hospital for nine days while their parents waited anxiously for their recovery.

When the boys' health was restored, the family eagerly made their way to Norfolk, Virginia. Abraham tried his hand at a number of occupations during his lifetime including several small grocery stores and a dry cleaning

Hazel Wilkomer

business where he also did alterations. While his father had been a master tailor in Poland, Abraham had not inherited his talent. There were few calls for tanners in this country, so Abraham discovered early on that the skill which was responsible for his success in Poland was useless to him in America. Raizel, all the while, worked side by side with Abraham in the businesses. Their customers did not understand Raizel's Polish name so they Americanized it to Hazel, hence, the name by which she has become known in this country.

In 1952, their third child, a daughter Renee had been born to them making their family complete. But they continued to struggle for many years both emotionally and financially. Like so many other survivors, because of the

pain, they could not speak about what had happened to them and they thought, "who would have believed that such a thing could happen." So their story is being told publicly for the first time. In 1991, Abraham passed away after a long, debilitating illness. In 1997, Raizel suffered a stroke which affected her speech and left her wheelchair bound. She continues to live in Norfolk with her devoted son, Michael, who is her caregiver. Oscar lives in Virginia Beach, and Renee lives in Maryland with her husband, Serge, their daughter, Ilana, who is fifteen, and son, David, age eleven. Hazel's grandchildren are the light of her life. Raizel's mother-in-law, Mary, eventually moved to Miami and kept in contact with the family. Renee, who met her several times, described her as funny and upbeat.

When Raizel's family fled from their home in Poland, they were able to leave their cherished family photos with trusted neighbors who accepted them at their own peril. Approximately six years ago, the family was in touch with a local woman who was traveling to Vilnius. The woman told the family that she and her traveling companions would try to recover the photos from so long ago. They were able to locate the village and find the neighbors' house but not the neighbors themselves. Thus, this family, like so many others to this day, has not a single photograph of the hundreds of relatives who perished in the Holocaust. They live with only their memories. ❖

Photo courtesy of Elsa Moed Weinman

After his release, Jules Moed, a passenger on the Quanza, called the Washington Post from the lobby of the Mayflower Hotel to thank the American people. His words were:

"WE HOPE TO REMAIN IN THIS GLORIOUS COUNTRY FOR A WHILE UNTIL WE GO ON TO OUR OWN RESPECTIVE COUNTRIES. WE SHALL TAKE WITH US THE MEMORY OF THE DEMOCRATIC AND HUMAN KINDNESS WHICH GAVE US THE COURAGE TO START LIFE AFRESH IN A NEW WORLD. WE THANK THE AMERICAN PEOPLE. GOD BLESS AMERICA."

The Saving of the S.S. Quanza

Admiralty lawyer, J. L. Morewitz, helped save refugees from Nazism

By Stephen J. Morewitz

Over 50 years ago, my father, Burt Morewitz was an 18-year-old student at William and Mary. On weekdays and Saturdays he would commute to Williamsburg from his home in Newport News. On September 11, 1940, my father's daily academic concerns were shattered when the controversial Nazi refugee ship, S.S. *Quanza*, put into Norfolk, and brought international attention to Hampton Roads.

His father, Jacob L. ("J. L.") Morewitz, of Morewitz and Morewitz, was asked to represent four *Quanza* refugees who were fleeing Nazi persecution and the war. He represented the four refugees despite the fact that helping the refugees' win their freedom was a very unpopular cause among some residents of Hampton Roads.

An experienced maritime lawyer in Newport News, J. L. had an unusual legal practice for that time because his partner was his wife, Sallie Rome Morewitz. In 1940 there were few women attorneys in the United States. Husband and wife partnerships were also very rare. Sallie Rome Morewitz had been a special law student in the William and Mary School of Law in

> *The Morewitz family had no idea that the controversial Quanza episode would be a prelude to the Holocaust.*

1930 and had been the first woman student from the school's main campus to be admitted to the bar.

On Saturday, September 14th, Burt got home from William and Mary to hear the persistent ringing of the phone. J. L. was calling to tell him to hurry over to Sewell's Point and catch a glimpse of the (80) Nazi refugees who were landing from the *Quanza*. After the telephone conversation, the young student dashed off to the coal piers and saw the jubilant passengers win their freedom. J. L. was a hero to his son, Burt.

J. L.'s youngest son, David E. Morewitz, also remembers vividly his father's

heroic rescue of the Nazi refugees. David was eight years old at the time and remembers manning the phone during the news media event. The youngest son took calls from Attorney Leon Seawell of Hughes, Little and Seawell, who represented the ship in U.S. District Court. Dr. Alan Morewitz, another son, drove J. L.'s clients to Washington after they landed.

The Morewitz family had no idea that the controversial *Quanza* episode would be a prelude to the Holocaust. Paradoxically, the incident resulted in a significant tightening of the already restrictive refugee immigration policy by the State Department. As a result of the *Quanza* affair, it became much harder for European refugees, both Christian and Jewish, to gain admission into the United States.

About 48 years later, David began researching the history of the *Quanza* affair. He requested U. S. Immigration and Naturalization Services to provide the vessel's manifests for New York and Norfolk and the immigration and naturalization records for every refugee from the ship. He also asked the National Archives and the State Department to provide any available

The S.S. Quanza

government documents related to the vessel.

In 1990, David provided me with these research documents and transcripts of court testimony and strongly encouraged me to write the first article on the *Quanza*. He felt that I should be the author since I was the family's only behavioral scientist. Despite my busy academic medicine and consulting schedule, I accepted my uncle's invitation and began combing the stacks of the University of Chicago Regenstein Library for books and articles on Nazi refugee ships. Eventually, I obtained additional government documents from the Franklin D. Roosevelt Library, the National Archives, Library of Congress and U. S. Immigration and Naturalization Services. Slowly, I was able to piece together the remarkable history of the *Quanza* refugees.

The Portuguese passenger steamer, *S. S. Quanza*, left Lisbon on August 9, 1940,

with about 317 European war refugees, many of who were prominent artists, civic leaders and intellectuals. About 196 passengers with either regular or acceptable "emergency" U. S. papers disembarked in New York on August 19. The remaining refugees had transit visas to Vera Cruz. Yet, when the ship arrived at Vera Cruz in late August, President Lazaro Cardenas of Mexico refused to accept most of the refugees despite the intervention of Josephus Daniels, the U. S. Ambassador to Mexico, and Rabbi Stephen Wise, President of the American Jewish Congress.

President Cardenas may have been unable or unwilling to save the refugees because anti-Semitism had emerged in his country. Moreover, Cardenas was nearing the end of his presidential term and he may have lacked the power to intervene on behalf of the refugees. At this time, Rabbi Wise pleaded with Secretary of State Cordell Hull and

Assistant Secretary of State Breckinridge Long to help rescue the refugees. They agreed to monitor the ship's whereabouts and do whatever they could to help in this matter. However, the State Department was apparently inept in monitoring the movement of the vessel after she left Vera Cruz. The State Department cabled its legation in Nicaragua that the ship was en route to Managua.

After being refused entry in Vera Cruz, the Portuguese passenger steamer actually headed for Hampton Roads to take on coal before going back to Lisbon the next day. Friends and relatives of the refugees wired attorneys in Hampton Roads and Mr. Roosevelt when they learned that the vessel would be docking there overnight for coal. A New York business associate of four passengers, the Rand family, asked Morewitz to provide legal representation for them.

When the ship put into Hampton Roads, Immigration slapped a detention order on Captain Alberto Harberts, ordering that all aboard not come ashore. Even before this issuance took place, Hillman Wolff, a German Jewish passenger, was so fearful for his life that he jumped overboard. Several hours later, local attorneys filed habeas corpus petitions on behalf of four passengers.

Morewitz took a different tack by attaching a $100,000 libel suit to the vessel. In this libel suit, Morewitz contended that the *Quanza* breached her contract with the Rand family because they were not allowed to land in Vera Cruz. In later testimony before U. S. District Judge Luther B. Way, Morewitz also asserted that the foreign ship owner violated the *Roxen* Doctrine, which provides shore leave for foreign seamen while a vessel is in a U. S. port, even if only to take on coal. Morewitz had been one of the attorneys in the 1925 landmark *Roxen* case.

According to Burt, his father's strategy was to tie up the ship in court long enough for refugee leaders in Washington to bring pressure on President Franklin Roosevelt. The U.S. District Court determined $5,000 as the amount of the bond needed to release the vessel from federal custody. The ship's agent and attorney had to wire Lisbon to obtain the bond money. This took several days, thus delaying the departure of the *Quanza*.

In a written opinion closing the case two years later, Judge Way noted that Morewitz's lawsuit delayed the ship in Hampton Roads long enough for the refugees to win their freedom. According to Judge Way, if the libel suit had not been filed, "that vessel would very probably have left this jurisdiction" with the refugees on board.

Roosevelt initially maintained a "hands-off" policy toward the *Quanza*. He was facing a precedent-setting third presidential term and did not want to upset the isolationists and anti-alien elements in the country. The President was especially concerned that there might be Nazi and Communist spies on

board the vessel. The American public during this period did not want the immigration quota raised or circumvented. The public feared that the admission of refugees would bring the U. S. into the despised European war and would take away scarce jobs from Americans.

Another major player in the *Quanza* episode was Professor Patrick Murphy Malin, a volunteer on the President's Advisory Committee for Political Refugees (PACPR). He met in Washington with Under Secretary of State Brekinridge Long, (who was "deputized" by FDR and Secretary of State Cordell Hull). Malin went on to Norfolk dockside. (Long only expected a few to be deemed "bona fide" political refugees). Malin "advised" Immigration that as to around half of the 80, the papers were in order. As to the other half, he suggested each be interviewed under oath (since he said there was no time to communicate with Europe). The result: "temporary" permits for all 80.

There were joyous celebrations on September 14th when word of the "temporary" permits became known. This day capped a major news media event, which had gripped the Hampton Roads community for several days. Because of warlike conditions (i.e., German U-Boats) in the Atlantic Ocean and abroad, none of the passengers was forced to go back to Nazi Europe.

Not surprisingly, some individuals were very upset by the admission of the

Photo courtesy of Norfolk Virginian-Pilot, (Staff Photographer Borjes).

Rose Schamroth and her daughters, Malvina and Annette gaze wistfully through a porthole at their husband and father, who is unable to get close enough to his loved ones to embrace them. This photo from the Norfolk Virginian-Pilot of September 12, 1940, shows the sad plight of over 80 refugees from Nazi persecution aboard the Portugese steamer Quanza, destined to be returned to Europe against their will.

European war refugees. In fact, Long vehemently opposed the admission of the *Quanza* refugees. Like Roosevelt, Long was fearful that there were Nazi and Communist spies on board the ship. Despite his opposition, Long sent a memo, (a "kosher" list), to the Justice Department mentioning he was recommending to the PACPR that *certain* individuals (including the Moed family and movie star, Marcel Dalio) be admitted. After the landing, Long vowed to get even with the refugee advocates who had disobeyed his orders with impunity.

In his published war diary entry dated September 18, (referring to events culminating in the 80 landing permits issued September 14), Long wrote: "I remonstrated violently; said that I thought it was a violation of the Law; that it was not in accord with my understanding with them; that it was not a proper interpretation of my agreement; that I would not be a party to it; that I would have no responsibility for it; and that if they did that I would have to take the matter up in some other way."

That same day Long, with Hull's authorization, obtained immediate approval from President Roosevelt to terminate the president's emergency visa program and close the lists of rabbis, intellectuals and labor leaders in imminent danger. Long took most of the authority to issue emergency visas out of the hands of the President's Committee and gave it back to the European consuls. He simultaneously ordered the consuls abroad to carefully screen all applicants, and reject them it there was any doubt whatsoever about their backgrounds. (Even before the *Quanza* incident Long cabled consulates to "delay, delay and delay").

Long justified his new emergency visa procedures by stating that the American consuls aboard were reporting that

Jacob L. (J.L.) Morewitz circa 1965 courtesy of David E. Morewitz.

undesirable individuals were being issued emergency visas. He did not cite the *Quanza* controversy as a specific reason for his September 18th proposal. The Assistant Secretary of State may not have wanted to use the affair as part of his official rationale because this would certainly have antagonized Eleanor Roosevelt. (The First Lady had received cables from the refugees while they were in port in Mexico; she passed a note on to FDR).

Long's sudden changes in immigration policy brought to a head a bitter schism between the President's Advisory Committee and the anti-alien State Department which had been simmering for the last several months. In fact, the entire President's Committee almost resigned in protest against the new State Department policy changes which they felt were made "unilaterally and without notice" to them.

In the aftermath of the September, 1940 event, James Grover McDonald, Chairman of the PACPR and George Warren, Executive Secretary, and others wrote letters and held meetings with the President and other officials to protest the new immigration policies that essentially terminated Roosevelt's emergency visa program. The anti-refugee policies of the U. S. and other nations in the late 1930s and early 1940s seemed to encourage Hitler to intensify his persecution of Jews and allowed him to devise the "Final Solution" to the Jewish problem.

After the *Quanza* affair, Morewitz and Morewitz continued to practice maritime law in Newport News. Burt followed in his parents' footsteps to become a maritime lawyer and has practiced law in Newport News for more than 45 years. David also followed the family tradition by graduating from William and Mary and becoming a lawyer. (His law degree is from the University of Illinois). He practices law and is a CPA in New York City. After receiving his undergraduate degree at William and Mary, Dr. Alan Morewitz received his Ph.D. from NYU and became a nuclear scientist. He is now a consultant in Los Angeles.❖

Editor's Note: The Quotation from *The War Diary of Breckinridge Long—Selections from the Years 1939-1941*, (Lincoln: University of Nebraska Press, 1966) p. 131, was used with permission from the University of Nebraska Press.

Tidewater Resident Recalls the National Council of Jewish Women's Response to the S.S. *Quanza*

By Sybil Friedberg

On September 11, 1940, the S.S. *Quanza* sailed into Norfolk to take on coal before returning to Lisbon. Relatives and friends of those left on board began to lobby for their release. Also fighting on behalf of the refugees was the Norfolk Chapter of the National Council of Jewish Women.

ELISE MARGOLIUS, President of the Council of Jewish Women from 1939-1946, remembers the *Quanza*. Her beautiful eyes cloud with the memory of World War II, then twinkle as she relives the times she, Justine Nusbaum, Doris Kaufman and others loaded their cars at midnight with refugees, and took them straight from the *Quanza* into their homes to sleep.

"On September 14, we got the call that the *Quanza* was here with 86 Jewish war refugees who were denied entry into the United States. The Portuguese freighter, *Quanza*, left Lisbon with over 300 passengers on August 9, 1940. Some refugees were released in New York, some in Mexico. When the *Quanza* stopped in Norfolk for coal, relatives, friends, and eventually Eleanor Roosevelt began crusading for the release of the 86 who were retained."

Elise remembers there were children aboard, with no fresh food. "We (NCJW) called a ship chandler and had fresh vegetables, fruit, canned goods and candy delivered onboard. Although they were not allowed off, we were invited on the *Quanza* for dinner." She also remembers the refugees as being frightened. "They had escaped Europe and the possibility of the death camps, had seen other passengers released onto American soil … they were steps away from freedom, and not allowed entry." The prospect of going back was terrifying. She recalls one passenger even attempted to jump overboard, but was restrained.

"There are young Jews today," Elise Margolius says, "who actually can't believe the atrocities happened. I remember a woman sitting right here in my living room 50 years ago, where we are sitting now. She told me the Nazis made her watch while they tore her infant from her arms and threw him into the gas chamber!"

Elise Margolius

Herbert Gertz

Justine Nusbaum

Doris Kaufman

authorities into allowing her to take them home for a Jewish meal and promised to return them by midnight. "I did return them at the stroke of midnight," she said. "I felt like Cinderella." This doctor was later released and established a practice in New York. His wife opened a millinery shop, Elise recalls. And in response to her hospitality, each year when she called to check on them, they would express their thanks by sending her a dozen roses. ❖

Doris Kaufman died November 9, 1987. Justine Nusbaum died April 16, 2000. Elise Margolius died February 5, 2002.

Later, the NCJW women were told the refugees could disembark if NCJW would assume financial responsibility. "We signed for their custody. At midnight, we all drove our cars to the ship and filled them to overflowing with people. Some were put up at the Fairfax Hotel. We took the rest home…."

At 1 am, she woke her husband and son, shifted everyone around and made room for her guests. "I can't remember if I changed the sheets," Elise smiles.

Herbert Gertz (of blessed memory), local chairman of the National Refugees Committee, invited all the refugees to breakfast at his home the next morning. Buses were chartered to drive many of them to waiting relatives in New York. "I will never forget that moment…! I can see their happy, smiling faces,

waving American flags as they waved good-bye and the bus pulled away … we all just wept!"

There were other ships after this, Elise recalls, but the *Quanza* was the first. One, a Portuguese freighter, held a 12-year-old girl because they felt they couldn't let a child leave the boat alone.

"Do you have the right to keep a 12-year-old child on a boat with all those seamen?" lise questioned the ship's officers. The girl was released when CJW Social Worker Cynthia Rice signed for her. Justine Nusbaum housed her awhile also, Elise recalls, until she was sent to relatives in New York.

At another time, a refugee physician and his wife and daughter were here briefly and were also not allowed to leave the ship. Elise talked the

EVELYN AND EMIL BRAND

Fleeing the Vise of Nazi Persecution

By Reba Karp

Evelyn and Emil Brand

Evelyn Brand came from Trembowla, Poland; her husband Emil was born in Cologne, Germany. She left her homeland in 1938; he, in 1937. Both were fleeing the vise of Nazi persecution which had begun to close in on them.

Although they feel their stories do not reflect the pain and suffering of other Holocaust survivors who were unable to escape, the terror they felt and were subject to was very real.

Evelyn Brand's story began in 1928 when her mother first applied to emigrate to America. Then, quotas were very restrictive and although they had the proper papers and support from cousins living in the United States, the quota was filled before their papers cleared.

"We were told that after 10 years, the quota would open again, to save the paperwork. Everyone laughed and told my mother to 'forget about it.'" But, her mother, aware of the threats surrounding them, decided to save the papers.

In 1933, with the rise of Hitler to power, persecution of the German Jews began to increase. Evelyn remembers that she was in the second grade when she experienced her first harassment by a friend – a classmate who walked to school with her each morning. When she neglected to stop and pick Evelyn up one day, Evelyn went to her house and was greeted with jeering laughter and a door that slammed in her face. "I was told I was *zydoka* (Jewish)." Frightened, she ran home.

In school, Jewish children were held back. "You never got a decent grade, you never were allowed to be on the honor roll. That hurt, for as a youngster you always tried hard. You wanted to compete. But you couldn't get anywhere."

But that was only one of many incidents to follow. The most frequent scare tactic occurred during Jewish holidays when, responding to a knock on the door, Jews would be greeted by a cat, a dog or turkey being thrown into their home. "If you didn't cover your windows, you would have no windows."

She remembers that a curfew for all Poles below a certain age required them to be off the streets at a particular time. Consequently, non-Jewish children held their meetings during the day.

"A car would park in front of our house almost every night ... It was there to make sure that you knew your life could end at any moment."

Jewish children, however, were not permitted to meet during the day. To get around this, a plan was devised which allowed the Jewish children to attend a group called Hanoar, sponsored by Hadassah. "We had very devoted fathers, one had a horse and buggy. He would drive up to the houses and at a signal, the children would jump into the back of the wagon and be covered with a black cloth."

The meetings were held in a basement lit by only one candle for fear of being caught. There, they were fed their lifeline to Judaism by learning Israeli songs and dances. "We were told stories about Israel. We became so enthralled we couldn't wait for the next week."

She remembers cousins, desperately trying to reach what was then Palestine, who attended special work camps to learn trades such as carpentry and plumbing skills, which were necessary in building a country. When it was time to emigrate, the young people went through a "mock" wedding ceremony enabling two to leave in the place of one. "When they arrived, they either were married officially or they parted ways."

When Polish law forbid the sale of kosher meat in 1938, Evelyn's mother pulled out her papers and reapplied to leave. She remembers that upon seeing friends off to the United States, she wrote a passionate letter to the cousin in New York who had originally sponsored them. "Because my brother was about to enter the army, my cousin hurried the process. We arrived in the United States in December, 1938."

After the war, she met her husband-to-be, Emil, at a summer camp in Connecticut. They met on a Sunday and although they were not married until six months later, she remembers that the following Tuesday they decided on what type of furniture they wanted in their home.

Emil arrived in America in 1937, also a refugee from the Nazi "Final Solution." "Two weeks before graduation, I was rejected from school and subsequent employment, for without a diploma in Germany you could not find work." At the time he was an artist, studying to become a clothing designer.

He remembers with gratitude the time his instructor saved his life by suddenly pushing him into the darkroom where photographs were being processed. When he came out, his instructor told him that the SS had been there looking for him. "It touched me. I cannot forget it."

In 1937 he became an "outsider." Jews were no longer allowed to belong to any organization or club, and as a Jew he could not go to the theater. Jews could only get a haircut on Mondays. This he refers to as "Hitler's overture" to the tragedy of the Holocaust.

"It is a very tragic story and very little is told about it," he began, explaining another incident of intimidation. "A car would park in front of our house almost every night. We knew it was the Nazi party because it had a flag. It was there just to make sure we didn't get any sleep; we had to be constantly on the alert. It was there to make sure that you knew your life could end at any moment."

It was also during this time that the Nazis confiscated his father's business of clothing stores. One day his general manager walked into the store, in uniform, and in a cold and impersonal manner demanded the keys and books to the business. The man had once been a trusted employee.

It was shortly after this incident that the family made plans to leave. Emil was to go first and his parents were to follow. But on *Kristallnacht* in 1938, Emil's father was picked up and deported to a concentration camp where he died. His mother left shortly after that for England and from there made her way to the United States. His brother, who had left Germany in 1936 for Palestine, later contracted malaria, but survived to join Emil in America.

Although he harbors no grudge against *young* Germans, "I will not shake hands with Germans who are my age," he said. "I do not know what his hand might have done during the Holocaust. I might be shaking hands with a mass murderer."

As a young man, Emil was an ardent soccer player who had aspirations of being in the 1936 Olympics. He was also a musician who dreamed of playing violin in an orchestra. Both of these dreams were destroyed by Hitler.

"I never completed what I set out to do. I loved sports. I loved music. I still do."

But during the Winter 2002 Olympics his oldest son Mark carried the Olympic torch part of the way in Boulder, Colorado, in his father's honor. When Mark told his father's story to a reporter, he was chosen out of a field of 40 to carry the torch dedicated to his father.

Proving it is never too late to make your dreams come true, when Emil retired 20

years ago, he found time to fulfill part of his dreams as a young man – to paint and participate in art shows. Before retirement, Emil and Evelyn lived in Connecticut where he was a layout designer for specialty stores.

Now Emil, 85, and Evelyn, 80, are living in Tidewater where they moved in March of 2001. Their son, David, and his wife, Bonnie, live in the area with their three children, Benjamin, Lauren, and Jenna. The Brands' other son is married to Maxine and they have two children, Rachel and Ali. ❖

Evelyn and Emil's son, Mark, carries the torch at the 2002 Winter Olympics.

ROZA AND MIKHAIL BLIKSHTEYN
From Russians to Americans

By Elena Barr Baum

To Americans, they are Russians, but growing up in Russia, they were known, even on their passports, simply as "Jews." When World War II began for Russia in 1941, the lives of ROZA AND MIKHAIL BLIKSHTEYN changed dramatically. They live in Norfolk today, but when Russia entered the War in Europe, Misha was seven and Roza was only five. They both grew up in Shargorod, a suburb of the city of Vinitza, militarily significant because Hitler kept a staff and a bunker there.

Shargorod was overwhelmingly Jewish, and was home to seven synagogues. When Roza's mother was a girl, these synagogues were all open and thriving. Between 1925 and 1930, most were closed down. This was the period after the Russian Revolution when the government was clamping down and trying to end all religious practice. Neither Roza nor Misha remembers practicing Judaism at home. Misha had an uncle who was more observant than his parents, and when things looked bad, he remembers his uncle saying, "We will perish here. I want you to die like a Jew." He taught Misha some rudimentary Hebrew, including how to count. Misha laughs at how easily he can still remember some of what he was taught, *"ehad, shtayim, shalosh,"* even now.

A little Hebrew was as far as Misha's Jewish education went, because in 1941 the Germans arrived in Shargorod, and life changed drastically. They built a fence around a good portion of the village, turned it into the Jewish ghetto, and mandated that all Jews live within its boundaries. Since most of the town's men, including both Misha's and Roza's fathers, were away serving in the Russian army, the ghetto was full of women and children. There was no time to evacuate, and nowhere to go. The Jews of Shargorod became "prisoners" in the ghetto.

Roza's house, a four-room single-family dwelling housed up to 40 people after the creation of the ghetto. The overcrowded, vermin-infested conditions led to a typhus epidemic in 1942 that killed many ghetto dwellers. Misha was one of the few who remained healthy, and he remembers going to hack pieces of ice from atop the frozen river to help fight the fevers of some of the ailing. It was a brutally cold winter that year, colder than usual, and there was no way to bury all of the epidemic's dead. Misha recalls that the ghetto's residents removed clothing from the dead bodies to help keep the living warm, and often, hungry dogs would eat the bodies that had been set aside awaiting burial. It was a horrific sight for a child to witness.

Though Misha's family made it through that long winter, his little sister died of diphtheria in 1944, when she was just five years old. There was medicine available to treat her illness, but one of the ghetto managers, known as the "Judenrat," withheld it, in case his own children got sick. The "Judenrat," were Jews hired by the Germans and the SS

Younger years: The Blikshteyns with their daughter, Juliana.

to "police" the ghetto. Despite the deaths from sickness, including the loss of his sister, Misha knows that Shargorod was lucky. Many surrounding villages had suffered slaughter at the hand of the Nazi killing squads. They were waiting, literally, for the axe to fall on them. Misha knows that these squads in another town buried his aunt and three of her children alive, so in a way, he feels lucky. Whether it was because of the city of Vinitza's strategic importance, or because they simply ran out of time, the Germans never launched a Jew-killing campaign in Shargorod.

Stalinist and spies surrounded the town. Even Roza's 15-year-old cousin was a partisan of the movement. Ironically, Stalin, the lesser of two evils, was the enemy of the Nazis, so it seemed

acceptable. The Russian people would learn after the War that Stalin was little better than Hitler. While they were aware of the War in Europe, the young people in Shargorod did not know the details of the death camps. They had no newspapers or radio, and they were far enough from the railroad that not much news reached them that the Germans didn't impart themselves.

The Russians eventually liberated Shargorod, but neither Roza's or Misha's father survived the War. Roza's father disappeared and was reported killed in 1941, and Misha's died in 1944. It was hard to raise a family on the minuscule pensions the government provided. Roza's mother tried to work in a bank after the War, but the salary was too small. She supplemented it by illegally making soap in her home.

> The Blikshteyns now see themselves as "products" of Soviet propaganda. Even after the War, they found it dangerous to speak out against Stalin. There was a strong feeling of anti-Semitism within the Soviet government. A special department of the KGB existed to destroy the Jewish population of Russia.

Both young people returned to school after the War, but had much to make up. Roza eventually entered the Kamensk Podolsk Institute in the Ukraine to study physics and mathematics, and later became a teacher for fifth through eighth grade. Misha, who had drawn posters at home to earn extra money while studying as an adult in high school, went on to college in Moscow. It was a technical school for builders, similar to a technical architecture school.

The Blikshteyns now see themselves as "products" of Soviet propaganda. Even after the War, they found it dangerous to speak out against Stalin. There was a strong feeling of anti-Semitism within the Soviet government. A special department of the KGB existed to destroy the Jewish population of Russia. Both Roza and Misha remember the KGB campaign to purge Russia of all Jewish doctors. They had been declared enemies of the state and arrested. Jews were often fired from their jobs for the smallest of reasons and those who lost their jobs often had trouble finding new ones. Though most of their friends and colleagues were Russians, the Blikshteyns do not ever recall their lives being personally affected by Soviet anti-Semitism. Both were urged to join the Communist Party many times, but never did. This did not seem to have any ill effect on their lives.

Although they knew each other as children, they did not date one another until college when they decided that they were destined to be together.

During one school break, Misha traveled back 1000 miles from Moscow to see her, "and that was it," the couple agrees. Married for 41 years, they have a daughter, Juliana. When Juliana and her husband Toli, with their two children, decided to emigrate, Roza and Misha stayed behind.

Though "comfortable" in Russia "their lives felt empty without children and grandchildren close by." In 1997, they finally joined their children in Virginia Beach and are very glad they did. In Russia they felt they had to hide their Judaism, but here, Roza and Misha are proud to call themselves Jews.

Their granddaughter Bela, 21, is a student at William and Mary, while their grandson Boris was at Hebrew Academy and after his Bar Mitzvah last year, moved on to Norfolk Collegiate.❖

Reprinted from *Renewal Magazine*, Winter 2002.

(Elena Baum interviewed Roza and Misha through an interpreter, Lev Shikhman, himself a veteran of the Russian Navy during World War II.)

By all accounts, DENA VERNIK, born with a Jewish name in March 1930, is an exceptional woman. Named for an uncle, who died serving Russia in the civil war of 1918, Dena had to use the Russian name, Yevdokiya, during and after World War II. Dena was raised in her grandparents' home in beautiful Odessa on the Black Sea where she developed a passion for books. Reading since the age of five, she excelled in school.

By 1937, even though Russia was not officially at war, Stalin had begun arresting many "enemies," and Dena's uncle was among them. To protect themselves, the family had to state that they didn't know him, but her father would not turn on his brother. Instead, when Dena's mother Tatyana was pregnant with her little brother, Yakov, he left home to hide so he would not be arrested.

Dena had finished fourth grade by the time the War began. In September of 1941, true enemies surrounded Odessa. The city was bombed constantly, and she remembers the synagogue on the corner of her street being blown up. She can still see in her mind the people trying respectfully to extricate the remnants of the shul's Torah. On October 16, 1941, the Nazis arrived with their Romanian allies to occupy Odessa. With her father still away, Dena remained with her grandparents, and her mother took care of three-year-old Yakov.

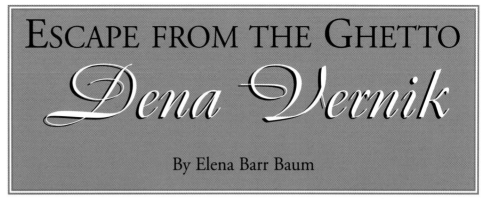

ESCAPE FROM THE GHETTO
Dena Vernik

By Elena Barr Baum

Dena Vernik, center, with her family — daughter, Galina Kastin, left; grandson, Tolya; son, Alexander; and son-in-law, Peter Kastin.

The Nazis gave an order that all Jews must leave their homes on October 24 or 25, taking with them a two to three day supply of food and clothing, and go towards a place in Odessa called, "Dalnik." Those who left their houses on the 24th never came back. After they had been gathered together, they were burned alive. By the luck of sheer numbers, the Jews who left home on October 25 were turned back; the Nazis were unequipped to kill the entire Jewish population as planned, because they had not expected it to be so large. In all, Dena says 90,000 Jews were killed in Odessa.

Needless to say, Dena's family was lucky not to have left on the first day. She remembers that later, on January 10, 1942, the Nazis "ghettoized" the suburb of Slobodka, and ordered all Jews not already living there to move there. Because of her grandparents' ill health, they decided not to go; they said they would rather die in their home. They sent Dena to live with a non-Jewish neighbor who was a teacher, while Tatyana and Yakov stayed with some friends, none of them following the Nazi order.

A few days later, the Nazis began searching for Jews outside the ghetto, and Dena's protectress became afraid for her own life. The teacher took Dena and gave her to a Jewish lady in the neighborhood, who was on her way to the ghetto with her own son. Twelve-year-old Dena had no choice but to go with them. When Tatyana came for her at the teacher's home, she found her

daughter gone. Distraught, she asked her parents for advice. Abraham sent his wife, Gitteli into the ghetto to look for Dena. After she had left the house, Dena's blind grandfather went down to his basement and hung himself, as he had said he no longer wanted to be a burden to his family.

"All of my life, I know my grandmother saved me, and I cannot remember [this] without tears."

Her grandmother found Dena, but now the two of them were in the ghetto while Tatyana and Yakov were on the outside. Gitteli knew that the ghetto probably meant death, and she couldn't bear the thought of this for her special granddaughter. Since only non-Jews had entry and exit privileges, her grandmother asked a local woman from Slobodka to take Dena out of the ghetto, pretending she was her own child, as if they were going shopping. She was then to seek out Tatyana. Since the woman who left with one child

would have to return with a child, Gitteli told the lady to ask Tatyana to keep Dena with her, and send Yakov back to the ghetto. Tatyana then made the agonizing decision, prompted by her own mother, to sacrifice one child for another. Since Yakov was circumcised, his Jewish heritage could not be denied. He was also too young to protect himself and anyone hiding him could be killed. The terrible but necessary plan worked, Dena and her mother reunited, and Yakov went back to the ghetto to stay with his grandmother. Dena has never learned the details of their deaths, be it hunger, cold, or murder, but she knows that neither of them survived. "All of my life, I know my grandmother saved me, and I cannot remember [this] without tears."

Even Dena's escape from the ghetto could not be celebrated, because not only did she lose contact with her brother and dear grandmother who had raised her, but she also contracted a terrible case of typhus, and almost died. With her mother's loving care, and probably a small miracle, she survived. She and her mother spent the next two years moving from home to home, Tatyana doing housework in exchange for their room and board. When people visited, they were hidden in basements. When it seemed to be getting too dangerous, they went to a new place. She will never forget those who risked their lives for them, including one woman, the wife of a man her father had once helped, who risked her own two children's lives by hiding them.

On April 10, 1944, the Russians arrived in force, and the Nazi reign of terror in Odessa ended. Dena and her mother were free. Her father, who had eventually joined the army, had been wounded in the War and when he returned home, he moved what was left of the family to Moscow. Dena had missed three years of the schooling so precious to her. With the help of a tutor, Dena was able to pass the exam for the 5th grade and go on to the 6th grade class. She finished high school in 1949, only two years behind schedule.

By then, Stalin was well into his campaign against Jews, partly due to the creation of Israel. He labeled Jews "cosmopolits," or persons who do not like their country. Because of her heritage, Dena's school would not give her the gold medal, equivalent to the valedictory award for the best student. Her math teacher, however, courageously stood up to party leadership for her, and she was awarded the medal, which she has to this day.

Such a medal was important, because it should have allowed someone entrance to a university without taking exams. Even though she finally had it in hand, Moscow University did not allow Jews. Instead, she enrolled in a chemical institute to study organic chemistry. When she arrived, her name was not on the organic chemistry list and she was shifted into "silica," or building materials. She realized quickly that the school had placed all Jews into that one division, regardless of their talents or interests. She studied there for five years, finishing in the top ten in her class. Even with her superb record, her lab placement was given to a Russian (non-Jew), and she was placed for work in a glass plant in a Moscow suburb, a two-and-one-half-hour commute from home.

"All of my life I felt I was Jewish," says Dena. "But as a Jew, a woman, and a non-party member, I rarely received a promotion, as Jews were not allowed to be anyone's boss." She worked days and continued to study at night. After the glass plant job, she worked for ten years as an engineer at another lab, helping inventors document their work and doing translations. She then earned a master's degree, becoming a special type of lawyer for inventors. She wrote applications for them and for lawyers for 19 years.

During the earliest of these times, she was raising a daughter, Galina, from her first marriage to Michael, an engineer. Their life was difficult and the marriage did not survive. She met and married David Vernik in 1962, and they had a son, Alexander. The children grew up, and both trained as computer programmers, and life went on. But when Galina and her husband, Peter, decided to move with their two sons to the United States in 1991, life in Moscow became emptier. Two years later, on September 24, 1993, Dena, David, and Alexander followed them to Virginia Beach.

Dena's love of learning has never left her and she immersed herself in learning English at the Adult Learning Center in Virginia Beach. After two years, Dena and David moved to Norfolk, where Dena continued studying at the Madison Career Center and at Temple Israel, where she and David were members before he passed away in September 1998. Her grandsons attend the University of Maryland and Virginia Tech studying computer programming like their parents and their Uncle Alexander.

Though Dena remembers her grandmother Gitteli praying, lighting candles, going to synagogue and fasting on Yom Kippur, she really knew nothing of Judaism until she came to America. She credits Rabbi Michael Panitz of Temple Israel, Rabbi Stu Warner of the JCC-Norfolk, and Elsa Borman, ESL teacher, for helping her learn about Judaism.

She knows she was lucky to survive the War and thanks God every day for America. ❖

Reprinted from *Renewal Magazine,* Winter 2002.

Hampton Roads Holocaust Survivors of Blessed Memory

Rabbi Israel Bornstein
Chana Bromberg
(Alexander Bromberg's first wife)
Alexander Bromberg
Anna Burk
Charles Burk
Alex Davis
(Eva Kramer's first husband)
Moses Dilbert
(Barbara Herman's first husband)
Morris Drucker
Etele Yoheved Ernstein
Ted Finder
David Floch
Edith Friedenbach
(Kitty Sak's mother)
Leo Friedenbach
(Kitty Sak's father)
Jan Frohlich
Charles Goldman
Esther Goldman
Simon Grossman
(Ruth Levinson's first husband)
Devorah Gutterman
Samuel Gutterman
Barbara Dilbert Herman
Giza Horowitz
Sam Horowitz
Irving Igdal
Sigmund Kolpan
Stefa Bercowizc Zarnowiecka Korn
(Charles Burk's sister)

Eva Davis Kramer
Sol Kushner
(Bluma Kushner Bromberg's first husband)
Harry Lefcoe
Lola Kolpan Levinson
Szaja Lida
Ber Luftrieber
Rosa Luftrieber
Max Melamed
Abe Okun
Sabina Miller Okun
Anna Perl
John Perl
Esther Schwarcz
(Eva Davis Kramer's sister)
Chaim Sendowski
Rela Sendowski
Israel Shapiro
Miriam Shapiro
Joseph Slivowitz
Leah Slivowitz
Shalom Steinbach
Halina Sternlicht
Freda Sygal
(Dana Cohen's mother)
Bella Weinstock
Moishe Weinstock
Annie Weisberg
Abraham Wilkomer

Residents of Blessed Memory Whose Stories Appear in *To Life*

Wallace Dreyer
Marie Knowles Ellifritz
Joseph Gertz
Doris Kaufman
Elise Margolius
J. L. Morewitz
Justine Nusbaum
Rocco Russo
Sam Sandler

"May their memory endure, inspiring truth and loyalty in our lives. May their souls thus be bound up in the bond of life."

Siddur Sim Shalom

Sam Althaus

Stephen P. Barna

Bronia Drucker

Cantor Joseph Gutherz

Bronia Hendler

David Hendler

Zipora Katz

Samuel Kessel

Nandor Lazar

Ruth Lida

Rachel Melamed

Margaret Newfield

Shimon Orlowski

Greta Rochkind

Cantor Harry Sterling

Bronia Drucker and her granddaughter.

"Many things in Jewish history are too terrible to be believed – but nothing in that history is too terrible not to have happened ...

"Yet, after all the massacres, the inquisitions, the Holocausts, the expulsions and the pogroms ... here we still are."

Abba Eban

Shimon Orlowski and his grandson.

DATES OF INFAMY
and The Jewish Response

1933
JANUARY 30   Adolf Hitler appointed Chancellor (Prime Minister) of Germany.

MARCH 23   First concentration camp, Dachau, established.

MARCH 27   Enabling Act suspends civil liberties.

APRIL 1   *The "Judische Rundschau," a German Jewish newspaper, publishes an article entitled "Wear the Yellow Badge with Pride," the first in a series entitled: "Saying 'Yes' to our Judaism." These slogans were adopted by the Jews of Germany.*

APRIL   Boycott of Jewish shops and businesses. Jewish professionals barred from entering offices. First anti-Jewish decree; the law for the establishment of the Civil Service. Gestapo established.

MAY 10   Public burning of books written by Jews, those of Jewish origin and opponents of Nazism.

SPRING-SUMMER   Jewish professors expelled from universities. Jewish writers and artists prohibited from practicing their professions.

AUGUST 20   *Boycott of Nazi Germany declared by American Jewish Congress.*

OCTOBER 19   Germany leaves the League of Nations.

1934
AUGUST 2   Hitler names himself "Fuhrer," following the death of German President von Hindenburg.

1935
MAY 31 - NOVEMBER 15   Jews barred from serving in German armed forces. "Nuremburg Laws" - anti-Jewish racial laws enacted. Jews could no longer be German citizens, marry Aryans, fly German flag or hire German maids under age of 45. Germans define "Jew" as anyone with three Jewish grandparents or someone with two Jewish grandparents who identifies as Jewish.

JUNE 30   *General strike of Polish Jews in protest against Anti-Semitism.*

OCTOBER 3   Italy invades Ethiopia. This event upset European alignments and brought Fascist and Nazi dictatorships into close accord.

1936
MARCH 3   Jewish doctors baned from practicing medicine in government institutions.

OCTOBER 25   Hitler and Mussolini form Rome-Berlin Axis.

1937
JULY 16   Buchenwald Concentration Camp opens.

1938
MARCH 13   Anschluss: annexation of Austria by Germany; all German anti-Semitic decrees immediately applied in Austria.

MARCH 15   *Mass anti-Nazi rally in New York under the auspices of the Joint Boycott Council.*

APRIL 26   Jews in Reich must register all property with authorities.

AUGUST 1   Adolf Eichmann establishes first Office of Jewish Emigration to speed up forced emigration.

AUGUST 17   Decrees that revoked all name changes by Jews and forced those Jews who did not have names recognized as Jewish by German authorities to add Israel (for males) and Sarah (for females) as middle name.

SEPTEMBER 25-30   Munich Conference - England and France agree to turn over Sudentenland (part of Czechoslovakia) to Germany.

NOVEMBER 7   Herschel Grynszpan assassinates Ernst von Rath, Third Secretary of the German Embassy in Paris.

NOVEMBER 9-10   *Kristallnacht*(Night of Broken Glass); Anti-Jewish pogrom in Germany and Austria. 267 synagogues destroyed, 7,500 Jewish shops looted. 30,000 male Jews arrested; many of them sent to concentration camps; 91 Jews are killed.

NOVEMBER 12-15   Decree forcing all Jews to transfer retail businesses to Aryan hands. All Jewish pupils expelled from German schools.

DECEMBER   *Establishment of "Aliya Beth" in Palestine.*

1939

JANUARY 30   Hitler's Reichstag speech states that if war erupts it will mean the Vernichtung(extermination) of European Jews.

AUGUST 23   Molotov-Ribbentrop Pact signed: non aggression pact between Russia and Germany.

SEPTEMBER 1   Beginning of World War II; Germany invades Poland.

SEPTEMBER 27   Heydrich orders establishment of ghettos and Jewish councils (Judenrat) in German-occupied Poland.

OCTOBER   *The Jewish Community of Palestine demands participation in the war against Nazism: 26,000 join the British Army.*

NOVEMBER 23   Jews in German-occupied Poland forced to wear distinguishing badge.

NOVEMBER   *Dr. Emanuel Ringelblum convenes a conference in Warsaw with representatives of underground parties in order to discuss provision of aid to Polish Jews.*

1940

JANUARY-FEBRUARY   *First underground activities by Jewish youth movements in Poland.*

MAY 7   Lodz Ghetto closed off; approximately 165,000 inhabitants in 1.6 square miles.

MAY 10   Germany invades Holland, Belgium and France.

MAY 20   Concentration camp established at Auschwitz.

JUNE 22   France surrenders to Nazis.

AUGUST 8   Battle of Britain begins.

AUGUST 17   *Mass demonstrations by starving people in Lodz Ghetto. Organization of "Forteresse Juive" (later "Armee Juive") begins in France.*

SEPTEMBER 27   Rome-Berlin-Tokyo Axis.

NOVEMBER 15   Warsaw Ghetto sealed off with approximately 500,000 inhabitants.

NOVEMBER 20-24   Hungary, Rumania and Slovakia join Rome-Berlin-Tokyo Axis.

DECEMBER   *Dr. Emanuel Ringelblum founds "Oneg Shabbat," secret archives in the Warsaw Ghetto.*

French resistance fighters.
Photo by Hugo Horvath

1941

American troops arrive in Europe
Photo by Hugo Horvath

APRIL   Germany occupies Greece and Yugoslavia.

JUNE 7-8   *Israeli Palmach units take part in Allied invasion in Syria.*

JUNE 22   Germany invades the Soviet Union.

END OF JUNE   Nazi Einsatzgruppen (special moblie killing units) carry out mass murder of Jews in German-occupied areas of Soviet Union.

JULY 31   Heydrich appointed by Goring as responsible for implemtation of "Final Solution."

SEPTEMBER 1   Jews in Third Reich must wear yellow Star of David as distinguishing mark.

OCTOBER   At Auschwitz, establishment of Birkenau camp, future site of mass extermination of Jews, Gypsies, Poles, Russians and others.

DECEMBER 7   Japanese attack on Pearl Harbor.

DECEMBER 11   *"Struma" sets sail from Rumania for Palestine. On 12 February 1942 it strikes a mine and sinks with all aboard .*

DECEMBER   *Formation of an underground Zionist Youth Movement in France (Mouvement de Jeunesse Sioniste). Armed underground organization established in the Minsk Ghetto: the first Jewish partisan group operates in the area.*

1942

A portion of the original electrified outer wall from Dachau Concentration Camp with photographic view of inmates at morning roll call, c. 1942. The section was donated to the Virginia War Museum in Newport News, Virginia by General Jacob Devers, Commander, 6th Army Group, whose troops liberated Dachau.

JANUARY 20   Wannsee Conference; Heydrich reveals official plan to murder all Jews on European continent.

JANUARY   *"Unified Partisan Organization" (FPO) set up in the Vilna Ghetto and Kovno Ghetto.*

JANUARY   *Tuvia Bielski organizes the first partisan base in the Naliwiki forests, Western Byelorussia.*

MARCH 1   Extermination by gas begins in Sobibor extermination camp; by October 1943 - 250,000 murdered.

MARCH 17   Extermination begins in Belzec extermination camp; by end of 1942 - 600,000 Jews murdered.

MARCH   *Belgian Jews establish a mutual aid organization ("Comite de Defense Juive").*

LATE MARCH   Deportations to Auschwitz extermination camp begin.

APRIL   *Anti-Fascist bloc established in the Warsaw Ghetto.*

JUNE 30   All Jewish Schools in Germany closed down.

JULY   *Gizi Fleischman organizes the underground "Working Group" in Czechoslovakia. Founding of the General Staff of the Jewish Maquis in Lyons, France.*

JULY 22   *Armed resistance during the liquidation of the Nieswiez Ghetto, Western Byelorussia.*

JULY 22   Treblinka extermination camp begins operations; by August1943, over 700,000 Jews murdered.

JULY 28   *"Jewish Fighting Organization" (Z.O.B.) set up in the Warsaw Ghetto.*

AUGUST   *Armed resistance during the liquidation of the Mir Ghetto, Western Byelorussia.*

SUMMER - WINTER   Deportation of Jews to extermination camps from Holland, Poland, France, Belgium, Croatia. Deportation of Jews from Norway, Germany and Greece to extermination camps.

SEPTEMBER 3   *Armed resistance during the liquidation of the Lahava Ghetto, Western Byelorussia.*

SEPTEMBER 23   *Armed resistance during the liquidation of the Tutzin Ghetto, Western Ukraine. An armed group organized and led by Moshe Geldenman escapes from the Kurtz Ghetto, Western Ukraine to engage in partisan operations in the area.*

NOVEMBER   Allied forces land in North Africa.

DECEMBER 22   *Jewish Combat Organization set up in Cracow: attacks on German soldiers.*

WINTER   *Jewish Partisan movement organized in forests near Lublin.*

1943

JANUARY 18-21   *First armed resistance in Warsaw Ghetto; street fighting under command of Mordechai Anielewicz.*

FEBRUARY 2   Germans surrender to Russians at Stalingrad.

MARCH   Liquidation of Cracow Ghetto.

APRIL 19   *Warsaw Ghetto revolt begins as Germans attempt to liquidate 70,000 ghetto inhabitants. Jewish underground fights Nazis until early June.*

SUMMER   *Hundreds of underground fighters leave the Vilna Ghetto for the forests. Armed resistance by Jews in Czestochowa, Lvov, Sedzir, Bialystok and Tarnow ghettos.*

JUNE   Himmler orders the liquidation of all ghettos in Poland and the Soviet Union.

AUGUST 2   *Armed revolt in Treblinka extermination camp.*

AUGUST 16   *Bialystock Ghetto revolt and breakout. Revolt at Krikov labour camp, Lublin district.*

FALL   Liquidation of large ghettos: Minsk, Vilna Riga.

OCTOBER 14   *Armed revolt in Sobibor extermination camp.*

Robert Middendorf, of the 289th Combat Engineers and father of Perry Deglandon, was a liberator. He died before telling his story.

1944

JANUARY   *The Jewish underground in Budapest sets up a workshop for forging documents for rescue purposes: by the end of 1944, over 10,000 people had been supplied with such documents.*

MARCH 14   *Group of Palestinian parachutists leave for Yugoslavia, Hungary and Rumania.*

MARCH 19   Germany occupies Hungary.

MAY 15   Nazis begin deporting Hungarian Jews. By July 9, 437,000 sent to Auschwitz.

JUNE 6   Allied invasion of Normandy - D-Day.

SPRING-SUMMER   Red Army repels Nazi forces.

JULY 20   Group of German officers attempt to assassinate Hitler.

JULY 24   Russians liberate Majdanek death camp.

SUMMER   Liquidation of ghettos in Kovno (Kaunas), Shavli (Slauliai) and Lodz. Inmates sent to concentration camps and death camps.

OCTOBER 7   *Sonderkommando uprising at Auschwitz: one crematorium blown up.*

OCTOBER 31   Remnants of Slovakian Jewry deported to Auschwitz

NOVEMBER 8   Beginning of Death March of approximately 40,000 Jews from Budapest to Austria.

NOVEMBER   Last Jews deported from Theresienstadt "model ghetto" to Auschwitz.

NOVEMBER 1   *Jewish brigade leaves for Italian front.*

Stationed on Tinian Island, Lt. Bill McDonald (father of Laura Miller) and Lt. Dan Stump plot a set of DF bearings on Japanese radar stations after a flight mission.

1945

JANUARY 17   Evacuation of Auschwitz; beginning of death march of camp inmates.

JANUARY 25   Beginning of death march of inmates of Stutthof.

APRIL 6-10   Death march of inmates of Buchenwald.

APRIL   Final Red Army offensive in Germany from East; Allies advance from West.

APRIL 30   Hitler commits suicide.

MAY 8   Germany surrenders. End of Third Reich.

AUGUST 6   U.S. atomic bomb is dropped on Hiroshima.

AUGUST 9   U.S. atomic bomb is dropped on Nagasaki.

SEPTEMBER 2   Military leaders sign surrender terms on the U.S.S. *Missouri* in Tokyo Bay.

GLOSSARY OF TERMS

Bar Mitzvah: The ceremony marking the assumption of adult religious responsibilities, at age thirteen.

B'shert: Yiddish word which literally means "fated".

Cheder: A religious elementary school; Hebrew school.

Chutzpah: Supreme self-confidence; nerve.

Daven: To recite Jewish prayers.

DP Displaced Persons: Individuals who did not return to live in their homes following World War II. DPs lived in temporary camps in the Allied zones and Italy.

Gendarmes: French police.

Gentile: Any person who is not Jewish.

Ghetto: An area of a city in which Jews were forced to live.

HIAS: Hebrew Immigrant Aid Society. Founded in 1881, it is the oldest international migration and refugee resettlement agency. As an expression of Jewish tradition and values, it responds to those who are threatened or oppressed.

JDC: Joint Distribution Committee-sponsors programs of relief, rescue, and reconstruction fulfilling its commitment to the idea that all Jews are responsible for one another and that "To save one person is to save a world" (Mishna, Sanhedrin 4:5).

Judenrat: Committee of Jews set up by the Nazis in Jewish communities and ghettos in occupied Europe to execute the Nazis' orders.

Kaddish: A Jewish prayer recited by mourners at public services after the death of a close relative.

Kiddush: A prayer of sanctifying time that is recited over wine on the Sabbath and festivals.

Kindertransport: About 10,000 children from Germany, Austria and Czechoslovakia were sent to foster homes in Great Britain by their parents to save them from the Nazi threat. Over 80 percent of the children never saw their parents again.

Kosher: Foods and other items that meet Jewish ritual requirements.

Kristallnacht: "Night of the broken glass"-organized destruction of synagogues, Jewish houses, and shops, accompanied by mass arrests of Jews, which took place in Germany and Austria under the Nazis on the night of November 9-10, 1938.

Kz: The abbreviation for the German word for concentration camp.

Lager system: System of camps that supported the death camps.

Magen David: Literally, the Shield of David. The six-pointed star is a universally recognized symbol of Jewry and it appears on the flag of the state of Israel.

Mensch: One who is respected. A descent, noble person.

Minyan: A quorum of ten Jewish men required for a communal religious service. Today women are included in non-orthodox movements.

OSE: Oeuvre de Secours aux Enfants-a Jewish organization whose mission was to rescue children from deportation and death.

OSS: Office of Strategic Services-US agency created in 1942 under the jurisdiction of the Joint Chiefs of Staff for the purpose of obtaining information about enemy nations and sabotaging their war potential and morale. Disbanded in 1945, many of its functions were assumed by the CIA.

Partisan: A member of a body of detached troops making forays and harassing an enemy within enemy lines by using hit-and-run guerilla tactics.

Sabra: A native-born Israeli.

Shabbat: The Sabbath, which for Jews begins at sunset Friday and ends after sundown Saturday.

Shivah: The seven days of mourning following burial of a close relative.

Shochet: Ritual slaughterer.

Shtetl: Jewish village in Eastern Europe.

Shul: Synagogue.

Tefillin: Small leather boxes, or phylacteries, containing written prayers. Observant Jews wear them when reciting morning prayers. Not worn on Shabbat or holidays.

Yahrzeit: The anniversary of the death of a close relative.

Yiddish: Everyday language of Eastern European Jews, combining elements of German, Hebrew and some Slavic languages.

Zionism: A national movement for the return of the Jewish people to their homeland and the establishment of Israel as the Jewish state.

Photo by Joseph Lust

"I cry out with all my heart against silence."

Elie Wiesel

Editor's Note: The information for this article was taken from an interview with Vic Pickett, the artist commissioned to design and create Tidewater's Holocaust Memorial sculpture. The interview was conducted by Telsa Leon, a Tidewater artist and member of the Holocaust Commission of the Community Relations Council of the UJFT. On July 7, 2001, Vic Pickett and Elizabeth Leeor were married.

Tidewater's Holocaust Memorial
A Community's Dream Becomes Reality
By Telsa Leon

The Tidewater Holocaust Memorial stands on the grounds of the Jewish Community Center of South Hampton Roads on Newport Avenue in Norfolk, Virginia. In 1989, Bootsie Goldmeier, President of the United Jewish Federation of Tidewater, appointed a Holocaust Memorial Committee to plan and commission an artist to design a Holocaust memorial. Vic Pickett, former Chairman of the Art Department at Old Dominion University, Norfolk, Virginia, was chosen to create a meaningful sculpture.

It took Pickett two-and-one-half years to complete the project. In the first phase, he designed a scaled-down model, with the concept being a memorial people could walk through. But this concept was to be altered as Pickett progressed.

"I had to deal with a single object that (would) become a symbol of the people who were killed in the Holocaust," Pickett begins, adding that "the artistic creation also had to serve as a remembrance of … the survivors."

Weaving together these two aspects of the Holocaust – six million Jews who perished with those who survived – became Pickett's goal. Unsure of the survivors' response, Pickett chose the reflective surface of stainless steel for the memorial. As one survivor notes, "… everyone who looks at it will be able to see that they are reflections of their forefathers."

Because he is not Jewish, the project has had a profound impact on him. This impact includes the conversion of a friend who worked with him on the project. As a result … she converted to Judaism. She later took the name of Elizabeth Faye Leeor.

The memorial is not only a dedication to those who perished, but a reminder of those who survived. "They are the ones who had such a great effect on me … an emotional pivot that the ideas worked from."

The Jewish community's devotion to the arts, he feels, is inherent in "a religion that is based on family, intellect and culture, of which the arts are a part." And it is family, intellect and culture combined with the intellectual like of the community that makes it all work.

Raising Rescuers
Heroes evolve, they aren't born.

By Sandra Porter Leon

"Our goal is to teach goodness. Our goal is to understand the mystery of goodness. Imagine what this world would be if we really succeeded in our goals." Rabbi Harold Schulweis

How do we as individuals open our hearts to the habit of caring? How do we as parents serve as models to fight anti-Semitism, racism, and prejudice and provide an environment that empowers a child to make a difference? Part of the answer may lie with the rescuers, men and women who risked their lives and those of their families to save fellow human beings during the Holocaust.

In our Jewish tradition, a person who saves but one life is considered as if he had saved the entire world. Rescuers numbered few during the Holocaust and paled in comparison to the majority of bystanders and perpetrators who allowed the destruction of two-thirds of European Jewry. Some people feel that by studying rescuers' deeds and moral acts of courage may detract from the real horror of the Holocaust; however, "we must realize," notes Rabbi Harold Schulweis, "that there are no heroes

without villains and that even a small light in a cave vividly illuminates the predators dark design."

Who were these rescuers and did they share commonalties that may provide us with some insight into what motivates good behavior?

"All rescuers were unique," notes Eva Fogelman who directed the Rescue Project, a study of 300 rescuers and survivors from Nazi occupied Europe. "If there is any commonalty," she notes, "it was not socio-economic in nature – such as political affiliation, social class, gender, education, or religion." Her research reveals that the rescuers were a diverse group, but there were patterns in their upbringing that can provide us useful clues to nurturing and promoting altruistic behavior in ourselves and our children.

"A majority of rescuers," continues Fogelman, identified strongly with one parent who was a "strong moralist – not necessarily religious but holding very firm opinions on moral issues and serving as a model of moral conduct." Eighty percent remember an altruistic role model from childhood.

Philip Hallie, in his book *Lest Innocent Blood Be Shed*, describes the inhabitants of Le Chambon, a little village in the mountains of central France, who saved over 5,000 Jewish children. Rescue was possible because of the spiritual leadership of Pastor Andre Trocme who inspired his villagers "to imitate Jesus' love for all mankind."

When asked recently why she and her fellow neighbors saved Jews, even at great personal risk, Madame Trocme said, "We did nothing out of the ordinary. We did what we had to do." The habit of service, the habit of hospitality, the habit of caring, says Hallie, allowed the people of Chambon to save so many lives. "Like physical courage, moral courage needs to be exercised, habitualized so it comes easily."

Besides having a role model, many rescuers also participated in helping activities as children. Eva Fogelman states that parents instilled in their children the importance of helping others when they enlisted the youngster's "hands-on" assistance in their own altruistic activity. Taking bread to a neighbor or providing less fortunate children with toys and clothes serve as examples.

So often parents or friends may perform good deeds without involving their children or explaining its meaning. The other day, my daughter received a beautiful certificate that a tree in Israel had been planted in her honor. Until she sowed her own seeds and harvested the fruits of her own garden, the significance of the gift was meaningless.

Another child-rearing practice typical of rescuer homes was a method of discipline known as "inductive reasoning." It seems as the overwhelming majority of rescuers studied by Pearl and Sam Oliner, authors of *The Altruistic Personality*, remembered one parent who enforced rules by explanation rather than punishment. "The child tends to be more compassionate when told why their actions are bad," says Oliner, "as opposed to brute force."

The Oliners' words remind me of the STEPS class, an acronym for Successful Tips for Effective Parenting, in which parents learn appropriate language tools to combat the screaming toddler or the aggressive five-year-old, no matter how frustrating. Instead of hitting a child or telling him that he is bad for poking his sister, the caretaker is encouraged to use feeling words. "Becky feels sad when you poke her" …"I love you, but I do not like your behavior." …"How would you feel if she poked you?" This method encourages the child to feel compassion and responsibility for his or her actions.

In her book, *When Light Pierces the Darkness*, Nechama Tec found that rescuers had a sense of individuality. They tended to be non-conformists and believed their actions made a difference. Rescuers tended to have an internal moral barometer of right and wrong. They often did not need the support and approval of others, but rather relied on their own self approval.

Rescuers also tended to bond within their family as well as the society at large. Children were able to extend their connections with relatives to include people who were different from them. In her study, Oliner reflects that tolerance of others is one of the shared attributes of many of the rescuers. "They protected," says Oliner, "not a believer or disbeliever, not a partisan, not a Jew, but a human being, a man, a woman, a child of God."

Eva Fleischner, who studied Catholic rescue in France, also echoes that "the oneness of all humanity^prompted some of the rescuers to act on the behalf of Jews. Rescuers saw themselves as individuals linked to others in a shared experience. They were able to go beyond their own group and embrace diversity.

Most rescuers would start their helping activities by providing some bread or clothes and only gradually take greater risks like sheltering or transporting Jews. In his study, Ervin Staub states that goodness, like evil, often begins in small steps. Heroes evolve; they aren't born. Very often the rescuers make only a small commitment at the start – to hide someone for a day or two, but once they have taken that step, they began to see themselves differently, as someone who helps.

Although there is much debate about rescue, all researchers agree that if we instruct our children to value all human life, empathize with people in distress, and embrace diversity, we would create a society in which the Holocaust could not germinate. I will conclude with a quote by Rabbi Harold Schulweis who eloquently states that "it makes no small difference whether from our youth, we form habits of one kind or another: it makes a very great difference, or rather, all the difference." ❖

FOR FURTHER INFORMATION:

LOCAL RESOURCE CENTERS
- United Jewish Federation of Tidewater, *Virginia Beach*
- Bonk Rivin Holocaust Library, *Temple Sinai, Portsmouth*
- Virginia War Museum, *Newport News*

HOLOCAUST RELATED WEB SITES
www.holocaust-trc.org

www.ushmm.org

www.holocaustcommission.org

www.holocaust-history.org

www.facing.org

www.wiesenthal.com

www.yad-vashem.org

A Holocuaust survivor is considered to be any Jew who lived in Germany, Austria or any of the countries occupied by the Nazis, and who emigrated after the following dates:

◆ Germany after October 1933

◆ Austria after March 1938

◆ Czechoslovakia after October 1938

◆ Poland after September 1939

◆ Denmark, Norway, Belgium, the Netherlands, Luxembourg and France after April/May 1940

◆ Yugoslavia and Greece after April 1941

◆ Bulgaria, Rumania and Hungary, as of April 1941 (when these governments enacted anti-Jewish measures upon the demands of the Nazi government)

◆ Former Soviet Union after June 1941

Conference on Jewish Material Claims against Germany, Inc.

"Lest We Forget; The Holocaust" by MaryAnne Katz

AFTERWORD

The Jewish people have been telling stories for 4000 years – ever since Eve took that first forbidden bite.

Nobel Laureate and Holocaust survivor Elie Wiesel has written that God created the human race because of God's love for stories. It is true that each of us has a story. But some stories we are *required* to tell, for it is possible that these stories will ensure the survival of mankind.

Such are the stories of Holocaust survivors, their rescuers and the liberators.

However, every honor brings with it the weight of responsibility. Truthfully, we did not realize the immensity of this project when we began over two years ago. We soon discovered there were many survivors, rescuers, and liberators whom we previously did not know and whose stories had not been recorded. The most difficult part of publishing this book, however, was dealing with our own anguish over whether we had conveyed, as well as words can, what the survivors had experienced, whether their voices could be heard over ours. And finally, we wanted the book to be user friendly, especially for young people, to whom it is dedicated.

In the late 1970's, long before most of the world had taken any notice of Holocaust survivors, Reba Karp, editor of the United Jewish Federation of Tidewater's *Southeastern Virginia Jewish News* and *Renewal Magazine*, had already begun recording and publishing the testimony of Holocaust survivors in the Tidewater area. Listening to their stories of persecution, unrelenting fear, separation and unbearable loss, death, despair, courage, goodness and sacrifice, Reba knew that she must become the vehicle to transmit them. Her resolve to share their stories with future generations took root and led to the publication of three short volumes.

Since then, time has diminished the ranks of the survivors. That reality and the looming threat of revisionism made Reba realize that the job was not finished. There were stories that needed to be told – and in a more permanent form. It was Reba who kept reminding us that these are not *our* stories to change and to polish. They belong to the survivors – in their own words. It is their legacy to us, to those who perished, and to those who will come after us.

Moving this project from interviews to press could not have occurred without a strong leader. Laura Miller, the Chairman of this project, has been the "engine" that has driven the process forward. It was her "Let's-just-do-it" attitude that took a dream and turned it into a reality. No task daunted her. Realizing that the book would need underwriting, Laura and her husband, Jerry, assumed responsibility for raising the necessary funds. They did it quietly and unassumingly. Add to that Laura's energy, her organizational skills, her relentless attention to detail, and her willingness to do *whatever* needed to be done – and you have the driving force of the project. *To Life,* as her family will attest, became Laura's full-time job for the past two years. Her selfless dedication to the project has inspired us all.

Everyone involved in this publication is aware of the critical role played by Perry Deglandon. Perry is a young woman cut from the same fabric as the rescuers or Righteous Gentiles. Although not Jewish, she has dedicated these past few years to the design and formatting of the book. Gathering a spiritual and emotional energy from the survivors, rescuers, and liberators – many of whom she came to know personally - she has transformed this book into a work of art and a reflection of her own inner beauty. Her commitment to the project, her calm in the midst of the storm, and her abiding friendship have been among the many blessings of working on *To Life*.

Many people were involved in the publication of *To Life*. Each of the writers gave countless hours of his/her time to interview and write these testimonies. We are grateful to them for understanding the importance of what we set out to do. The artwork on the cover of *To Life* and that which embellishes the stories is the creation of MaryAnne Katz. Her artistry and passion for Jewish life have added greatly to the beauty of the book. The technical and formatting expertise of Brenda Hall has also been indispensable and deeply appreciated. And to the proofreaders – Moira Wright, Wendy Juren Auerbach, Victoria Weinstein, and Joan DeLarosa – who did the "grunt" work that no one loves doing, you too have contributed to the professional quality of our final product.

We have been fortunate to have the wise and generous counsel of Norfolk attorney, Stephen E. Noona. The UJFT Holocaust Commission is indebted to him for sharing his time and talent to address the complexities of publishing this book.

Our publisher, Howard Unger, has ensured that *To Life* is a high quality publication, and also affordable. Thank you, Letton Gooch.

Finally, we wish to express our gratitude to all of our donors for your trust, your vision and your generosity. You have enabled us to produce a resource to inspire the humanity in a new generation. We hope you are as proud of this work as we are.

To Life: Stories of Courage and Survival is a tribute to the resilience and the indomitable spirit of all who witnessed and experienced the consequences of Nazi hatred and destruction. It is also a tribute to the determination, love, and great compassion of those who have dedicated themselves to learning from the past and educating for the future.

To Life!

Betsy Karotkin
Assistant Executive Director
United Jewish Federation
of Tidewater
Virginia Beach, Virginia

ACKNOWLEDGEMENTS

To Life wishes to acknowledge those who contributed to the production of this book — the writers, photographers, and artists. They are part of this historical endeavor.

MARYANNE KATZ provided the art for the cover of *To Life* and the original art drawings throughout the book. She has produced three one-woman shows. After studying in Paris, France she returned to her home in Buffalo, New York, where she was an adjunct professor at Buffalo State College. She and her husband David, a Holocaust survivor, now make their home in Chesapeake.

SUSAN HIRSCHBIEL studied photography in New York at the International Center of Photography before moving to Hampton Roads in late 1997. Her community work, in addition to the Holocaust Commission, includes the Virginia Arts Festival, the Contemporary Art Center of Virginia, the Chrysler Museum of Art, the Hampton Roads Youth Center, ACCESS/Tidewater Scholarship Foundation, and the Virginia Beach Foundation.

HUGO HORVATH, First Lieutenant with the 3355QM, an amphibious unit, has photographically recorded an American soldier's experiences during World War II. Perhaps the most fascinating aspect of the collection is that the film was developed in the field on moonless nights, using three army helmets as baths for the processing. His chemicals consisted of whatever he could find, even vinegar from the field kitchen. Due to the make-shift developing process and unrefined solutions, the film is showing signs of age. Mr. Horvath, a resident of Virginia Beach, is working toward preserving his extensive photographic collection (numbering in the thousands) before this portion of history fades into the past.

STEPHEN JAY FRIEDMAN, a local photographer, has won numerous awards and has earned a degree from Virginia Professional Photographers Association.

ECHARD WHEELER is a native of Louisiana where his love of photography was born. He enjoys capturing the spirit of the varied surrounding cultures and documenting life's great journey – "frozen moments in time (which) will forever tell the story."

PAULA ALPERIN, a registered nurse is a long-term care insurance representative. She is a former chairman of the Holocaust Commission of the United Jewish Federation of Tidewater and continues to be an active member of the Commission. She and her husband, Ervin, have three children and four grandchildren.

WENDY JUREN AUERBACH is the Director of Public Affairs and Community Marketing at WVEC-TV and a past chairperson of the Holocaust Commission of the United Jewish Federation of Tidewater. She produced the Emmy Award Winning educational documentary, "Surviving Hatred: Witness to the Holocaust," which has been distributed both regionally and nationally in hundreds of schools.

BARBARA BRANTLEY BAILEY, a graduate from Southwest Missouri State College and Old Dominion University, lives with her two sons in York County. She is the author of *Feeling Guilty*, the memoirs of Holocaust survivor, Esther Goldman (of blessed memory). She has been teaching for 28 years and instructs her students to honor all of mankind and humanity.

ELENA BARR BAUM, editor, writer and mother was instrumental in the development of an educational campaign in Dallas, Texas, on Infant Brain Development, "Babies First!" Elena is a member of the Holocaust Commission.

ERIC BERRYMAN At the time Berryman interviewed Shalom Steinbach in 1984, Berryman was a LCDR and Deputy Chief of Public Information for Supreme Allied Command Atlantic.

LISA BERTINI is a partner at Hofheimer Nusbaum. Her main passion is joining her husband, Jack Siegel, in teaching their children the beautiful faith of Judaism. She became active in the Holocaust Commission after a mission sponsored by the United Jewish Federation of Tidewater to Eastern Europe where she visited Auschwitz and Thereisenstadt.

GINNY SEALEY BOBBY, former member of the staff of *Renewal Magazine*, is Director of AIDSCare at Eastern Virginia Medical School. She lives with her husband, Christopher, and daughter, Lilly, in Norfolk.

MOIRA WRIGHT BODNER is a local freelance writer. She received her MA from Old Dominion University and lives with her husband, Ivan, in Norfolk.

PERRY DEGLANDON, a freelance designer, received her BFA from the University of Southwestern Louisiana and was the founder of Chautauqua Design Group in Ruston, Louisiana. She and her husband, Terry, have two daughters and reside in Virginia Beach.

SYBIL FRIEDBERG, a former teacher, is a past contributing writer to *Renewal Magazine*. She is the mother of three daughters and four grandchildren.

EILEEN FREY, a Norfolk native, teaches eighth-grade English at Great Neck Middle School in Virginia Beach. She also enjoys her roles as wife to her husband, Howard, and as mother to two nearly grown daughters, Allison and Kelsey.

MICHAEL FUTCH has been a full-time reporter with The Fayetteville Observer since January 1983. He and his wife, Anne, have one son, Carson. They live in North Carolina with their good dog, Molly.

ERIC FUTTERMAN is President of EAF Productions in Richmond, Virginia. He is a two-time Emmy Award winning writer and director.

ORA BAER GERSTL is now married and lives in Canada with her husband Eliyahu Gerstl and daughter Temima Tova.

LYNDA GONSENHAUSER holds Masters Degrees in both Humanities and Holocaust Studies. She was a freelance writer and a trained interviewer for the Stephen Spielberg Survivors of the Shoah Visual History Foundation.

FRIEDA IGDAL is a pharmacist and child of Holocaust survivors Ruth Igdal and Irving Igdal (of blessed memory).

REBA KARP, a former reporter and assistant editor of the *Norfolk Ledger Star*, is the editor of the *Southeastern Virginia Jewish News* and *Renewal Magazine*. She is the author of three published books, one of

which, *The Edgar Cayce Encyclopedia of Healing* (Warner Books) has been translated into three languages, French, German and Japanese.

FRED KIRSCH has been with the Virginian-Pilot for 22 years. He and his wife, Flax, live in Norfolk with their three daughters. Meeting Anna Perl was one of the highlights of his career.

PAUL LANKFORD is a member of the Upper School faculty at Cape Henry Collegiate School in Virginia Beach. He is the author of several textbooks and curriculum guides, and was recognized as the Virginia English Teacher of the Year in 1982 and the Hampton Roads Teacher of the Year in 1990.

SANDRA PORTER LEON is currently a Professor at Tidewater Community College in the Department of Health Science Technologies. An active volunteer in the community, she is a past chairman of the Holocaust Commission of the United Jewish Federation of Tidewater. Married to Miles Leon, she is the mother of two children, Erin and Ben.

TELSA LEON is a Tidewater artist who has exhibited locally in the Irene Leach Competition. She has commissioned artwork at the University of Virginia Law School. A member of the Holocaust Commission, she is married to attorney Arnold Leon and is the mother of three sons and four grandchildren.

DONNA KENWORTHY LEVY is the former advertising manager of the *Southeastern Virginia Jewish News* and *Renewal Magazine* and has written for both publications. She now lives in Venture, California, with her husband and works as a teacher in a California high school.

MARGIE MARCUS currently lives in Bethesda, Maryland, and works as a planner to preserve historic buildings at Walter Reed Army Hospital Center in Washington, D.C.

RICHARD MARTEN is a writer and businessman living in Virginia Beach.

DR. STEPHEN J. MOREWITZ is the President of the litigation-educational consulting firm, STEPHEN J. MOREWITZ, PH.D., & ASSOCIATES, Buffalo Grove, IL, San Francisco and Tarzana, CA. Dr. Morewitz is also Professor and Dean of Research at the California College of Podiatric Medicine.

ELLIE PORTER, a graduate of The University of Pennsylvania School of Medical Technology, began her career as a lab technician. With the birth of her children, Michael, Janet, and Sandra, she turned to volunteer activities, serving as president of B'nai Brith Women and Jewish Family Service where she was instrumental in the resettlement of twenty-six Russian families in the late seventies.

LISA RICHMON is a freelance copywriter and journalist, specializing in lifestyle and human interest stories. She lives with her husband, Wayne, and two dogs, Sophie and Ruthie.

ABBOTT SAKS is an adjunct professor of Spanish at Old Dominion University. He enjoys writing puns, poetry and studying etymology. He is married and has two children and two grandchildren.

VALERIE FREEMAN SAMSELL teaches art and nutrition and serves on many educational boards and committees. She and her husband Darryl have three children.

PATTY SLOTNICK is a past chairman of the Elie Wiesel Student Writing Competition and a past chair of the Holocaust Commission of the United Jewish Federation of Tidewater. She is a registered nurse and is married to physician, Nathan Slotnick. They have one son.

KAREN YEVLOVE STOUT is a high school counselor at Ocean Lakes High School. She lives with her husband Tom and daughter in Virginia Beach.

REBECCA TABAKIN is Library Coordinator for ECPI College System headquartered in Virginia Beach. She and her husband Mark have two children.

WILLIAM WALKER is Director of University Relations at the College of William and Mary in Williamsburg.

LOIS WINTER holds masters degrees in Early Childhood Education from Old Dominion University and in Counseling from the College of William and Mary. She teaches gifted children in Newport News.

KITTY WOLF is Director of Dependent Care Services for The Planning Council and is Principal of Portsmouth United Religious School. She reviews books of Jewish content for the JCC at Barnes and Noble monthly.

RABBI ISRAEL ZOBERMAN is the spiritual leader of Congregation Beth Chaverim in Virginia Beach. Son of Polish Holocaust survivors, he was born in Chu Kazakhstan on November 12, 1945. From 1947 to 1949, his family lived in the Wetzlar Displaced Persons Camp in Frankfurt, Germany.

RACHEL ZOBERMAN, a frequent contributor to the *Southeastern Virginia Jewish News* and *Renewal Magazine*, received her BA degree in English from William and Mary in Williamsburg. She is currently working on her MA in Journalism and Public Affairs at American University in Washington, D.C.

And be a blessing.
Genesis 12:2

Throughout your day – and your life – you
will feel pulled in more than one direction by
competing forces. It may be difficult to
decide what to do. But remembering to "be
a blessing" will guide you to act in a loving
fashion – in thought, word, and action.

Rabbi Levi Meier